DAILY LIFE IN BIBLICAL TIMES

Liora Ravid

ל. ניסן כסלי תש״ג.

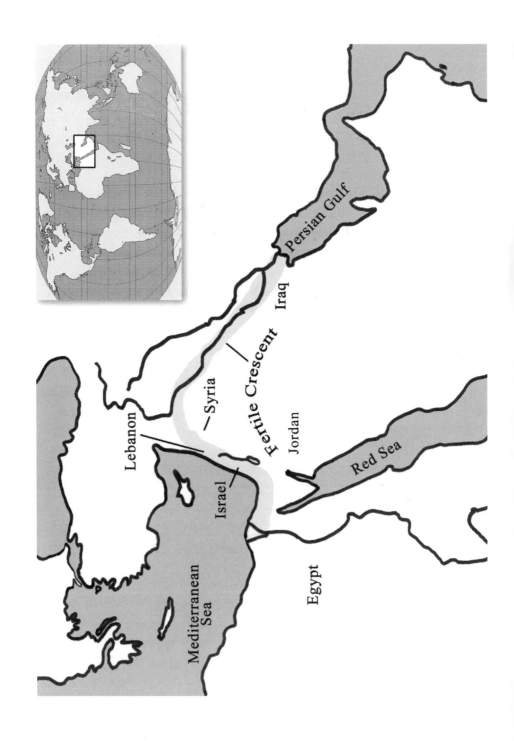

Liora Ravid

DAILY LIFE IN BIBLICAL TIMES

Translated by Jessica Setbon

gefen publishing house
JERUSALEM • NEW YORK   Est. 1981

COVER DESIGN: Shaul Tsemach
TYPESETTING: Benjie Herskowitz, Etc. Studios
MAPS: Tali Sherman

ISBN: 978-965-229-609-2

3 5 7 9 8 6 4 2

Gefen Publishing House Ltd.
6 Hatzvi Street
Jerusalem 94386, Israel
972-2-538-0247
orders@gefenpublishing.com

Gefen Books
11 Edison Place
Springfield, NJ 07081
516-593-1234
orders@gefenpublishing.com

www.gefenpublishing.com

Printed in Israel

Library of Congress Cataloging-in-Publication Data

Ravid, Liora.
    [Tanakh hayah be-emet. English]
    Daily life in Biblical times / by Liora Ravid ; translated by Jessica Setbon.
    pages cm
    Includes bibliographical references.
    ISBN 978-965-229-609-2
    1. Bible. O.T. – Criticism, interpretation, etc. 2. Bible. O.T. – History. I.
Setbon, Jessica, translator. II. Title.
BS1178.H4R3813 2013
221.6 – dc23
                    2013006742

CONTENTS

INTRODUCTION

For almost four thousand years, Abraham and Sarah, Isaac and Rebecca, Jacob and his wives, and the other biblical characters have walked alongside us, their stories and deeds forming the backbone of Judeo-Christian culture. The ocean of time that separates us from these ancient heroes has not tarnished their images, nor has the tumult of the modern age obliterated them from our minds. They stand beside us today just as they stood beside our ancestors before us, and just as they will stand beside our children and the generations of the future.

Yet although the hand of time has not erased the biblical characters from our minds, it has obscured the customs of their days that reveal why they acted in certain ways and not others. As a result, their story stands alone, disconnected from where they lived and the way of life they followed in ancient times. We know the story of what they did, but most of us are unaware of the way of life that dictated their actions.

Daily Life in Biblical Times brings the well-known stories that have wandered afar back to their place of birth and to the ground from which they sprouted. This book carefully shakes the dust of time from a world that was, but that ended and is no longer. It reconnects the stories to the cultural reality,

1

social norms, and legal systems that were in place during the period when the biblical characters lived, but that no longer exist in Western culture.

Today we live in cultures with government institutions that have replaced the traditional roles of the family. We live in a society with armies, police forces, legal systems, and educational and social welfare institutions. Each of us is represented by a name and identification number appearing on a computer screen in countless offices and institutions of which we may be unaware. All our lives, we purchase from and supply services to people whom we do not know, who for us are no more than dry data on a computer screen. This is the framework within which we live and in which we raise our children – but this is not the life people experienced during biblical times.

The biblical patriarchs and matriarchs lived in a world that had not yet established any government institution. In ancient times, the family, not the state, was the supreme body in society. The family was responsible for the safety of its living area and the welfare of each of its members. It was society's only economic and legal system. It also served as the main pool of brides and grooms from which the fathers selected partners for their children. Because life took place entirely within the family, a person who was expelled from it found himself in an ungoverned space in which he had no defense, no means of economic support, and no social network.

The fact that the family was the highest body in society, duty-bound and defined by the blood relationships among its members, explains why all the social laws in the Bible are laws of family, not state. It explains why the elders who led the family fulfilled the role of the legal authority and judged their relatives, which would be unacceptable in our time. In the case of severe crime, the elders permitted a blood redeemer to take revenge against the criminal, and this redeemer fulfilled the role of today's executive authority. The redeemer, in most cases a brother of the murder victim or of a raped girl, was responsible for executing the criminal. This explains why, for example, after Tamar was raped, her brother Absalom was responsible for killing the man who had harmed her (II Sam. 13).

In modern, enlightened society, the law considers that women have rights equal to those of men, and this situation seems natural to us. We are oblivious to the fact that equal rights for women, as well as the feminist principles that underlie this concept, are new ideas, unknown to people in the ancient world and in a traditional society that functioned according to strict behavioral codes.

In the period in which our foremothers lived, a girl was married at age ten or eleven. Before she even began to menstruate, she was married to a man chosen by her father. From the day of her wedding, she became the absolute property of her husband, who paid her father a dowry, thus in effect purchasing her from him. Her body, her sexuality, and the children she bore belonged, of course, to her husband. The stories of Tamar (Gen. 38) and Ruth and Orpah (in the book of Ruth) reveal that even when the husband died, his family continued to hold the power of ownership over the wife.

The biblical characters lived in a society that permitted and even encouraged men to marry numerous women, an act prohibited in modern, Western society. A polygamous household operated according to a strict hierarchy in which each woman had her place. This book explains why it was preferable for a man to take many wives, and defines the code that determined the status of the wife in her husband's home. This code demonstrates that in contrast to what many of us may have been taught, Leah, not Rachel, was Jacob's senior wife and the one with the higher status.

The sole function of the woman in the ancient world was to bear children to her husband. The stories of Sarah, Rachel, and Hannah reveal that women who had difficulty becoming pregnant occupied the lowest rung on the social ladder. A barren woman was a disgrace to herself and to her husband. His other wives exploited her weakness, mocking her and bolsting their own superior status.

The Bible makes only brief, casual mention of several issues that are fundamental to understanding it, whose influence transcends the boundaries of the book and continues to our day. One example is the story of the journey of Abraham and his family from Ur, known to many as Ur of the Chaldees, to Canaan, the modern State of Israel. The idea has taken root in our minds that the forefathers of Genesis came to Canaan from the area of the Tigris and the Euphrates Rivers (in today's Iraq). On the basis of this distant collective memory, a tradition developed within Judaism and Christianity that the journey to Canaan represented the watershed between the pagan worldview and the concept of a world ruled by one God.

Is there any foundation to this collective memory?

Was it really possible for Abraham and his family to walk thousands of miles, carrying all their possessions with them? Could people really cover such an enormous distance in one lifetime? Or perhaps, as many Bible researchers argue, the story of the journey to Canaan is a myth, not an event that ever really happened?

In order to offer an authoritative answer to these questions, I examined every detail that the Bible provides about the journey. I measured the walking distance, solved the question of how the walkers obtained food and water, and took into account the difficult conditions of the path and the ravages of the climate. Finally, I determined a key according to which I calculated the number of years the journey must have taken, if it did really happen.

To my surprise, and in contrast to what I had first conjectured, my reconstruction returned a positive answer: it was possible for people to make this journey in one lifetime! The journey stands the test of time and logic, contradicting the argument that the story is a myth and not a real-life event. If we accept this conclusion, then the section that reconstructs the journey illuminates one of the most heroic and mysterious adventures that ever took place during the biblical period. In addition, the reconstruction shows that Sarah's protracted barrenness resulted from a combination of the exertion of the journey, her poor diet, and the young marriage age practiced in the ancient world.

Another major question that the Bible leaves unanswered is the issue of what lay behind the choice of central characters. Why was it important to the biblical author to write about shepherds and simple farmers like Abraham, Isaac, Jacob, and Judah? Why did a work with such a clear masculine orientation bother to record the stories of the foremothers and other women such as Ruth and Naomi? What was so special about these women, who at first glance seem so unimportant?

Chapter 15, which addresses this question, reveals the fact that from creation until the "end of time," the Bible follows the story of one specific dynasty: the Davidic line. The forefathers and foremothers belonged to this noble dynasty, and their story is part of David's story. The New Testament also asserts that Jesus belonged to this dynasty. The characters that did not belong to this important dynasty mounted the stage of history for a fleeting moment, but their sons did not inherit their positions. The Bible does not mention them, and therefore we do not know what became of them. Following in the footsteps of David's dynasty reveals that although Rachel belonged to the family of this dynasty, she was not one of David's forebears. This explains Rachel's low status in comparison to Leah, and explains why Jacob's mistaken love for her led to disaster instead of blessing.

This book also presents a new analysis of the period of David's ascension to kingship. The Bible does not explain the reason for the strained relationship between Saul and Jonathan, Saul's eldest son, who was supposed to inherit his position. We also find no explanation of why Saul, who loved David at first, later tried to kill him, nor why Jonathan joined David and helped him flee from his father.

This book offers answers to these questions, and proves that Saul's endless wars against the Philistines were a grave mistake, and almost led his nation to ruin. I argue here that Saul fought until his dying day against the wrong enemy, and that this almost led to a fatal error. I also show that in order to save Saul's kingdom from destruction, David had to replace him – and this is the reason why Jonathan joined his side.

ಲೃೞೞ

The forefathers and foremothers, prophets, judges, and kings lived on a strip of land measuring just 37 by 60 miles (60 by 100 km). On this microscopic spot on the globe the Bible was recorded in the original Hebrew, and from that it was translated into every language in the world.

It is a well-known rule that while a translation of a written work from one language to another may aspire to be exact and high in quality, the range of meanings enabled by the original language is inevitably lost. This rule is especially applicable to translations of the Bible, which was written in a language as elegant as it is ancient.

The stories in the Bible are very short, often comprising only several verses. The longer stories may take up several chapters. In order to broaden the scope of the story, the biblical authors often used wordplays and double, even triple entendres which allow multiple interpretations of the story. These wordplays expand the story, adding a depth possible only in the original Hebrew. Because translators of the Bible were careful to translate word for word, the reader who relies on a translation of the Bible into his own language misses the wordplays and the range of meanings present in the original language. For this reason, I and the translator of the book, Jessica Setbon, dedicated substantial space in the English translation of the book to translation of selected wordplays that have double and triple meanings, and to the special role they play in the stories in which they were integrated.

In this book, the reader will be exposed, probably for the first time, to these wordplays and the range of meanings that are lost in translation. In addition, the reader will find here a comprehensive explanation of the biblical writing style, which is completely different from our modern method of writing.

Finally, I would like to add one point that is relevant to the opinions of many present-day Bible scholars. I will also return to this idea in the last chapter of the book.

The belief in the existence of one God Who created and rules the world developed from within a pagan environment that believed in the existence of multiple gods. Above all else, the purpose of the Bible is to declare to the world the existence of one God. Three major religions have developed from it: Judaism, Christianity, and much later, Islam. This fact, singular within human history, is enough to indicate its enormous importance.

Yet despite the importance of the Bible, in the last few decades, most Bible researchers at the world's major universities have asserted that the family stories that took place before the time of David never really took place. Extremists among them argue obstinately that everything written in the Bible, from beginning to end, never happened at all. Both the extremist researchers and their more moderate colleagues agree that the family stories in the Bible are legends, and thus we cannot learn anything from them about the biblical period.

This consensus is largely due to the many legendary elements in the stories that are unacceptable to scientific logic. Examples of this are the statements that the forefathers lived hundreds of years, or the story that Sarah was ninety years old and Abraham one hundred years old when Sarah became pregnant. The academic opinion is also strengthened by the fact that we have no archeological evidence from the period of the patriarchs and matriarchs, which might somehow authorize their story.

But when we carefully peel away the legendary overlay from the stories, we find a social picture recognizable to us from other traditional societies, including some that persist today. The new layer that emerges from the mythical covering reveals a reliable and logical picture of a living, breathing society, a picture that is appropriate to the biblical period and to the way of life practiced during that time. This picture exactly fits the scorched landscape in which the biblical characters lived, and no other place in the world.

The thousands of years separating us from the time of our forefathers, as well as the lack of any archeological evidence that might support the biblical text, ensure that we will never be able scientifically to prove the veracity of their story. Still, this absence of proof does not change the fact that ever since human beings began to draw on the walls of their cave dwellings, they have recorded their stories. Because humans have told their stories in every time and in every place where they have lived, there is no reason to assume that they stopped doing so only in the biblical period. There is no reason to presume that the biblical authors wrote myths, while other peoples who lived during the same time wrote about events that took place in reality. Just as in our time people write legends alongside descriptions of important contemporary issues, such was the case with all ancient peoples, including the biblical authors.

A society that recounts the reality of its time is no myth or legend. Rather, this is a society that truly existed and recorded its story in its own unique style and language. Thus even if we cannot prove the truth of each individual story, as a whole the collection of stories in the Bible offers fascinating and credible testimony about the beginnings of a nation on its land.

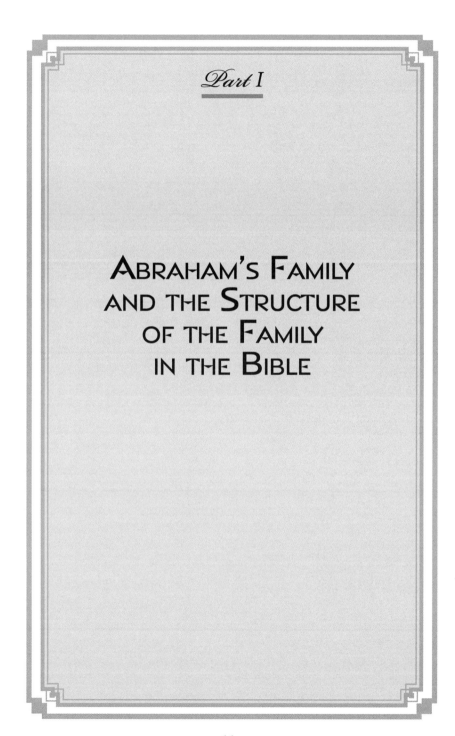

Part I

ABRAHAM'S FAMILY AND THE STRUCTURE OF THE FAMILY IN THE BIBLE

Chapter One

THE TIME OF ABRAHAM

braham is the most important character in the book
of Genesis, as well as one of the major figures in the
Bible and in the history of the three monotheistic
religions. Jews, Christians, and Muslims all view him as their
patriarch, and thus his importance transcends the boundaries
that the Bible defines. Due to Abraham's role in the biblical
narrative, we know about other members of his family as
well: his father Terah, his brother Nahor, and his nephew Lot
(his brother's son). If not for Abraham, Sarah's life would
have been considered unimportant, and her story would have
been written out of the holy book.

But what do we really know about Abraham? What do
we know about Ur (of the Chaldees)[1] – Abraham's birthplace
– and the land of Canaan to which he journeyed? Where was
Haran, where God first revealed Himself to Abraham and
commanded him to go to the land that He promised to him
and his descendants forever?

According to the tradition that developed among the Jews
hundreds of years after the biblical period, the journey from
Ur to the land of Canaan was a pilgrimage from a world of

---

[1] On the difference between "Ur" and "Ur of the Chaldees," see chapter 3, p. 47.

paganism to the land of the One God. In Christian tradition, a pilgrimage to holy sites was called a Crusade, and its goal was religious and ritual. Because the New Testament asserts that Jesus was descended from Abraham, the journey to Canaan determined the path for the masses of Crusaders who made the pilgrimage behind the cross to the land of Israel, which is the biblical land of Canaan. But what do we actually know about this important journey? What do we know about the travelers, our forefather Abraham and foremother Sarah?

Ur, Birthplace of Abraham

Our journey in the footsteps of Abraham and his family begins in Ur, where they were born. Many researchers (even those who believe the story is a myth) date the period of their journey to approximately 1800 BCE. Other researchers date the story one century earlier, or two centuries later. Because the exact date is not important for the purpose of our discussion, we will accept the majority opinion that the story of Abraham and his family refers to 1800 BCE, about four thousand years before our time.

Ur, where Abraham and his family were born, was an ancient city-state[2] located in Aram Naharaim in today's southern Iraq. Much later in time, it became known as Ur of the Chaldees, and it is still known by this name today. The book of Genesis mentions Ur in an aside, as if it were

---

[2] As its name implies, the ancient city-state was an independent state comprised of one city ruled by a king. With the aid of his family and the army he commanded, the king directed both the internal and external affairs of his tiny kingdom. Due to their small size, the ancient city-states did not survive for long. The kings had difficulty defending the cities they ruled, and were easily defeated by more powerful kings or warrior tribes. In Greece, the ancient city-states were known as "polis," with Athens and Sparta the most well-known examples. The principalities that existed in Europe throughout the Middle Ages were an almost exact replica of the ancient city-states, except for their larger territory. Monaco is the best example of a modern city-state. Singapore and the Vatican City are also autonomous city-states, although they are not governed by kings.

an unimportant town, unworthy of mention had it not been related to the history of Abraham. But the opposite is the case. Ur was a major city-state, one of the most splendid and advanced in the ancient Near East. It was a bustling, wealthy metropolis, a modern-day New York, London, or Paris.

Ur was founded on a small hill, about 230 miles (370 km) south of today's Baghdad and 155 miles (250 km) north of the Persian Gulf, beside the delta created by the two great rivers, the Tigris and the Euphrates, before they spill into the waters of the Gulf. Long after the time of Abraham, this area was renamed Mesopotamia, meaning "the land between the rivers."

About eight thousand years ago, the first permanent settlements of the ancient Near East were established there, and thousands of years later, this was where Abraham's ancestors were born. Not far from Ur, on both sides of the Tigris and the Euphrates, other major city-states were founded, including Babylon, Erech, Eridu, Larsa, and Isin, all equally advanced and impressive.

Today, Iraq has four distinctive characteristics: the enormous oil reserves buried deep beneath its surface, its poverty, the reigning political chaos, and its cruel and bloody wars. Yet ages ago, the oil reserves slumbered quietly in their depths while the local inhabitants worked the land between the two rivers, a fertile Garden of Eden. Groups of nomads whose wanderings led them to this area were the first to pitch their tents and settle there, and the wandering shepherds who ended their travels became farmers who settled permanently on the land.

Years passed, then more. Other groups of nomads traveled through the area, envying the permanent residents and eventually joining them. They also began to devote their lives to working the fertile earth. And so, in a long, slow process that took place over thousands of years, the tiny villages grew into small city-states, then large kingdoms, and finally into two enormous empires that inspired dread throughout the ancient Near East: Assyria and Babylon.

The first settlement in Ur began around 4000–3500 BCE, about two thousand years before the time of Abraham, so that by his time, Ur was already an ancient city-state with a long, splendid history. In excavations in the region, archeologists have discovered massive palaces and temple towers, called ziggurats, which towered to over sixty-five feet (20 m).[3] On the walls and pillars of these structures, ancient artists etched plaster carvings in the form of fine lace and beautiful, refined geometric patterns. They also made paintings that illustrated the exploits of their revered kings. Stunning jewelry, musical instruments, and war implements decorated with gold and precious stones were used by the kings during their lifetimes, and accompanied them after death to the silent land of the shadows. These ornaments adorn the major museums of the world, serving as impressive self-testimony to the advanced level of the artists and metalworkers who created them.

The colossal palaces and temples that survived the ravages of time and the wounds of war bear witness to the architectural, engineering, and mathematical skills of the engineers and builders who constructed them. Only in Egypt do we find structures comparable in splendor, sophistication, and impressiveness to the treasures found within.

Among the treasures found in Ur and the city-states nearby are thousands of clay tablets. This clay is made from a mixture of muddy earth, or silt, which was originally used

---

[3] A ziggurat is a tower-temple with a wide base and narrow apex, built on a man-made dirt mound. The residents of the ancient city-states constructed these enormous mounds for two reasons. First, they thought that the gods wanted to feel exalted and enormous, and so they needed high dwellings to which believers would have to lift their gazes (like the cathedrals of Europe and America). The second reason is practical: The area on both sides of the Tigris and Euphrates is at sea level, and so it was repeatedly inundated by the flooding rivers. The goal of the mounds was to prevent the shrines and palaces from being swept into the waters of the Persian Gulf.

for pots. The ancients formed this clay into tablets and used them as writing surfaces. After the scholars finished carving their words in the wet tablets, they left them to dry in the sun or heated them in a kiln. Thanks to this process, as well as the dry climate, their writings have been preserved to this day. Cuneiform, the script used by the people who lived between the Tigris and the Euphrates, is considered the most ancient form of written expression in human history. Scholars have deciphered this script, enabling us to read compositions and documents written by people who lived thousands of years before Abraham's time.

The clay tablets found in Mesopotamia describe the methods of rule of the major ancient city-states and the legal system they followed. They detail the inhabitants' economic life, method of household management, and daily routine. From the distance of the millennia that have passed since the scribes of Ur bent over their wet tablets and used small reeds to press into them the first recorded texts, we are able to learn about the full range of life of the inhabitants of the ancient city-states. This knowledge will serve us when we pack our bags and follow in the footsteps of Abraham and his family (chapter 3).

The deciphered clay tablets give us a very good picture of the components of the Mesopotamian diet, and thus we know for certain that barley, wheat, and dates were main staples. The region's inhabitants used wheat and barley to make bread and cakes (they also made beer from barley). From dates, they made wine and jam – and used these to sweeten the barley cakes they baked. Archeologists have discovered enclosures for domestic animals, revealing that the inhabitants domesticated the goat and the sheep, and so we know that the villagers benefited from meat and dairy products. Their menu also included fish and birds that swam in the water or nested serenely among the cane branches in the delta valley marshes.

The pastoral image I have created here is somewhat exaggerated. The fertile area between the two rivers suffered wars during the time of Abraham, as well as before him. The great wealth of Ur and the neighboring city-states was the constant target of foreign kings, who tried to dominate them and their treasures. Warring tribes and conquering armies who envied the villagers' fertile earth and treasures invaded their homes, plundering them of their possessions. The inhabitants were uprooted from their lands and forced to become either refugees or slaves to the new masters. But history does repeat itself, although it strikes with greater intensity and savagery each time. Although the new masters settled on the land they conquered and began to enjoy the new wealth that fell into their hands, they themselves were conquered by other invaders, stronger and crueler than they, who also desired the lands and treasures of Ur and its neighbors. At the end of a long process that continued for many centuries, conquerors and conquered assimilated into one entity, one cord woven from numerous separate strands.

About fourteen hundred years after the time of Abraham, Alexander the Macedonian entered the center stage of history, and the spotlight focused on him. When his mighty army conquered the fertile region, the ancient city-states and kingdoms received new passports bearing the new, inclusive name of Mesopotamia. The individual names of Ur, Larsa, Isin, Uruk, Erech, and Nippur were forgotten, relegated to the sidelines of history. Rigid and determined, the proud Greek rulers imposed their glorious new Hellenistic culture on the lands they occupied, while the indigenous culture that had developed over thousands of years in one place was defeated, sinking silently under a thick layer of earth and slowly disappearing. An entire way of life was pushed off the stage of history, while the curtain was lifted on Greek culture.

Compared to Ur, the land of Canaan, to which Abraham, Sarah, and Lot arrived after long, exhausting years on foot, was a remote corner, miserable and desolate, located at the back edge of the world and populated by a group of small, poor tribes known as Canaanites.

From a historical, cultural, and economic perspective, the journey of Abraham and his family was a crossing from a rich, prosperous land to a poor, empty area. It was a journey from a place where water was plentiful and the earth soft and fertile to a dry region where the hard, desolate earth tortured the farmer who attempted to plow it. This was a journey from a place where kings lived in lofty palaces and adorned themselves with golden jewelry inlaid with precious stones to a place where the wealthiest inhabitants toiled to build small stone houses that have long since crumbled.

This was a journey from a place where the gods were worshipped in enormous, magnificent temples to a place where the worship of God was performed under the open skies, on an altar made of a small pile of stones collected quickly and abandoned immediately after the ritual. Abraham built such altars at the places he passed along his journey (Gen. 12:7–8; 13:4, 18), as did Isaac and Jacob. The Israelites did so as well, until Solomon built a small, modest Temple in Jerusalem (c. 960–940 BCE). Over the years, this Temple grew in our collective memory until it became a spacious, majestic structure that never could have existed. Abraham's journey to the land of Canaan was one more thing: a journey to the land where the most well-known book in the Western world, the Bible, was written.

It seems obvious to ask why Abraham and his family left the verdant region between the Tigris and the Euphrates and traveled to a distant, barren, empty land. The answer present in our collective consciousness is that God commanded Abraham to go. But in truth, it was not Abraham, but his father Terah who left Ur and directed his steps toward the land of Canaan (Gen. 11:31–32).

Terah did not complete the passage, because he died in Haran. But when we ask why he gathered his family in the first place and began the journey to a foreign, distant land with which he had no connection, our question demands an answer.

Chapter Two

LEAVING UR

Terah took his son Abram; and Lot the son of Haran, his grandson; and his daughter-in-law Sarai, the wife of Abram his son; and they departed with them from Ur of the Chaldees to go to the land of Canaan, and they came as far as Haran and settled there. The days of Terah were two hundred and five years, and Terah died in Haran.

(Gen. 11:31–32)

The historical story of the journey from Ur to the land of Canaan begins on the day Terah, Abraham's father, gathered together his family and his meager possessions and took to the road. According to the text in Genesis, the family's first stop was the city of Haran, still in existence today in southern Turkey. Terah died in Haran, after which his small family parted ways. Nahor and his wife Milcah settled in Haran, where they built their home, while Abraham, Sarah, and Lot continued their journey to the distant land.

The Bible does not explain why Terah and his family decided to leave their native land and move to a foreign place. Perhaps this is why previous researchers have neglected this issue. But the move from Ur and the story of the journey,

21

which were compressed into the two verses above, contain one of the most heroic and important dramas in the history of both Judaism and Christianity.

When we open the atlas and calculate the distance between Ur and Haran, we see that the two cities are located about 808 miles (1300 km) from each other. Once the travelers reached Haran they had to cross the plains of Urfa (Sanli-urfa in modern Turkey), the chain of the Lebanon mountains, and the land of Canaan. They then went down to Egypt, the farthest stop on their journey, and from there, they returned to the land of Canaan. As we will see in detail in the next chapter, they walked at least 2175 miles (3500 km). This is a vast distance, especially when we take into consideration the topographic conditions of the route and the fact that the group traveled on foot. This detail serves to intensify the first question: Why did Terah decide to gather his family and leave for the land of Canaan? Why did he leave behind his way of life and all his possessions, and set out on this journey? The book of Genesis does not answer this question, nor will it reveal any answers below.

The only thing we can say for certain is that Terah did not make his journey due to divine command, since God never revealed Himself to Terah and never commanded him to do anything. Any answer we suggest must be based on the social and economic reality of that time. Our proposal must accord with the knowledge we possess about the way of life practiced in Mesopotamia four thousand years ago.

LAND AND SOCIAL HIERARCHY

The economic life of inhabitants of the ancient world was based only on agriculture. Thus the land was their most important economic asset as well as their principal source of wealth. Because ownership of land determined a person's social and economic status, we will use this fact as a reliable measure in order to identify the status of Terah and his family.

In the ancient world, the kings were the owners of the largest estates and the wealthiest people in their kingdoms. If their kingdom dominated a central crossroads, they collected taxes from caravan drivers in exchange for the right to pass through and stop inside their kingdom. Second on the ladder of wealth and power were the priests, traditionally both the enemies and partners of the kings. The priests controlled the temples, and they also owned extensive land. The gods of Mesopotamia and Egypt were not satisfied with small stone altars such as the one Abraham built. Instead, they developed a penchant for enormous houses of worship and valuable gifts – and this craving, as we are aware, has continued throughout the world to this day.[4] In addition to income from offerings and other payments that worshippers brought to the temples, the priests also received significant income from the lands they owned. In third place on the social ladder stood the king's family and his followers. Many of them were army officers who fought alongside the king and aided him in ruling the kingdom, although they often rebelled against him at the first opportunity in an attempt to improve their social and economic status.

In fourth place in the social hierarchy were middle-class citizens who owned small plots of land. Fifth place was occupied by a large class of poor, who were free citizens but did not own their own land. The poor lived with their families on the landowners' estates. In exchange for this privilege, they worked the fields and compensated the landowners with agricultural produce, like the tenant farmers of the feudal period

---

[4] For example, the Vatican in Rome has the status of a state, and it owns one of the wealthiest banks in the world. The Catholic Church also owns land in many countries, which comprises a significant part of its substantial wealth.

in Europe. As usual, slaves occupied the bottom rung of the social ladder. Slaves had no civil rights; they were the property of their masters, and like any merchandise lying on a shelf, they also bore a price tag. Owners could buy and sell their slaves just like donkeys, sheep, or cows. Owners could marry male slaves to female slaves so that they would give birth to the next generation of slaves. Like their parents, the children of slaves were property that could be traded.

The poor and the slaves were the engine that turned the wheels of the economy in the ancient world. They built the pyramids of Egypt, the palaces and temples of Mesopotamia, and the Great Wall of China. Thousands of years later, they built the palaces and cathedrals of Europe. Six thousand years ago slaves picked cotton in Egypt, and two hundred years ago they did the same in the United States.

The poor and the slaves worked side by side, but the poor still had one advantage: they were free citizens, and so they could not be bought or sold. A landowner who was not satisfied with a poor tenant's work had the right to throw him off his land, but he could not dismantle his family and sell each member separately. By contrast, a slave lived in constant fear that his family would be torn apart and sold off one by one, and this served as a particularly efficient means of banishing any foolish thoughts of freedom from his mind.

In addition to the population that lived permanently in one location, the ancient world included another large social group – the nomads. In the time of Abraham (early second millennium BCE), large groups of people wandered with their herds of goats from one pasture to another, until finally they also took possession of land and exchanged the nomadic life for permanent settlement. By definition, nomads owned no land of their own, and so they lacked the most important source of wealth. Although they were very poor, the nomads possessed herds of goats, which were their major source of sustenance. They also owned donkeys, which carried their owners' possessions on their backs.[5]

In the land of Canaan to which Abraham journeyed, the social stratification was much simpler. The Canaanite tribes that lived there at the beginning of the second millennium BCE were mainly concentrated in the few areas that had water. Due to their poverty and because of the small number of inhabitants, the social classes that developed in Canaan were not the same as those of contemporary Egypt and Mesopotamia. In Abraham's day, there were no kings, priests, or nobles in Canaan. At the top of the social hierarchy stood the elders, who were the leaders of the privileged families. The wealthy among them lived in small houses, which they built by gathering stones in the fields and placing them one on top of the other, then filling the cracks with dirt. The rest of the population lived in tents. Number two in the social hierarchy were the nomadic shepherds who followed their goats. Last place, of course, was reserved for the slaves.

Now, with the socioeconomic hierarchy of the inhabitants of Mesopotamia clear in our minds, we are able to determine the social and economic status of Terah and his family with a large measure of probability. We can also suggest an explanation for why they left Ur.

A reliable socioeconomic test must account for the fact that ownership of land was the only measure of wealth in ancient times. Such a test must conclude that Terah did not have land of his own. A person who lived in an agricultural society, whose entire existence and livelihood relied on the land he owned, was not suddenly overcome by the strange desire to wander afar and look for a new place to settle. He did

---

[5] A socioeconomic hierarchy based on land ownership was common throughout the world until the beginning of the Industrial Revolution, which led to mass movement of populations from villages to cities (first in England in 1760, then throughout Europe). When mechanized industry developed and the influence of monetary capital on economics increased, ownership of land ceased to be the sole measure of wealth.

not leave his land of his own free will, but rather remained to live and work on it. Further, in ancient times, land was never only an economic asset, but a cultural one as well. A person's cultural heritage was closely connected to the land on which his ancestors had settled, on which he lived and raised his children. The family land always had sacred value to its owners, and this sanctity was passed down through generations along with legends of miracles that had taken place in a hidden cave or under an ancient tree that grew on the land.

Due to the great importance of the land, we may comfortably assume that if Terah had owned land, he would not have left it. The fact that he did leave his place of birth shows that he apparently was lacking this asset. If Terah and his family did not own land, then they must not have belonged to any of the four upper classes we defined. They were not kings, priests, or nobles, nor were they members of the middle class, who also owned small farms of their own. According to our class hierarchy, Terah and his family must have been either poor, or slaves who had managed to flee to freedom, or nomads who had not yet settled in one location.

We will examine these possibilities below.

The possibility that this was a family of slaves who had fled their owners is unreasonable. A slave who attempted to run off but was caught faced execution, and his family was divided and sold to other owners. Alternatively, if the owner had mercy on his slave's life, he would cut off his ear or brand him, so that all would recognize that this was a runaway slave. Furthermore, according to ancient law, landowners were forbidden to shelter runaway slaves, and a landowner who was caught doing so was subject to the death punishment.[6] These severe punishments undoubtedly had a deterrent effect. Still, there were always some slaves who managed to flee, and

---

[6] Hammurabi, laws 16, 19.

there were always some landowners who were glad to take them in for free and reintroduce them into the cycle of slavery. A lone slave was easily absorbed by a distant estate and could disappear within it, but such an opportunity was not available to a family of slaves that tried to flee together and preserve its unity. Because the Bible describes the departure of Terah's family members as a calm process and not as an escape, we can assume that they did not belong to the class of slaves that lived in Ur.

Possibly, Terah and his family were nomadic shepherds, like much of the population of the ancient Near East in the second millennium BCE. This possibility might explain why they did not own land and why they were not in flight, but we must reject it as well. The wandering pattern of traditional nomads is territorial, or circular. Although nomads are not landowners themselves, they do return to regular pastures. Nomads' traditional stories are connected to the regions where they wander, the wells to which they return at the end of their circle to draw water, or the palm trees that they repeatedly visit in order to gather fruit. Nomads do not walk 808 miles (1300 km), the distance between Ur and Haran, in order to return to the same pastures and wells. Certainly they do not walk 2175 miles (3500 km) as far as Egypt, the farthest stop in the journey of Abraham and his family. Because regular, cyclical travel is a major characteristic of nomadic society, we can assert with certainty that Terah and his family did not belong to this social group. Our family of travelers walked forward, always advancing, never returning to where they had been before.

A family that leaves its homeland in order to reach a distant destination and rebuild its life there is a family of emigrants. Throughout human history, emigrants have traveled long distances to settle in a new land, and the usual reason for this phenomenon is well known. The motive for emigration in times of peace (as opposed to during war) is almost always economic. In most cases, emigrants are poor people looking for new economic opportunities in faraway places. They set their sights toward the place they want to reach, and never return to their previous habitation. The day they leave their homeland, they cut themselves off from their previous lives, unravel the connections of the past, and leave behind the people they know. Emigrants do not settle near their original dwelling; rather, they aim for a distant location, hoping to rebuild their lives anew there.

A good example of this is the settlement of the United States of America. Three hundred years ago, waves of immigrants from Europe came to the relatively empty young country. In those days, Europe was the "Old World," urbanized and wealthy – the parallel of Ur and its sophisticated neighbors. Just as the distant land of Canaan was not the land of Terah and Abraham's ancestors, so America across the ocean was not the ancestral land of any individual in the multitude that streamed toward it. And just as Abraham and his family had no historical connection to the land of Canaan, so America was not "the Holy Land" for any of the immigrants who knocked on its doors. America was "the New World." It was the holy land of the dollar and of economic opportunity, and the poor of Europe flowed toward it because they were poor, because America opened its doors with jobs and income that were unavailable in the country they had left. Indeed, the desperate immigrants who grasped at a distant hope had to cross the ocean in small, dilapidated boats to reach that faraway continent.

Their desire to escape the economic troubles they had suffered in their home countries overcame their fear of crossing the ocean and the hazards of the journey. Eventually, Western Europe – one of the most significant sources of immigrants to the United States – itself became flooded with immigrants.

Since the Second World War, tens of millions of Muslims have moved to Western Europe from Arab countries, in the hopes of improving their economic condition, although that region lacks any religious or historical importance for them.

Because economic immigration has a regular pattern that repeats itself throughout history, we may assume that this was the case for Terah's family as well. Apparently, economic hardship was the reason why Terah and his family left magnificent Ur and began to walk to a new place, in the hopes of finding economic opportunities unavailable to them in the wealthy "Old World." The fact that Terah left a prosperous, advanced city-state does not mean that he himself was a wealthy man, or that any crumbs from the magnificent treasures of the kings and nobles fell into his lap.

The possibilities we have analyzed above lead to the conclusion that Terah and his family belonged to the poor class, and that they left Ur because they lacked the most important economic resource of every agricultural society: land.

We do not know the reason for Terah's poverty, and from a distance of almost four thousand years, we can offer only several conjectures. Possibly, his ancestors had always been poor. Another possibility is that they had been wealthy, but lost their property due to a natural disaster. Every type of natural disaster that causes loss of life and property today also took place in Terah's time, and may have been the reason for the family's poverty. Heavy rains that fell on the high mountains of what is now modern Turkey and Kurdistan may have pooled into the enormous mouths of the Tigris and Euphrates, creating a gigantic wave that flooded the low plain where Ur was located. Perhaps one of the floods that often ravaged the area swept the family property into the Persian Gulf. Locusts, one of the most severe plagues of the ancient world, may have blanketed the fields of Terah or his ancestors. One swarm of locusts landing en masse in one field instead of another was enough to impoverish the family who depended on that field for their bread.

Perhaps Terah was not his father's eldest son, and thus he did not inherit the family's property and was forced to look for a new place to settle. Either way, we can assume that like countless impoverished emigrants who lived before and after him, Terah packed his bags and went off to seek his luck in another land because he was poor. The only difference between Terah's family and any other family of displaced persons about whom we know nothing seems to be that this unique family gave birth to one of the most important and well-known characters in the history of the monotheistic world: Abraham.

Chapter Three

THE ODYSSEY: THE JOURNEY FROM UR TO THE LAND OF CANAAN

Terah took his son Abram; and Lot the son of Haran, his grandson; and his daughter-in-law Sarai, the wife of Abram his son; and they departed with them from Ur of the Chaldees to go to the land of Canaan, and they came as far as Haran and settled there...and Terah died in Haran.

(Gen. 11:31–32)

The Lord said to Abram, "Go forth from your land and your birthplace and your father's house to the land that I will show you. And I will make you a great nation; I will bless you, and make your name great, and you shall be a blessing...." So Abram went as the Lord had spoken to him.... Abram took Sarai his wife and Lot his brother's son, and all their wealth that they had acquired, and the souls they had acquired in Haran, and they set out on the way to the land of Canaan, and they came to the land of Canaan. Abram crossed through the land to the site of Shechem, to the plain of Moreh.... He moved from there to the mountain east of Beth-el and pitched his tent with Beth-el to the west and Ai to the east.... Then Abram journeyed on, journeying steadily southward. There was a famine in the land, and Abram went down to Egypt to sojourn there, for the famine was severe in the land.

(Gen. 12:1–10)

The journey of Abraham, Sarah, and Lot, from Ur in today's southern Iraq to the land of Canaan, is the most important journey in the history of the monotheistic world.[7] According to the Jewish tradition that developed hundreds and thousands of years after the biblical period, this was a journey from the world of idol worshippers to the land of the One God, where the Bible was written in order to inform the world of His existence. According to Christian tradition, Jesus was a descendant of Abraham, and thus the journey to the land of Canaan became a pilgrimage to the place where Jesus was born. Throngs of Crusaders from throughout the Christian world swarmed to the Holy Land in the footsteps of their savior, and faithful Christians still do so today.

Yet despite the enormous importance of this journey for followers of these two religions, we know almost nothing about it. The story of the entire journey is compressed with simplicity into names of several regions and settlements that mean very little to most readers, and conceals every other detail from us. The text tells us only that Terah led the family from Ur to Haran, where they split up. Nahor, Abraham's

---

[7] Because the first part of the journey, which was led by Terah, is also part of the journey made by Abraham, Sarah, and Lot, I relate to the journey as a whole and do not consider the first section as a separate unit.

brother, and his wife Milcah pitched their tent in Haran and remained there, while Abraham, Sarah, and Lot continued on their way to the land of Canaan. From there Abraham's group went down to Egypt, and after an unknown length of time they turned around, returned to the land of Canaan, and settled in Hebron (13:18), an important city in biblical times.

The text that records these scant details does not reveal what distance the three traveled, or how many years they were on the road. It does not say what baggage they carried, or how they renewed equipment that wore out from heavy use. It ignores the great obstacle that stood in their way: how to obtain food on the endless roads.

Not one word.

The biblical text says nothing about the emotional lives of any of the three. It does not reveal in what direction Abraham's thoughts wandered on the days when he walked the roads, nor does it mention a word about the feelings of Sarah and Lot, whose fate was bound up with him.

The Bible does not always use such concise language. For example, the story of the journey of Moses and the people who left Egypt with him offers many more details, and thus we have a fairly full picture of the Israelites' travails in the desert. But Moses and his followers crossed the Sinai Desert only once, while Abraham and his two companions did so twice – once on the way to Egypt and once on the way back. Yet we know nothing about their days on the road.

In the previous chapter, we noted the tendency of the biblical authors to condense entire biographies into several words, and pointed out that we do not know why Terah and his family left Ur. How can it be that the Bible documents the chain of events preceding the Exodus from Egypt, while it says nothing of the events before the departure of Terah and his family from Ur? Here we meet with this phenomenon once again, and we will encounter it repeatedly in the following chapters.

This concise writing style has many disadvantages. It conceals from the reader vital details about the protagonist's past and inner world. Only on occasion, for a brief moment, does the text cast a thin ray of light on a character's feelings, but it immediately disappears before we can absorb exact details from the general picture. The reader who desires a complete picture is left frustrated and dissatisfied. As a rule, the Bible gives only the result, without the chain of circumstances that preceded the event it describes. As if that is not enough, the biblical writers did not place the story in any historical, social, or legal context that would aid the reader in understanding it. The biblical stories dangle by a thread, unattached from any meaningful background. For example, if we read the text alone, we do not know that Abraham and his family left one of the most advanced city-states in the ancient Near East and set out for one of the most remote areas of that period.

Nevertheless, the spare writing style also has a major advantage: every word in the story contributes to our comprehension of the text, for if a word were superfluous, it would have been spared. The Bible does not include blather or endless, unnecessary descriptions; it does not contain gossip, or pornography in the guise of artistic writing. To the biblical authors, every word was worth its weight in gold, and they considered each word carefully before placing it in its exact designated position. Thus the limited details that the text does give about the journey enable us to reconstruct it with a high degree of probability.

Since the stops along the journey were noted, we can calculate the distance between them and find that the three walked about 2175 miles (3500 km). This is equal to the distance on foot from Moscow through Berlin and then to

Madrid, or between New York and Miami – and back. Based on this data, we will calculate how many years the journey took. Maps and atlases will illuminate the landscapes and regions through which the group traveled, and the weather conditions that prevailed along their path.

A quick peek at the map reveals that the lion's share of the journey passed through mountains whose highest peaks reached 3000 m (9800 ft). It also reveals that the second half of the trip passed through hot, arid areas, and so we may conclude that in that part of the journey, the travelers suffered from a shortage of food and water.

Archeological findings also make an important contribution to the project of reconstructing the journey. Thanks to lists that the ancients carved on clay tablets, we can estimate with great likelihood the components of the food basket available to the family, the equipment they took with them, and the way they replenished their supplies. In general, when we spread the few details that the book of Genesis gives us across a broad cultural map, we obtain a key that opens many doors. Careful use of this valuable key will open the door to one of the most fascinating, mysterious, and heroic dramas in the history of the Bible: the journey from Ur to the land of Canaan.

JOURNEY TO THE LAND OF CANAAN

The first stage of the journey began in Ur and ended in Haran: "They went forth with them from Ur of the Chaldees to go to the land of Canaan, and they came as far as Haran and settled there" (11:31).

The historical Ur was located in modern-day Iraq, on a small hill on the banks of the Euphrates River in southern Mesopotamia, about 168 miles (270 km) from the Persian Gulf. Haran, the family's first stop, still stands today, in southeast Turkey near the Syrian border. Ur and Haran are connected by the long, curving Euphrates River, and as we already mentioned, the distance between the two cities is about 808 miles (1300 km). Because caravans always traveled alongside rivers, we can state with certainty that Terah and his family walked up the Euphrates toward Haran. The river marked their route and ensured that they would not lose their way. In addition, it provided ample water and pastures for the goats and donkeys that walked in front of them, and whose praises we will sing below.

Haran, located at the upper end of the Euphrates, was a key stopping point. Although it was not a magnificent city-state like Ur, it was an important, well-developed city that dominated one of the most vital commercial thoroughfares in the ancient Near East. The wise men of Haran were well known throughout the region for their knowledge of astronomy – upon which we still rely today.

From a theological point of view, the first section of the journey, led by Terah, was insignificant. God did not reveal Himself to Terah, nor did He command him to leave his birthplace and go "to the land that I will show you." According to the order of events determined by the book of Genesis, God reveals Himself to Abraham for the first time after Terah's death, when the travelers reach Haran. In Haran, God gives the command that became engraved in the collective mind of the Jewish people:

> The Lord said to Abram, "Go forth from your land and your birthplace and your father's house to the land that I will show you. And I will make you a great nation; I will bless you, and make your name great, and you shall be a blessing. I will bless those who bless you, and those who curse you I will curse; and all the families of the earth shall be blessed through you." So Abram went as the Lord had spoken to him, and Lot went with him; Abram was seventy-five years old when he left Haran. Abram took

Sarai his wife and Lot his brother's son, and all their wealth
that they had acquired, and the souls they had acquired in
Haran, and they set out on the way to the land of Canaan,
and they came to the land of Canaan. (Gen. 12:1–5)

When faithful Abraham heard God's word, he gathered
his meager belongings, parted from his brother Nahor and
Nahor's wife Milcah, and set out together with his wife Sarah
and nephew Lot. Theologically speaking, this act began the
journey from the "Old World" of idol worshippers to the
"New World" governed by the One God. The three travelers
turned their backs on Haran and began to walk toward the
land of Canaan.

The second half of the journey, from Haran to Canaan,
was much longer and more tortuous than its predecessor.
Abraham and his entourage had to add another 1400 miles
(2250 km) to the 810 miles (1300 km) they had already covered, until they finally completed their journey and unloaded
their travelers' bags from their shoulders.

In the first part of the journey led by Terah, the family
walked northwest: from the southern city of Ur to Haran,
the northernmost point on their path. In the second half,
Abraham led the group, and they turned from Haran toward
the west and walked toward the "Great Sea," as the ancients
referred to the Mediterranean. The three crossed the plains
of Urfa where Haran is located, and 186 miles (300 km) later,
the Mediterranean winked at them with shining blue eyes.
After reaching the plateau above the sea, they turned south
and walked to Canaan.

At this point, Abraham had to choose between two paths
that were well frequented in his day. He and his small group
could descend from the Urfa plains to the coastal region, and
walk along the water line toward Canaan. Alternatively, they
could remain more or less at the same height (about 765

yards [700 m] above sea level) and cross the Lebanon mountain range that stretches from north to south, parallel to the
Mediterranean Sea. The route along the open plain, beside
the water, was much easier to walk than the path through the
mountains, but it had one major disadvantage: it was exposed
to the nomad's greatest enemy ever – highway robbers. In the
ancient world, highway robbers were such a serious threat
that royal trade caravans traveled with guard corps. Because
the three did not enjoy such protection, they apparently
chose the path that was more difficult but safer – through
the mountains. Among the colossal rocks and thick brush of
the Lebanon mountains, they could find hiding places from
highway robbers. They could stop for the night in mountain
caves, take shelter from the ravages of the climate, and light
a fire without fearing the gaze of hostile eyes. Apparently, the
mapmakers of historic atlases also followed this logic, since
they traced the probable journey of the group through the
mountains and not along the sea.

We will thus follow the mapmakers' lead, and assume
that after the family crossed the Urfa plateau, they turned
south and continued on the path that divides the Lebanon
mountain chain. This route added another 292 miles (470
km) to the journey. They then descended the mountains and
continued through the northern entrance into the land of
Canaan.

When the three entered Canaan, after 1286 miles (2070
km) of wandering, Abraham had reached the land to which
God commanded him to go. With this, his religious mission
was completed. Undoubtedly, at this stage he and his fellow
travelers were tired of long roads, and wished to unpack their
bags and settle in one place. But this is not what happened.
The three did not settle in the Land that God had promised Abraham he would inherit. They did not drive their
tent stakes into its earth, nor did they plant olive trees or

grapevines. The travelers did not wash the dust from their blazing faces, nor cool their swollen feet in clear spring water. They allowed no rest for their weary bodies, covered only by a thin layer of skin, sticky with sweat, which kept their bones together in one package. To their great misfortune, they reached the Promised Land in a time of severe famine, and thus they had to continue walking. The text reads:

> There was a famine in the land, and Abram descended to Egypt to sojourn there, for the famine was severe in the land. (12:10)

In Canaan and the neighboring lands, famine was a result of drought, which followed lack of rain, the sole source of water: "A land of mountains and valleys; from the rain of heaven it drinks water" (Deut. 11:11). In order for rain to fall in this part of the world, the wind has to push the clouds that gather over the Mediterranean Sea toward the east, over the shoreline. But in drought years, the wind does not push the clouds over the shoreline, and they drop their water into the sea. As a result, the regions east of the coast remain dry. Farmers then have no choice but to stand back and watch, brows furrowed with worry, as their fields turn yellow and wither with thirst, and the wheat they had sowed at the end of the summer refuses to sprout. They observe the waning flow of water in the rivers, and the emptying of the pits they had dug to collect rainwater. The farmers and shepherds have no water for themselves or their herds to drink. When rain does not fall for one year, the inhabitants suffer, but when rain stays away for several years in a row, disaster ensues: domestic animals die of hunger and thirst, and the human population along with them.[8]

---

[8] The Bible offers dozens of examples of how the inhabitants of the land of Canaan suffered from hunger after several consecutive years of drought, and even resorted to cannibalism (II Kings 6:24–30).

There is no water.

In just such a year, following several consecutive years of drought, Abraham and his entourage reached the land of Canaan. Those who are familiar with the water cycle that dominates this region will realize that they should have ended their journey as soon as they entered the land. The three travelers had just descended the Lebanon mountain range and reached the northern part of Canaan, which is rich in water when compared to the southern region. So they should have unpacked their bags and stayed in place until the next rainy season arrived, hoping it would be more blessed than its predecessor. But strangely, they acted in opposition to all logic and continued to walk south. Continuously south. As they moved south, they penetrated ever deeper into the heart of the Negev desert, the driest part of the land throughout the year, whose inhabitants are the first to suffer during years of drought.

In light of these facts, it seems obvious to ask why Abraham and his group did not remain in northern Canaan. Apparently, the answer is that they had no choice. At that time, the land was populated by a sparse, impoverished group of Canaanites, which naturally concentrated around the scarce bodies of water. During drought years, those inhabitants who did not flee to Egypt crowded beside the water sources and tried to reduce their usage to the minimum necessary to remain alive. A population that is counting the last remaining drops of water in the wells and rivers does not welcome strangers who knock on their doors, even if God has sent them. Logic dictates that the longtime residents were unwilling to share their remaining water reserves with the newcomers, and pushed them south to the arid areas of the Negev, thus adding an additional 168 miles (270 km) to their journey.

When the three reached the Negev, they suffered from a famine so severe that they were forced to continue fleeing to the verdant strip along the Nile River in Egypt, the bread basket of the ancient world (in sharp contrast to our time). But in order to do so, they had to cross the deathly Sinai Desert, adding another 150 miles (400 km) to their journey.

All the hardships they suffered from the day they left Ur until crossing the Negev do not compare to what awaited them in the Sinai Desert – a land in which a cruel yellow sun is pinned in the everlastingly blue sky from dawn until dusk.

The desert landscape is stunning and dreadful. At this point, our three travelers, who had already experienced a variety of scenery throughout the years of their journey, encountered the barrenness of the desert.

The desert changes its appearance and its colors, but one color is never seen: green. Yellow, brown, red, and black dominate, changing places with surprising subtlety and creating a feeling of movement, within stillness that lacks even the motion of shadow. Curved mounds of soft yellow sand are broken at horizon's edge by plains of shattered stone that give rise to black hills of granite, fractured and razor-sharp. Once, hundreds of thousands, perhaps millions of years ago, the broken stones were proud, whole rocks. But the sun roasted them in the fires of hell, cleaving deep grooves within their cores. The wind completed the work of destruction by smashing them into small pieces, then sprayed them in all directions.

Adventurers and modern-day lovers of wilderness landscapes are drawn to the monstrous power of the desert that lies as flat as a corpse. Yet they know that if they stare patiently at the scenery spread before them, they will discover signs of life. A few beetles and a frightened lizard may dart quickly past, in search of a shady corner. Should they turn over a large rock, a snake or a scorpion may grin at them in surprise, and the terrifying hiss of its whispering escape will bore its way into their mental store of mysterious desert melodies.

Perhaps it is the midday glare of the wilderness, or the radiance of night, clean and clear, that calls out to these adventurers. Perhaps it is the howling of jackals, appearing at dusk to sing a dissonant lullaby to the moon, audible from one end of the world to another, that momentarily awakens the ancestral memories these daredevils try in vain to erase from their minds. Refugees from the big cities know that if they wait a bit longer, the soft landscape, in which movement is expressed through changes in light and shadow, will be transformed in an instant. From within the glassy silence, suddenly a sharp whistle will burst forth. A wild wind awakens in a panic, hurling to the skies mounds of sand mixed with small, sharp stones. A deep blue ocean of sky will breathe the sand clouds into its lungs, and a murky darkness will descend upon the earth. For one moment, one hour, the sandstorm will fill the adventurers with a feeling of powerful satisfaction that they vainly pursue in cities packed with people and cars and trains, and everything that moves, honks, and spits out black smoke. When the storm abates, the whistling will cease, the silence will return. Clouds of stones that were lifted on high will fall to the ground like raindrops, and the fine sand will slowly descend and create new dunes in places they did not exist mere hours previously. The adventurers of the modern world visit the desert for a week. They photograph the shattered landscape, and when they have had enough of its silence or wildness, they load their belongings into their backpacks and return home, to recount their experiences in the wilderness.

Abraham, Sarah, and Lot were not adventure lovers who escaped to the wild in the hopes that the blazing sun would alleviate an irksome longing for which there is no real relief. They did not forget their past in the desert; no distant memory engraved in the back of their minds, or deep within their hearts, suddenly awakened and called them to return to it. They reached the desert because they were hungry, and because they knew that their only chance to remain alive was to cross it. But the sun beating down from the accursed blue skies burned their brains and roasted their shoulders from early morning to sunset. When the desert awoke and began its crazy dance, they were not filled with ecstatic joy, but with horror. They fled in panic to a cave dug into the rock that protected their starving, emaciated bodies, and waited for the storm to abate. When night came, they did not gather inside a tent purchased in an upmarket store for high-tech camping equipment, but took shelter together with the goats and donkeys inside a simple tent, and curled up on a thin straw mat that Sarah wove from dry weeds she gathered on the way. They covered themselves with a hide cloak, worn and full of holes from age and use. In the last moment between wakefulness and sleep, they thanked God for having mercy on them and allowing them another day of life. Then nothing else was important, and they plunged into a dreamless sleep, from which they awoke the next day as weary as if they had never slept, as if no rest could ever banish their fatigue.

We do not know how long the three remained in Egypt, until one day they retraced their footsteps and returned to the land of Canaan and the Negev. In order to go back, they had to cross the Sinai Desert a second time and add another 250 miles (400 km) to their journey. When they reached the region of Sodom, an oasis in the heart of the Negev, Lot took his leave from Abraham and Sarah, and the longtime partnership between them reached its end. Abraham and Sarah continued for another 62 miles (100 km), and when they reached Hebron, they finally stopped walking (13:18).

Totaling the distances above reveals that from the day they left Ur until they arrived in Hebron, the group crossed

2015 miles (3240 km). But this is the distance by air, and
they were on foot. Therefore we must add to this measure
the bends in the road as well as the climbs up and down
mountains. We must take into account that errors in naviga-
tion and short excursions to wells or to gather the scattered
herd of goats added another 160 miles (260 km) to the distance they walked. Apparently, then, the estimate that the
three walked about 2175 miles (3500 km) is close to the true
distance.

THE FERTILE CRESCENT

The map reveals another detail that we must take into
account. The settlements through which the three travelers
passed were located along one of the most ancient and important routes in the ancient Near East. This route spanned the
Fertile Crescent,[9] an enormous envelope that embraces the
mighty Syrian Desert, strewn with sand and endless fields
of gravel. In order to bypass the Syrian Desert, compared
to which the Sinai Desert is a flowering garden, travelers in
ancient caravans walked along a route that stretched across
the Fertile Crescent and passed through Haran – one of the
northern stations on the road.[10] Thousands of years before
Abraham, and after him, as well, this route served caravans
of traders and nomads as well as fighting armies. The fact
that the author of the story of the biblical journey mentions
names of settlements along the ancient caravan route, and
emphasized that the family reached Haran and stopped there,

[9] The Fertile Crescent is so named for its crescent shape, which resembles a bow
with two legs of differing lengths. One leg stands in the delta of the Tigris and the
Euphrates Rivers, near Ur, where the journey began. The other leg stands in the delta
formed by the Nile before it drains into the Mediterranean Sea – the farthest point the
three reached. The northern part of the Crescent is in the region of Haran, and it bends
toward the west.

[10] Today's Haran is identified with a small village and archeological site located in
northeast Turkey, near the Syrian border, next to the Euphrates River.

stands up under any historical test. It illustrates that the author did not fabricate an illogical path, but rather recorded that the family followed one of the most important routes of the ancient Near East.

PREPARING FOR THE JOURNEY: CAMELS AND HISTORICAL WRITING

Analysis of the journey's route raises additional questions, aside from the one of distance we examined above. For example, how did a family that lived almost four thousand years ago prepare for such a long journey? What equipment did they take with them, and how did they transport it? What were the components of their diet? How did they travel – on the backs of donkeys, horses, or camels, or on foot?

The book of Genesis mentions the camel several times, and even relates that Abraham's faithful servant Eliezer went to Haran at the head of a caravan of ten camels (24:10). This suggests the possibility that the journey to Canaan was made on camelback, which would have significantly lessened its travails and the great drama we describe here. But in Terah and Abraham's time, the camel was not yet domesticated, and so they could not have used them.

Researchers assert that wild camels lived in the ancient Near East forty thousand years ago and perhaps even earlier. But domestication of the camel began tens of thousands of years later. The first evidence that humans used the camel for their own purposes is from around 1300 BCE, by the earliest estimate – about five hundred years after the time of Terah and Abraham. In order to explain the contradiction between the biblical description and the researchers' contention, I must give a short explanation of one of the most complicated and fascinating problems in the field of biblical studies: the question of when the Bible stories were written.

Academics assert that the Bible is not the homogenous composition of one author, but rather a work that was written over a period of about 1350 years (c. 1800 BCE–450 BCE, with some parts dating even later), by as many as hundreds of authors. They argue that the Bible is a collection of numerous texts of various types that were transmitted orally over a period of one thousand years before they were written down. This means that we must relate to the Bible stories as works that were recorded in the collective memory of the Israelites over a very long period, and not as news reports broadcasted moments after the events took place.

Literature that is transmitted orally from generation to generation has a tendency to change. We may assume that each individual in the chain of transmission altered a few details of the story he inherited from his predecessor, and added aromas and flavors of his own. Possibly, he may have forgotten some of the details of what he heard. The person transmitting the story might have intentionally omitted information that he considered unimportant, or emphasized other details that his ancestors considered marginal. Certainly, he may also have transmitted to his listeners an exact replica of what he heard from his predecessors.

For an oral composition, the dramatic stage takes place at the point of its transformation into a written work. Theoretically, from this stage on, every scribe could make an exact replica of the story he received from his predecessor, but this is not exactly so. Although the "scribe-copyists," as they are called in academic parlance, aspired to preserve the Bible's accuracy, they added or deleted parts of the text according to their own understanding, and so the text was changed. Only after the invention of the printing press (the first Bible was printed in Italy in 1488) was the "living" text that was previously copied by hand transformed into a "fixed" text that did not pass through the hands of copyists, and from which countless identical copies could be made.

Academic researchers therefore assume that Abraham's story, which was transmitted orally in the first generations, is not identical to the story that was recorded in writing about 800 or even 1000 years later. Details of his life may have been omitted, while other details were added. Possibly, the story of the journey to the land of Canaan, which we are trying to reconstruct here very carefully, was originally told with greater detail, but over the years was shortened and condensed into a handful of points on the map.

Biblical researchers believe that due to the many metamorphoses the text underwent, we do not possess the original text. They attempt to identify which sections of the text were recorded earlier and which were added later. For this purpose, they developed several criteria for identifying earlier layers of the story, on top of which a later story may have been placed by a copyist who lived generations later. Here I will mention two simple principles that are important for our purposes.

According to the first principle, a section that revises previous statements represents a later addition to the original story. The second criterion specifies that a section that reveals an underlying purpose and contradicts other elements in the story is also a later addition.

The first example I will give here is Ur – Abraham's birthplace, known to us as "Ur of the Chaldees." The historical Ur was founded c. 3400 BCE, and for more than two millennia was known by that original name. In 900 BCE (900 years after Abraham's time), Ur was conquered by warriors from a tribe or group called Chaldeans, and at that time its name was changed to Ur of the Chaldees. The fact that in the book of Genesis, Ur is known as Ur of the Chaldees (11:28, 31; 15:7) reveals that the version of the text we have today was recorded after the Chaldean conquest, almost thousand years after Abraham's time.

The Bible contains other examples of settlement names that were updated to the name known in the copyist's time. For example, Hebron is the name of a settlement that was previously known by two other names: Alonei Mamre and Kiryat Arba (Gen. 13:18, Josh. 14:15, Judg. 1:10). Luz was the ancient name for Beth-El (Gen. 28:19, Judg. 1:23, and elsewhere), and Alon Moreh was the ancient name for Shechem (Gen. 12:6). Dan was first known as Laish: "And they called the name of the city Dan, after the name of Dan their father... *but Laish was the name of the city at first*" (Judg. 18:29). A copyist who lived after the "updater" copied the old name and the new name as well, or else deleted the old name. This method of updating names explains how historical Ur was forgotten, and only the commonly known name Ur of the Chaldees was preserved.

The story of Abraham sending ten camels loaded with abundant gifts to his family in Haran (24:10) is an example of the second principle: a section that contradicts a previous story and reveals an underlying purpose was probably altered by a copyist.

The description of Abraham as a very rich man (chapter 24) contradicts the description of him as a poor shepherd who wandered from place to place and lived in a tent (chapter 18). At the very least, it contradicts the fact that in Abraham's time, the camel was not yet domesticated. How can we understand this contradiction?

Hundreds of years after the domestication of the camel, one of the copyists seems to have made this "small" addition to Abraham's story, with the purpose of describing him as a wealthy man. Possibly, the copyist was not able to accept the fact that such an important figure as Abraham, to whom God had promised the land of Canaan, did not own land on which he could settle.[11] The description of Abraham sending his servant at the head of a caravan of ten camels carrying valuable merchandise corrects the impression that he was a poor, homeless nomad, and transforms him in several sentences into one of the wealthiest men in the ancient Near East. For in the period in which the story of his journey was written, camels were so costly that only kings were able to acquire them. The assertion that Abraham owned at least ten camels is comparable in today's terms to the bank statement of the owner of a dozen luxury cars, numerous private planes, and a string of estates in various countries.

Now that we have clarified the academic theories of different periods and purposes in authorship, we can better comprehend the issue of the camel. We can return to the story of the journey and determine with certainty that Terah and his family did not use camels – unfortunately for them. If the family of travelers had owned camels on which they could have ridden, their suffering during the long years of wandering would have been greatly eased.

DONKEYS AND GOATS

We now return to the questions we asked earlier: what equipment did the family take with them, how did they carry it, and how did they obtain food? The answer to these questions leads us to two small but remarkable animals: donkeys and goats.

Donkeys were the most important beasts of burden in Abraham's time, as well as much earlier. For thousands of years, donkeys paced at the head of the caravans that crossed the commercial routes of the ancient Near East. They accompanied the Israelites when they left Egypt and crossed the Sinai Desert on their way to the land of Canaan (Num. 20:4, 8, 11), until camels arrived on the scene and replaced them.

---

[11] Although Abraham purchased a field and burial cave in Hebron, he did not live there.

The small, grayish donkey is a strong beast with extraordinary survival ability, requiring only small quantities of water and dry grass for nourishment. The Bible mentions the donkey dozens of times, which reveals the important role it fulfilled in the households of ancient society. Thanks to its hardiness, we can assert with certainty that the family relied on several small, bent-headed donkeys to carry its baggage. The donkeys carried tents for shelter at night; sleeping mats of braided straw; sacks of wheat, dates, and olive oil for food; a few clay pots for cooking; and some items of clothing. In addition, we can be sure that before they entered the Sinai Desert, the three travelers loaded the donkeys' backs with goatskin water jugs,[12] which they refilled from wells and cisterns located on the way.

Since we have determined that donkeys accompanied the family on the journey, why have we decided that the three travelers walked, instead of riding on the donkeys' backs? A donkey can carry a load of 110 to 130 pounds (50 to 60 kg), about the weight of a small adult. But if the three had ridden their donkeys, their convenience would have come at the expense of the equipment and provisions necessary for their very existence.

Archeological findings such as cuneiform clay tablets reveal that in ancient times, permanent inhabitants who lived alongside the great rivers enjoyed a rich and varied diet, which included all the major food groups needed for their survival. But let us not delude ourselves into thinking that this menu was available to people who spent their days on the road. The nomads' diet was based on the amount of baggage they could take with them, in addition to whatever game they hunted and the assortment of fruits and edible plants they gathered on the road.

---

[12] Even today, inhabitants of the desert still use goatskin water jugs.

We may assume that Terah and his family prepared as best they could for the journey, for if not, they would not have survived it. Almost certainly, in order to enrich the meager menu available to them, they also gathered wild fruit and barley, and on the days when they walked along the Euphrates, they caught fish. But this food is incidental, and luck might not always have been on their side. We may assume that usually, the travelers had to rely on the provisions they carried with them: grains of wheat, dates, and olive oil. This diet lacks calcium and protein, which is vital for the proper functioning of the human body and continued survival. The absence of these components is especially grave when we consider the constant physical effort demanded from them throughout the many years of walking. Without a reliable, regular supply of protein and calcium, our three travelers would have died of malnutrition, and this leads us to the heroine of the journey: the Arabian goat, whose praises we will sing now.

The Arabian goat is a remarkable creature. With a long, matted black coat, it is about the size of a German shepherd, much smaller than its short-haired, white European cousin. Although the goat produces less milk than the sheep or cow, its physiology enables it to walk long distances and cross deserts.[13] Thus, alongside the donkey, the goat serves as the nomads' faithful escort. Like its white-haired cousins, the Arabian goat is expert at climbing cliffs and mountains, and even climbs trees like a monkey. Travelers in the villages of Morocco, for example, might catch sight of groves of low trees with what looks like black soccer balls hanging from their branches. From up close, the amazed tourist will discover that these are not, in fact, wayward balls, but rather diligent goats that have climbed the trees and are now decimating

---

[13] By contrast, the physiology of cows and sheep is not suited to extensive walking, and so they never accompanied nomads on their wanderings.

the green leaves and fruit, much to the distress of the grove owner.

The black goat is the queen of the desert, and has no equal. In a desolate landscape scorched by the sun's burning rays, it always knows where to find the last leaf that has managed to survive among the rocks. A few stalks, a couple of dry thorns, and a little water are enough to keep its milk machine in action. Thus even under the extremely stressful conditions of the desert, under which it barely survives, the goat is still able to produce a few drops of milk that can revive human beings.

The goat's long, black hair contains natural oils that swell in the cold and when in contact with water, helping it withstand extreme weather conditions. The swelled hair also traps air, acting as a layer of insulation that preserves body heat. On rainy, cold days, this hair swells, and the oil trapped within prevents water from penetrating to the goat's skin (similar to a bird's feathers). On warm days, the opposite mechanism occurs: the hair contracts, allowing the breeze to pass through and cool the goat's body. Because goat hair preserves its natural qualities even after it has been cut, it was the material of choice for high-quality tents, until the age of nylon fiber. Because the black goat, like the donkey, has accompanied nomads for thousands of years, we can state with certainty that a flock of dusty black goats proudly marched at the head of our weary band of travelers. We can also affirm that Sarah, as dusty as they, ran behind them, collecting every clump of hair they shed in order to patch the tent sides and the family's tattered clothing.

On their narrow shoulders, the goats bore the mighty responsibility of providing the family with a small amount of milk, offered from tiny teats hidden under their cloak of wild hair. The goats were the travelers' only stable source of calcium and protein – but that was not all they provided.

The generous goat contributed its final offerings upon death: its lean meat was roasted on the fire and eaten; its hide was skinned and transformed into clothing, shoes, or cloaks; and its hair was woven into the warp and woof of the tents.

Undoubtedly, the importance of the goats for the travelers' survival reached its peak when they crossed the famine-struck land of Canaan and the barren Sinai Desert. During that time, the family was completely dependent on the goats, since these animals were the only source of calcium and protein available to them. We can assert that without goats, the travelers' health would deteriorate even further and the deficiencies in their diet would spell disaster. Thus when we say that the black goat that bared its teats to Sarah was the great heroine of the journey, we do so with sincerity and a gesture of respect. We should bow deeply before it in thanks for its kindheartedness and for supporting our forefathers in those times. And if, heaven forbid, we have forgotten to thank a few small, gray donkeys as well, we bow our heads in esteem and gratitude to them as well.

DAYS OF WALKING

The author of the Bible compressed the story of the journey from Ur to the names of a few settlements through which the travelers passed, leaving us, in the end, with a valuable key with which we have already succeeded in opening several doors. Now the time has come to decipher the code that seals the most complex lock: we must calculate the length of the odyssey of Abraham, Sarah, and Lot, from the day they began their journey until they unpacked their bags and rested from their travels. The answer depends on two factors: the pace of the journey, and the number of days the travelers stopped in each place.

On days when the family took down its tents at dawn and put them up again for the night in a new location, they moved at the same speed as the slowest link in the group – the flock of goats, whose importance for the family's survival we noted above. Although the Arabian goat is able to cross mountains and deserts, it walks slowly and can manage only four hours of walking a day, with many stops. Under generous pasture conditions, with plentiful grass and water, the goat can walk about 3 miles (5 km) per day. The grazing day begins in the morning, when the shepherds escort the herd out of the paddock, and ends in early afternoon when they bring it back for milking and nightly rest. On such a happy day, the she-goat is spoiled. Head bent, it devours grass in delight. It rips off first one stalk, then another, lies around lazily and gossips with its companions about the handsomest billy goat in the herd. Under kind conditions, when the donkeys do not have to carry loads on their backs, they stand in place, chomping grass and listening quietly to the goats' conversation.

The herd that accompanied our family of travelers did not enjoy such days of ease. Ragged and exhausted, like the masters who led them, the goats scaled the massive cliffs and mountains that overlooked both sides of the Euphrates. They crossed the chain of the Lebanon mountains, the drought-ridden land of Canaan, and the Sinai Desert twice. In relying on the goats' walking speed to determine the pace of the journey, we must also consider the difficult road conditions, the ravages of the climate, and the resources for daily sustenance available to the herd along the route. We must also consider the young kids following behind their mothers, and the fact that the goats suffered from a shortage of water and pasture and needed time to search for them. These conditions force us to reduce the pace of the journey from an average of 3 miles (5 km) per day to 1.2 miles (2 km). To this we must add the travelers' excursions for collecting twigs, drawing water, gathering plants, and assembling the herd. Here we should point out another important consideration: of course a goatherd could drive the herd to double or even triple its pace. But if the goat travels 6 miles (10 km) every day, it will not be able to consume the amount of food it needs in order to continue. Eventually, it will starve to death, while the kids will die in just one day. Clearly, if the travelers did not take into account the needs of the herd, the goats would die first, and they would follow suit.[14]

DAYS OF LABOR

Despite the great importance of the herd for the family's sustenance, it is not possible that their diet consisted only of a few milk products, the plants they gathered, and occasional goat meat. Abraham, Sarah, and Lot must have filled their tattered bags with wheat and dates, the ancient world's main source of carbohydrates and sugar, which are vital for the functioning of the human body. They had to refill the goatskin jugs with olive oil and renew other essential items that wore out from hard use. But how does one purchase food products and equipment in a world without cash or credit cards?

The answer is through barter – the most ancient form of commerce. Since barter was common in the ancient world, and farms were strung all along the route, it is highly probable that the three stopped at farms and offered themselves as laborers for hire.

In the ancient world, the economy was based solely on manual labor. Work in fields and dairy farms, spinning

---

[14] We find evidence of this in Jacob's parting words to Esau: "And [Jacob] said to him, 'My master knows that the children are tender, and the flocks and the cattle, which are raising their young, depend upon me, *and if they overdrive them one day, all the flocks will die*. Now, let my master go ahead before his servant, and I will move at my own slow pace, according to the pace of the work that is before me and according to the pace of the children, until I come to my master, to Seir'" (Gen. 33:13–14). Jacob's statement demonstrates that the walking speed of an adult is much faster than that of the flocks, the children, and the young animals. As far as we know, Abraham's group included no children, and so the goat herd must have determined the pace.

wool, drawing water, curing hides, weaving and sewing, cutting down trees, paving roads, building palaces and shrines
– all these were accomplished through manual labor. Such
an economy demands as many workers as possible. Thus
labor contracts are one of the main topics of the clay tablets
found in Mesopotamia: contracts for the purchase and sale of
slaves, and contracts for temporary hired laborers and their
employment conditions.

The employment contracts reveal that farm owners
kept slaves as a permanent workforce living on their farms.
During peak agricultural seasons, such as plowing and harvest times, they hired additional laborers, most probably from
among the poor classes that did not own land of their own.
The employment contracts address employment conditions
and duration. Some of the contracts are for one agricultural
season (five months), while others are for two or even three
years. A worker's payment was determined according to the
period of his employment, and included sacks of dry food
such as wheat, barley, and dates. If a laborer and his family
stayed on the farm for several years in a row, their wages
included clothing, shoes, a few sheep, and on occasion, a precious bar of metal.

The travelers' need to refill empty sacks of food and
renew used equipment is clear. Because labor power was the
only item of trade available to Abraham, Sarah, and Lot,[15]

---

[15] Many researchers believe that Abraham, Isaac, and Jacob were "half nomads" –
meaning that they maintained reciprocal relationships with the permanent residents
of Canaan. These researchers hold that the forefathers sold milk products to farmers,
and received agricultural products in exchange. I disagree with this opinion, since the
farmers may have owned their own herd animals and cattle that provided them with
a daily supply of milk. It is not logical to assume that the farm owners depended for
their milk supply on the nomads, who were in one place one day, and another the next.
We also must recall that nomadic society is nonproductive, and nomads do not carry
around surplus food for sale. When the nomads wandered near agricultural settlements, they raided the farmers' fields and stole produce. We find evidence of this in
chapter 6 of Judges, which recounts Gideon's battle against the Midianites, nomadic
tribes that raided the Israelites' fields during harvests and stole their produce.

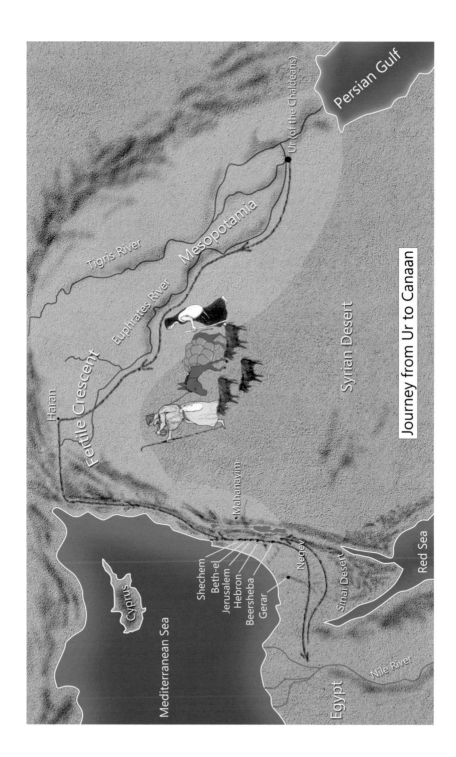

Journey from Ur to Canaan

Persian Gulf

Ur (of the Chaldeans)

Tigris River

Mesopotamia

Euphrates River

Fertile Crescent

Syrian Desert

Haran

Mahanayim

Mediterranean Sea

Cyprus

Shechem
Beth-el
Jerusalem
Hebron
Beersheba
Gerar

Negev

Sinai Desert

Red Sea

Egypt

Nile River

and because they had no other way to obtain the items they needed, we conclude that they must have broken up their journey from time to time in order to work at farms along the way.

Every method of calculation I have performed has led me to conclude that for each day of walking, on which the family advanced about 1.2 miles (2 km), they stopped for an average of three days. In my estimation, these stopover days were not only more numerous than the walking days, they were also more exhausting.

In order to explain this conclusion, I will focus on one detail: the production of bread, humanity's simplest and most basic food.

On the day God banished Adam and Eve from the Garden of Eden, He cursed them with a misfortune that still applies to their descendants:

> *Cursed be the ground for your sake; with toil shall you eat of it all the days of your life. It will sprout thorns and thistles for you, and you shall eat the herbs of the field. By the sweat of your brow shall you eat bread, until you return to the ground.... (Gen. 3:17–19)*

Only two ingredients are needed in order to make bread: flour and a little water, which are mixed and kneaded into dough. To improve the flavor, oil and salt may be added. The dough is rolled out and placed for a few moments on a burning hot surface, then eaten while still hot. But in order to perform this simple act, months of toil must precede it.

In the Near East, grains of wheat are sown at the beginning of the fall, before the rainy season begins. But at the end of summer, the ground is dry, hard, stubborn, and hot as a furnace. In order to make furrows within it, it must be plowed with force. In Abraham's time, plowing was performed with a small, wooden, L-shaped spike, which was hitched to an ox or donkey. Two people were needed to guide the plow: one held the animal's halter and led it forward, while the other leaned his entire body weight on the wooden spike and pushed it into the ground. If a farmer did not own an animal, he hitched the wooden plow to a human assistant.

After the plowing stage was completed, it was time to sow. So as not to waste the precious seeds of wheat, the farmer placed them into the furrows one by one, and covered them by hand with dry clods of earth. Then he had to wait for the rainy season to arrive. In a blessed year, when the rains fell on time and the wheat sprouted and grew, the farmers harvested it in the spring, some five months after sowing.

Because metal was still rare and very expensive in Abraham's time, we cannot assume that small farm owners used metal tools such as scythes. Logic dictates that harvesting was done by pulling the sheaves from the ground, not by cutting them. After the harvest, the wheat was taken to the granary, where it was laid out to dry in order to prevent fermentation and rotting.

After the harvested wheat dried, it was time for threshing, the act of separating the grains of wheat from the stalks and chaff. In the ancient world, threshing was done using a special implement – a heavy wooden board with basalt stones attached to the underside. The thresher was hitched to an animal (or a human being), which was tied to a post. Then the animal dragged the thresher around in circles over a pile of sheaves. If a farmer did not own a thresher, he beat the sheaves against a hard stone, as did the biblical Gideon and Ruth the Moabite (Judg. 6:11, Ruth 2:17). When the threshing or beating was finished, the result was a mixture of cut straw and grains of wheat that had to be separated, or winnowed, from each other. The winnowing was done by tossing the mixture against a light breeze (Ruth 3:2, Is. 41:15–16). The straw and the chaff flew off in the breeze, while the heavier grains of wheat fell at the winnower's feet. After separating the grains from the straw, the farmer gathered the grains into one pile, and the carbohydrate-rich stalks, used for animal fodder, into another. Then the farmer had to sift the grains of wheat from the dirt and ground thresher stones that stuck to them. This cleaning process was performed using a sifter or by hand.

After the grains of wheat were cleaned came the grinding stage. The grains were placed between two flat, heavy stones. The farmer turned the upper stone, which rode on top of the lower stone, grinding the grains into flour. After this exhausting labor was finished, he could finally make the flour into bread, in just five minutes of pleasurable work.

The primitive work methods and lack of knowledge about enhancing the quality of the soil meant that the fields did not yield bountiful produce, even in years with ample rain. Thus a farmer could not pay his laborers with multiple sacks of grain. Indeed, the Bible addresses this state of affairs: "You shall not oppress your fellow; you shall not rob; the hired worker's wage shall not remain with you overnight until morning" (Lev. 19:13). The farmers may not have intentionally exploited the workers, but often they did not have enough to pay their wages, especially during drought years. We may thus conclude that when Abraham, Sarah, and Lot stopped at farms and performed hard labor, the wages they received were meager in comparison to the salaries of all those who perform intense physical work, even today. From this we reason that in order to purchase necessities, they had to stop their journey on occasion and hire themselves out to work for a full five-month agricultural season, and sometimes even for several seasons, for one or two years in a row. To the stopover periods we must add days when the family had to stop for other reasons, such as bad weather, kidding season, or other reasons of which we are unaware. These stopover days must be included in our calculation of the length of the journey, justifying the estimation that for every day of walking, the family paused for an average of three days.

DURATION OF THE JOURNEY

It is now time to assemble the data we have collected and address the last question that still remains unanswered: How long did it take for Abraham and his two escorts to cover 2175 miles (3500 km)?

We have divided the journey into two parts: days of walking and progress, on which they took down the tents, and days of labor, during which they remained in one place.

On walking days, the goat herd dictated the rate of progress. As we explained, the difficult route, the lack of pasture and water, the fatigue of the herd, and the need to preserve its health produced a rate of 1.24 miles (2 km) per day, on average. The need to renew supplies of food and equipment meant that for every day of walking, the band had to stop for an average of three days in order to work on the farms along their route.

According to this calculation, Abraham and his entourage traveled 1.24 miles (2 km) in four days. Multiplying the distance of the journey by the number of days required to cover one mile results in the estimate that the group was on the road for about 7000 days (4/1.24 x 2175), which we may round off to twenty years (7000/365=19.178).

CONCLUSION

We have reconstructed the story of the journey to the land of Canaan to the best of our ability. According to Jewish and Christian tradition, this journey represents a watershed separating the worlds of paganism and monotheism. We have analyzed every significant detail we imagined might be of use, and undoubtedly, we have also inadvertently omitted many valuable details. The goal that stood before us was to form an image of this formative journey that is close to the truth.

We will never know why the author who recorded the narrative of this journey compressed his words to a minimum, from which we may omit not even one letter lest we risk obliterating the story altogether. By contrast, the books of Exodus and Numbers give expansive descriptions of the difficulties of the route and the suffering of Moses and those who followed him out of Egypt. But Moses and the Israelites walked some 310–370 miles (500–600 km), or about one-sixth to one-seventh of the distance that Abraham, Sarah, and Lot walked. Moses and the Israelites crossed the Sinai Desert only once, while Abraham and his group did so twice. Although the books of Exodus and Numbers relate negatively to the complaints of those who left Egypt, the hardships mentioned in those books describe the real experience of walking in the desert. This experience remains the same, whether the traveler crossed the desert four thousand years ago, or yesterday, or today. It is exactly the same accursed desert, and whoever attempts to reconstruct on foot the journey of those who made the Exodus from Egypt will cry out in anguish just as they did.

While the laments of the Exodus were immortalized in the holy book, none of us knows what Abraham experienced on the days when he walked paved and unpaved roads. Sarah's voice was hushed, and no one knows what she felt on the days when she walked, silent as the grave, as the desert stretched beneath her feet and in front of her glowing black eyes. Before she lay down to sleep, did she shake the sand from her tattered, wretched clothes, as full of holes as a sifter from the hardships of the route? Did she comb her hair and wash her face to remove the sand that stuck to her black eyelashes? And where did the young woman who almost died each day of thirst find water? No one knows whether she fell asleep sobbing from hunger, the afflictions of the journey, exhaustion and loneliness, or because the skin stretched across her lean frame was scorched day after day under the rays of a merciless yellow sun stuck to a wicked blue sky. No one knows whether Abraham tried to comfort her, and no one knows if she was indeed comforted. No one knows the thoughts of Lot, whose fate was bound up in theirs; nor will anyone ever know. Their voices have been silenced, and the epic story of their journey has been compressed into a container too small to contain it.

Today, as the heroes of this valiant expedition rest in the dust, the time has come for us to try to appreciate what they experienced on the long journey from Ur to the land of Canaan. I have offered my suggestion here, and the methods I have used are open to the reader's criticism. Anyone can argue with me, and anyone can offer better solutions. Either way, the story of the heroic expedition is worthy of appreciation, and the time has come for it to receive that recognition.

Chapter Four

FAMILY COHESION AND LIFE EXPECTANCY

The main characters whom the Bible describes were ordinary people. The Bible depicts the struggle for survival of individuals who lived in tents and who spread sleeping mats on the hard, dusty ground from which they eked out their living. It tells of shepherds and farmers, not, as in Greek mythology, of gods who were endowed with superhuman powers and characteristics. The argument that the Bible preserves the earthly origins of its protagonists will accompany us throughout this book. This assumption enables us to view each one of the biblical heroes as representative of all shepherds and farmers who lived in that time and place. We can relate to the family of Genesis as typical of other families who lived in the same era and environment.

The Bible mainly focuses on the isolated protagonist, mentioning his family as an aside. Still, the family, the most important social organization of ancient times, filters through and is always located in the background. Because the biblical figures lived in a time when the world moved as slowly as the herd of black goats that marched at the head of the caravan, the eight hundred years separating the time of the first forefathers and the time of David do not matter for our purposes. Family, social norms, and the pace of life remained constant throughout this period, and so the story of the first main character sheds light on the story of the great king, born to a family of simple farmers who lived in Bethlehem.

The families that the Bible describes are similar to other families who lived in the ancient world, and to families who still live today in remote traditional societies, but they cannot be compared to the modern family. The biblical characters are unlike any of us. The ways of life and social and legal norms practiced in those days do not exist in permissive, modern Western society – and the gaping chasm between them and us cannot and should not be bridged. We share only our basic characteristics with the ancient heroes: our ability to love, hate, envy, and desire the permitted and the forbidden. Thus we feel toward them a strange affinity, but in all else, we are different from them. The Bible heroes acted differently from us because they lived in a world unlike ours, a world that was, ended, and is no longer. If we wish to know them, we must turn our backs on the windows overlooking streets thronged with people, to avoid seeing the swarms of cars streaming into roads too narrow to contain them. If we want to comprehend the biblical figures of thousands of years ago, we must return to the time when they lived and to the social behavior customary in that time. Above all, we must understand the family, the most important social group of biblical times.

In our days, the term "family" is very much open to personal interpretation. The family can follow the traditional definition, in which a man and woman who are married to each other raise the children they have together. A family can also be a man and woman who raise children born to each of them in previous marriages. A modern family may refer to a woman alone raising children born to her from a past marriage, or to a woman raising children born to her from several men, to whom she was never married and whom she barely recalls. A family can mean a woman raising children born to her through a sperm donation from a man she has never met. In this case, she has reduced the father to his combination of genetic characteristics, chosen from a "Daddy-by-order" pamphlet in an artificial insemination clinic. In our time, a family can mean a man raising his children alone without a partner, or two men or two women living together as a married couple. In many countries, same-sex partners are considered a family according to the law, as well as by social norms. A family can also refer to a group or cult that a person joins and considers his family.

Some of us may have decided that our parents or siblings are no longer our "family," but we may relate to close friends as family. Some also feel that they would be the last to stand beside a relative in time of need, but the first to come to the aid of a dear friend. In general, the modern family includes a much broader range of relationships than the genetic connection between individuals, and it largely depends on individual choice. The family of our day is in many ways like a supermarket cart to which we can add or remove people as desired. It is like play dough that can be molded and shaped into many different forms.

None of the characteristics I have mentioned here fits the family that lived in the period of the Bible. The family in the ancient world was traditional. By definition, tradition is a fixed way of life, closed to personal interpretation and choice. In the ancient world, a person could not delete from his life a family member he did not desire, nor could he decide that his friends were closer to him than family members. The family was a group of people who shared the blood flowing through their veins, and the relationship between them was binding and defined. The family was a functional unit that

fulfilled clear goals: survival, expansion, and the establish-
ment of stability and order in human life. Terms such as
"happiness," "self-fulfillment," and "successful relationship
with a partner" were not part of the roles the family played
for its members.

In order for us to follow in the footsteps of the biblical
characters, we must first understand the structure of the
family in which they lived. The patriarchal household is the
first family unit the Bible describes.[16] "Patriarchal household"
means a nuclear family led by a man.

This term is not equivalent to the modern-day "nuclear
family," since the latter term allows for a woman to lead the
family, and permits the variant familial structures described
above. "Patriarchal household" emphasizes that the leader
of the family is a man, not a woman, even if that family
is comprised of a widow and mother of children. In such a
case, the widow and her children belong to the household of
her deceased husband's family, led by his father or one of his
brothers.

In biblical times, a patriarchal household included the
father of the family, his wives, and his sons, but not his
engaged or married daughters. It included the wives of his sons
and grandsons, but not his engaged or married granddaugh-
ters. Girls were counted as part of their father's patriarchal
household until their engagement, but from that day onward,
they belonged to the patriarchal household of the groom. For
example, if a father betrothed his daughter on the day of her
birth or during the early years of her childhood, then the girl
belonged to the patriarchal household of her future groom,

---

[16] The term "father's household" appears repeatedly in the Bible. Some examples are
Gen. 38:11, 46:31; Num. 3:24, 30, 35; Josh. 2, 12, 18; II Sam. 3:29; 14:9. Gen. 46:31
reads: "And Joseph said to his brothers and to his father's household: I will go up and
tell Pharaoh, and I will say to him, 'My brothers and my father's household who were
in the land of Canaan have come to me.'" In this chapter and subsequently, I use the
term "patriarchal household" to mean the biblical "father's household."

even though she continued to live in her father's home. On the day of her marriage, the daughter moved into her husband's home, and she and her children were counted along with the members of their father's patriarchal household.

The second family unit in place during the biblical period was what in today's parlance is known as the "extended family." The extended family was the most important social organization, and it included all the households that were related by blood. Brothers, uncles, and male cousins of first, second, and third degree, along with their families, all belonged to the extended family.

Under ideal circumstances, which did not always exist, sons remained close to their father's home and to the other extended family members.[17] Like grapes, which cannot live when detached from their stem, the sons established their own patriarchal households near their birth family, and near their brothers and other relatives. And so while we are proud when our adult children leave us for independent lives of their own, members of the ancient world aspired to unite and live together as a cluster of patriarchal households, like traditional families today in extreme Third World countries. The main reason for this desire was that during the biblical period there was no government body that superseded the family, and so the family, not the state, was the supreme social institution.

The bigger and more united the family, the greater its strength. Its chances of survival were higher, and every household and individual within it was stronger and more protected. In order to preserve its cohesion, the family established a number of mechanisms in order to keep its members within it. Here I will list the three most important of these,

---

[17] When we discuss laws of inheritance in the Bible, we will describe the limitations of reality on this ideal model. See chapter 22.

and this will give us the infrastructure we will need in the subsequent chapters.

I call the first and most important mechanism of the three "the institutional mechanism," and I have already hinted at it above. We members of modern society live in a state or country with defined borders. We do not know what it means to live in a world without a "state," without a central regime that has established governmental or other institutions located outside the family and superseding it. We cannot conceive of a way of life without an army, a police force, courts of law, schools, hospitals, shopping centers to supply our every need, and banks and communications services to connect us to each of these institutions. All our lives, we purchase services from people outside the family, and we provide services to people who are no more to us than a name and identification details appearing on a computer monitor.

The biblical characters lived in a society that had not yet established any of these institutions, and this did not change much during the period of kingship.[18] The extended family, not the state or the king, fulfilled the roles of all our social institutions, and was the only supplier of services to each of its member households. An individual who was distanced from his family was expelled into an empty, vulnerable space, without any institution to protect him. He was ejected into a lawless expanse of nothingness with no means of defense. Perhaps this state is best expressed by Cain's words after God decreed his exile:

> *Then He said, "What have you done? Hark! The voice of your brother's blood cries out to Me from the ground!*

---

[18] The role of the king in ancient history was to defend the borders of his kingdom, and to expand it by conquering new lands. The king built walls, fortified the major cities, and paved roads. But he was not responsible for the economic welfare of his people. He did not establish hospitals, welfare institutions, schools, or banks. The king did not supply services related to the daily lives of the citizens of his land.

Therefore, you are cursed even more than the ground, which opened wide its mouth to receive your brother's blood from your hand. When you till the ground, it will no longer yield its strength to you; you shall be a wanderer and an exile in the land." Cain said to the Lord, "Is my iniquity too great to bear? Behold, You have banished me today from the face of the earth – can I be hidden from before Your face? **I must become a wanderer and an exile on earth; whoever meets me will slay me!**" *The Lord said to him, "Therefore, whoever kills Cain, vengeance will be wrought upon him sevenfold." The Lord placed a mark on Cain, so that none who met him should slay him. (Gen. 4:10–15)*

Another example of the misfortune of an individual who was expelled from his family is found in the story of David's flight from Saul. When David lived outside his family, he described himself as a dead dog or a flea: "After whom has the king of Israel gone out? Whom are you pursuing? A dead dog, a single flea" (I Sam. 24:14).

The family, like every social organization, developed an internal leadership that stood at its helm and managed its affairs. In the biblical period, the leaders were the heads of the respected families, the "elders," whose importance we will emphasize in the following chapters. In addition to being leaders of their families, the elders fulfilled the role of today's judiciary authority, and their power and status was preserved even when ancient Israelite society became a monarchy. But the elders judged only members of their own families, which is inconceivable today. The laws of punishment scattered throughout the Bible reveal that the elders had judiciary authority over a range of cases, from the most minor infraction to the most severe. The elders presided over family matters (Deut. 21–25) and resolved everyday disputes between neighbors. They determined the punishment of a person who hit another and caused disability, and of one whose donkey wandered into a neighbor's field and caused damage (Ex. 21–22). In the case of a serious crime such as the killing of another person, the elders had to determine whether the case was defined as murder or manslaughter. If they decided that the victim was intentionally murdered, they permitted the blood redeemer to execute the murderer. The redeemer acted under the authority of the elders, and was not considered a murderer. In a society with no government institution higher than the family, the blood redeemer, usually the brother or cousin of the victim, took the place of today's executive authority. But if the elders decided that the victim was killed unintentionally, they allowed the killer to take shelter in a "city of refuge" ("city" in biblical language is what we would call a small village). As long as the killer remained within the boundaries of the city of refuge, he enjoyed the protection of the elders of the settlement, and the blood redeemer was forbidden to take revenge against him (Num. 35:9–34, Deut. 19, Josh. 20).

The fact that the elders of a certain clan offered their protection to a member of another family demonstrates their high status, as well as the fact that leaders of neighboring families maintained reciprocal, cooperative relationships. One instructive example of such cooperation was the decision of the tribal elders to demand that Samuel appoint a king over ancient Israel, thus preventing Samuel from transferring his authority to his sons (I Sam. 8:1–7).

The elders did not lead their families or mete out justice because they were incapable of doing anything else, like many of today's vacuous power chasers. The elders were wise. They were the balancing power that preserved the unity of the extended family and the households it included, and so the members of their clan respected them and accepted their authority.

The second mechanism that preserved family cohesion was economic. In chapter 2, we discussed the economic importance of the land on which the family lived and from which it took its bread. Because the land belonged to the family, a son who was expelled from his father's household and his extended family was cut off from the heart of economic life and left roofless. The only way left for him to earn his bread was to go off to an unrelated farm and offer himself as a hired laborer, as Jacob did (Gen. 29:14–30; 31:1–13, and elsewhere). Alternatively, he could join a group of mercenaries who protected other families in exchange for food and lodgings, as David and Jephthah did (I Sam. 22:1-2, 25; Judg. 11).

The third mechanism of cohesion was the family's control over the available brides. This control ensured that young men took wives from within the extended family. In the ancient world, fathers chose their children's spouses (at least for their first marriages). They usually married their daughters to a member of the extended family. Repeated marriage ties between households that belonged to the same extended family tightened the relationships among them and strengthened their social group. Nevertheless, marriage between households belonging to two unrelated families was also acceptable (Judg. 12:9),[19] although apparently less common. After two or three generations of repeated intermarriage between two unrelated households, they combined into one extended family, and this strengthened both sides.

In general, when we speak of the "family" in biblical times, we are referring to a society that was traditional, organized, and based on a framework of patriarchal households and extended families that maintained cooperative relationships, in which members took responsibility for each other. In addition, we mean a society that had yet to establish social

---

[19] "Ibzan of Bethlehem judged Israel. He had thirty sons and he sent out thirty daughters; he brought thirty daughters for his sons from without."

and economic institutions outside the family. The social group into which an individual was born performed all the roles that we in the Western world have placed in the hands of outside, alien institutions.

LIFE EXPECTANCY

The functional explanation I discussed above gives only a partial explanation of the need for family unity. The other part is the low life expectancy of people in the ancient world. Until about 150 years ago, the life expectancy of residents of the United States and Europe was about forty-five years. Improvements in diet, living conditions, hygiene, sanitation, and the availability of medical services to the entire population (especially children) have produced a huge leap in the life expectancy of residents of Western countries.

The women among us are expected to live an average of eighty-two years, and men an average of seventy-nine years. By contrast, the life expectancy of residents of the Third World who lack these advantages is about forty years.

Scientific studies have attempted to calculate the life expectancy of the people who lived in the ancient world. According to studies with maximum age results, men lived thirty-five years on average, while women lived thirty years. More cautious studies argue that men lived to age thirty on average, women to twenty-seven.[20] Studies agree that hunger, the greatest mass murderer in human history, is the most significant factor in explaining the vast difference between the life expectancy of modern humans and that of our ancestors. After hunger follow plagues and infectious diseases, that also wiped out masses of people at one blow. Last in importance are wars and natural disasters.[21] Researchers agree

---

[20] I agree with the maximum estimate, and so I rely on it in this book.

[21] In the ancient world, genocide, as practiced in our enlightened society, would have been considered wild, illogical behavior. Conquering peoples did not destroy the

that on average, women in the ancient world lived shorter lives than men, because of death in childbirth or postnatal complications.

Research shows that until three hundred years ago, about fifty percent of infants died before they reached their fifth birthday. About forty percent of the population reached age twenty, twenty percent reached fifty, and only eight percent lived to age seventy. In other words, until three hundred years ago, about eighty percent of the population died before they reached age fifty. This data shows that a woman who gave birth ten times was considered lucky if she remained alive and if two or three of her children survived and reached adulthood.

Although the Bible does not directly address issues of life expectancy and mortality rates of the population, it does mention hundreds of times that hunger, plague, and war decimated multitudes. The conclusion is clear: a population in which only twenty percent ordinarily reached age fifty depended on the next generation for its strength. Such a population, in contrast to modern society, did not age, as the high birthrate did not change the fact that life expectancy was low. It was thus critical for ancient society to establish mechanisms of cohesion in order to support and maintain its member households. It also had to keep within the fold those members of the younger generation who successfully survived their childhoods, since its continued existence depended on them. Under the conditions of ancient times, the extended family had to do everything possible in order

---

nations they occupied, but rather made them into slaves. Slaves were an important labor force, and from the conqueror's point of view, decimation of a population that was defeated in war was a waste of precious economic resources. The Bible describes mighty victories (and losses) of the Israelites, in which they killed tens of thousands of their enemies, but these are impossible glorifications. Such masses of people can be decimated only with the weapons of mass destruction that modern, enlightened humans have tragically invented.

to strengthen the human foundations that bound it together. Furthermore, such a society determined that a woman's sole purpose was to give birth through her husband to as many children as possible. This assertion will accompany us to the end of this book.

Chapter Five

TERAH AND HIS FAMILY:
A FAMILY PROFILE

I n chapter 2, we investigated the possible reasons for the departure of Terah and his family from Ur. Now that we understand the importance of the extended family and the mechanisms of cohesion the family created to preserve its unity, we can analyze the consequences of the departure on our family of emigrants.

We may establish with certainty that on the day the travelers turned their backs on the palaces and shrines of wealthy, splendid Ur, they severed all connections with their past, and these were never retied. The departure from Ur disconnected them from the ways of life they had known previously. The mechanisms of cohesion and mutual support that held extended families together were no longer available to them. Terah and his sons were ejected into a vulnerable space, in which kings did not grant protection to citizens who lived in the territories under their control. We may assume that an isolated family wandering the roads like a satellite lost in space paid a heavy price for leaving. This implication is supported by the description of the marriages of Terah's sons. The text reads:

And Abram and Nahor took themselves wives; the name of Abram's wife was Sarai, and the name of Nahor's wife was Milcah, the daughter of Haran, the father of Milcah and the father of Iscah. (Gen. 11:29)

The Bible recounts that Terah had three sons: Abraham, Nahor, and Haran. Haran died before the family left Ur, leaving two children: Milcah and Lot. Nahor married Milcah, Haran's daughter and therefore his niece; Abraham married Sarah, who was his half-sister. The text reads:

Abraham said of Sarah his wife, "She is my sister." *So Abimelech, king of Gerar, sent, and took Sarah. And God came to Abimelech in a dream by night and said to him, "Behold, you are to die because of the woman you have taken; moreover she is a married woman." Now Abimelech had not approached her; so he said, "...**Did not he himself tell me: 'She is my sister'? And she, too, herself said: 'He is my brother!'** ...And Abraham said, "...Moreover, she is indeed my sister, my father's daughter, though not my mother's daughter; and she became my wife.** And so it was, when God caused me to wander from my father's house, I said to her, 'Let this be your kindness which you shall do for me – to whatever place we come, say of me: **He is my brother."** ...And to Sarah, [Abimelech] said, "Behold, I have given your brother a thousand pieces of silver." (Gen. 20:1–16; see also 12:13, 18–20)*

Generations of readers have asked whether Abraham and Nahor's marriages were incestuous, and we will address this issue below. For now, we will clarify what we can learn about the strength of this important family from their marriages.

In the previous chapter, we discussed how the extended family acted as the natural and primary source of brides from which fathers preferred to choose wives for their sons. We noted that marriage alliances were also common between patriarchal families who were not related to each other, in order to unify and become one extended family. Yet the portrait of marriages in Terah's household stands in stark contrast to these customs, and also conflicts with its own existential interests.

For some unknown reason, Terah did not find spouses for his children from his extended family's supply of brides and grooms, and so he did not strengthen the mutual ties between himself and his relatives. Nor did he create marriage alliances with other patriarchal households. He did not annex any other family, and he did not join together with any other family. As a result, Abraham's and Nahor's marriages with women of their father's household did not give Terah the advantages that the extended family usually granted its members. Furthermore, the fact that Terah married off his sons before they departed on their journey strengthens the supposition that even while living in Ur, the nuclear family he led was weak and disconnected from its environment. The family's isolation inspires the conjecture that Terah recognized his family's weakness, and in order to prevent its extinction in his own generation, he had his children marry each other.

We would expect that a small family whose entire existence hung by a thread would do everything to preserve its unity, but the opposite took place. After Terah died, his sons separated. Nahor and Milcah settled in Haran, while Abraham, Sarah, and Lot continued their journey to the land of Canaan. On the day the brothers separated, the fragile coalition that had existed between them fell apart, and from then on, each one stood at the head of a tiny patriarchal household of its own. Each continued his life without the support and assistance of his brothers, and thus their chances of survival decreased significantly. Despite this risk, Nahor's move to Haran proved to be a great success. Thanks to the plentiful water sources and pasturelands of Haran (the region of Turkey today), Nahor quickly established a successful sheep and goat farm. His wife and concubine gave him many children and transformed him into a man leading a stable, well-established patriarchal household (Gen. 22:20–24).

In comparison to Nahor, Abraham's chances of survival were poor, almost hopeless. While Nahor was beginning to establish himself, Abraham continued to walk the roads, leading a tiny, sad family that did not give birth to even one child. Though God had promised Abraham a land in which to settle and children as numerous as the sands of the sea, for the time being it seemed that this promise was actually fulfilled with Nahor. Abraham's muted and melancholy protest against God, who shunted him from here to there like an empty tin can, demonstrates his awareness that his branch of the family stood at the brink of extinction:

> *After these events, the word of God came to Abram in a vision, saying, "Fear not, Abram, I am a shield for you; your reward is very great." And Abram said, **"My Lord, God, what can You give me, seeing that I go childless, and the steward of my house is the Damascene Eliezer?"** Then Abram said, **"See, to me You have given no offspring; and see, my steward inherits me."** (Gen. 15:1–3)*

FORBIDDEN SEXUAL RELATIONS

The question of whether Abraham and Sarah's marriage was incestuous has fired the imaginations of many of our predecessors. In order to offer a responsible answer to this question, we must take a few minutes' rest from our journey in the footsteps of the forefathers, and explain forbidden sexual relations in biblical terms.

Biblical law permits a man to marry multiple wives, and takes a positive view of the formation of marriage alliances within the extended family. We noted the primary reason for this in the previous chapter: ancient families, who usually lost half their children before they reached their fifth year, needed as many children as possible in order to improve their chances of survival. Yet despite the desperate need for children, ancient society was organized and did not permit a man to marry any woman he desired. The lawmaker, or God according to the Bible, strictly limited the women with whom a man was permitted to have sexual contact or marry. He surrounded them with high fences, on which he hung clear red warning signs. Whoever violated the prohibitions was considered to have violated a sexual prohibition, for which the punishment was death.

The first and most severe sexual prohibition in the Bible is adultery. The woman was the absolute property of her husband and no one but he was permitted to have relations with her. Adultery was a severe, intentional violation of a man's right of ownership over his wife's body and sexuality. The recognition that adultery endangers family unity explains why one of the Ten Commandments is dedicated exclusively to this sin: "You shall not commit adultery." The commandment "You shall not covet your fellow's wife, his manservant, his maidservant, his ox, his donkey, nor anything that belongs to your fellow" (Ex. 20:13–14) complements this prohibition and supports the concept that the wife was the property of her husband, just like his slave, ox, or donkey.

The books of Leviticus (18, 20:10–22) and Deuteronomy (23:1–2) expand the circle of prohibitions that Exodus defines, enumerating additional women with whom a man was forbidden to have sexual relations (the Bible is written in masculine language, but these prohibitions also apply to women). The Bible forbids a man from having relations with his mother, his father's wives, his brother's wives, his daughters, and his son's wives. It forbids a man from marrying both a mother and her daughter, and forbids him from marrying his sister, even if she is his half-sister:

> The nakedness of your sister – whether your father's daughter or your mother's daughter, whether born to one who may remain in the home or born to one who must remain outside of it – you shall not uncover their nakedness. (Lev. 18:9)

> A man who shall take his sister, the daughter of his father or the daughter of his mother, and he shall see her nakedness and she shall see his nakedness, it is a disgrace and they shall be cut off in the sight of the members of their people; he will have uncovered the nakedness of his sister, he shall bear his iniquity. (Lev. 20:17)

Another law prohibits a man from marrying his aunt (Lev. 18:12; 20:21–22). If marital relations between aunt and nephew are forbidden, then logic would dictate that an uncle is also prohibited from marrying his niece.

The laws governing sexual relations were created in order to maintain proper family relationships and preserve family unity, not in order to prevent the birth of children with genetic defects, of which the ancients were unaware. The great importance that the Bible places on the unity of the family reveals the fear that its disintegration would leave the individual without a social framework, on which he depended in order to exist. In order to preserve the unity of the family, the Bible relates to forbidden relations as sexual pollution, comparable to the practices of the foreign peoples who lived alongside the Israelites – and this demands a short explanation.

The Bible describes various types of impurities created throughout the normal course of life. Because these impurities are of natural origin, a person cannot and is not required to avoid them. Bodily secretions, sexual relations between man and wife, and various diseases are considered to create impurity (the book of Leviticus explains these in detail). The moment a person dies, his corpse becomes impure (Num. 19). The Bible does not consider these natural impurities as sinful or improper. The only requirement for a person who becomes impure in this manner is to undergo the process of purification specified in the Bible.

Aside from the natural sources of impurity, there are three types of impurity derived from intentional sin, direct transgression of the prohibitions listed in the Bible: idol worship, or worship of other gods aside from the God of Israel; murder (rape of a woman is equivalent to murder, and I will discuss this in part 4); and forbidden sexual relations.

In contrast to the other types of impurity, these intentional sins create impurity from which a person cannot be cleansed. This impurity passes from the body of the sinner to the land and pollutes it. Since, according to the Bible, God is master over the land of Israel, His holiness is transferred to His land (hence the expression "the holy land"). If the Israelites sin through idol worship, murder, or forbidden sexual practices, the impurity created by their sin will pass to the holy land and pollute it. The only way to purify the land from the defilement attached to it is to execute the sinner (Num. 35:31–34), or else the land will expunge its inhabitants from within it:

> Do not become contaminated through any of these [forbidden sexual relations]; for through all of these the nations that I expel before you became contaminated. The land became contaminated and I recalled its iniquity upon it; and the land disgorged its inhabitants. But you shall safeguard My decrees and My judgments, and not commit any of these abominations – the native or the proselyte who lives among you. **For the inhabitants of the land who are before you committed all these abominations, and**

*the land became contaminated. Let not the land disgorge
you for having contaminated it, as it disgorged the nation
that was before you. For if anyone commits any of these
abominations, the people doing so will be cut off from
among their people.* You shall safeguard My charge not to
do any of the abominable traditions that were done before
you so that you will not contaminate yourselves through
them; I am the Lord, your God. (Lev. 18:24–30).[22]

In light of the Bible's negative view of forbidden marriages, it
appears that Abraham committed a serious sin in marrying
his half-sister Sarah. But instead of the sinners paying with
their lives for their crime, God reveals Himself to Abraham
and sends him to the Holy Land, whose purity was preserved
by the restrictions on sexual relations.

The contradiction I am presenting here is only apparent, since the Bible must be studied from many contexts,
not from the narrow viewpoint I have presented here. The
forbidden relations in Leviticus are only one part of a much
broader complex of forbidden relationships. If we study them

---

[22] According to the biblical story, God gave the laws in the Torah at Mount Sinai (Ex.
19–20). This has led many readers to believe that up until that time the Israelites lived
in a lawless world, in which everything was permitted. This is untrue, and the Bible
never says this. If murder, moral corruption, and sexual depravity had been permitted
before the laws were given at Sinai, God would not have punished Cain. He would not
have opened the heavens and purified the world of humanity's sins, nor would He have
rained down fire and brimstone on Sodom and Gomorrah. According to the Bible, at
Sinai the Israelites received religious laws, such as the command to exclusively worship the God of Israel and the command to sanctify the Sabbath as a day of rest. Aside
from these laws, God also commanded the Israelites regarding social issues, including murder, theft, and adultery. The religious laws were new, and at the ceremonial
occasion of Sinai they received formal status. In contrast, the social laws are known to
have been practiced long before in the ancient world. At Sinai, the two types of laws,
religious and social, received the standing of divine command – and this is a very
important development. From this point on, whoever violated social laws not only
committed a social crime, but also sinned against God, the Lord of law and guardian
of social justice. In addition, we must consider that human beings are social creatures
– and no human society, even the most primitive, allows its members to murder and
steal. Every known society has clear family structures. Ancient society was traditional, and thus it was also highly organized (see previous chapter). Unfortunately, we
cannot make the same assertion about modern, permissive society.

from a comprehensive point of view, we realize that over the generations, these prohibitions change with respect to the size of the family and society to which they apply.

As the story described in the Bible advances in time and the society grows, the circle of forbidden marriages becomes wider and more rigid. In contrast, when we examine the earlier biblical periods, we find that the laws were more flexible, and at times even nonexistent – except for the prohibition against adultery, which was always in force. In my opinion, the flexibility or rigidity of these prohibitions depends on the size of the pool of marriageable women in each particular period.

We may easily show that the marriage prohibitions in Leviticus are limited to first-degree relatives, and that they do not extend to second-degree relatives (cousins). Furthermore, while Leviticus uses extreme language to describe the sexual lawlessness of foreign nations, it does not prohibit the Israelites from intermarrying with them. The book of Deuteronomy repeats the prohibitions of Leviticus, but adds additional stringencies of its own.

According to the Bible, the text of Deuteronomy is comprised of Moses' parting speeches to the Israelites before he dies and they enter the land of Canaan (c. 1250 BCE). However, researchers believe that Deuteronomy was written about six hundred years after Moses' lifetime, about 630 BCE. These researchers hold that the authors of Deuteronomy repeat the Leviticus prohibitions as if dictated by Moses because they wanted to make Deuteronomy seem ancient. The fact that Deuteronomy expands on the restrictions delineated in Leviticus supports the argument that it was written in a much later period. According to Deuteronomy, the Israelites were forbidden to marry women from the Canaanite, Moabite, Ammonite, and Egyptian peoples, a restriction which was not in place earlier: "An Ammonite or Moabite shall not enter the congregation of the Lord, even their tenth generation shall not enter the congregation of the Lord, for eternity" (Deut. 23:4; see also Deut. 7:1–3; Judg. 3:5–7).[23] The expansion and increased rigidity of the circle of forbidden marriages gives support for the late date of Deuteronomy. (Moses himself married an Egyptian woman.)

The justification for marriage prohibitions between Israel and foreign nations is exactly identical to that of the other marriage restrictions: marriages with women from the nations forbidden to the Israelites produce impurity that defiles the holy land. In other words, at the time when Deuteronomy was written, the distinction between marriage to a first-degree relative and marriage to a woman from a foreign nation no longer existed. Both were considered forbidden marriages that transferred impurity to the land and polluted it.

The circle of marriage prohibitions could only be expanded on condition that the pool of brides and grooms within a social group was large enough. The best examples of this are the marriages of David and Solomon. Eight hundred years after Abraham and Sarah, David married many Israelite women, as well as women from among the neighboring nations (II Sam. 3:2–5; 5:13–15). Yet he did not marry Canaanite or Egyptian women, who were forbidden to the Israelites. Indeed, the Bible finds no fault in David's foreign wives. It does, however, condemn him for desiring Bathsheba, as she was a married woman, which meant he violated the prohibition against adultery. Solomon, David's son through this infamous beauty, began a successful career as king, but ended his days a bitter failure. Solomon built the First Temple

---

[23] The claim that marriage with the neighboring nations was not prohibited in the time of the forefathers raises the question of why Abraham commanded his servant not to choose a bride for Isaac from the Canaanites, but instead to travel to Abraham's family in Haran. I discuss this in chapter 15.

in Jerusalem, the holiest place on earth, and therefore also the most sensitive to impurity. Yet the first to defile it was none other than Solomon himself, who in his later years married foreign women, including some from nations forbidden to Israel.

The book of Kings rebukes Solomon for building shrines for the gods of his foreign wives next to the Temple in Jerusalem. The impurity created by this act seeped into the holy land and defiled the Temple, and so God decreed that the kingdom founded by David would disintegrate and disappear:

> King Solomon loved many foreign women, in addition to the [Egyptian] daughter of Pharaoh – Moabites, Ammonites, Edomites, Sidonians, and Hittites – from the nations of which the Lord had said to the Children of Israel, "Do not come [into marriage with] them, and they shall not come into [marriage with] you…. **Then Solomon built a high place for Chemosh, the abomination of Moab, on the mountain facing Jerusalem; and for Molech, the abomination of the Children of Ammon; and he did likewise for all his foreign wives, they burned incense and sacrificed to their gods.** So the Lord became angry with Solomon, for his heart had strayed from the Lord, the God of Israel, Who had appeared to him twice and commanded him regarding this matter – that he not go after the gods of others – but he did not heed that which the Lord had commanded him. So the Lord said to Solomon, "Since this has happened to you, and you have not kept My covenant and My decrees that I have commanded you, I shall surely tear away the kingship from you…. In your days, however, I will not do it, because of your father David; from the hand of your son will I tear it away. (I Kings 11:1–12)

Indeed, during the reign of Rehoboam, son of Solomon and grandson of David, the kingdom of Saul separated from the kingdom of Judah, as was prophesied (I Kings 12). In later times, King Josiah purified the Temple of the defilement Solomon had introduced (II Kings 23:13–14).

From this summary, we understand that prohibited marriages included not only marriages between first-degree relations, but other types of forbidden marriages as well. The impurity created by prohibited marriages extended to the holy land and defiled it. Yet we must also take into account that as the society described in the Bible grew and expanded, it raised the standards for prohibited marriages. At the stage when the pool of marriageable women was large enough, the lawmaker saw no difference between a man marrying his sister or a girl from the forbidden foreign nations – both were considered prohibited marriages, and both were considered by God as impure and defiling to the land.[24]

When we return to the ancient origins of Israel and the period of Abraham and Sarah, the system of prohibited relations we have surveyed here disappears. The book of Genesis describes small, isolated families. Naturally, the pool of marriageable women was limited in such families; thus the forefathers of early times had no choice but to marry women from nations that in a later period were forbidden to Israel. For example, Abraham married Hagar the Egyptian in addition to Sarah; Joseph, Jacob's son, married Osnat, daughter of an Egyptian priest (Gen. 41:45); Judah, Jacob's fourth son, married the daughter of Shua the Canaanite (Gen. 38:1–2); and Moses, the most prominent leader in Jewish history, in whose name Deuteronomy speaks, married Zipporah, daughter of the Midianite priest Jethro (Ex. 2:21). If these characters had lived in a later period, the Biblical authors would have

---

[24] Ezra and Nehemiah, the major leaders of that period, feared that the Israelites would follow Solomon's lead. If so, the impurity created by marriage connections with women from forbidden nations would affect the Second Temple as well, leading to a similar fate as that of the First Temple (Neh. 13:23–27).

rebuked them as they did Solomon, instead of treating their wives' origins with indifference.

The connection between family size and sexual prohibitions finds additional support in one of the most well-known stories in Genesis. After the journey from Ur to Canaan, the longtime partnership between Abraham and Lot came to an end. Abraham and Sarah went to Hebron, while Lot went to Sodom, in those days a verdant oasis in the heart of the desert. Shortly afterward, God decided to rain down fire and brimstone on the inhabitants of Sodom and Gomorrah, because their sins defiled His holy land. But before beginning the work of purification, God saved three "righteous" individuals from the destruction: Lot and his two daughters.

The three refugees fled the devastation of Sodom and found shelter in a far-off, isolated cave. After the fires died down and the sky-high pillars of smoke dissipated, the two young women were overwhelmed with fear that God had destroyed all the men in the world, except for their father. Because in their world, a woman's sole purpose in life was to bear children, they found a creative way to fulfill their duty: they plied their father with wine, and when he was drunk, they lay with him and became pregnant. This abominable act led to the births of Moab and Ben-Ammi. According to the tradition recorded in Genesis, these two sons became the founding fathers of two nations defined as impure and forbidden in marriage to Israelites:

> Now Lot went up from Zoar and settled on the mountain, his two daughters with him…; he dwelt in a cave, he with his two daughters. The older one said to the younger, "Our father is old and there is no man in the land to marry us in the usual manner. Come, let us ply our father with wine and lay with him that we may give life to offspring through our father.… Thus Lot's two daughters conceived from their father. The older bore a son and she called his name

Moab; he is the ancestor of Moab until this day. And the younger one also bore a son and she called his name Ben-Ammi; he is the ancestor of the Children of Ammon until this day. (Gen. 19:30–38)

The story of the perverted behavior of these two young women and the dubious origins of Ammon and Moab has a doubtful basis. The author who wrote this story intended to slander two nations that were bitter enemies of Israel, not to describe an incident that actually took place. But interestingly, the critical tone of the story here is directed against the origin of the two nations, not against the participants in incest. This leads us to note that while the Bible excoriates Solomon for marrying forbidden women, it mentions not a word of criticism against Lot and his daughters, who lived in complete isolation. We must also note that the incestuous relations among these three took place immediately after God destroyed the inhabitants of Sodom and Gomorrah for their sins. All that was necessary in order to purify the land from the family's sins was to send down a second volley of brimstone. The fact that this did not happen shows that from the author's perspective, the young women's fear that their father was the last male left alive was adequate justification for their shocking act.

To summarize this chapter, marriage prohibitions in the Bible were not determined in outer space. They took into account the reality of the pool of marriageable women, and this also applies to Terah's family. Abraham and Nahor took wives from their father's household out of the constraints of reality – because they were unable to find women from their extended family or from unrelated families, and because their own family was small and isolated. Their marriages to women from within their immediate family did not strengthen their father's household, nor did it improve their chances of survival, but it did prevent the immediate extinction of their patriarchal household in that generation. And so, although we do not know why the family was so isolated, the image of marriage within Terah's household supports the profile of his family as forlorn and fragile.

Part II

THE WORLD OF THE WOMAN

Chapter Six

WOMEN'S POSITION IN BIBLICAL SOCIETY

Т he Bible is a masculine work, written by men for a male audience. It was written in a time when feminism and the ideas underlying this term had not yet entered anyone's consciousness. Thus, the stories of women, and women in general, occupy a secondary position in the Bible. The books of Joshua, Samuel, Kings, and the Prophets are all named after men and recount the exploits of men. But what do they say of the deeds of their wives and daughters?

Almost nothing.

In most cases, their names are not even mentioned, and they are referred to, if at all, with the general term "women." In addition, the Hebrew language clearly differentiates between masculine and feminine language, and this distinction reveals that the magnificent poetry of the book of Psalms is written in masculine language addressed to men, not to men and women together. This is also the case in the book of Proverbs and in the two daring philosophical works of Ecclesiastes and Job.

Within the extensive list of male characters, we find two rare wildflowers: the books of Esther and Ruth. Aside from these two charming daisies, the women in the Bible are mentioned only by virtue of being the wives of the main male characters. They are always shadowy supporting characters, never central figures standing on their own. The story of the heroism of Sarah who traveled the roads was recorded only because she accompanied Abraham. If that had not been the case, she would have been erased from the holy book, just as she was erased from the story of the binding of Isaac, whom the Bible, not surprisingly, presents as the only son of Abraham (Gen. 22:1–2). In general, God did not reveal himself to women in nighttime visions nor in a burning bush, nor did He grant them any mission. Women were not queens, and they did not lead armies that went out to war as the kings did. They were not prophetesses, and certainly not priestesses. True, Deborah was a prophetess, as well as a woman judge and leader (Judg. 4–5). There was also one biblical queen. Not Esther, who was a harem wife, but Atalia, daughter of Ahab, who managed to grip the reigns of leadership for six years until she was executed (II Kings 11). So while we may count on one hand the number of women who stood out for a moment on their own merit, these individual incidents do not dilute the masculine majority that stride powerfully across the entire Bible.

The Bible was written within a traditional, patriarchal society, in which a dim-witted man was superior to an intelligent woman, simply because he was born a man. It was written in a period when a woman was blessed if she had sons, not both sons and daughters. Infertility in the Bible was a deficiency of women only, not of both women and men. Because the Bible was written in a time when women were inferior to men, it is mainly concerned with men's deeds.

Yet although women's stories were pushed to the back of the black tents in and around which they spent their lives, their voice is somehow heard. Even if it is hushed, weak, and uncertain, it manages to emerge from between the tents, like the rustle of leaves on a distant tree. Their voice never shouts or accuses, and it never reveals the modest way of life that was practiced inside those black tents. The voice of the woman in the Bible is a restrained sigh swallowed behind compressed lips. So as much as we may aspire to approach our ancient foremothers, they will forever remain hidden behind the mists of an ocean of time and silence.

Despite this, I intend to draw aside the edges of the women's tents and shine a delicate beam of light inside. I would like to collect the stories that the authors scattered with a tightly closed fist and put them together. Like joining pieces of a puzzle, I propose to create an image of the woman whose only purpose in life was to bear as many children as possible for her husband – and yet despite the need for children, the Bible considers the blood of her monthly period and of childbirth as impure and polluting (Lev. 12).[1]

The work of putting together the pieces of the puzzle is paved with objective difficulties, and with one severe limitation that I have chosen to take upon myself. I have already described the first objective difficulty above: the Bible was written by men who lived in a traditional society, and thus they had no interest in detailed explanations of women's issues. The second difficulty is the concise writing style of the biblical authors. Their succinct language has already tormented us in the previous chapters, and it will continue to do so in the chapters to come. As if these challenges were not enough, the authors excluded several pieces of the puzzle that

---

[1] Today many view the laws of impurity after childbirth and menstruation as primitive and degrading. In my opinion, the opposite is the case, and this law is designed to protect the woman and her health. In the ancient world, the woman was the property of her husband, and he was permitted to have sexual relations with her at any time (and this is still the case in the Third World). The biblical lawmaker placed a limit on the husband's right over his wife's body, and defined certain days when he was forbidden to touch her. In my view, this law is designed to protect the woman's health and allow her time to recover her strength.

are vital to completing the image of our foremothers' world. Although fitting together the pieces found in the Bible will give us a reliable idea of the complete picture, the final image will always remain incomplete and riddled with holes.

An additional difficulty is the vast gap in time between the biblical writers and us. We were born in a different age, and our language and conceptual world is different from theirs. The concept of egalitarianism that has become a fundamental part of Western society's worldview has led us to forget the fact that the biblical characters had their own worldview, one which we cannot always comprehend. Just as we had to reconstruct the meaning of the term "family," in the following chapters we will have to reconstruct other expressions that have disappeared from today's language, or that have taken on other meanings from those which the Bible intended.

The limitation that I have chosen to take upon myself is as follows: in the past few years, a new trend has developed – writing novels about the characters in the Bible. Some authors have used their fertile imaginations to embroider exaggerated plots that never took place, and applied them to the biblical characters. Some of them have gone even further, and imposed the sexual fantasies that run wild in their minds on our ancient foremothers. Yet anyone familiar with life in the ancient world will realize that such fantasies never could have taken place in a traditional society that followed a strict code of behavior. These authors weave impossible events and pornographic episodes into the biblical stories, and impose them on individuals who lived thousands of years ago. Their distorted diligence in transforming these inventions into "historical truth" is nothing less than historical vandalism, deluded and dreadful. Such authors take cynical advantage of freedom of expression. They exploit the fact that although the Bible has the status of a holy book, it has no author's rights and thus does not enjoy the privilege of legal defense. The limitation I have placed on myself in this book is to avoid the crooked paths of these fiction writers. I will not join those who publish books that denigrate whichever biblical characters they disdain. I will not stain the edges of our ancient mothers' frocks with meaningless rubbish and present it as historical truth that took place in reality.

Although the biblical authors did push the female biblical characters into the wings, they preserved their honor, and I will follow their lead. If we want Sarah, Leah, and Rachel to permit us to approach them one step in their direction, we must keep them within the social, cultural, and legal framework in which they lived. If we wish for them to stretch out their arms, weary from harsh labor and travails, across the mists of time, and tenderly stroke the lashes of our eyes before we fall asleep, then we must respect the limitations that the Bible defined. We must recognize that while perhaps we can roll back the edges of their tents, we will never be able to open them wide.

FERTILITY AND MARRIAGE AGE

Each Western country that belongs to UNICEF, a United Nations affiliate,[2] has passed its own law regarding "the age of consent." The goal of this law is to ensure the basic rights of a young woman over her body, her right to choose the people with whom she has sexual relations, whom she marries, and with whom she wants to have children. One of the most important goals of this law is to protect young girls

---

[2] UNICEF was established in 1946. Its goal is to create laws relating to the legal status of minors, and to help high-risk children around the world. The first article of the Convention on the Rights of the Child, passed in 1989, defines a "child" as an individual below the age of eighteen, and places responsibility for his welfare on the country in which he resides. UNICEF works on behalf of boys and girls equally. Here I relate only to girls. The "age of consent" is usually defined as the age at which a female is legally capable of agreeing to sexual intercourse. A male who engages in consensual sex with a woman above this age cannot be prosecuted for statutory rape.

from sexual abuse, and to ensure that their age will not be exploited for the purpose of forced sexual relations.

The age of consent defines the minimum age under which a girl is considered a minor, or too immature to have sexual relations of her own free will. In Western countries, the age of consent varies between fifteen and eighteen. In most of these countries, the minimum age for marriage is eighteen, slightly higher than the age of consent. Because a young woman's physical development is complete around this age, marriage prior to the legal age is considered marriage to a minor. Thus a young woman who wants to get married before this age must appeal to a court and justify her request in order to obtain a marriage license.

In our time, many young women who live in permissive, modern Western societies have never heard of the age of consent and have no idea what it is. The widespread social reality is that many girls are beginning to have sexual relations before the minimum legal age in their country, but they also are delaying marriage to ever higher ages, much beyond the legal age. Furthermore, Western society no longer upholds the close relationship between marriage, sexual relations, and childbearing, which existed and still exists in traditional societies. In our permissive society, these three components are no longer related to each other and do not necessarily take place in this order.

We can restate a well-known truth about modern Western women: the higher the level of a woman's education, the more she will aspire to achieve in her career and reach economic independence, and the higher the age of her first pregnancy will climb. Today, this age can reach thirty or even higher. Whether she is married and has sex is not the concern of the legal system, nor of anyone but herself.

The law requiring ten-year-old girls to attend school and forbidding others from having sex with them and marrying

them seems fundamental to us, so much so that we have forgotten it was an innovation of UNICEF in the late twentieth
century. We have forgotten that our grandmothers married
when they were sixteen, and that their grandmothers married at fourteen, thirteen, or even earlier. We have forgotten
that their father chose their husbands, and the question of
whether they wanted to marry these men was irrelevant. In
ancient Greece, Rome, Japan, Mesopotamia, and Egypt, girls
often married at ten, eleven, or twelve years of age, and we
have ample evidence that they sometimes married even earlier (marriage at such ages and younger is still practiced in
Third World countries). And so, as we stride backward in
time, we return to a reality in which the marriage age was
early and a young girl became a woman in one cheerless day.
The days of youth, exploited in our time for studies, outings
with friends, and endless battles with parents, served in the
ancient world for bearing children.

The Bible does not record the marriage ages of our foremothers, but we may assume that they were between ten and
twelve, because this was common practice for their time and
lifestyle. We find a hint of this in the story of Rebecca's marriage to Isaac (Gen. 24). Abraham, so we are told, sends his
servant, Eliezer, to his family in Haran to find a bride from
among them for his son Isaac. The faithful servant obeys his
master's command, and returns to Canaan accompanied by
Rebecca and her nursemaid Deborah (24:59). The fact that
Rebecca's nursemaid accompanies her does not mean that
Rebecca was a baby who was still nursing, but that she was
very young. This assumption explains why Laban, Rebecca's
brother, asks Eliezer to delay her departure for several years,
perhaps even until she reached the age of ten:

> Her brother and mother said, "Let the maiden remain with
> us for some years, even ten; then she will go." (Gen. 24:55)

The Song of Songs also alludes to a very young marriage age:

We have a little sister who has no breasts; what shall we do for our sister on the day she is spoken for? (8:8)

Elsewhere, we find clues that males also married in early adolescence. For example, when Jacob felt that his days were coming to an end, he gathered his sons and delivered a parting blessing. He first addressed his eldest son Reuben: "Reuben, you are my firstborn, my strength and the first of my potency..." (Gen. 49:3) The Hebrew word for "potency" means fertility, the ability to impregnate a woman. A boy reaches the age of sexual potency, or puberty, around age fourteen. The book of II Kings recounts that Amon, king of Judah, was crowned king at age twenty-two. Two years later, he was murdered, and his son Josiah inherited the throne at age eight (II Kings 21:19–26; 22:1). If Amon was twenty-four when Josiah was eight, then he was sixteen when his son was born. Thus Amon must have married at age fifteen at the latest.

The writings of Maimonides (Rabbi Moses ben Maimon, 1138–1204) provide important evidence for the assumption that our foremothers married before age twelve, and that childhood marriages were practiced up until several hundred years ago. Maimonides wore two hats: he served as personal physician to the Egyptian sultan, and he was also one of the most important and well-known legal authorities in Jewish history.

One of his major works is called Mishneh Torah, which is comprised of fourteen comprehensive books, collections of laws from the Mishnah and the Talmud, which preceded Maimonides by six hundred to one thousand years.[3]

---

[3] The Mishnah is a Jewish work composed approximately between the first and third centuries AD. The main purpose of the Mishnah is to clarify the biblical laws. The Talmud was written after the Mishnah was canonized, approximately during the third to eighth centuries (at the latest). Its principle goal is to expand on and reinterpret the laws of the Mishnah.

Maimonides recorded these laws in clear language, with the goal of determining a uniform Jewish legal code that would apply to all Jews. One of these fourteen books is entitled *Nashim* (Women), and it contains laws related to a woman's life from the day she is born until the day she dies. One of the topics this book addresses is the appropriate age of marriage for boys and girls.[4] Maimonides repeats the position of the Talmud, written about six hundred years before his time, and establishes that a girl is considered a minor until she reaches the age of twelve years and one day. From the age of twelve years, six months, and one day, she is considered a mature adult, and she has the right to refuse to marry a man chosen by her father.

From Maimonides' explanation, we learn that the age of marriage and the age at which a girl is considered an adult are two different, unrelated concepts. According to him (and following the Talmud's reasoning), the appropriate age of marriage for a girl is related to the beginning of her sexual development, not to her age. A girl is considered ready for marriage from the day she grows her first two pubic hairs, called "the lower sign." Girls generally grow their first pubic hairs around age ten. In other words, Maimonides supported the ancient custom of girls marrying between the time they developed the first sign of physical maturity and age twelve and a half, at which time they would have the right to refuse to marry the groom their father chose for them.

My reliance on Maimonides is deliberate. He was a renowned physician, exceptional in his generation, and recognized by his community for his authority to make Jewish legal decisions. A man of such medical background was undoubtedly aware of the vast difference between the beginning of

---

[4] Maimonides does not explicitly say that he intends to rule on the appropriate age of marriage, but based on his source and the issue he discusses, we can conclude that this was his intention.

a girl's sexual development and her full physical maturity around age eighteen. Certainly, a man of his education was well aware that sending a girl of age ten (or even earlier) to her husband's bed might cause her serious physical harm. He must have known that if she conceived shortly after the onset of her menstrual cycle, this might endanger her life, or even prove fatal. He also must have known that at this stage, a girl's pelvis is still narrow, and her body is not strong enough to withstand the burden of nine months of pregnancy and the difficulties of childbirth. Indeed, the death of young women during or following childbirth was the main reason for the low life expectancy of women in the ancient world as compared to men. Here we should add that Maimonides left behind detailed medical books, but none of them addresses women's health or the dangers to a girl who conceived before completing her physical development. Apparently, this disregard is not coincidental. If he had been considering the girl's health, instead of the Jewish legal decision, he would have adopted a physician's point of view and taken a stand against the position of the Talmud and the customs of his time.

The question of why people in ancient times married off their daughters at such a young age demands explanation. Although I have not found any studies specifically addressing this subject, the answer seems to lie in the short life expectancy of women. In ancient society, a woman of fifteen to twenty was considered to have reached the middle of her life. At age thirty, she was already approaching the end of her life (in modern Western society, the middle of the average woman's life is forty). Apparently, then, in times when women were expected to live an average of thirty years, they had to utilize as much of their fertile years as possible in order to bear children. A girl who began her menstrual cycle around age twelve was expected to have her first child at fourteen or fifteen, followed by numerous additional pregnancies.

But child marriages created several cyclical problems. First, the younger the girls were when they conceived, the more their lives were endangered, since their pregnancies and childbirths were much more difficult and complicated than those of women who had reached full physical maturity. Indeed, in many cases the pregnancy ended with the death of the mother, the infant, or both. In other cases, girls were unable to bear nine full months of pregnancy and gave birth prematurely to small, weak babies. These babies often did not survive, which contributed to the high infant mortality rate. (As noted, until about three hundred years ago, about half of all infants died before age five.) Sometimes, young women suffered repeated, multiple miscarriages, again endangering their lives.

A young woman who lost her baby felt a bitter sense of disappointment. Social pressure and the fact that she needed to have a child in order to establish a position in her husband's household pressured her to conceive again quickly. A girl who did not have time to recover from her first miscarriage before again conceiving doubled and tripled the danger to her life.

This picture of things sharpens our understanding of the enormous gap between a woman in the ancient world and her modern daughter who puts off her first pregnancy by many long years. In a society in which most women begin their first pregnancy after age twenty or more, the question of whether they have reached full physical maturity in order to bear the pregnancy safely is no longer relevant. And so, at an age when modern women begin to consider whether they are ready to bring a child into the world, their ancient foremothers had already given birth between five and eight times, and miscarried the same number. Before reaching thirty, they had used their own hands to dig many small pits, in which to bury the babies they had borne and lost. At thirty, they were old,

worn women, considered lucky if they still had two or three
healthy children left after the relentless cycle of pregnancies,
births, and miscarriages. If they lost all their children, they
were considered unlucky.

Our ancient foremothers were assembly-line workers in
a giant baby factory, and this factory ended their lives prematurely. They lived in a time and place when child marriages
were the accepted custom. They lived in a short-term, cyclical world, in which maturity was forced upon them in one
day. They married and began to have sexual relations at an
early age, which today's legal authorities assume the right to
prohibit. The law of "marriage age" and other laws designed
to protect girls from arranged marriages had not yet been
passed in their time, nor were these listed in any book.

SENIOR WIVES, CONCUBINES, AND SLAVES

A society whose inhabitants have such short life spans must
renew itself quickly. Such a society encourages its men to
marry multiple women so that they will have many children,
in the hopes that some will manage to survive childhood and
reach maturity. Naturally, a household with many children,
such as that of Gideon, who had many wives and seventy
sons (Judg. 8:30), had a much higher chance of survival than
a household such as that of Abraham, who had two wives and
only two sons.

The Bible reveals that men married women from three
social classes: senior wives, concubines, and slaves. If men
took female captives in war, they married them as well (Deut.
21:10–14).[5] The problem is that the Bible does not define the

[5] Because of the high mortality rate, marrying multiple wives was both desirable and
necessary. Yet we can be reasonably certain that only wealthy men married multiple
wives. If the practice of marrying multiple wives had been widespread throughout all
social sectors, this would have resulted in a serious shortage of brides and a long line of
bachelors. Because the Bible does not describe a society suffering from a shortage of
brides, apparently the social balance was preserved and most men had only one wife.

difference between these three classes, nor does it explain the advantages and disadvantages of each. Almost certainly, this is because at the time it was written, everyone knew the difference between these categories. Just as in our time, no writer explains to his readers the difference between a bicycle and a motorcycle, the biblical authors did not bother to explain the meanings of everyday terms. But as we pointed out earlier, time went on, and society and concepts changed, while the Bible remained constant. Today, if we want to understand these terms in context, we must reconstruct their biblical meaning.

SENIOR WIFE

When the Bible wants to emphasize a woman's status in her husband's home, it uses the term "lady" (*gevirah*) (I Kings 11:19; II Kings 10:13; Jer. 13:18) or "senior wife" (*sarah*) (Judg. 5:29; I Kings 11:3; Is. 49:23; Esther 1:18). In other cases, the Bible uses basic terminology, calling the senior wife simply "wife" (*ishah*). Because the term "senior wife" clarifies the difference between the three classes, I will use it here instead of the general term "wife."

A senior wife could be the daughter of kings. She could also be descended from paupers, like Sarah, whose name reflects her status (*sarah* means "senior wife"). She could be the only wife of her husband, such as Rebecca, Isaac's wife, or one of several senior wives who crowded his home. Jacob, for example, had four wives. Leah and Rachel were senior wives, while Bilhah and Zilpah were slaves.

Apparently, two conditions were necessary for a wife to be considered senior: first, she had to be born to a free father; second, the groom or his family had to pay her father a bride-price, which means payment given in exchange for the bride.[6] The bride-price was apparently in the form of a silver

---

[6] This is why a man's household did not include his daughters, but did include his sons' wives.

bar, a rare commodity in those times, or other merchandise of equal value (Gen. 20:16; 34:11–21; Ex. 22:15–16; Deut. 22:27–28).

For example, Abraham gave gifts and precious gold jewelry to his family in Haran in exchange for the bride he took for his son Isaac. Jacob paid Laban with two seven-year series of labor in order to marry the beautiful Rachel. Saul, Israel's first king, agreed to have his daughter Michal marry David in exchange for an unusual bride-price: one hundred foreskins from his most bitter enemies, the Philistines. David brought Saul twice the price, and married Michal (I Sam. 18:25–27).

Although the Bible does not indicate this, the most common method of paying the bride-price seems to have been bride exchanges between families of equal status. Each household "paid" the other with a bride, thus ensuring that its daughter would enjoy the status of a senior wife. (I believe that the bride-price was actually paid only in cases when bride exchange was not possible. Meaning, the groom's family did not have a girl to offer as a bride in exchange for the girl they were receiving.)

In a household where a man had several wives, including concubines and slaves, the senior wife had the highest status. But if the man had several senior wives, then the one who gave birth to his firstborn son occupied the top rung of the hierarchy. According to the social norms practiced in the ancient world (preserved in traditional societies today), the firstborn son was the father's inheritor and successor. Therefore his status was higher than that of his brothers, and this improved his mother's status in relation to his father's other wives. But the status of "mother of the successor" was fragile. If her son died at a young age, the status of firstborn was transferred to the son who stood next in line, even if his mother was a different senior wife. The most well-known case of birthright transfer was that of Solomon, David's youngest son, who inherited his throne. A somewhat less well-known instance of birthright transfer is Reuben, Jacob's oldest son, whose position of firstborn was taken away and given to Judah, the fourth son.

A senior wife gained advantage over her husband's other wives by bearing him children, thus "earning" the bride-price paid for her. A barren senior wife lost her status – and her entire world. She did not strengthen her husband's household, and so she did not earn the bread she ate. Such a woman suffered severe helpings of shame and contempt from her husband's other wives, who exploited her weakness in order to take advantage of her and flaunt their superiority. When we reach the stories of Sarah, Rachel, and Hannah, we will appreciate the extent of the misery suffered by senior wives who had trouble conceiving.

CONCUBINES

Concubines have faded from existence – simply vanished. Until several decades ago, a concubine was an unmarried woman who had a relationship with a man to whom she was not married, usually because he was already married to another woman. She trailed behind her a thick train of shame and disgrace, and many thought of her as a private whore. As times have changed, so have definitions, and the dishonorable concubines of the past now carry their heads high and bear the title "lovers" or "partners for life."

In biblical times, a concubine was not the single lover of a married man. She was not his "partner for life" and certainly not his private whore. The Bible mentions concubines dozens of times, always in a positive tone, which shows that concubines were a common phenomenon that carried no dishonor.

The biblical concubine was a married woman whose father was a free man. Her status in her husband's home was lower than that of the senior wife, apparently because she

was given to him without a bride-price (the Bible mentions a
bride-price only in relation to senior wives). Almost certainly,
a father who relinquished his daughter's bride-price married
her to a wealthy man who promised her and her children food
on their plates and a roof over their heads (or else the bride's
father used the marriage to pay a debt, as in Ex. 21:7–11).
For example, Saul, the first king of Israel, was married to one
senior wife and one concubine. His senior wife was Ahinoam
daughter of Ahimaaz, and his concubine was Rizpah[7] daughter of Aiah, who bore him two sons. David, who was much
wealthier than Saul, married at least six senior wives (II Sam.
3:2–5) and ten concubines (II Sam. 15:16; 20:3). The family
status of Bathsheba, Solomon's mother, is difficult to decipher. Since no bride-price was paid for her, we can conclude
that she was married to David as a concubine, and that due
to her intelligence and cunning, she acquired power in the
royal court and pushed her son to a status he did not deserve
according to the order of inheritance. Solomon, the son of
this energetic woman, married seven hundred "noblewomen"
and three hundred concubines (I Kings 11:3).[8]

The intense need for children implies another source for
concubines. Apparently, disabled girls born to free men also
married as concubines. In our time, disabled women often
remain without partners or children, or else they marry other
disabled men, but this was not the case in a time when society begged for children. Logic dictates that a disabled girl who
could bear children was given to her husband as a concubine.
Her father did not receive payment for her, but if she gave

---

[7] The name Rizpah is another example of changes in the Hebrew language that took
place over thousands of years. In today's parlance, *rizpah* means a paved area of stone,
wood, or glass on which people walk. In biblical language, *rizpah* means ember or
flame (Is. 6:6). The meaning of Rizpah, Saul's concubine, is flame, not pavement.

[8] When the Bible wishes to give an expansive description of a character's wealth, it says
that he has many wives and sons. This is the case with King Ahasuerus in the book
of Esther, and Gideon, who had seventy sons (Judg. 8:30–31; also see Songs 6:8–9).

her husband children, her status in his household was firmly established. We will return to this issue when we sing the praises of "tender-eyed" Leah.

FEMALE SLAVES

Female slaves, like their male counterparts, have always occupied the lowest position in society and family. The female slave, like a male slave, was part of the household property. She was an object that could be bought and sold. If she had children with a man who was also a slave, they inherited the slave status of their parents. The children of slaves belonged to the master of the household. If he wanted to, he could take them away from their parents and sell them, just as the white masters in the United States did when slavery was practiced, and as is still the case in several Third World countries. Because female slaves were property and lacked all civil rights, their masters could do what they wanted with them. The masters could have the female slaves marry male slaves, or use them for their own purposes and have children with them – every female slave's sweetest dream.

A female slave who conceived through a free man remained a slave because she was the daughter of slaves, but the price tag was removed from her, and she could no longer be sold. The biggest advantage gained by such a lucky slave woman was that her son was born free, by right of his father's status. The status of a slave's son was lower than that of his brothers born to senior wives and concubines, but in daily life, this had little practical expression. Ishmael, for example, the son of Abraham through an Egyptian slave, was of lower status than Isaac. But thanks to his father, Ishmael was a free man and not a slave. The four sons born to Jacob through the slave wives Bilhah and Zilpah (Dan, Naftali, Gad, and Asher) were free men. Each one gave his name to a tribe of Israel, just like their brothers who were born to Jacob's senior wives, Leah and Rachel.

Adultery

In the chapter on family structure in biblical times (chapter 4), we pointed out that permissive modern Western society recognizes marriage arrangements that were not possible in a traditional society with a strict code of behavior. Yet despite the freedom of choice of which we are so proud, the law dictates that only two people can marry each other. Bigamy is prohibited in our time, even if it is carried out with the cooperation and agreement of all parties. A person who wishes to marry a second time must first get divorced, thus formally freeing himself from the previous marriage. But in the biblical era, a man who wanted to marry another woman did not divorce his first wife; rather, he simply took a second or third wife at will. Thus in the Bible, we find no incident of a man divorcing his wife. The wife certainly could not divorce her husband, since she was his property.

Western society, the bastion of moral, liberal values, has forbidden multiple wives, but it permits adultery. Adultery in our day often improves the adulterer's prestige in the estimation of his friends and himself. At most, it can serve as a reason for divorce, but not for a lawsuit.[9] In the ancient world, adultery was not considered a reason for divorce, but rather the most severe sin in the area of family life, and a justification for execution:

> *A man who commits adultery with a man's wife, who commits adultery with his fellow's wife; the adulterer and the adulteress shall be put to death. (Lev. 20:10; 18:20)*

---

[9] In traditional Muslim societies today, adultery is still considered a severe sin, and women suspected of having sexual relations or any type of relationship with another man are executed, usually by their brothers.

But what constituted adultery in a society that held a positive view of multiple wives? According to the Bible, adultery is a one-way situation. A man could not commit adultery toward his wife, because the woman did not have sole rights over her husband's sexuality. As mentioned before, the husband had the right to marry as many women as he could afford. Jacob, for example, was married to four women, and did not commit adultery against any of them. However, a married woman (or an engaged woman) who had sexual relations with another man committed adultery against her husband, since she was his property (or the property of the man to whom she was engaged), and permitted only to him. A man who secretly caressed the thighs of such a lady committed adultery against her husband, but not against his wives.

The most well-known act of adultery that demonstrates these facts is the story of David and Bathsheba (II Sam. 11).

One sleepy afternoon in Jerusalem, King David went up to the rooftop of his home and beheld the landscape below. The sun setting in the west shone its last red light among the city's vanishing hills, which recalled the fleshy buttocks of a full-bodied woman reclining on her stomach. Against the background of the quiet scenery slowly falling into slumber, the tired king sensed the intoxicating, heavy scent of the white jasmine plants, or perhaps of the yellow acacia flowers. It reached his nostrils, erasing the bloody memories of wars that suffused his brain.

The quiet afternoon hours in Jerusalem, today tumultuous and rank with the sweat of the chafing, teeming masses, were calming in the king's time. They relaxed the king, who bore a heavy burden on his shoulders: the wars he had fought, the kingdom he had founded, the mistakes he had made with his sons, and the weight of history that would transform him, unwillingly, into the savior king. For a moment, he was freed from the disturbing thought that the Jebusite land of

Jerusalem, which he had transformed into his capital, would eventually become a holy city. He ignored the future of Jerusalem, which like a magnet would attract armies of believers who slaughtered each other in the name of a sanctity he never intended it deserve. For that one moment, he also forgot the prattle of the many future Bible researchers and archeologists who would make light of his achievements, or argue audaciously and obstinately that the greatest king ever in Israelite history was no more than a myth. David took a deep breath, imbibing the sweet, intoxicating scent of jasmine or acacia, and his thoughts wandered among the soft posteriors of the sleeping city's hills.

All at once, his musings were interrupted by the tempting sight of a naked woman bathing on one of the roofs across the way. The sight of the woman's body lit with the red and gold light of sunset inflamed the desire of the king, who had already experienced many women in his lifetime. And in one foolish moment, he added the least deserving woman of all to the trunk in which his many wives were packed.

What a pity.

David was well aware that Bathsheba was a married woman and that it was forbidden for him to have relations with her, but the long shadow she sent toward him caressed his face and whispered a soft, lustful melody in his ears. David took the wife of Uriah the Hittite, and by doing so, both of them violated the severe prohibition against adultery.

The Bible does not blame David for committing adultery toward his wives, but rather for committing adultery toward Uriah, with Uriah's wife. According to biblical law, the two adulterers should have paid with their lives for their sin. This did not happen, since the status of the sinner always mitigates the punishment dictated by law. David was not executed, but Nathan the prophet, who served in his house, cursed him for his wicked act:

And now, the sword shall not cease from your house forever, because you have scorned Me and have taken the wife of Uriah the Hittite to be a wife unto you. So says the Lord: Behold! I shall raise evil against you from your own household, I shall take your wives away in front of your eyes and give them to your fellowman, who will lie with them in the sight of this sun. Though you have acted in secrecy, I shall perform this deed in the presence of all Israel and before the sun! (II Sam. 12:10–12)

The prophet Nathan's curse was realized, and the sword smote the house of David time and again. The only one who ended up benefiting from the whole story was Bathsheba: Solomon, her son with David, became Israel's third king.

Chapter Seven

FERTILITY IN THE BIBLE AND THE ANCIENT WORLD

The world is divided into two spheres: upper and lower. The upper sphere is in the heavens, and it is the location of the pantheon, dwelling place of the gods according to the beliefs of pagan nations. The lower sphere is the earth, home of human beings with all their misfortune and suffering.

The gods, residents of the heavenly pantheon, lived an eternal life, and so they were freed from the dread of death. They had no fear that it would suddenly sneak up on them, or crawl with agonizing slowness into their bones to take their souls and the souls of their loved ones. The gods did not need to put aside a few coins for the day their teeth fell out, their backs became bent, and their steps became hesitant, shaky, and fragile. They did not know the meaning of fear, or grief, or worry. Eternal happiness reigned in their heavenly abode, and they held boisterous, merry parties in their home from one dawn to the next. The male gods dedicated their lives to pleasure and celebration. They cheerfully quarreled over the graces of the beautiful goddesses, who were just as bored and wild as their male counterparts. Before going out to parties, the goddesses would stand before the mirror hung in the sky, admiring their eternal radiance and the smooth texture of their skin, stretched forever across their young faces with nary a wrinkle or blemish. Then, blowing themselves a loving kiss in the air, they glided off with a flutter of wings to join the heavenly crowd.

Meanwhile, in the lower sphere on earth, humans lived out their lives of sorrow and anxiety. Each morning they loaded onto their backs the burden of the fear of death in all its terrible forms, and went out to their daily labors. One plowed his fields; another led his sheep to pasture, using sticks and stones to drive away the wolves who howled for a piece of meat for their pups. Another nursed his feverish son throughout the night. Still another rose at first light to dig a pit in which to bury his wife, who had passed away a short while earlier. Toward evening, when the inhabitants of the land returned to their homes, they poured out their prayers to the inhabitants of the upper sphere. They begged to be favored with the graces of the gods, for among those beings who floated aimlessly in the heavens were several gods and goddesses who played a central role in the lives of humans. These, of course, were the gods of fertility, who controlled the fertility of human beings, animals, and plants.

The gods of fertility were seemingly generous. Thanks to their blessing, human beings and domestic animals multiplied, and the fields yielded their produce. But in truth, the gods of fertility were mainly busy with themselves and the internecine battles they waged with idle brothers and sisters.

The suffering of human beings, who raised their palms in supplication to the fertility gods and implored their assistance, bored them and did not succeed in opening their hearts. Like their siblings, the fertility gods also suffered from megalomania. They were angry, spoiled, capricious, and subject to sudden, strange whims. They sold the fertility blessing to human beings grudgingly, with a tightly closed fist and at an exaggerated price, while at the same time distributing misery and suffering generously and free of charge.[10] The gods of fertility loved expensive gifts as demonstrations of honor and flattery, and the human beings, fearing the gods' harsh retribution, scurried to satisfy their desires. They sacrificed the fruits of their labors to the gods, dedicated their festivals to them, and praised them upon rising in the morning and when lying down to sleep at nightfall.

But still, the gluttonous desires of the gods knew no fulfillment and their bellies remained insatiable. Even when human beings wept over the death of their children, or went hungry for bread when their crops withered, the gods continued to gorge themselves joyfully on the sacrifices and offerings they were served – and they constantly asked for more and received more. Only every once in a while, when their desires were fulfilled and their stomachs swollen with contentment, did they grant the humans tiny portions of plenitude so that they could barely survive for one more day, or one more year. But when it seemed to them that the humans were neglecting their duties or giving too much attention to one of the competing gods, they retracted their blessings and smote them mercilessly. Sometimes they struck the humans just because they had an argument among themselves. Every bit of foolishness that incited commotion in heaven sent tongues of fire down below, and the sparks of their anger reached the humans, scattering death and destruction among them.

When the tumult died down, the fertility gods suddenly recalled that without their blessing, the cycle of life in the lower sphere would come to an end, and the humans'

---

[10] Prometheus was the one god who loved human beings, and he gave them the only gift they ever received for free – fire, which he stole from the gods. For this he was severely punished: Zeus commanded that he be chained to a high rock in the Caucasus mountains for eternity.

offerings would stop flowing to their tables. The fear that their cups would not be refilled with red wine and liquor was the only reason for them to renew their blessings. And so, in years when the gods were placated, the humans gave birth to healthy children and even enjoyed observing their grandchildren's mischievous antics. The domestic animals multiplied, the fields yielded grain, and the olive trees bore ample fruit. But the gods' contentment never lasted for long, and the plentiful years were quickly followed by desolate ones, in which the humans suffered curses and misery, and the bad years outnumbered the good.

Yet despite the fertility gods' volatile and angry character, they had one merit: they never asserted that they were punishing the humans justly or for any sin committed against them. Questions of justice and judgment made them yawn from boredom. Humans composed songs of praise honoring the gods' beauty and power, but never lauded their justice or honesty.

The Israelites lived within the cultural realm of the nations that surrounded them, and were influenced by their beliefs – but at the same time, they developed their own independent beliefs. One of the greatest differences between the pagan worldview I have presented above and that of the Bible is the concept of multiplicity versus uniqueness. Another is the concept of justice. In contrast to the pagans, who believed that the forces active in the universe were distributed among multiple gods, including the gods of fertility, the Israelites believed that all these forces were concentrated in the hands of one God Who had no equal and Whose power was eternal. Still, despite the vast differences between the two forms of belief, they have much in common.

Just as the pagans believed that their gods desired sacrifices and foods, the God of Israel commanded His people to give him sacrifices and offerings (the book of Leviticus discusses this at length). The firstborn son symbolically belonged to God. The firstborn of the cattle and sheep, as well as the first fruits of the barley and wheat harvests, were literally given to God (Ex. 13:12–13; Lev. 23:10–20, and elsewhere).

Like the pagans, the Israelites also believed (and many continue to believe) that when God was pleased with their behavior, He blessed them, their domestic animals, and their fields. Like the blessing of the pagan gods, God's blessing to the Israelites is not eternal life or happiness, but fertility, without which the cycle of life would stop. Similarly to the beliefs of the neighboring peoples, the Bible also emphasizes the view that when God was content with Israel's behavior, He permitted them to raise their children in peace and plow their fields unhindered. But when He was not satisfied with them, he removed the blessing of fertility and smote them harshly. God sent plagues to kill the Israelites, clouds of locusts to destroy their fields, and enemy armies to sow death and destruction among them. He stopped the rains and dried up their wells. God used exactly the same punishments with which the angry gods punished the pagans.

But here, in all related to reward and punishment (in academic terms, the concept of retribution), we find another big difference between the two beliefs: while the pagans believed that their gods were capricious, volatile, and dishonest, their hands soaked in blood, the Israelites believed in the absolute justice of God. The idea that justice is one of the outstanding characteristics of God, that nothing is hidden from Him and that He judges Israel with honesty and fairness, is one of the cornerstones of the Bible – and continues to be a pillar of religious belief today. The belief in the absolute justice of the One God did not permit the Israelites the escape available to the neighboring nations. While the pagans could blame their suffering on the gods' injustice and cruelty, the Israelites had to take personal responsibility for all their troubles. Every disaster that befell them was considered a punishment for sins they had committed, even if they did not know what those sins were (the book of Job is an outstanding example of the philosophical challenges posed by this belief).

The Bible is scattered with dozens of examples showing that God's punishment fits the individual's sin, and conversely, that the level of recompense He offers is equal to the level of the person's righteousness. The reward for good deeds is always fertility, while the punishment for sins is infertility, which leads to annihilation. Chapter 28 of Deuteronomy gives ample expression to this concept. In this chapter, God blesses His believers, and also details the punishments of those who stray from His path. This is the text of the blessing:

> *It shall be that if you hearken to the voice of the Lord, your God, to observe, to perform all of His commandments.... All these blessings will come upon you and overtake you, if you hearken to the voice of the Lord, your God: Blessed shall you be in the city and blessed shall you be in the field.* **Blessed shall be the fruit of your womb, and the fruit of your ground, and the fruit of your animals; the offspring of your cattle and the flocks of your sheep and goats. Blessed shall be your fruit basket and your kneading bowl**.... *(Deut. 28:1–14; also 11:11–14)*

Following is the text of the curse – death and the annulment of fertility:

> *But it will be that if you do not hearken to the voice of the Lord, your God, to observe, to perform all His commandments and all His decrees that I command you today, then all these curses will come upon you and overtake you: Accursed will you be in the city and accursed will you be in the field.* **Accursed will be your fruit basket**

*and your kneading bowl. Accursed will be the fruit of
your womb and the fruit of your ground, the offspring of
your cattle and the flocks of your sheep and goats.* (Deut.
28:15–68; 11:15–17, and elsewhere)

The idea that God (or the gods, according to pagan belief)
rules over the world's abundance, that He gives from it to His
believers and withholds it from those who deny Him, is an
expression of theological, religious thinking.

In a world in which God (or the gods) controls fertility, infertility in the physiological sense does not exist. The
barren woman has no defect in her reproductive system that
prevents her from conceiving; rather, God has "closed" her
womb.[11] In contrast, a fertile woman is righteous, and God
has blessed her and "opened" her womb. Her many, healthy
children, who enjoy long lives and the birth of descendants
after them, are proof of God's approval of her behavior.

The argument that barrenness is evidence of divine
punishment places us in a dangerous trap that the biblical
authors preferred to ignore rather than confront. In the Bible
we find not one word or hint that Sarah, Rachel, or Hannah
sinned, and therefore God closed their wombs. Even so, we
have only to recall the equation specifying that the punishment fits the sin. It is sufficient for us to know that God's
eye is watching over human beings, and that He judges them
with justice, in order to deduce on our own the reason for the
prolonged barrenness of these women. The True Judge does
not punish righteous women who have no fault. He does not
block from them the only path through which they may fulfill their duty to their husbands and to the society in which
they lived. Indeed, Sarah, Rachel, and Hannah did not blame
their barrenness on their health. They did not know how they

---

[11] As we have said, the Bible is a masculine work, and so barrenness is only found in
women.

had sinned or why they were being punished, but they did know that for some reason, the God Who judged them with absolute justice had decreed they would be barren. For reasons that they could not fathom, they had to bow their heads and stiffen their shoulders while arrows of scorn pierced their hearts.

Chapter Eight

SARAH'S LIFE

Abram and Nahor took themselves wives; the name of Abram's wife was Sarai, and the name of Nahor's wife was Milcah.... And Sarai was barren; she had no child.

(Gen. 11:29–30)

*Now Sarai, Abram's wife, had not borne to him, and she had an Egyptian handmaid named Hagar. And Sarai said to Abram, "**Behold now, the Lord has restrained me from bearing**; please come to my handmaid; perhaps I will be built up from her." And Abram hearkened to Sarai's voice.*

(Gen. 16:1–2)

One of God's outstanding attributes is justice. God sees everything, knows everything, and always passes fair judgment. He punishes the wicked according to their degree of wickedness, and rewards the righteous according to their level of righteousness. God judged Sarah, found her guilty, and imposed on her the harshest punishment a woman could earn: He prevented her from having children. He took from her both motherhood and the possibility of fulfilling the only obligation of a woman who lived in the ancient world. Without children, Sarah could not establish her position in Abraham's household. She did not earn the bread she put in her mouth, and there was no justification for her existence or recompense for her suffering.

We have already mentioned that the biblical writers did not accuse Sarah of any sin. But they were the ones who determined the equation specifying that every sin deserves punishment, and that the punishment fits the severity of the sin. Clearly, if the Supreme Judge prevented Sarah from bearing children, this must mean that she sinned against Him in some unknown manner. Something in her belief, perhaps in her personality, or in her deeds, was defective.

From a theological point of view, Sarah's barrenness raises a serious difficulty. Abraham is the only character in the Bible who merited God's promise that his descendants would outnumber the sand of the sea and the stars of the sky. But how could God fulfill this promise if He prevented Sarah from having children?

Abraham did not earn these celebratory promises for no reason. Jewish tradition, which developed hundreds of years after the period of the Genesis characters, examined every detail the Bible gives about Abraham's life under a magnifying glass, and found that God tested him with ten difficult and bitter trials. According to tradition, these trials included the departure from Ur, the journey to the land of Canaan, the famine, and taking Sarah to Pharaoh's house (Gen. 12:11–20). Sarah's barrenness, Abraham's circumcision, and the banishment of Ishmael and Hagar from his house are also among the trials. The authors of these traditions carefully examined Abraham's every act, and ruled confidently that faithful Abraham passed all the trials that came his way with flying colors. He thus deserved the fulfillment of God's promises. But the only reward he received for his steadfastness was a wife whose womb was closed by God Himself for some unknown reason.

The tradition is lavish in its praise for Abraham, who withstood every trial.

But where is Sarah?

For a reason I cannot explain, the collective memory of the biblical peoples, both Jewish and Christian, does not include her. The entrance to the palace of glorification is blocked to her, and we have forgotten that every trial that Abraham underwent affected her as well.

Abraham is righteous. Sarah is barren.

Sarah was excluded from the descriptions of the trials Abraham withstood. She was silenced and disgraced. Her place remained in the wings, behind the sides of the black tent that she so meticulously patched from goat hair. The diminution of her image was so successful that for almost four thousand years we have forgotten that her childhood and youth withered on the roads before it budded and sprouted. We have forgotten that Sarah walked beside Abraham the entire route from Ur to the land of Canaan, and that she missed not one step of the entire 2175 miles (3500 km) that her righteous husband walked (see chapter 3).

In comparison to Abraham's courage, the story of her bravery has been dwarfed in our minds. The fact that she shared all the trials he withstood so bravely has disappeared from our consciousness. We praise Abraham for his powerful belief in God, but we forget that on the nights when he spread a thin straw mat on the hard ground and curled up on it to sleep, Sarah was beside him. Only a tattered goatskin coverlet and the thin tent sides separated between this lonely, hungry girl and the stars in the skies – but still, we do not consider this a trial for her. Even the sacrifice of Isaac, the only son born to Sarah after long years of barrenness, was a trial for Abraham, not for her.

This distant girl who has vanished from our minds, who wandered ravenous on empty roads, whom the dry east wind tossed around like a tumbleweed, whose black hair was painted by the dust with the sandy colors of the desert, was our ancient, brave foremother. But if God punished her, why should we try to defend her? Why should we open the gates of our memory to her, and allow her to enter and stand beside such a righteous man as Abraham?

When we set aside the Bible's theological way of thinking and adopt a practical worldview that does not ascribe Sarah's barrenness to God, a new possibility arises that explains why she was unable to conceive for so many years.

As we recall, Sarah was born in Ur, one of the most magnificent and prosperous cities of the ancient world. Almost certainly, like all girls of her time, she was married around age eleven, even before commencing her menstrual cycle, simply because that was the custom of the time.

As we showed in chapter 1, the nutritional resources available to the residents of Ur were ample and varied, and included all the food groups needed by humans. Even if we agree that Terah's family was poor, while they lived in Ur their nutrition was much better than that of nomads who wandered the roads. Their diet certainly included everything needed by a girl in the years of her preliminary sexual development. If Sarah had remained in Ur and not gone on the journey, she would have received the nutrition necessary for proper development. Given ample nutrition, she would have conceived for the first time around age fourteen or fifteen, like most girls. She would then have continued to give birth until around age thirty, when she died of exhaustion and premature old age. If that had happened, the story of her life would have been an exact copy of that of every other girl of her time.

But Sarah's story is not that of just another girl who lived almost four thousand years ago. Shortly after her marriage, she joined her family on the trek to the land of Canaan. Sarah was then eleven or twelve years old. From the day she left Ur and for the next twenty years, she walked thousands of miles and worked at manual labor in order to purchase a bit of food.

Throughout these years, Sarah was mainly nourished by the barley she gathered on the roads, a little wheat, some dates, olive oil, and milk products supplied by the small herd of goats that accompanied the family. When a faithful goat happened to die, she could gnaw on a piece of meat, which supplied her with some protein and fat. Such a diet would enable her to survive, but it hardly made up for the enormous amount of calories she burned on the days when she walked, or when she stopped in one place to work at manual labor.

When I presented this data to physicians, they all agreed that Sarah's chances of conceiving were minimal, almost nonexistent. In their opinion, the combination of poor diet, which sometimes reached famine level, and intense physical effort over a period of twenty years meant that Sarah was in very poor physical condition. In the reality described here, every crumb of food she placed in her mouth was transformed into energy that was immediately channeled toward one purpose: ensuring the continued functioning of the life systems necessary for her survival (brain, heart, kidneys, liver, and lungs). Termination of the functioning of these systems would mean death. According to the doctors, the continual scarcity of food had a devastating effect on Sarah's fertility: it suppressed all systems not immediately necessary for her survival. Above all, her near-starvation diet suppressed her reproductive system, a natural consumer of abundant energy. Under Sarah's deprived living conditions, she had no chance of becoming pregnant, or of growing a healthy fetus in her womb and providing the nutrition it needed to build its body – and the fact is that she did not conceive.

In addition to her poor diet, we must add the environmental conditions, also voracious consumers of calories. During the years of the journey, Sarah slept under the open sky, in a cave, or in a hut she happened to come across on one of the farms where the family camped. Winter in the Lebanon mountains is cold and snowy, while summer in the Sinai Desert is as hot as a fiery furnace. Although during the fall and winter months, mornings in the desert are warm and pleasant, the temperature drops toward nightfall and freezing cold slowly creeps into the bones and the body they support. Undoubtedly, during the daytime Sarah suffered from thirst and the blood in her veins boiled, but at night her bones shook from cold and no clothing she might wear was enough to warm her. Survival in such climate conditions demands enormous energy and requires consumption of food rich in protein and fat. But where would a girl living under extremely deprived circumstances obtain such rich food?

According to the physicians I consulted, if Sarah had conceived in such a situation, chances were high that her body would abort the fetus in her womb, and almost certainly she would die of weakness, along with the fetus. The doctors compared her condition to that of an anorexic girl whose menstrual cycle ceases due to her low-calorie and low-protein diet. Sportswomen, dancers, and models, who live on a strict diet and consume high amounts of energy, often face similar results.

But although severe malnutrition for an extended period causes a woman's menstrual cycle to cease, this process is usually reversible. If the anorexic gradually returns to eating and enjoys a rich diet, and if the sportswoman abandons exhausting sports that burn energy like a furnace, there is a good chance that their menstrual cycle will return to normal and they will be able to conceive and bear healthy children – and thank God, this was so for Sarah as well.

Sarah was not an anorexic, a model, or a sportswoman. She was a hungry girl, used to suffering and privation. But because her physical condition was very similar to such women, she also had a chance to recuperate and conceive. The conditions for this were rest from the journey and a significant improvement in her diet – and this is exactly what happened! When she reached Hebron with Abraham, an end came to the terribly taxing period of walking that almost took her life each day. The continuous physical effort was considerably reduced, and her diet apparently improved significantly. After several years of rehabilitation, just like anorexics undergo, Sarah recuperated and conceived.[12]

We find a hint of support for this argument in the story of the three angels who visited Abraham and Sarah's tent to inform them that she would conceive and give birth to a son. Sarah listened secretly to their conversation, and laughed to herself in disbelief:

> *Now Abraham and Sarah were old, coming on in years; Sarah had ceased to have the way of the women. And Sarah laughed within herself, saying, "After I have become withered [meaning cessation of the menstrual cycle], will I have restoration [of "the way of women"]?[13] And also, my master is old." (Gen. 18:11–12)*

---

[12] The Bible says that ten years after Abraham and Sarah lived in Hebron, Sarah was still childless (Gen. 16:3). Ten years is considered a round number in the Bible, not an exact number.

[13] The traditional translation of Sarah's rhetorical question is "After I become withered will I have pleasure?" But this does not reflect the meaning of the Hebrew or the author's intention, and so I have emended the translation.

The Hebrew word for "withered" with regard to a woman means the cessation of her monthly menstrual cycle, or menopause. The word *ednah* is usually translated into English as "restoration," but that is only one of its meanings. In Hebrew, the Garden of Eden means a garden of plentiful, abundant fertility. *Ednah*, in Sarah's case, means fertility, youth and renewal, and this is Sarah's meaning here: she is referring to the restoration of her monthly cycle, "the way of women." Elderly Sarah laughed incredulously, because the messengers implied that her youth, and her monthly cycle along with it, would return to her after she had grown old, and she would be able to

The exact meaning of the Hebrew text is that after the long, wearing years during which Sarah's body fought so that her life-maintaining systems would function, her reproductive system began to operate once again. Sarah received her menstrual period – "the way of women" – and was able to conceive. If Sarah had lived in our time, her doctor would have instructed her to follow the same regimen of rest and diet that she observed on her own.

THE MIRACLE IN THE BIBLE: SARAH IS NINETY, ABRAHAM IS ONE HUNDRED

> *The Lord visited Sarah as He had said, and the Lord did to Sarah as He had spoken. Sarah conceived and bore a son to Abraham in his old age, at the time of which God had spoken to him. Abraham named his son who had been born to him, whom Sarah had borne to him, Isaac.... Abraham was a hundred years old when his son Isaac was born to him. Sarah said, "God has made joy for me; whoever hears will rejoice over me." She said, "Who would have said to Abraham that Sarah would nurse children, for I have borne a son to his old age!" (Gen. 21:1–7)*

The book of Genesis recounts that when Sarah reached ninety, she conceived and bore a child to Abraham, then one hundred years old, thanks to God, Who "visited" her. Secular readers relate to this with scorn, as a ridiculous story that could not possibly have happened in reality. In contrast to them, readers with a deep religious worldview believe that God performed a miracle. Since according to the Bible, the story of Isaac's birth is a miracle, I must explain what a miracle is.

According to popular conception, a miracle is a welcome event that takes place in an unexpected manner. Some

---

conceive. The meaning "restoration" cannot fit here because it is not the opposite of "withered." It does not describe Sarah's situation, and it is not her intention.

examples are sudden recovery from a serious illness, surviving a fatal traffic accident without injury, or falling from a top story of a building and landing on a soft bush instead of on the sidewalk pavement. These examples, like the big win in the lottery, belong to the world of probability, because they can take place by chance. They are rare, but they are not divine miracles.

A divine miracle, according to the theology that the Bible presents, is something completely different. It is God's way of revealing Himself to human beings. This revelation always involves a change in the laws of nature, which God Himself determined during the six days of creation of the world. One of the goals of the divine miracle is to prove that God exists beyond nature, and that He is not subject to the laws He determined for nature. When God wants to reveals Himself to human beings, He bends the laws of nature to His will, and this bending is a "miracle." It involves a dramatic change in the course of nature as known to human beings in their everyday lives. A miracle inspires surprise and intense emotion at the infinite power of God.

For example, no one would notice if a thorny, dry bush that grew in the desert suddenly caught fire and disappeared in the blink of an eye, leaving no trace. But when a dry bush, containing almost no consumable matter, burns continuously and is not consumed – this is a phenomenon that contradicts the physical law that nothing can burn more than the amount of flammable matter it contains, and thus it is a divine miracle (Ex. 3:1–4). Another example: when the shade that a sundial casts moves in opposition to the direction of the sun, as if the sun rose in the west and set in the east, this is a miracle. Only God can cause shade to move in the opposite direction of the sun's progress (Is. 38:4–8). Of course, God is visible through major events as well, as in the ten plagues with which He smote Egypt, and the cessation of the sun and moon's movement (Josh. 10:12–14). In general, a miracle in the Bible is an event that contradicts nature's routine as known to human beings. It is proof of the infinite power of God, and of His ability to transform the impossible into the possible. (This conception is particularly evident in the books of the Prophets and Psalms, and especially in the New Testament.)[14]

If we had read in Genesis that Sarah was around thirty-three when she conceived Isaac, as our calculations indicate, we would not consider her pregnancy such a surprising or shocking event. We would not believe it was proof of God's ability to perform powerful deeds that did not normally happen in a woman's life. Indeed, in Sarah's time, a woman of thirty-three was considered to have lived above the average number of years (thirty). But although it might be a rare occurrence, such a woman could still conceive.

However, the biblical authors did not write about the rare but possible. They were interested in the impossible, that wonderful realm in which God's power was revealed in public, inspiring awe and trembling. Thus they wrote that Sarah conceived at age ninety, when Abraham was one hundred. Such a pregnancy could take place only when God decided to reveal His unlimited power – and this was the goal of the story of Isaac's birth. The New Testament went one step further and inspired additional awe, recounting that Jesus was born as a result of the Holy Spirit of God actually visiting his mother, the Virgin Mary (Luke 1:26–38).

But when we consider Isaac's conception from a point of view that does not follow the biblical authors' aim to glorify God's greatness, we find that the "miracles" Sarah experienced were pedestrian, not divine. The first miracle involved the biological systems that suppressed her reproductive system

---

[14] The miracle is one of the basic principles of every religion and belief. Every religion has its own traditions that demonstrate the supernatural powers of its gods.

and prevented her from conceiving. If Sarah had conceived during the days when she wandered the roads, the pregnancy would have taxed her already poor physical condition and to the physical exertion she had to expend every day. If this had happened, it is highly likely that Sarah would have shared the same miserable fate of countless nomads who died on the roads from exhaustion and hunger, and that of wretched Rachel, who died in childbirth and was buried on the side of the road (Gen. 35:16–20). From a practical viewpoint, the miracle that Sarah experienced was that she did not conceive until she completed the journey and regained her strength.

The second miracle took place several years later. After Sarah rested, recuperated, and added some fat under the thin layer of her skin, her reproductive system, which had been suppressed for so many years, awakened and began to function once again. From a practical point of view, the chances of conceiving at the end of the journey were almost nonexistent, yet still Sarah became pregnant and gave birth to a son – and that was a miracle!

The cynics among us will certainly say that this was not a "miracle," but rather a statistical probability. But I insist that it was a miracle!

CONCLUSION

From the calculation we have detailed above, we may estimate that Sarah was around eleven years old when she began the journey, and thirty-three or thirty-four when she conceived. In our days, pregnancy at this age is routine. But Sarah did not live in our time, and in the reality of her era, a woman past the age of thirty was considered old, at the end of her life. Indeed, at age thirty-three, Sarah was a tired woman, and according to the physicians with whom I have consulted, the long years of privation undoubtedly did significant damage to her health. Still, from a purely biological point of view,

she was not an old woman. Surprisingly, almost paradoxi-
cally, her lengthy "barrenness" was to her benefit in the end.
The unique circumstances of her life meant that her youth
was not used for bearing children. Despite her advanced
age, her condition was not much worse than that of most
of her contemporaries, whose bodies were worn down from
many pregnancies and miscarriages. Sarah still had a chance
to recover enough to conceive, and she did in fact conceive
and give birth. Given that in the ancient world babies nursed
until age three, Sarah must have been around thirty-seven
when Isaac was weaned. Almost certainly she died soon afterward, a very old woman.

From a practical point of view, the life story of this brave
little nomad exactly fits the reality in which nomads and
refugees lived then, and still live today, ending their lives on
the roads. It fits the harsh landscape in which she walked for
twenty years, step after step after step.

Sarah was a heroine. She withstood all the trials with
which God tested Abraham. Still, in the collective memory
of her ungrateful descendants, the trials she bore were forgotten, and she is remembered mainly as a barren woman,
jealous and angry. To me, however, of all the women the Bible
describes, Sarah is the one I admire most. She is my heroic
foremother.

Chapter Nine

SARAH AND HAGAR

S arah did not fulfill her duty toward Abraham. She did not bear him children, and did not strengthen the patriarchal household he headed. For some reason of which she was unaware, God punished her. He closed her womb and stamped a mark of disgrace on her forehead: barren.

This mark of disgrace pierced her heart during the long years when she wandered the roads, when each day she awoke to exhaust herself in harsh labor for a bag of flour and a little olive oil. The shame of her childlessness affixed itself to this silent woman and did not desert her for a moment. Almost four thousand years have passed, and this shame continues to suck her blood like a parasite. Sarah, the most well-known barren woman in the Western world, remained silent then, and she remains silent today as well. Perhaps only at bedtime, when she spread a straw mat on the hard ground and curled up under a soft blanket of stars, did a heartbreaking sigh of insult, heard by none, escape from between her cracked lips. Perhaps one tear, shining like one of the stars in the endless clear sky above her, rinsed a thin trail of the road's dust from her face.

But if God decreed barrenness for her, why should we pity her?

Sarah lived in a quiet, empty world that needed as many children as possible in order to continue. She lived in a world in which men wanted to marry multiple women, hoping that some of the sons they bore would safely survive their childhoods and reach maturity. In her world, pity for a childless woman was doled out in measured amounts, if at all.

Long years passed.

One day, Sarah stood still; she rested her traveling bag on the ground and stopped walking. She was already thirty years old, an old woman who despaired of the hope that she would ever be able to clutch a child of her own to her breast. Because of her, the man she had married twenty years earlier in magnificent Ur headed a sad, tiny patriarchal household, to which not even one child had been born. This situation went on for too long, and a solution had to be found. When Sarah reached the bottom, she approached Abraham and asked him to have a child with her Egyptian maidservant, Hagar, who had apparently joined them when they returned from Egypt:

> Now Sarai, Abram's wife, had not borne to him, and she had an Egyptian slave woman named Hagar. And Sarai said to Abram, "Behold now, the Lord has restrained me from bearing; **please go in to my slave woman; perhaps I will be built up through her.**" And Abram hearkened to Sarai's voice. (Gen. 16:1–2)

Sarah's request to Abraham is clear: she asked to be "built up," or strengthened, through the child that her slave woman would bear, and thus benefit herself. Yet for some unclear reason, authors of ancient legends who lived in the land of Israel more than fifteen hundred years after Abraham and Sarah's time changed the intention of the text. They transformed Sarah's words, and asserted that she spoke only out of love and anxiety for Abraham. Since then, we remember their words, not the words of the Bible. Foremost among the legend writers in the land of Israel around 250 BCE was the author of a small, ingenious book – the book of Jubilees – which will assist us in the following chapters as well. According to the author of Jubilees, Sarah's intention was to benefit Abraham, not herself:

> *Sarai advised her husband Abram, and said to him: "Go in to my Egyptian slave-girl Hagar; perhaps I will build up descendants for you from her." Abram listened to his wife Sarai's suggestion, and said to her, "Do (as you suggest)." So Sarai took her Egyptian slave-girl Hagar, and gave her to her husband Abram, to be his wife. (Jubilees 14, 22–23)*[15]

The Jewish commentator Philo of Alexandria, who lived in Egypt about two hundred years after the author of Jubilees, went one step further. According to him, when Sarah realized she was unable to conceive, she decided to give her slave woman to her beloved husband, so that he would obtain the child they yearned for:

> *[This] demonstrates her great love for her husband, for since she was considered barren, she thought it unjust that her barrenness would be detrimental to her husband's household. Thus she placed his [Abraham's] interests over her own status. (Philo 16:2)*

It is an open secret that a woman in love is capable of doing many things in order to satisfy her beloved's will, except for one: marrying him to another woman so that she will bear a child for him, instead of her! Indeed, according to the biblical text, Sarah asked Abraham to marry Hagar for her own benefit, and not for anyone else's: "Please go in to my slave

---

[15] J.C. VanderKam, *The Book of Jubilees* (academic translation) (Lovanii:1989).

woman; perhaps *I will be built up* through her." Abraham acquiesced, and Hagar the Egyptian was given to him as a wife.

In what way did Sarah hope to be built up through her slave woman? What profit did she expect? To answer this question, we must stop for a moment at the side of the road, to sip some cool water and consider the laws of the ancient world and the writing style of the biblical authors.

We have already mentioned that biblical writing is characterized by extreme conciseness. The Bible does not waste words, and any word that can be spared – is spared. Yet surprisingly, alongside the Spartan economy that characterizes most of the stories, on occasion we encounter the opposite phenomenon, when a word or sentence is repeated a number of times. Such repetitions are always a red light ordering the reader to stop. They signal that the author wanted to emphasize an especially important issue. The following passage is one of these red lights – the phrases highlighted here specify nine different times, using various phrasings, that Hagar was Sarah's slave woman:

> *Now Sarai, Abram's wife, had not borne to him, and **she had an Egyptian slave woman** named Hagar. And Sarai said to Abram, "Behold now, the Lord has restrained me from bearing; please go in to **my slave woman**; perhaps I will be built up through her." And Abram hearkened to Sarai's voice. So Sarai, Abram's wife, took Hagar the Egyptian, **her slave woman**, at the end of ten years of Abram's dwelling in the land of Canaan, and she gave her to Abram her husband for a wife. And he came to Hagar, and she conceived, and she saw that she was pregnant, and **her mistress** became slight in her eyes. And Sarai said to Abram, "This outrage against me is because of you! I myself put **my slave woman** in your embrace, and when she saw that she had conceived, and I became slight in her*

*eyes. Let the Lord judge between you and me!" And Abram said to Sarai, "Here, **your slave woman** is in your hands; do to her that which is proper in your eyes." And Sarai afflicted her, and she fled from before her. And an angel of the Lord found her by a water fountain in the desert, by the fountain on the road to Shur. And he said, "**Hagar, Sarai's slave woman**, where are you coming from, and where are you going to?" And she said, "I am fleeing from before **Sarai, my mistress**." And the angel of the Lord said to her, "Return to **your mistress**, and allow yourself to be afflicted under her hands." (Gen. 16:1–9)*

The Bible and ancient legal books dedicate considerable space to the legal relationship between masters and servants, both male and female. Therefore, if the author found it important to emphasize the legal relationship between the two women so many times, this means that the relationship between them played a central role, and we must investigate its nature.

We have already noted that during the biblical period, marrying multiple wives was permitted and desirable, and men did not need to obtain their wives' permission in order to marry additional women. Abraham could have married as many women as he wanted – except for Hagar, because Hagar was not his servant, but Sarah's! She was Sarah's property, not Abraham's, and the passage above emphasizes this fact in nine different ways. Sarah had the right to do what she wanted with Hagar: she could sell her, banish her, or have her marry one of their other slaves and then sell her children. She could have her marry Abraham so that she would conceive through him. The children born to a slave woman belonged to her master, as she did, and not to their biological mother. This is what Sarah meant when she said, "Please go in to my slave woman; perhaps I will be built up through her." The great profit that Sarah hoped for was motherhood to a child she was prevented from conceiving herself. She intended to recognize her slave woman's son as her own, and to grant him the special status reserved for the firstborn son of the senior wife.

In many aspects, Sarah's act reminds us of today's practice of surrogate motherhood, in which a woman who cannot conceive uses the womb of another woman in order to gain a child for herself. Even in our time, a woman who uses a surrogate mother does so as a last resort. Like every last resort, surrogacy is an act that follows long years of despair and misery – and Sarah was desperate and miserable.

But despite the similarity, modern surrogacy is completely different from the ancient form. Today's surrogate mother is not married to the husband of the barren woman, and she has no legal rights over the child she bears. She detaches herself from the baby immediately following the birth, and this rapid separation symbolizes that her role has ended. The surrogate mother is not allowed to take part in the life of the baby and the family, and is not permitted to breathe down the neck of the woman who raises him. After the birth, the surrogate mother returns to her home, and with this, her connection with the baby and its legal parents ends. Unfortunately, Sarah did not enjoy any of these advantages.

Ancient surrogacy was a package deal in which the biological mother was married to the baby's father, but because she was a servant, she had no rights over the baby. The baby belonged to the mistress, not to the woman who gave birth to it, and this is true in our case as well. Although Hagar was given to Abraham in the status of a wife ("and she [Sarai] gave her to Abram her husband for a wife"), she remained Sarah's slave both legally and in practice, and the author saw fit to emphasize this point nine times. If Hagar's legal status had changed as a result of her marriage to Abraham, Sarah would never have given her to him. Sarah did not intend to "build up" Hagar, but rather herself. Still, at this juncture the slave woman was the big winner. The profit Hagar gained by marrying Abraham, a free man, was that the price tag was removed from around her neck. Sarah no longer had the right to sell her or separate her from her son, like an ordinary slave woman.[16] The lucky slave woman earned additional gain from conceiving a child to a free man – thanks to his father, her son was born free, not a slave.

Thus, while formally Ishmael was considered Sarah's son, he grew up alongside his biological mother, right before her eyes. Her blood flowed in his veins, and no one could take this away from her. Furthermore, Hagar knew that Sarah, Abraham's senior wife, gave her son the special status reserved for the family's firstborn son of a senior wife. He would benefit from the rights that legally belonged to the firstborn, and inherit Abraham's property and status.

Hagar's Audacity

Sarah hoped to be built up through Ishmael, and to strengthen her shaky place in Abraham's home. She hoped that mothering the child she adopted as a son would remove the shame that adhered to her. But in reality, the opposite took place. She was disgraced even further. Seemingly, she had a son, but in fact, Sarah succeeded in building up Hagar instead of herself. From the day this daughter of slaves conceived and ensured her place in Abraham's home, her self-confidence swelled, and she became arrogant toward her mistress. Hagar hit Sarah at her weak point, her barrenness: "She saw that she was pregnant, and *her mistress became slight in her eyes*."

The term "slight" as used here means "foolish" or "silly." Sarah was furious at Hagar because the slave treated her as a stupid woman deserving of ridicule, whose orders could be

---

[16] When Sarah gave Hagar to Abraham in marriage, she gave up the right to sell her. Indeed, when relations between the two women reached boiling point, Sarah afflicted her slave woman, and later even banished her to the desert. But at no point in the story was Hagar given up for sale.

ignored. Hagar felt, apparently with justification, that she had the power to treat Sarah insolently, and this reveals that her pregnancy through Abraham changed the social order in his home. From Hagar's point of view, at that point she became the senior wife, and she had the right to humiliate her mistress and treat her arrogantly.

In truth, Hagar did nothing apart from joining the crowd of people who ridiculed Sarah and poured salt on the bleeding wound inside her heart. But foolish Hagar forgot that she was not actually a member of this crowd. When Sarah had had her fill, she went to Abraham and lashed out at him:

> **This outrage against me is because of you!** *I myself put my slave woman in your embrace, and when she saw that she had conceived, I became slight in her eyes.* **Let the Lord judge between you and me!**" *And Abram said to Sarai, "Here, your slave woman is in your hands; do to her that which is proper in your eyes." And Sarai afflicted her, and she fled from before her. (Gen. 16:5–6)*

The Hebrew term for Sarah's outrage is *hamas*. Although this translation is correct, "outrage" is only the secondary meaning of this word in biblical language. The primary meaning, which is lost in translation, is "sin against God." For example, due to the acts of "outrage" committed during the time of Noah, God opened the skies and washed away all the inhabitants of the earth:

> *And God said to Noah, "The end of all flesh has come before Me, for the earth is filled with outrage (*hamas*) because of them, and behold, I am destroying them from the earth." (Gen. 6:13)*

In using the term outrage (*hamas*), the author chose to use one of the harshest expressions of anger in biblical language to express Sarah's bitterness. Understanding this word and

the demand that Abraham stand trial before God shows that
Sarah interpreted her husband's support of Hagar as a sin
against God.

In addition, we must take into account the social and
cultural reality in which these things were said. The women
in the Bible were not like modern women. They did not raise
their voices to scream at their husbands. The documenta-
tion of this outburst of fury by one of the most important
biblical characters is a singular occurrence, unrepeated in the
book. The expression "This outrage against me is because
of you" shows that Sarah blamed Abraham for allowing the
slave woman to transform the household hierarchy and treat
her with insolence. Without backup from him, Hagar would
never dare to be so audacious. The fact that she did so shows
that Hagar had support for her behavior. Sarah's fury also
clarifies another issue: she had reached the bottom, and was
waging a lost battle against her servant in her own home.

But why should Abraham be responsible for preserving
his wife's honor? She had not preserved his honor by fulfilling
her duty toward him, while the slave woman given him as a
wife conceived easily and was about to bear his firstborn son.
So in Abraham's opinion, Sarah had nothing to complain
about. But when she called him to stand trial before God,
he had to respond. Abraham's dry reply is recognition of his
wife's official position in relation to Hagar, but not an admission that he agrees with the justice of her argument: "Here,
your slave woman is in your hands; do to her that which is
proper in your eyes."

Hagar was a foolish slave woman. If she had been blessed
with a shred of intelligence, she would have recalled that
although she had been given to Abraham as a wife, and Ishmael was considered his firstborn son, she remained Sarah's
slave. If only she had remembered that her marriage did not
change that fact, her situation would have been supreme. If

she had exercised caution with her mistress's honor, then she could have borne more sons to Abraham, thus further strengthening her own status in his household. But silly Hagar forgot who was the slave woman and who was the mistress. From the day Abraham removed his protection from her, she was at her mistress's mercy – and Sarah had no mercy. Perhaps Sarah was not able to avenge the protracted mistreatment of those who mocked her, but she could vent her full fury upon her slave woman. The moment she was given permission, Sarah unleashed twenty years of insult on the miserable servant, until Hagar fled from her into the desert.

God sent an angel to instruct Hagar to return to Sarah's home and continue to suffer at her mistress's hands. But even without the angel, Hagar would have returned to Sarah's home, which was nothing more than a shabby tent woven from goat hair. After all, that home, woven of warp and woof, was the only home Hagar knew. If she had not returned to Sarah, she would have died of thirst long before the sands of the desert stretched their gaping maws and swallowed her whole. Thus Hagar returned to Sarah's home and continued to suffer the abuse of her mistress, who never forgave the slave woman for taking advantage of her barrenness in order to treat her with arrogance.

THE BIRTHS OF ISHMAEL AND ISAAC

Ishmael (meaning "God will hear"), the son through whom Sarah hoped to be built up, was born. Because Sarah recognized him as her firstborn son, Abraham had a successor "born" to his senior wife. But in reality, Sarah did not strengthen her shaky position. She could not banish Hagar and develop a preliminary bond with the baby, for her withered breasts were dry as the desert through which she walked, and she could not supply the baby with the basic food needed for his existence. The ancients, who buried many children, recognized the importance of long-term nursing. They knew that mother's milk supplied all the ingredients the baby needed, and improved his chances of survival. They also knew that nursing created the first close relationship between mother and baby – and Sarah was not able to supply any of this to Ishmael. The only thing she could do for her little son was to give him to his biological mother and look on, eyes torn with pain and jealousy, as the baby latched its mouth onto the nipple of her hated slave woman. Women in the ancient world usually nursed their babies for three years. Every single day throughout that period, like continuous torture, Sarah was forced to watch as Hagar clutched to her breast the child through whom she hoped to be built up. Sarah saw with her own eyes how the child nurtured a natural and deep relationship with his mother. Formally, little Ishmael was her son, but apparently this was as far as their relationship went. Sarah granted him her status, but she received nothing in return.

The Bible says that thirteen years passed from the day Ishmael was born until Sarah experienced a miracle: she conceived and bore a son. After nine months of pregnancy that were so late in coming, Sarah finally was able to clutch to her tortured heart a son of her own – Isaac. She felt how her breasts filled and how the baby in her arms drew her milk from them. She pressed her cracked lips to his silky skin, tasting him again and again, as if begging for the flavor of his skin on her lips to erase the long years of suffering from her soul. And so, the silent groans of sorrow to which no one bothered to listen were slowly healed, and exchanged with cries of joy:

And Sarah said, "Laughter has God made me; whoever hears will laugh at me." And she said, "Who would have

said to Abraham that Sarah would nurse children, for I
have borne a son to his old age!" (Gen. 21:6–7)

We know nothing about the relations that prevailed between
the two women from the day Ishmael was born until Sarah
gave birth to Isaac. We do not know if Sarah continued to
treat her thoughtless servant with cruelty, or if she became
accustomed to her presence and left her alone. One thing we
can say for certain: Sarah stood guard and did not allow Hagar
to become pregnant again.

Until Isaac's birth, Hagar's place was ensured, thanks to
Ishmael, who was considered Abraham's firstborn son and
inheritor. But after Isaac was born, this situation changed.
Sarah no longer needed the slave woman's son in order to be
"built up" through him, and so she removed her protection
from him and took away the rights reserved to the firstborn.
From that point on, Isaac was considered Abraham's firstborn son and successor. Ishmael, born to a slave woman,
stood far behind him.

Almost certainly, had the relationship between the
two women been ordinary, Hagar and Ishmael could have
remained in Abraham's home until the end of their lives, as
part of the patriarchal household he headed. But apparently,
the relations between them remained strained, and Hagar
and Ishmael were ordered to leave the home.

The book of Genesis recounts that one day, after Isaac
was weaned (this means he was about three years old), Sarah
sees Ishmael "laughing":

And Sarah saw the son of Hagar the Egyptian, whom she
had borne to Abraham, laughing. (21:9)

The meaning of the word "laughing" has never been completely clarified, and we cannot understand it from the text.
Ishmael's laughter is mentioned so vaguely that we cannot

tell if he was laughing at Isaac or with Isaac, or if Isaac was present when he laughed. There is no clue whether something in Ishmael's laughter hurt Isaac. Still, this ambiguous laughter ignites Sarah's fury, and she demands that Abraham banish him and his mother from their home.

Later in history, commentators pounced on this laughter in order to justify the banishment of mother and son. Some said that the laughter implied a sexual offense against Isaac, while others argued that the laughter was clear proof that Ishmael was an idol worshipper. Of course, the text does not support either of these interpretations, for according to the Bible, it was not possible for Abraham's son to be either a sexual offender or an idol worshipper. In essence, it does not matter what Ishmael's laughter meant, or even if he laughed at all. Either way, Sarah would have banished him and his mother from the home.

Isaac was the only love and joy Sarah ever knew in her bitter life. He was born toward the end of her life, and she had to ensure that Ishmael and his mother would not threaten his firstborn status and his inheritance. If Isaac had been born to Abraham first, his status as firstborn would have been clear and unchallenged. But in Abraham's household, the social order was reversed, and until Isaac was born, firstborn status was promised to Ishmael. Sarah feared that if she and Abraham died while Ishmael and his mother were still living in their home, the two would take advantage of Isaac's tender age and prevent him from inheriting his due. Indeed, the text shows clearly that Sarah did not desire to banish Ishmael because of his laughter, but because she feared for her son's inheritance:

*And Sarah said to Abraham, "Drive out this slave woman and her son, for **the son of this slave woman shall not*** *inherit with my son, with Isaac." But the matter seemed evil to Abraham, concerning his son. (Gen. 21:10–11)*

According to the text, Abraham thought Sarah's request was evil – and this should not surprise us. Hagar and Ishmael were an inseparable part of the small patriarchal household that he led, and it was natural for Abraham to love his son deeply. The text says that he capitulated to Sarah's demand only after God intervened in the argument between them and ruled in her favor:

God said to Abraham, "Let it not seem evil in your eyes on account of the lad and on account of your slave woman. Whatever Sarah says to you, listen to her voice, for through Isaac will your seed be called. But the slave woman's son, too, I will make a nation, for he is your seed." (Gen. 21:12–13)

Abraham's position was tragic. In the depths of his heart, he was well aware that even if God had not intervened in the argument between him and Sarah, he had to choose one of his two sons and one of his two women. If he wanted to ensure that the firstborn status would pass to Isaac, born to him through his senior wife, who was also his half-sister, and not to the son whose mother was a slave woman, then he had to banish Ishmael. Abraham could not ignore the logic in Sarah's words, or the fact that the continued presence of both in his home endangered Isaac's firstborn status. The moment of truth arrived, and even without God's ruling, he had to decide on a course of action.

But could he banish one son in order to leave the way open for the other? The answer is yes, and the Bible offers support for this practice in other incidents.

Genesis relates the strange story that after Sarah died, Abraham took another wife named Keturah. In addition to her, he took concubines (Gen. 25:1–6). His many wives gave Abraham numerous sons, brothers to Isaac, his firstborn son.

Undoubtedly, the story of Abraham's sons who were born after Sarah's death is unrelated to the main story in Genesis, which relates that Abraham was childless for most of his life and had two sons in his old age. The story of the multiple wives he took after Sarah's death is apparently a satellite story, added at a later date to the main story we have discussed here – and this requires explanation.

Researchers of the Bible have noted that the Bible stories, especially those in Genesis, are not homogenous or consistent. Sometimes, sentences from one story are repeated in another. Sometimes the same story appears in several versions, and sometimes one version contradicts another.

For example, Genesis offers two different versions of the story of the creation of humanity. According to one version, on the sixth day of the creation of the world, God created man and woman in His image (1:26–27). The second version detaches the creation of humanity from the creation of the world. It recounts that at some point after the creation of the world, God created man from the earth and breathed life into him. Then God brought man into the Garden of Eden, so that he would cultivate it. Observing man's solitude, God put him to sleep and created woman from his rib (2:18–23). We may easily demonstrate that according to the first version, the creation of the first man and woman was part of the creation of the world. According to the second version, however, the creation of man is unrelated to the creation of the world. God creates him from dust, not in His image. Eve was created at an even later stage, from a rib in her husband's chest.

In another example, before God brought the flood upon the earth, He commanded Noah to bring into the ark seven pairs of pure animals and birds. In addition, Noah had to bring one pair from each of the other kinds of animals (7:2–3). Later, we read that Noah brought only one pair of pure animals and birds into the ark, like the other animals (7:9, 14–16). An additional example is the story of how Jacob earned the birthright in Isaac's household. According to the first version, Esau, Jacob's twin brother, sold his birthright for a bowl of lentil stew (25:27–34). The second version of this story is completely different: Jacob stole the birthright from Esau, and was forced to flee to Haran (chapter 27).

Based on dozens of similar examples in the Bible, researchers have concluded that different groups in ancient Israel recorded variant versions of the same story. At some point, these variant versions reached the Bible's editors, and they placed the different versions of the same stories side by side.

The story of Abraham taking many wives and having many children after Sarah's death is a good example of how one variant preserved by one group contradicts the main story, which says that Abraham had only two sons in his old age. Almost certainly, at some point this variant reached the Bible editors, and they attached it to the text after the main story, like a tail.

For our purposes, this variant is important for one reason: it exemplifies the custom of inheritance practiced during biblical times. According to this source, when it came time for Abraham to put his affairs in order before leaving this world, he sent his many sons away from Isaac to "the land of the east" (not a country, but a general eastward direction). He did this because he wanted to block any threat to Isaac's firstborn status:

> *Abraham gave everything he had to Isaac. And to the sons of Abraham's concubines, Abraham gave gifts; then he sent them away from Isaac his son while he was still alive, eastward, to the land of the east. (Gen. 25:5–6)*

According to the version before us, the author was apparently aware of the moral problem that lay behind Hagar and Ishmael's banishment from their home. In order to solve it in a reasonable manner, the author recounts that God took Sarah's part, and promised Abraham that no harm would come to Hagar and Ishmael. But what would have happened if God had not intervened in the argument between the elderly loving couple? Abraham would have banished Hagar and Ishmael anyway! For if he had not done so, he would have been placing Isaac in great danger. We must recall that although we have been focusing on Abraham and Sarah, Hagar also has a key role in this great drama. We may not have taken her considerations into account, but Sarah undoubtedly did so. Sarah knew that just as she wanted to ensure Isaac's firstborn position, so Hagar wanted to ensure the same for Ishmael – this was the very reason she had been given to Abraham in the first place. If Isaac had not been born, Ishmael would have preserved the status of firstborn, just as Sarah would have remained in her position of disgrace. But once the power relationships changed, Sarah had good reason to suspect Hagar and Ishmael. Only after the two were banished from her home did the astute woman's fears subside. She ensured the position of her only son, whom she loved, and then she could die in peace.

CONCLUSION

Sarah's story describes a girl who had to fight alone in a ring much larger than her small size, from the day she knew her own mind. Her story takes place in a world where a woman's only purpose in life was to bear children to her husband, and whoever did not do so paid a heavy price. After the slave woman conceived through the master of the household, she felt she could humiliate her mistress and act arrogantly toward her. This reveals the disgraced status of the barren senior wife. Sarah could abuse her slave, but this would not restore her honor or her status. Only after she gave birth to Isaac could she put the slave woman in her place and restore her own senior status in Abraham's home.

Sarah was a poor, lonely girl, with no assets but one: she was Abraham's senior wife and his blood relative. When she finally conceived, she had to struggle to ensure that her son would inherit her status and the firstborn position in his father's household.

Two derogatory nicknames have stuck to Sarah throughout history: Sarah the barren, and Sarah the jealous and heartless, who banished Hagar and Ishmael to certain death in the desert.

Was she really a jealous woman?

Perhaps.

But to me, Sarah is the symbol of a fighting woman: she had to battle in order to win – and she won. If I had been in her position, and if I had to fight for the life of my child like she fought for her son's life, I would have behaved exactly as she did.

I would have sent Hagar and Ishmael into the desert, and shut the doors of the wilderness firmly behind them!

Chapter Ten

JACOB, LEAH, AND RACHEL

(GENESIS 29 – 31)

W e are about to don our diving suits and grab our masks, oxygen tanks, and any other equipment we might need, and take a long dive into the story of Jacob and his two wives, Leah and Rachel. This veritable soap opera has all the essential elements: love, hate, violence, cheating, ups and downs, upheavals, jealousy, and broken hearts – and if I've forgotten something on this list, I'm sure it's there, too.

According to Genesis, Isaac married Rebecca, his cousin from Haran, and the couple had twin sons: Esau and Jacob. Esau burst out into the morning air first, and according to the custom of the time, he was supposed to inherit Isaac's position. Furthermore, the Bible says that Esau was Isaac's favorite son, while Jacob, who was born second, was Rebecca's favorite.

Years passed.

The twins grew up, and their parents aged. When Isaac sensed his last day approaching, he decided the time had come to bless his elder son, Esau. The blessing, so we gather from the text, was a humble ceremony in which Isaac intended to declare that Esau would inherit his property and his status as head of the household. The custom of the firstborn son succeeding his father placed Esau before Jacob, much to the distress of Rebecca, who had her own priorities. She thus made the decision to reverse the accepted order of inheritance, according to which the firstborn son of the senior wife became his father's successor.

Rebecca resolved to take advantage of elderly Isaac's weak and blind state to remove the blessing from Esau and transfer it to Jacob. She approached her favorite son and convinced him to join her scheme. Mother and son contrived a plot: Jacob would disguise himself as Esau and present himself to his father as if he were his twin brother. Isaac fell into the trap and blessed Jacob, and so the birthright passed to him. Shortly afterward, Esau stood before his father to receive the blessing that had just escaped his grasp. When he discovered his twin brother's deception, he swore to kill him (chapter 27). Jacob had no choice but to flee for his life and take shelter in the home of Laban, his mother's brother. Laban, as we recall, lived in Haran (in today's Turkey), to which his grandfather Nahor had emigrated two generations earlier.

The great drama that we will address in the next two chapters began on the day the refugee reached the home of his uncle Laban and met his two cousins, Leah and Rachel. Leah, the elder, had "tender eyes," while her younger sister was "beautiful of form and beautiful of appearance" (29:16–17). When Jacob's eyes met those of the lovely Rachel, he fell deeply in love with her, and so he asked her father's permission to marry her.

In biblical times, a wealthy man was entitled to receive a bride-price for his attractive, healthy daughter, and thus she married with the status of a senior wife. Because Rachel was pretty and healthy, naturally her father expected to receive a sizeable bride-price for her. From the text, we understand that this was clear to Jacob, and he never dreamed of obtaining her for free.

But where would he get the money to pay Laban the bride-price for his little beloved?

The fact that Jacob arrived in Haran as a refugee, his pockets tattered and empty, did not discourage him or detract from his resolve to obtain this expensive bride, no matter her price. He thus promised to work on Laban's farm without payment for seven full years, and to give up his salary as payment for Rachel's bride-price. Laban agreed to the deal, and Jacob, who up to then had lived a life of sweet idleness in his father's home, energetically put his shoulder to the yoke and began to count the days that separated him from his beloved. Seven years later, the bride-price was paid, and Jacob demanded that Laban fulfill his end of the bargain:

Jacob said to Laban, "Give me my wife, for my term is fulfilled, so I may go in to her." (Gen. 29:21)

Like his sister Rebecca, Laban had his own set of priorities. When he agreed to the marriage of his younger daughter before her elder sister, he ignored the custom of time and place. After Laban received a respectable bride-price for his beautiful younger daughter, he suddenly recalled that first he must marry off his elder daughter, who was apparently less attractive. Just as his good sister had switched her two sons on the day of Isaac's blessing, Laban switched his two daughters.

The long-awaited wedding night arrived, and Laban held a festive banquet, inviting the whole town to celebrate along with him and his son-in-law. Jacob's joy at the anticipated union with the princess of his dreams mingled with anxiety in anticipation of their first night alone together, so he drank some wine in order to calm his nerves. Then he took another sip, and perhaps another glass, and maybe even one last glass of wine for dessert. When his anxiety dissolved and the vise around his throat relaxed, Jacob was ready to go out and fulfill the groom's wedding night obligation. But at that moment, he was no longer able to distinguish between his beautiful Rachel and her tender-eyed sister who was waiting quietly in his bed. For while Jacob swallowed one glass, and then one or two more, Laban placed Leah in his wedding bed. When morning arrived, the contented groom awoke and turned to kiss his beloved bride, whose delightful body he had tasted for the first time just hours earlier – but to his shock, on his bed lay a woman he had never intended to marry!

This was not the bride he had awaited.

This was not the bride he had dreamed about each night as he lay in bed, exhausted from his day's labor. Not for her did he rise before daybreak, and not for her did he break his back in harsh labor for seven years!

Undoubtedly, his marriage to Leah, who at that point may have suffered the first blow from his hands, was a cruel and unexpected joke. Shocked and mortified, Jacob rushed to his father-in-law in order to protest the swindle.

Laban, who apparently had prepared for the meeting with his furious son-in-law, answered him calmly that it was not the accepted custom to marry off the younger daughter before her elder sister. If he still insisted on marrying Rachel, he would have to gird his loins a second time and begin to count seven more years of labor. Jacob had set his heart on marrying the girl he loved, and so he started all over again, thus doubling Rachel's bride-price. When those seven years of labor ended, she was finally given to him in marriage.

BETROTHAL AND MARRIAGE

For fourteen years Jacob worked tirelessly for his beloved bride. For fourteen years Rachel waited until Jacob had paid her price and took her as his wife. Rachel's long waiting period raises the question of her legal status throughout that period.

According to the tradition accepted in Judaism after the biblical period, a woman was given to her husband through one of three customs: payment of the bride-price, legal contract, or sexual intercourse. This tradition was apparently based on the marriage procedure as practiced during biblical times. The bride-price was silver or other valuable property that the groom's father gave for the specific bride he chose for his son. The father of the desired bride was not permitted to take the payment he received for one daughter and give the groom another daughter, as Laban did. So according to the accepted custom, the marriage agreement between the two related specifically to Rachel. Not surprisingly, Jacob felt cheated when he discovered that he had received Leah in exchange for Rachel's bride-price:

He said, "I will work for you seven years, for Rachel your younger daughter."
Laban said, "It is better that I give her to you than that I give her to another man; remain with me." (29:18–19)

The "contract" was a document or any other type of legal obligation (during biblical times this must have been oral) that the father of the bride gave to the father of the groom, in which he promised to give his daughter in marriage to the groom. The obligation could be given on the day the intended bride was born, and could be a way of repaying a debt that the girl's father owed to the groom's father. We do not know whether the contract was given for a specific girl or for any one of the girls in the family.

The third way in which a young woman was given to her husband was sexual intercourse. From the day the man had relations with the woman given to him and pierced her hymen, she became his wife. Concubines, female slaves, and war captives were married in this matter (Deut. 21:10–14). Sarah gave Hagar to Abraham in this type of marriage, and Rachel and Leah gave their slaves Bilhah and Zilpah to Jacob as wives through this practice.

Because Jacob paid Rachel's bride-price to Laban, she must have married him as a senior wife. The difficulty we face is that Jacob did not pay Rachel's bride-price one day and marry her the next, but only after fourteen years had passed. This leads us to ask, what was her legal status during those years?

During biblical times, and for hundreds of years afterward, from the day that the father betrothed his daughter, her status was equivalent to that of a married woman. If she was still very young, she continued to live in his home. Her "wedding" took place on the day she left her father's home, went to live with her husband, and had relations with him for the first time.

The great advantage of separating betrothal from the wedding lies in the delay. This waiting period allowed the father to betroth his daughter conditionally before she was born, on the day of her birth, after she was weaned, or at any later stage. Because the girl continued to live in her father's home until she went to live with her husband, the age of betrothal was insignificant. The delay was also beneficial for the groom's family, as it gave them time to accumulate the bride-price.

The definition of a betrothed girl as a wife not yet given to her husband describes Rachel's status exactly. During the fourteen years she waited for Jacob, Rachel was considered a man's wife, and was forbidden to any other man. By contrast, Jacob was not betrothed to Rachel, for in the ancient world betrothal, like adultery, was a one-way situation: the woman could be betrothed, but not the man. A woman did not have sole rights over her husband's sexuality, and so he was permitted to marry as many additional women as he pleased and as he was able to purchase. Indeed, before Jacob finished repaying his debt to Laban, he had already married Leah, and this was not considered betrayal or adultery toward Rachel.

The Bible offers dual evidence regarding what took place on the wedding night. Apparently, in most cases, the bride left her father's home and went to live with her husband. Quite simply, without celebration or ceremony, he had sexual relations with her and pierced her hymen, and in this way their married life began. Sometimes, as in Jacob's first wedding, celebrations were held (Judg. 14; Jer. 7:34; 16:9), but apparently this custom was not widespread. The understanding that marriage ceremonies were rare explains why after Jacob finished paying Rachel's bride-price, he simply requested to fulfill his right to have relations with her, and did not ask for a wedding feast:

> Jacob said to Laban, "Give me my wife, for my term is fulfilled, so I may go in to her." (Gen. 29:21)

The feast Laban held in honor of Jacob's first wedding was like the bachelor party of today, to which only men are invited. In our time, the groom's friends do their best to get him drunk – and this is what happened at Jacob's wedding feast. Because Rachel and Leah did not participate in the celebration, their father could easily have slipped away from the revelers and secretly switched between them. After the party ended, Jacob must have been so inebriated that he did not notice he had pierced the hymen of the wrong bride, and thus made her his wife. The second wedding night, this time to the desired bride, was less festive than the first, and amounted to nothing more than Rachel moving to his tent and Jacob having relations with her.

Another example illustrating a betrothed woman not yet given to her husband and the transition to marriage symbolized by the sexual act is the marriage of Isaac and Rebecca.

Chapter 24 of Genesis recounts that Abraham sent his servant Eliezer to the home of his brother, Nahor, in Haran to find a bride for his son Isaac. In order to purchase a suitable bride, Abraham equipped Eliezer with a respectable bride-price, and the faithful servant went on his way to fulfill his master's command. Because the brothers had parted ways many years earlier, Abraham did not know the daughters who had been born and raised in Nahor's home. This meant the servant had to choose the girl who was right for Isaac. In order to identify a bride of admirable character, the astute servant chose a sign that would serve as proof of the desired qualities of the girl: the one who gave him and his camels water to drink[17] would demonstrate through her good deed that she was the one who deserved the high bride-price. Rebecca passed the test with flying colors, and the servant asked that she, and only she, become Isaac's wife. From the moment the bride-price exchanged hands, Rebecca became betrothed to a man whom she and her family had never met. Her status changed and she was transformed from an unattached girl into a wife, and due to this, Rebecca was then able to leave her father's home and go to a foreign land. When she reached Abraham's camp, Isaac led her to Sarah's tent and had relations with her, and in this way, without ceremony or celebration, their married life began:

> And Rebecca raised her eyes and saw Isaac; she inclined while on the camel. And she said to the servant, "Who is that man walking in the field toward us?" And the servant said, "He is my master." She then took the veil and covered herself. The servant told Isaac all the things he had done.

---

[17] See chapter 3 for discussion of the camels.

And Isaac brought her into the tent of Sarah his mother; he took Rebecca, she became his wife, and he loved her; and thus Isaac was consoled after his mother. (Gen. 24:64–67)

DID JACOB REALLY WORK FOURTEEN YEARS FOR RACHEL?

For fourteen years, Jacob gave up his salary in order to pay Laban the price of his daughter Rachel. As the novels say, great love demands great sacrifice. In reality, of course, things are different. Only rarely does a man pursue a woman he loves as stubbornly and tirelessly as Jacob pursued Rachel. Perhaps this is why his love has managed to touch our jaded, cynical hearts. It has moved us so deeply that we have overlooked the fact that something about the two groups of seven years of labor does not tally, that they do not stand the test of history and the accepted custom of that period. Absurd arguments have penetrated the most well-known love story in the Bible, and it collapses like a house of cards when the supporting card at the base is pulled out. Because we do not want to pronounce that the well-known love story is impossible, we will attempt to return the base card to the collapsed house and rebuild it. For this purpose, we will need to overhaul the entire structure. We will also need to repeat the assumption we made when we spoke in praise of Sarah – that Rachel and Leah married at the age accepted in their time.

Previously we asserted that the usual marriage age for girls who lived in the ancient world was ten or eleven. Unlucky girls married younger than this, while lucky ones married as late as twelve. If we accept the hypothesis that the two sisters married according to prevalent custom, we must subtract ten years from the fourteen years of labor Jacob gave for Rachel. We must give up on romance, and agree that Jacob worked for four years at most, two years for each of his two wives. We must agree that even great love is not worth an exaggerated price in a world that needed children.

When Jacob reached Haran, he met young Rachel, who was a shepherdess. In traditional societies, such as those of the Bedouin shepherds who live in the Negev and the Sinai Desert today, girls of seven and eight years old tend the flocks. We may thus infer Rachel's age when Jacob first laid eyes on her. Because Rachel was herding her father's sheep, she could not have been a baby, and had not yet reached the age of marriage. Therefore we assume that she was around age eight. This supposition explains why Laban did not rush to marry her off, but was willing to wait several years until Jacob paid his debt. According to the text, Leah was older than Rachel, so we might assume that she was nine years old (the two could have been born to different mothers). If Jacob arrived in Haran when the girls were eight and nine, then the question of when and whom they would marry could not be put off for long – and here lies the first obstacle.

If Jacob had married Rachel after seven years of labor, he would have been marrying a young woman of fifteen, who was already well past the accepted age of marriage. But Laban did not give him Rachel, he gave him Leah, who was by then sixteen, a very late age for marriage.

Then, after Jacob married Leah, Rachel had to wait another seven years until her turn came. From this we conclude that she had reached the age of twenty-two, twice the usual marriage age of her contemporaries.

Considering that women in the ancient world lived an average of thirty years, under this scenario most of Rachel's life was wasted in useless waiting for a groom who was available, lived in her father's home, and was officially considered her husband. A miserable old virgin of twenty-two, she had long since lost her worth, and never again would she warrant a bride-price. At most, Rachel could have been given away for free to an old widower with many orphans at home.

The two sets of seven years of labor create a situation in which the two sisters passed the prevalent marriage age, lost their value, and were no longer worth a bride-price. Leah, who married at sixteen, was already considered an old bride. The situation of Rachel, at twenty-two, was defined in one word: catastrophe.[18]

The two labor periods lead to another contradiction that makes them completely impossible. As we know, Jacob did not marry two wives, but four, since Rachel gave him her slave Bilhah as a wife, and Leah gave him her slave Zilpah as a wife. The four wives bore thirteen children to Jacob: Leah had six sons and one daughter; Bilhah and Zilpah had two sons each; and finally, after long years of barrenness, Rachel had Joseph and Benjamin.

According to the order of events the Bible relates, Leah began her pregnancies and births only after Rachel was

---

[18] Later in history, Jewish commentators attempted to resolve the problem of the fourteen years of labor. In order to shorten Rachel's waiting period, they said that she married Jacob one week after Leah, and that Jacob completed payment of his debt to Laban in the seven years that followed. They base their argument on the verse, "*Complete the* shavua *[week] of this one* and we will give you the other one too, for the work which you will perform for me yet another seven years. So Jacob did so and *he completed the* shavua *[week] for her*; and he gave him Rachel his daughter to him as a wife" (Gen. 29:26–28).

In modern Hebrew, the term *shavua* means "week." Thus the commentators (and most translations) render this phrase as "complete the week," meaning that Jacob married Rachel one week after he married Leah. But this interpretation creates a host of problems. Firstly, the term "week" did not exist in biblical times, and does not appear in the Bible. In biblical terminology, the concept of "seven days" is rendered literally as "seven days," not "one week."

Secondly, the argument that Jacob married Rachel one week after her sister creates an absurd situation in which Rachel was married without payment, although according to the text, Jacob did in fact pay her bride-price. The solution that these commentators proposed creates a legal situation in which Leah was Jacob's only senior wife, while Rachel was his concubine.

We must also recall that today's installment method, in which an item is purchased in the present but paid for in the future, applies only to modern economics, and was not practiced in the ancient world (nor in the time of the commentators).

married. Thus her eldest son was born in the eighth year of her marriage, at the earliest. After him, she had three more sons one after another, then stopped giving birth. During the years when Leah brought child after child into the world, her sister's self-confidence collapsed, for she had not conceived even once. Miserable, Rachel did what Sarah had done before her, and gave Jacob her slave, Bilhah, as a wife. Bilhah had two sons. When Leah saw two adorable boys running around in her sister's tent, she hurried to give Jacob her slave Zilpah, who also had two adorable boys. After an extended vacation during which the slaves' sons were born, industrious Leah returned to the fertility race with renewed strength, and bore two boys and one girl to Jacob. Now Jacob had eleven children, seven of whom were born to Leah. Only after the children of the three wives were born did God "remember" despairing Rachel, who crept around the family camp, shoulders drawn and wearing a humiliated expression. Finally, she gave birth to Joseph, then Benjamin.

The Bible does not calculate the order of births in Jacob's household according to years – but we will do so. We want to know Leah's age when she gave birth for the first and last times, and Rachel's age when she had Joseph and Benjamin.

If Leah was sixteen when she got married, and her first pregnancy was after Rachel's marriage, she must have had her eldest son when she was twenty-four. After him, Jacob had ten more children, one after the other. For a minimalist calculation, we will agree that the difference in ages among the eleven children was not the accepted three years, but only two.[19] From this we conclude that Dina was born twenty years after Reuben, Leah's eldest. If Leah was twenty-four when she had Reuben, she must have been forty-four when she gave birth to Dina, her last child.

---

[19] In the ancient world, women nursed their children for three years. Here I am reducing the nursing time by one year. If I do not do so, the results would be even more absurd.

According to our calculation, Rachel married at twenty-two. Then she had to wait twenty-two years for Jacob's first eleven children to be born, until she herself conceived for the first time. Therefore, she must have been forty-four at the very least when she became pregnant with Joseph, and forty-six when she became pregnant with Benjamin.

Such a situation is completely impossible in the reality of those times. Even in our day, with high-tech fertility treatments and with Western women living an average of eighty-two years, few women have their first pregnancy around age forty-five – and Rachel lived more than thirty-five hundred years ago. She lived in a world that did not have the advantages of modern medicine; in Rachel's world women gave birth in tents, fields, or at the sides of dusty roads. It is illogical to assume that women who lived an average of thirty years became pregnant at age forty-four or even later.

In addition, a small but charming mathematical mistake emphasizes to what extent the data the Bible gives is impossible. According to the story, after twenty years of staying in Laban's home, Jacob had had enough of his father-in-law and wanted to return to the land of Canaan. So he collected his wives and children and fled from Haran in secret. When Laban found out, he pursued and overtook them. A harsh dispute broke out between the two men, who had never shared any affection. During the argument, Jacob accused his father-in-law:

> This is my twenty years in your household: I served you fourteen years for your two daughters, and six years for your flocks. (Gen. 31:41)

Jacob lived in Haran for twenty years, of which he worked fourteen for two of his wives. The text states that his eldest son was born after he had finished paying Laban the double bride-price, and after he had married Rachel (29:27–32).

Thus Reuben was born in the fifteenth year of his father's stay in Haran (at the earliest). According to this citation, in the five years after Reuben was born, Jacob fathered eleven more children, one after another.[20] Of these, Leah gave birth to seven, born two years apart from each other....

THE NUMBER SEVEN IN THE BIBLE

Readers of the Bible have been so enraptured by the romance of the story of Jacob and Rachel that they have ignored the fact that Jacob did not hand over silver bars to Laban in payment for the bride-price. Instead, he paid with work that extended over many years, during which Rachel and Leah passed the accepted age of marriage and became the objects of ridicule. At that point, it was doubtful if any man would agree to take them, even for free.

The conclusion is clear: if we want to preserve the story of the two sisters within a logical framework and within the reality of their time, we must reorganize it. First of all, we must subtract ten years from the fourteen that Jacob supposedly worked. In order to justify such an outrageous step, I must explain the role of the number seven in the Bible.

The significance of the number seven in the Bible is symbolic, not necessarily quantitative. According to the story in Genesis, God created the world in six days, and sanctified the seventh to Himself as a day of rest (Gen. 2:2–3). This is how the number seven acquired its symbolic, sacred meaning. Because the number seven appears in the Bible hundreds of times with its symbolic meaning, we may assume that it preserves this symbolic meaning for the two periods of Jacob's labor. In other words, the biblical text supports the argument that the two periods of seven years of labor are symbolic, not quantitative.

---

[20] Benjamin was born in the land of Canaan.

The proposal that Jacob worked only two years for each of his wives enables us to determine that Leah and Rachel married at the accepted age of their time – and this was the underlying assumption that we made at the beginning.

If Jacob arrived in Haran when Leah was nine and Rachel eight, then according to our proposal, Leah married at age eleven, while Rachel married at age twelve. Such a suggestion rudely expunges the romance out of the story, but it works in favor of all the characters in the story, most of all Rachel. It preserves the worth of the sisters, and prevents them from becoming a pair of silly old virgins, waiting out their lives in useless expectation for the groom who lived in their home.

However, even if Rachel was married at the age of twelve, as we propose, she still had to wait twenty-two years until Jacob's eleven sons were born and her turn came to conceive. In order to extricate her from such a long stay in that tormented waiting room where barren women pace from one end of the corridor to the other, and in order to place her first pregnancy at an age conceivable for her time, we must reduce these twenty-two years as much as possible.

According to the order specified in the Bible, Jacob's sons were born consecutively, one after the other. Leah had four sons, then stopped giving birth. While she rested from her pregnancies, the two slave women had four sons. After them, Leah bore her last three children.

The contraction of time we are performing here means that Leah, the most fertile woman in the Bible, had her seven children with a difference of two years between each one, and only then stopped giving birth. Our time contraction also means that the four sons of the slave women were born during the same years as Leah's seven children. In order to justify this reasoning, we rely on the fact that during this period, Jacob and his wives were living in the home of Laban, owner of a successful sheep and goat farm. Thus the pregnant women enjoyed relatively comfortable circumstances and a rich, varied diet.

If, as we propose, Leah was married at eleven and gave birth to her first son when she was fourteen, then she gave birth for the last time at twenty-six (during that period, the sons of the slave women were born concurrently). According to our new calculation, Rachel, who was one year younger than Leah, first conceived when she was twenty-five or twenty-six. At twenty-eight or twenty-nine, she conceived again.

Let us summarize the process we have just been through. The story of Jacob who labored fourteen years for Rachel has been engraved in our memories as symbolic of a love that conquers all. But the author of this story seems to have pulled the wool over our eyes. He did not dally over the fact that two seven-year sets of labor worked to the disadvantage of each one of the characters in the story – especially Rachel. The order of events set by the author requires us to agree that Leah bore her three last children after age forty, and that Rachel bore her two sons around age fifty. Such a situation is unacceptable, and stands in contrast to the reality of the time in which the story's characters lived. Indeed, our proposal does abolish the romance in the story and minimizes Jacob's great sacrifice, but it renders an absurd story possible. It stands the test of logic and of the time period in which the characters of the story lived.

Yet even after we have reduced, as far as possible, Rachel's years of waiting to have her own child, her situation was tragic. Even if Rachel gave birth to her first son at age twenty-six, she still suffered long years of misery, shrinking into herself until one sad shoulder touched the other sad one. Throughout these years, she looked on in humiliation as her fertile sister and the slave women lifted their bellies proudly and established their positions in the home of the man who poured all his strength into marrying her. The bustling familial picture of Jacob's household darkened her days and poisoned her nights – for Rachel, there was no sunrise, and no sun would ever shine on her.

To repeat Jacob's declaration to Laban one last time:

> *This is my twenty years in your household: I served you fourteen years for your two daughters, and six years for your flocks. (Gen. 31:41)*

Our proposition assumes that Jacob worked the first four years in order to pay Rachel's double bride-price. In the next sixteen years Leah bore her seven children in rapid succession (while the sons of the female slaves were born concurrently), and Rachel had Joseph (Benjamin was born in Canaan). Assuming this chronology allows us to fit the story, if barely, into the twenty years that Jacob lived in Haran.

Before ending our discussion of this topic, we must address one remaining question: Why did the author decide that Jacob worked for two sets of seven years?

Almost certainly, the author assumed that his readers were well-acquainted with the symbolic meaning of the number seven, and thus did not bother to explain that it applied here as well. Another possibility is that the frequent use of the number seven in the Bible shows that this was an accepted writing style, no more. Over the years that passed since the Bible was recorded in writing, the meaning of the language changed, and later generations ignored the symbolic significance of the number seven and related to it as quantitative.

JACOB'S POSITION IN LABAN'S HOME

Jacob's sojourn in Laban's home returns us to our previous discussion regarding the role of the family in the ancient world. Before the age of national institutions that superseded the family, the extended family was a person's only source of strength, the only organization that supplied all his needs. A person was born, grew up, married, and spent his entire life within his family group. He contributed to the group's strength, and the group contributed to his. In contrast, a person who was expelled from his family was thrust into the null and void. From the moment he detached himself from his father's home and his extended family, he was left with no roof over his head and no basis for existence.

Such a person became a pauper without means, since his family land, the most important source of wealth in the ancient world, remained under the ownership of the family he left behind. In order to obtain a new framework that would provide him with protection and sustenance, he had to hire himself out for contract labor on an agricultural farm, where he performed the most demanding work. Such a person was technically free, but in actuality, he lived the life of a slave – and this was how Jacob lived in Haran.

After Jacob fled from his father's home, he was no longer part of a family framework that protected him and gave him a place to live and an economic foundation. To survive, he had no choice but to do what he indeed did: hire himself out as a laborer on one of the agricultural farms that always needed working hands. The home that gave Jacob shelter did indeed offer him an organized framework, but this did not render him equal in status to his uncle Laban. In this case, the family relationship gave Jacob no advantage. The geographical distance between the two families, one in the land of Canaan and the other in Haran, prevented them from acting as an extended family, which usually maintained relations of unity and mutual responsibility. From Laban's viewpoint, his charming nephew was no more than just another poor man who knocked on his gates with empty hands and asked for work and a place to live. Laban gave Jacob shelter only because he virtually enslaved himself. Indeed, every detail the text gives reveals that Laban related to Jacob with utter scorn, just as a master related to his slaves.

The manner in which Laban appropriated Jacob's salary and exchanged the brides is evidence of Jacob's weakness and the deep contempt Laban harbored toward him. We must recall that not only did Laban switch his daughters, but he also gained a bride-price for Leah, instead of giving her away for free. When Jacob protested the swindle, Laban replied calmly that if he wanted to marry Rachel, he would have to start at the beginning and count seven years of labor once again (according to our method, two years). Almost certainly, if relations of mutual responsibility had prevailed between Laban and Jacob's families, as accepted in extended families, it never would have entered his mind to take one daughter's bride-price in exchange for the other. But in this case, Laban never dreamed that Jacob even deserved an apology.

And Jacob?

Destitute Jacob, who had insisted on purchasing a beautiful, expensive wife, behaved like any other poor man. Like every day laborer, he bowed his head in submission and silently accepted his master's ruling – what else could he do?

We must note another fascinating detail that demonstrates Jacob's subordinate position. Laban belittled Jacob and exploited him as much as he could. Still, he preferred to marry his two daughters to Jacob rather than to another man: "Laban said, 'Better I give her to you than to another man; remain with me'" (29:19).

Laban was a clever man of sharp business acumen. If he married his daughters to any other man, in the usual "give and take" arrangement, they and their slave women would leave his home and go to live in the homes of their grooms. Following the custom of that time and place, the many children born to them would strengthen the patriarchal household of the man they married. The marriage transaction that Laban made with Jacob was "take and take": he received a double bride-price, his two daughters remained in his home, and their multiple children strengthened the extended family he headed. The assumption that Laban profited twice – both from the bride-price and from Jacob's sons – explains his daughters' grievance against him:

> Then Rachel and Leah replied and said to him [Jacob], "Have we then still a share and an inheritance in our father's house? Are we not considered by him as strangers? For he has sold us and even totally consumed our money!" (Gen. 31:14–15)

When Jacob decided to leave Haran and return to Canaan, he suspected that Laban would try to foil his plans. He called Leah and Rachel to the field, and revealed to them in secret that he planned to flee. When Laban discovered their escape, he gathered his kinsmen and pursued the fugitives. After overtaking them, he searched their belongings as if they were petty thieves. An argument broke out between the two men:

> Then Jacob became angered and he took up his grievance with Laban. Jacob spoke up and said to Laban, "What is my transgression? What is my sin that you have hotly pursued me? When you rummaged through all my things, what did you find of all your household objects? Set it here before my kinsmen and your kinsmen, and let them decide between the two of us. These twenty years I have been with you, your ewes and she-goats never miscarried, nor did I eat rams of your flock. That which was mangled I never brought you – I myself would bear the loss, from me you would exact it, whether it was stolen by day or stolen by night. Often, by day scorching heat consumed me, and frost by night; my sleep drifted from my eyes. This is my twenty years in your household: I served you fourteen years for your two daughters, and six years for your flocks; and you changed my wages ten times over. (Gen. 31:36–42)

Possibly, the assertion that Jacob's status in Laban's home was like that of a weak beggar whose master cheated him will offend some readers, since in our collective memory Jacob is depicted as a strong, romantic man. But the biblical author speaks for himself – and these are not his last words about Jacob, nor are they the worst.

Chapter Eleven

RACHEL AND LEAH

Jacob married two sisters who envied and fought each other for their position in his home. Each lacked something that her sister had, and that something embittered her life. Leah was given to Jacob in exchange for Rachel's bride-price, and Jacob could not forgive her this. He could not forgive Leah the fact that his payment for the exhausting years of labor he performed for Rachel was stolen from him, and exchanged for a woman of "tender eyes." He could not forgive Leah the fact that because of her, his marriage to his beloved was delayed, and he was forced to double his years of work for Laban. He could not forgive Laban for humiliating and exploiting him. And because Jacob could not stand up to his father-in-law, he took out all his anger and bitterness on Leah.

Legendary material that developed in Jewish tradition hundreds of years after the biblical period describes Jacob as a peaceful and studious man of pleasant character. Yet although the authors of legends viewed miserable Jacob with mercy, the book of Genesis depicts him as a harsh man who took out his anger on the woman who bore him seven healthy children.

In reality, if Jacob enjoyed one hour of happiness in his life, it was thanks to Leah – and yet we have preferred to forget his severe treatment of her. Now our feeble memory will have to confront the testimony of the biblical author, who says that because ungrateful Jacob loved Rachel, he avenged his bitterness on the good woman given to him by God in His kindness. Indeed, when God witnessed Jacob's mistreatment of the woman He destined for him, He closed Rachel's womb and opened Leah's:

> *The Lord saw that Leah was hated, so He opened her womb; but Rachel remained barren. (Gen. 29:31)*

Undoubtedly, the spurned Leah longed for some of the love her husband lavished on her sister. She had good reason to envy the beautiful, beloved Rachel – and the opposite is even more true. Hated as she was, Leah bore many children, so her position in Jacob's home was firm. Rachel, by contrast, disappointed him. Jacob performed hard labor in order to purchase a woman whose price was beyond his means, only to discover that she could not bear him children.

What had he worked for?

Beautiful Rachel, whom Jacob longed for so intensely, walked a thin line. One day, the ground dropped out from under her feet, and she fell into the abyss of desperation:

> *Rachel saw that she had not borne children to Jacob, so Rachel became envious of her sister; she said to Jacob,* **"Give me children – otherwise I am dead."** *Jacob's anger flared up at Rachel, and he said, "Am I instead of God, Who has withheld from you the fruit of the womb?" (Gen. 30:1–2)*

A woman whose husband hates her is a miserable woman. But if there is a scale that defines a miserable woman, the barren one stands at the top. This was the way of the world four thousand years ago, and the same applies today. But in Rachel's world, a full measure of shame and disgrace was added to the tortuous longing of the barren woman for her own child. And so, while Leah filled Jacob's home with many sons, Rachel became a stone around his neck, and like her sister, she found no comfort or refuge.

RACHEL'S ENVY

Rachel's beauty and Leah's apparent ugliness, the former's barrenness and the latter's fertility, Jacob's love for Rachel and hatred for Leah – all these fed the fire of mutual envy that burned between the two sisters (we already noted that this story has all the ingredients of a soap opera). But the text offers the impression that Rachel's jealousy intensified, developing into hatred for her sister.

Why?

Leah and Rachel lived in a world in which multiple women divided one husband among them. On nights when Jacob slept in the tent of one sister, the other was not considered betrayed or cheated. Nevertheless, Rachel had good reason to hate her sister – and in order to explain this, we must return again to the key that determines a woman's position in her husband's home.

In chapter 6, we noted that all references to bride-price refer to payment given only for women who married at the status of "senior wife." In contrast, concubines were given to their husbands for free, and thus their status was inferior to that of senior wives. Because the status of the son was determined by that of his mother, a concubine's son was inferior in status to his brothers, sons of the senior wives. Almost certainly, most concubines were given free of charge because their fathers were poor men whose economic status was lower than that of the grooms.

However, I believe that women were also given as concubines due to physical disability. In a world starving for children, it was not logical to "waste" the womb of a fertile woman who could bear healthy children, just because she was blind, crippled, or born with a harelip that ruined her face. We may conclude that in biblical times, a lame but fertile concubine was worth more than a senior wife who was beautiful but barren. We have already noted that even an ignorant but fertile daughter of slaves like Hagar thought herself more worthy than her barren mistress, and apparently she was justified in this self-evaluation.

The significant difference between the senior wife and the concubine was in the inheritance status of their sons. According to the order of inheritance, sons of senior wives had superior status to sons of concubines and slave women, even if they were born later. For this reason, Isaac was considered Abraham's firstborn son, even though he was born many years after Ishmael, the son of a slave woman.

Birth order played an especially important role when a man had several senior wives. The senior wife who bore his firstborn son – the future heir who would become head of the family – was superior to the other senior wives. Still, the status of the heir's mother was vulnerable. If her son died, the primogeniture passed to the son born after him, even if his mother was a different senior wife. If the second son also died, firstborn status went to the third son, and so forth.

The principle of primogeniture explains Rachel's hatred for her sister. Since Leah was married in exchange for Rachel's bride-price, she had the status of senior wife, and thus all six of her sons were higher in rank than Joseph and Benjamin.

Apparently, Rachel did not hate her sister only because she was more fertile, but because Leah married as a senior wife at Rachel's expense. From Rachel's point of view, Leah should have married as a concubine, not as a senior wife.

If Leah had married Jacob as his concubine, the status of Rachel's sons, although they were born last, would have been higher than that of Leah's sons, born first. In order to demonstrate how these issues fit the text, we must take a detour off the main road, find a shady spot under an old tree, and shed light on another aspect of the hidden charms of the biblical writing style, which never fails to surprise and amaze.

The biblical authors never wrote long descriptions of a character's physical appearance. Only on occasion, when a character's looks contributed to understanding the story, did they add a single identifying detail. They often used a literary technique of contrast in order to emphasize a detail that distinguished one character as opposed to another character or characters. For example, the text reports that Saul was tall, because his height differentiated him from his brothers (I Sam. 9:2). David is described as "ruddy" and of "fair eyes" (I Sam. 16:12), because his charming young face stood in intended contrast to that of the giant Goliath (I Sam. 17). The author emphasized David's faith in God and bravery by describing him as a youth, almost a child, half-naked, who used just one slingshot stone to defeat a colossal fighter, armed head to toe. The text describes Esau as hairy, while Jacob was smooth. The former's hairiness and the latter's smoothness played a vital role when Jacob stood before his blind father and declared that he was his brother (Gen. 27). Further, the woman who raised Samuel's soul from the dead described him as an old man enveloped in a cloak, thus enabling the terrified Saul to recognize Samuel through the cloak that the irate old man used to wear (I Sam. 28:13–14).

When a character's appearance did not contribute to understanding the story, the author ignored this aspect, and so we know nothing about the looks of Abraham, Isaac, Moshe, Joshua, or many other characters.

The biblical authors described the female characters with even greater brevity. Three women earn the description "beautiful." Rachel and Esther are called "beautiful of form and beautiful of appearance," while Abigail is said to have been "intelligent and beautiful." As we can see, these are general descriptions, not individual characteristics that might distinguish one woman from another. We do not know if these heroines were tall or short; we know nothing of the color of their eyes or of their hair. Even Esther, who was chosen as Ahaseurus's wife by virtue of her beauty, is not described with any detail that might distinguish her from the myriads of other women brought before him. All that is said of her is that she was "beautiful of form and beautiful of appearance" (Esther 2:7). Tamar (Gen. 38), Hannah, Peninah, Deborah, and Ruth did not merit even these few words.

Against the background of the uniformly succinct depiction of women's appearances, two examples stand out, and both are negative portrayals. Zipporah, Moses' wife, of whom Miriam and Aaron speak derogatively, is described as a Cushite (Num. 12:1). The land of Cush was in southern Egypt, on the border of what is today northern Sudan. The second woman for whom this refined and polished author gave an identifying sign was Leah. In order to direct our attention to the defect in her eyes, the biblical author used a technique of contrast, like that used to differentiate Jacob from Esau, and David from Goliath:

*Laban had two daughters. The name of the older one was Leah and the name of the younger one was Rachel. **Leah's eyes were tender, while Rachel was beautiful of form and beautiful of appearance.** (Gen. 29:16–17)*

The author uses two phrases to describe Rachel's beauty, specifying that she was attractive both in body and in appearance. From the proximity of this description to Leah's "tender eyes," we learn that only one of Laban's two daughters was attractive. Through this contrast technique, the author hints that something about Leah's appearance was defective. We will never know whether Leah was blind, or perhaps suffered from a severe eye disease. Either way, the defect in her eyes was so prominent that it became a sign that distinguished her from her sister and from all the other women in the Bible.

The hypothesis that Leah had a physical defect explains why Laban agreed to marry his younger daughter before the eldest, in opposition to accepted custom. This supposition may also explain why Laban stole Rachel's bride-price for Leah, and placed her in Rachel's bridal bed after getting Jacob drunk. The assumption that it was appropriate to marry Leah at the status of concubine also explains Jacob and Rachel's hatred for her. Because Jacob knew that any other man might have received Leah for free as a concubine, he felt foolish for paying full price for a defective wife. If Rachel had been the only senior wife in Jacob's home, her lengthy years of barrenness would not have affected the status of Joseph and Benjamin, who were born last. Apparently, then, Rachel hated Leah because the bride-price paid for her was exchanged for her sister, which lowered her two sons' status. According to the order of inheritance, Joseph and Benjamin came in seventh and eighth place, not first and second (the sons of the slave women did not count). So, if Rachel felt that her sister stole from her, she had good reason.

THE MARRIED LIVES OF LEAH AND RACHEL THROUGH THE NAMES OF THEIR SONS

The author of this section was a master artist. He was able to create new layers of meaning from combinations of words, comparable to what rare and unique artists like Rembrandt and Mozart achieved with a single brushstroke or note. Like the other authors of the family stories in the Bible, this writer carefully guarded the modesty and dignity of the characters whose story he recounts. He did not lift the layers of cloth that concealed the entrances to Leah and Rachel's tents, nor did he expose the intimacies of their physical organs to the reader. Like the other biblical authors, he left voyeurism and pornographic writing, which invaded the hidden regions of the human body, to writers born thousands of years after his time. The author mentioned not one word about Leah's personal experiences in the home of a man who did not want to marry her, nor of Rachel's life with the man who so longed to marry her that no obstacle in his path diminished his determination. Yet in a restrained and brilliant manner, the author left a small, hidden crack through which we can peek from a distance of thousands of years at the married life of the two sisters, to some extent satisfying our voyeuristic desire. In order to do this, we must delve once again into the mysteries of biblical writing, which never readily exposes itself to the reader.

The succinct biblical writing style obligated the authors to develop advanced methods for expanding the narrow framework of the story. This expansion is based on wordplays and double entendres that are possible in the original language, but which are lost in the literal and meticulous translation that the Bible has undergone.

One method the biblical writers used in order to "expand" the story was to give meaning to the characters' names. For example, God made the first man from dust, or earth, and called him Adam (meaning "earth"), recalling the substance from which he was created:

And the Lord God formed the man of dust from the earth (**adam**ah)*, and He blew into his nostrils the soul of life; and man* (adam) *became a living being. (Gen. 2:7)*

In our last moments of life, these ancient words come back to us, reminding us from what we were created, and to what we will return after completing our days on earth:

> By the sweat of your brow shall you eat bread until you return to the earth, from which you were taken: **for you are dust, and to dust** (adamah) **shall you return**. *(Gen. 3:19)*

Within Ishmael's name, the son Hagar bore for Abraham and Sarah, the author encoded the couple's protracted longing for a child: Ishma-el means "God will listen" or "grant." Isaac, in Hebrew Yizhak, is based on the root meaning "laughter" (*z.h.k.*). Yizhak (Isaac) is given that name because Abraham and Sarah laughed in disbelief when they were informed that Sarah would conceive (Gen. 17:17; 18:11–13).[21] The brothers Mahlon and Chilion, sons of Naomi and Elimelech, died prematurely (Ruth 1:5). In English their names are meaningless, but in Hebrew Mahlon meaning "illness," while Chilion means "annihilation" (Ruth 1:2). Undoubtedly, these were literary names that dropped a hint to the reader about the brothers' premature demise, for no parents in their right minds would give their children names that represented curses and predicted their early deaths by plague. In the same way, no parent would ever call his son "Naval" (meaning "villain"), revealing that the boy is evil from birth, and yet the biblical author applies this name to one of the characters:

> There was a man in Maon whose business was in Carmel. The man was very wealthy…. The man's name was Naval [villain] and his wife's name was Abigail; the woman was

---

[21] After the birth of her son, a thrilled Sarah repeats his name using the connotation of laughter: "Sarah said, 'God has made me *laugh* (*z.h.k.*) – He has given me both cause to rejoice, and a heart to rejoice.'" She added, "Who would have said to Abraham that Sarah would nurse children? Yet I have borne him a son in his old age."

*intelligent and beautiful, but **the man was difficult and an evildoer**. (I Sam. 25:2–3)*

Abigail, Naval's loving wife, condemned him in her explanation:

Let my lord not set his heart against this base man, this Naval, for he is as his name implies – Naval [villain] is his name and villainy is his trait. (I Sam. 25:25)

Translators of the Bible transcribed the names of the characters phonetically, but with this method, they could not include the meanings of the names. As a result, the reader who relies on a translation of the Bible into his native tongue remains unaware that the characters' names play an important role in the story and expand its framework.

Although the names of the characters we have listed above both amplify the stories and contribute to our understanding of them, they are not particularly complex. But when we examine the names of Jacob's family members, we discover a brilliant, shrewd phenomenon that is unique to this author. He used the names to record a hidden story underneath the exterior one. The names of Rebecca, Jacob, Laban, Rachel, and Leah double and even triple the breadth of the story. The names of the twelve sons of Jacob are twelve fascinating way stations in the married lives of Leah and Rachel. The reader who fails to comprehend this loses the marvelous wordplay within the names. He overlooks the hidden crack that sheds a thin ray of light on Leah and Rachel's experiences while living in Jacob's household. Such a reader reads the exterior story, but misses the story within the story.

We will begin by interpreting the simpler names and advance to the more complex. In Hebrew, the name "Rebecca" comes from the Hebrew root *marbek*, meaning fattened calf, or in our case, a woman with an ample, healthy body.

In the ancient world, full-bodied women were considered beautiful, as their bodies showed they were well fed and not suffering from starvation. The name Rebecca reveals that she was a plump and beautiful woman. The name Leah is derived from Akkadian, the language spoken in her native Haran, and it means "cow."[22] The name Rachel means "ewe." The names Rebecca, Leah, and Rachel reveal that these women were born onto successful farms, and thus they were named for milk-producing animals.

The name Jacob (Ya'akov) comes from the Hebrew root *'a.k.v.* This root has three meanings, and each one plays a role in the story. The first meaning is the back part of the foot, or "heel" (*'akev*). Jacob was given this name since he was born grasping onto the heel of his brother:

> *After that his brother emerged with his hand grasping onto the heel ['akev] of Esau; so he called his name Jacob [Ya'akov]. (Gen. 25:26)*

The second meaning is "to follow" (*la'akov*) or to walk in someone's footsteps – Jacob followed his brother out of their mother's womb. The first two meanings are explained in the story and repeat the descriptive type of name we explained above. These meanings are understandable to anyone who can read basic Hebrew. The third meaning is understood only by those with a strong command of the ancient language of the Bible, which is as different from modern Hebrew as Shakespeare's English is from modern English.

The biblical author, unlike the tradition many of us grew up with, harbored no affection for Jacob and lost no opportunity to disparage him, and the third meaning of his name reveals the writer's opinion of him. In Hebrew, as in English,

---

[22] Akkadian was the language of the region encompassing modern-day Iraq and Syria, from the fourth millennium BCE to the early 1st century AD – and then disappeared and was never used again. Many Hebrew words originate from Akkadian, including Leah's name.

one who speaks the truth is called "straight." A straight person is one who follows a straight path, who can be trusted and believed. In Hebrew, the opposite of straight is 'akov, "crooked" (like the shape of the heel). Again as in English, a dishonest person is called a "crook," or 'akov; a cheater or thief pursues a crooked, twisted path. For example, when Isaiah describes his vision of God's salvation of Israel, he describes a journey in which God levels the obstacles standing in the path of the travelers. The crooked path (passing through hills and valleys) becomes straight and smooth:

> A voice calls out in the wilderness, "Clear the way of the Lord; make a straight path in the desert, a road for our God." Every valley will be raised, and every mountain and hill will be lowered; **the crooked ['akov] will become straight** and heights will become valley." (Is. 40:3–4)

The prophet Jeremiah uses a range of images, including the word 'akov, to describe lies and betrayal:

> Let each man beware of his fellow; do not trust any kin! **For every kinsman acts crookedly ['akov ya'akov]** and every acquaintance mongers slander. Each man mocks his fellow and they do not speak truth; they train their tongue to speak falsehood, striving to be iniquitous. Your dwelling is amid deceit; because of their deceit they refuse to know Me – the word of the Lord. (Jer. 9:3–5; see also 17:9)

When the author of the psalm below asks for God's help to save him from his enemies, he relies on the third meaning of this root in describing betrayal:

> Together, all my enemies whisper against me, against me they devise my harm [saying], "The result of his lawlessness is poured over him...." Even my ally in whom

I trusted, who ate my bread, has **betrayed ['akev]** *me. (Ps. 41:8–10)*[23]

Following the third meaning of this root, a person whose name is Ya'akov must be "crooked" or deceitful. This inspires us to ask whether the choice of this name means the author is implying something about Jacob's character. The text itself gives us the answer.

After Isaac and Esau (the meaning of which is unknown) discover Jacob's deception in stealing the birthright, the author places these words in Esau's mouth:

> *When Esau heard his father's words, he cried out an exceedingly great and bitter cry.... But he [Isaac] said, "Your brother came with cunning and took your blessing." He said, "**Is it because his name was called Ya'akov that he deceived me these two times?** He took away my birthright and see, now he took away my blessing." (Gen. 27:34–36)*

When Jacob and his family flee Haran, Laban pursues and overtakes them. In describing Jacob's flight, the text employs another expression, "to deceive," which is a synonym for *'a.k.v.*:

> *Jacob deceived Laban the Aramean by not telling him that he was fleeing.... Laban said to Jacob, "What have you done that you have deceived me and led my daughters away like captives of the sword? Why have you fled so stealthily, and cheated me? For I would have sent you off with joy and song, with timbrel and lyre! (Gen. 31:20–27)*

---

[23] Most English translations of Psalms render verse 10 as "Even my ally in whom I trusted, who ate my bread, *has raised his heel against me.*" In so doing, they rely on the first meaning of the root *'a.k.v.* But when we examine the context, we find that the text actually follows the third meaning, betrayal, and this is how we have rendered the translation here. The Psalmist laments the betrayal of his close ally.

The most problematic name in this section is Laban, since the word *laban* means "white," the symbol of purity and honesty. The prophet Isaiah uses this word in exhorting sinners to repent their evil ways, assuring that God will forgive and purify their sins:

> *If your sins are like scarlet, they will become white [laban] as snow. (Is. 1:18)*

In Psalms, we read:

> *Behold the truth that You desire is in the concealed parts, and in the covered part is the wisdom that You teach me. Purge me of sin with hyssop and I will be pure; cleanse me and I will be whiter [laban] than snow. (Ps. 51:8–9)*

The name Laban symbolizes purity and honesty, while the name Jacob means the opposite. Can it be that Laban, who stole Jacob's wages and fraudulently gave him Leah in marriage, boasts a name that symbolizes honesty?

Of course!

When we reach chapter 15, which discusses the concept of the dynasty in the Bible, we will discover that Laban acted in accordance with the divine plan, thus justifying the positive connotation of his name. In the meantime, we will only remark that to the author, Laban is like the stick that beats Jacob in punishment, teaching him the principle of "measure for measure." Just as Jacob stole Esau's birthright, so Laban steals Jacob's wages. Equipped with an understanding of the contrast technique we have explained, the reader will readily see that the names Jacob and Laban are direct opposites. It is not surprising, then, that the two harbored no affection for each other.

The author reached the height of sophistication with the names of Jacob's twelve sons, which represent twelve chapters in the married lives of Leah and Rachel. According to the story, the two women, not Jacob, named their sons and gave the reasons for choosing those specific names. Leah named the sons born to her and her slave woman Zilpah (since the sons of the slave woman belonged to the mistress), and explained their names. Rachel named her sons and Bilhah's, and she also explained the reasons why she chose those names.

We will begin by examining the names of the eight sons who belonged to Leah's camp, and through them, we will listen to the voice of a woman describing the progress of her life, from the time her father deceptively placed her in her sister's bridal bed.

According to the story, Jacob hated Leah and loved Rachel. In recompense, God, who controlled fertility in the universe, interfered by "opening" Leah's womb and "closing" Rachel's:

> *[Jacob] came also to Rachel and loved Rachel even more than Leah.... The Lord saw that Leah was hated, so He opened her womb; but Rachel remained barren. (29:30–31)*

Despite Jacob's hatred, he did not avoid Leah, and she conceived and bore his firstborn son. The birth of a healthy son is a happy event in any family, but in a world in which the mortality rate of newborns and mothers was very high, every pregnancy that began and ended safely was considered a merciful act of God. For this reason, many biblical characters used the sons' names to express their thanks to God for granting them a healthy son. Ishmael means "God heard"; Joshua, Isaiah, and Hosea mean "God's salvation." The name Jesus in Hebrew is *Yeshua*, meaning "redeemer." Samuel means "his name is God"; and the Bible contains many other examples.

At the beginning, God opened the spurned Leah's womb, placing her before Rachel. Thus we might have expected Leah to thank God for His benevolence in giving her a firstborn son. But Leah did not thank God. She explained Reuben's

name in a voice shattered with pain, making God a witness
to her suffering:

> Leah conceived and bore a son, and she called his name
> Reuben, as she had declared, "Because the Lord has
> discerned my **humiliation [’onyi]**, for now my husband
> will love me." (29:32)

The term *’onyi* is derived from the root *’a.n.h.*, which has
several usages in the Bible (like the root *’a.k.v.*). *’A.n.h.* means
to answer, but Leah used a different meaning of this word:
"physical abuse," "cause of suffering," and "humiliation and
disgrace." The meanings of Reuben's name testify to what
the hated Leah endured at the hands of her good husband
in the first years of their marriage: "Because the LORD has
discerned my humiliation." However, in biblical language
the root *’a.n.h.* has an additional meaning, which has disappeared in modern Hebrew – "rape."

In biblical Hebrew, the word "rape" is always designated by the root *’a.n.h.* For example, Shechem, son of Hamor,
raped Dinah, Jacob's daughter (Gen. 34:2). Amnon, David's
eldest son, raped Tamar, his half-sister (II Sam. 13:12–14).
In both cases, the text uses the term *’a.n.h.* Using the same
term, the book of Deuteronomy rules that a man who has
raped a non-betrothed woman must marry her (Deut. 22:23–
24, 29). Another law uses this word in requiring a man who
has raped a female prisoner of war to marry her, or else allow
her to go free (Deut. 21:10–14; also Judg. 19:24; 20:5).

Since the Bible consistently uses the root *’a.n.h.* to mean
rape, may we deduce this meaning here and ask, did Leah use
the Bible's language to say that Jacob raped her?

Possibly.

Under ancient law, rape did not exist between husband
and wife. Once he had paid her bride-price, she became his
property. A man was permitted to have relations with his

wife at any time, except during her menstrual period (Lev. 15:19–28). We may thus absolve Jacob from rape according to the modern legal definition. Still, in the name Leah gave Reuben, she revealed that she suffered at the hands of her merciful husband. We cannot deny that in naming her first-born son, Leah used a term that in biblical language means rape, physical abuse, disgrace, and humiliation. The contrast technique we pointed out earlier emphasizes the treatment Leah received, as opposed to her sister:

> *He came also to Rachel, and he loved Rachel even more than Leah. (29:30)*

Jacob loved Rachel, but abused Leah. His treatment of her was so harsh that Leah did not have the strength to thank God for giving her a healthy firstborn son, who ensured her position in her husband's household. All she asked for was a little of the love he showered upon her sister: "For now my husband will love me." Yet her request was not fulfilled, and Jacob continued to abuse her even after she bore him a second son, Simeon:

> *And she conceived again and bore a son, and declared,* **"Because the LORD has heard that I am hated,** *He has given me this one also," and she called his name Simeon. (29:33)*

Through Simeon's name, the woman whose husband left his marks on her body cried out to God to bear witness to Jacob's continued spurning of her, despite the two sons she had borne him. God heard her cry, and granted her a third son, Levi:

> *Again she conceived, and bore a son and declared, "This time* **my husband will join me**, *for I have borne him three sons;" therefore his name was called Levi [lit., "join"]. (29:34)*

Even after Leah gave birth a third time, she still did not
thank God, but in Levi's name, the knives are no longer cutting her skin. "Levi" comes from the root *l.v.h.*, meaning
"attachment" or "joining a companion"; or in this case, "My
husband will join me." The meaning of Levi's name reveals a
modest change in Leah's status. It conceals a soft undertone
not found in the accusatory names of his two elder brothers.
Something in Leah's voice softened and relaxed.

Fertile Leah conceived a fourth time and gave birth to
Judah, whose name is based on the words *hudah-yah*, meaning "thanks to God" or "thank God for giving me this son."
In Judah's name, the dramatic change that began in her life
becomes explicit. Leah, who until this point was preoccupied
with her pain, finally found the strength to lift her head and
thank God for the great kindness He did for her:

> She conceived again, and bore a son and declared, "This
> time let me **gratefully praise the Lord**"; therefore she
> called his name Judah. Then she stopped giving birth.
> (29:35)

At last, the name Judah expresses true joy and gratitude to
God! Leah gradually became a happy woman.

How wonderful!

According to the order of events in Genesis, the spotlight now passes to Rachel's tent. But we will wait with the
names that Rachel gave her sons, and continue to follow the
joyful changes that took place in the courtyard of Leah's tent.
The next two sons born in her growing camp were born to
her slave woman Zilpah. Because the sons of a slave woman
belonged to her mistress, Leah was responsible for naming
them. She called the first son Gad:

> When Leah saw that she had stopped giving birth, she took
> Zilpah her slave woman and gave her to Jacob as a wife.
> Zilpah, Leah's slave woman, bore Jacob a son. And Leah

*declared, "**Good luck** has come!" So she called his name
Gad. (30:9–11)*

"Gad" means "luck," and Leah said, "Good luck has come."
At this point, Leah had given Jacob five sons, and she was
indeed a lucky woman. When the slave woman bore Jacob a
second son, Leah's happiness surpassed all bounds:

*Zilpah, Leah's slave woman, bore a second son to Jacob.
Leah declared, "**Happy am I**, for women will call me
happy!" So she called his name Asher. (30:12–13)*

The Hebrew word *asher* means "joy" or "great happiness."
Leah exclaimed, "Women will call me happy" – the women
who had known me as an abused woman, wretched and humiliated, would now exclaim: "Look, what a happy woman!"
Possibly, even though Leah used the plural "women" in this
sentence, she was referring to just one woman: her beautiful,
beloved, but miserable sister who looked on, eyes reddened
with pain and envy. At that point, Leah had all the reason in
the world to thank God and to bless her good luck and happiness. At this stage in her life, she stood at the head of a strong
camp that numbered six sons, and to further increase her joy,
God gave her three more children:

*God hearkened to Leah; and she conceived and bore Jacob
a fifth son. And Leah declared, "**God has granted me my
reward**, because I gave my slave woman to my husband."
So she called his name Issachar. (30:17–18)*

The name Issachar contains the word *sachar*, meaning
"reward" or "wages." Leah welcomed this new member of her
camp as a reward for giving her slave woman to Jacob. She
then gave birth a sixth time:

*Then Leah conceived again and bore Jacob a sixth son. Leah
said, "**God has endowed me with a good endowment;**

now my husband will make his palace with me, for I have borne him six sons." So she called his name Zebulun. (30:19–20)

The high status Leah had reached is easily recognizable in her explanation of the name Zebulun. The term *zebul* means "shrine" or "palace." When Leah explained her choice of the name of her sixth son, she said, "God has endowed me with a good endowment." She meant, "God has granted me an especially superior and fine gift." She added, "This time my husband will make his palace [*zebul*] with me, for I have borne him six sons." Could she be saying that after giving her husband eight sons, six of them from her own womb, she considered herself as important as a queen in her palace?

I would like to believe that this is how she felt.

Finally, Leah gave birth to a girl, whose name she did not explain:

Afterwards, she bore a daughter and she called her name Dinah. (30:21)

We have followed in the footsteps of Leah. The meanings of her sons' names reveal how her status slowly ascended from the lowest to the highest level. The names reflect the misery of her first years of marriage and the wonderful transformations that took place from birth to birth.

But now we must exchange joy for sorrow.

Before entering the courtyard of beautiful Rachel, whose womb God closed, we must tear our clothes, don sackcloth, and sprinkle ashes on our heads, as was the custom of mourners during biblical times. In Rachel's darkened courtyard, there was no happiness, nor would there ever be. Candles burned inside it for a moment, only to flicker and die the next.

Beloved Rachel witnessed with her own eyes how her sister's status in Jacob's home rose with each birth. She understood the significance of the names Leah gave her sons, and observed how her spurned, humiliated sister became a happy woman. From the tent next door, she heard how Leah's cries of pain were transformed gradually into exclamations of joy. Rachel knew that despite her smooth skin and beautiful face, the true disability lay not in Leah's tender eyes, but in her own flat, empty stomach. Rachel became a sad woman. In her distress, she sounded from the depths of her heart the miserable call of all her sisters in fate:

> *Rachel saw that she had not borne children to Jacob, so Rachel became envious of her sister; she said to Jacob, "Give me children – otherwise I am dead." (30:1)*

We might have expected that the most well-known lover in the Bible would calm and comfort his desperate wife. But from the meaning of Jacob's name and the names of Reuben and Simeon, we know that Jacob had too little patience and too strong a fist. Yet perhaps this judgment is unfair, for Jacob believed in the same value system that was upheld by his contemporaries. He worked at hard labor in order to buy an expensive, exceptional wife, but when he opened the package, he realized he had made a bad purchase. Ironically, the very woman given to him in deception, as an act of scorn and ridicule, added to Jacob's honor. Thanks to Leah, he became the leader of a strong, established patriarchal household. But Jacob had no patience for her barren sister's tears, and so he lashed out at her in fury:

> *Jacob's **anger was kindled** against Rachel, and he said, "Am I instead of God, Who has withheld from you fruit of the womb?" (30:2)*

Jacob's answer illuminates two issues. Firstly, like his contemporaries, he believed that God controlled fertility in the
world, and so Rachel's barrenness was a divine punishment.
The second issue involves the Hebrew expression used to
express Jacob's outburst of anger: *haron af*, "to kindle anger."
This expression appears dozens of times in the Bible. It does
not mean momentary, passing anger between husband and
wife, but rather, a dreadful, violent eruption of fury. In the
Hebrew Bible, most usages of this term refer to God's terrible
anger, and His desire to smash and destroy everything in His
path. As we have seen, the biblical author used advanced,
state-of-the-art techniques in order to expand the framework
of the story. Undoubtedly, he purposely chose one of the most
extreme expressions of anger for this passage. The use of this
term here teaches us that Jacob did not just lose his patience
at Rachel's bitter weeping. It means that all of the anger he
had accumulated from the day he set foot on Laban's threshold exploded in the face of his miserable wife, who pleaded
for her life.[24]

Shocked by her good husband's outburst, Rachel realized
what she had to do. Like Sarah before her, Rachel gave him
her slave woman as a wife. Bilhah conceived and gave birth
to a son, and Rachel called him Dan.

> *She said, "Here is my maid Bilhah, go to her, that she may
> bear on my knees and I too may be built up through her."
> So she gave him Bilhah her slave woman as a wife, and
> Jacob went to her. Bilhah conceived and bore Jacob a son.*

---

[24] Jacob's fury, and his accusation of Rachel, "Am I instead of God, Who has withheld
from you fruit of the womb?" offer a good example of the contrast technique we have
explained above. Like Rachel, Hannah wept bitterly because she had difficulty conceiving. Witnessing his beloved wife's sorrow, her husband Elkanah tried to comfort
her: "Elkanah, her husband, said to her, 'Hannah, why do you cry and why do you
not eat? Why is your heart broken? Am I not better to you than ten children?'" (I
Sam. 1:8). When we are aware of the contrast method in biblical writing, we readily
observe that the author has chosen to describe these two men as completely opposite
in character.

*Then Rachel said, "**God has judged me**, He has also heard
my voice and has given me a son." She therefore called his
name Dan. (30:3–6)*

The word *dan* means "judge." In this context, "God has
judged (*dan*) me for continued barrenness." Like Sarah and
Hannah, Rachel did not know why God judged her for barrenness, but in the name she gave to her slave woman's son,
she expressed her understanding that her childlessness was
a divine punishment. Bilhah conceived again, and Rachel
called the new baby Naphtali:

*Bilhah, Rachel's maidservant, conceived again and bore
Jacob a second son. And Rachel said, "Awesome grapplings
have **I grappled with my sister**, and I have also prevailed!"
And she called his name Naphtali. (30:7–8)*

The meaning of the name "Naphtali" is "grapple," "clash,"
or "strife." In Naphtali's name, Rachel immortalized the
competition and struggle with her sister for status in Jacob's
household.

The third son born in Rachel's camp was finally her own.
To this son, for whom she had waited so many years, Rachel
gave the name Joseph:

*God remembered Rachel; God hearkened to her and He
opened her womb. She conceived and bore a son, and said,
"God has removed [a.s.f.] my disgrace." So she called his
name Joseph, saying, "May the Lord add [yosef] on for me
another son." (30:22–24)*

Joseph's name has two different meanings. One recalls the
fact that her barrenness, like that of every childless woman of
her time, was considered a disgrace: "God has removed [a.s.f.]
my disgrace." Another meaning of the same root is "to add
to." Rachel asked that God "add" for her a second son: "May
the Lord add on [*yosef*] for me another son."

How terrible was her wish, how accursed.

If only we could have placed our hand over her mouth and hushed her. If only we could have prevented her from asking for a second child, and begged her to make do with one. Unfortunately, we were not beside Rachel. God did grant her request – but disastrously. Rachel conceived a second time, but during the birth, something went wrong. In her last moments, as her short, tragic life dwindled, she managed to give her second son his terrible name:

> Rachel went into labor and had difficulty in her childbirth. And it was when she had difficulty in her labor that the midwife said to her, "Have no fear, for this one, too, is a son for you." And it came to pass, as her soul was departing – for she died – that she called his name **Ben-oni**, but his father called him **Benjamin** [ben-yamin]. (35:17–18)

The word *ben* means son. The word *on* has two conflicting meanings. *On* means "power" and "strength" (Gen. 49:3), but it also means "death," "sorrow," and "mourning." From the mouth of a dying woman who uttered this statement with her last breath, the name Ben-oni cannot mean power or strength. Instead, Rachel must have intended the second meaning: "the son who announces my death" or "the son who brings my death." With this name that commemorates her demise, Rachel's life ended and she returned her tortured soul to her Creator. Understandably, Jacob changed the name of the son born in his old age, and called him Benjamin [*ben-yamin*], meaning "son of the south," since Benjamin was born in Canaan, south of Haran.[25]

---

[25] The biblical authors determined the directions while standing facing the rising sun in the east. Thus *kedem* (forward) means east (Gen. 25:6). West is toward the sea [*yam*]. *Yamin* ["right"] means south, and *smol* ["left"] means north. When Abraham reaches the decision that he must part from Lot, he says: "Let there be no strife…between me and you…. Is not the whole land before you? Separate yourself, I pray you, from me: if you will take the **left hand** [north], then I will go to the **right** [south]; or if you depart to the right [south] hand, then I will go to the left [north]" (Gen. 13:8–9).

CONCLUSION

Most names in the Bible have meaning, but not all of them expand the edges of the story in which they appear. But when we read a story in which all the characters' names have meaning, we must recognize that these names may play a role. This becomes especially important when the author gives a woman the right to speak. In such a case, we must listen with particular care to her words, because the Bible is a masculine work, and women's voices are almost never heard. Clearly, if the author gave Leah and Rachel the privilege of saying their pieces, he must have done so intentionally.

Bible translations transliterate the names of Jacob's twelve sons phonetically, without explaining their original meaning. As a result, a reader who does not understand the meanings of the names and their important role remains unaware of the author's genius touch in weaving a hidden story underneath the surface one. He cannot recognize the brilliant name game that reveals the exchange of status between Leah and Rachel in Jacob's home. Such a reader never notices that the names of Jacob's sons tell the story of one woman's great victory and her sister's sad defeat.

Now that we have clarified the meanings of the names, we can easily see how the names Leah gave her sons indicate grounding and growth. Having sons was the only way she could win a place in her husband's home – and through their names, Leah reveals that she was the big winner.

By contrast, the names Rachel gave her sons express defeat and sorrow. They begin in a low place, and descend ever lower, down to the grave.

The names of Rachel's sons reveal the downfall of a beautiful woman, whose husband's mistaken love for her led to her ruin, bringing disaster instead of blessing. As we will see in detail in chapter 15, according to the biblical story, God decided that Leah, not Rachel, would be Jacob's most valued wife, and so Rachel is the big loser. Before taking our leave of her, we must rest our heads on her grave and allow our grief over the death of this beautiful young woman to overcome us. We must follow the custom of our ancestors, and grasp a handful of earth in our fists to sprinkle on her grave. Our love for Rachel will seep down into the earth, reaching her resting-place and demonstrating that we have never forgotten her. Perhaps our memory will be sufficient to comfort her.

We return for the last time to the love story of Jacob and Rachel. This story has touched our hearts – because we like love stories. Because every once in a while, just for a moment, a caressing hand lit the darkness in our cynical, sober souls. Here and there, we have also lit a small candle in our lives, but like Rachel's, ours was extinguished, leaving a scorched, scarred spot in our hearts as a remembrance.

We admire Jacob's love for Rachel, but if a person's last wish has any value, we would do well to remember his. Before Jacob died, he gathered together his sons and instructed them to bury him beside Leah, not Rachel:

> Then he instructed them; and he said to them, "I shall be gathered to my people; **bury me with my fathers** in the cave that is in the field of Ephron the Hittite. In the cave that is in the field of Machpelah, which faces Mamre, in the land of Canaan.... There they buried Abraham and Sarah his wife, there they buried Isaac and Rebecca his wife; and **there I buried Leah**...." When Jacob finished instructing his sons, he drew his feet onto the bed; he expired and was gathered to his people. (Gen. 49:29–33)

Chapter Twelve

HANNAH, PENINAH, AND ELKANAH

(I SAMUEL I)

Abraham and Jacob and their wives stood at the tips of the two relationship triangles we studied in the previous chapters. The third triangle is composed of Elkanah and his two senior wives, Peninah and Hannah.

Over six hundred years separate the period of Abraham and Jacob from that of Elkanah. Abraham's era is usually estimated at the eighteenth century BCE, while Jacob lived about fifty years later. Elkanah and his two wives lived at the beginning of the eleventh century BCE. The gap in time between Abraham and Elkanah is readily observable in their way of life and method of worshipping God, but not in the status of women, which remained static throughout ancient history. During these six hundred years, important social changes took place in Israelite society, and I would like to dedicate several words to describing these transformations.

Abraham and Jacob lived in Canaan as nomadic shepherds, following their flocks of goats from one pasture to another. Although Abraham did purchase a piece of land in

Hebron, and Jacob purchased land outside Shechem, neither of them ever worked that land or settled on it. By contrast, Elkanah and his two wives represent a more advanced way of life, of villagers who lived permanently in one place.

One of the most important and fascinating changes that took place during those six hundred years is in the method of religious worship. The forefathers of Genesis wandered from one place to another, and took their worship with them. They built altars from collections of stones they gathered on their journey, which they used for a single ceremony. When the ceremony had ended, they left the place and never returned. The forefathers sanctified God, not the place of worship, and this is easily understandable, since they did not put down roots in the new land to which they had arrived. God's holiness was present in their souls, and it was expressed in their immediate, personal, almost intimate connection with Him. God accompanied them on their journeys, and played a central role in the lives of their families. He spoke to them, and even sent them divine messengers in the form of men. But above all, God loved the small, modest altars they erected in His honor under the open blue skies, in order to commemorate important events in their lives and thank Him for His goodness.

The direct, unmediated worship of God that characterized the forefathers' worship was appropriate for a nomadic society that did not have an established base on the land. It characterized a society that had not developed a hierarchical, organized priestly institution, led by professional priests whose only job was to lead religious rituals. As we learn from Leviticus, the Israelite priests eventually appropriated this job for themselves alone, as happened everywhere in the world. (In the more advanced stage of religious evolution, religious leaders were considered by their flocks to be saints and miracle workers. The elevation of professional religious leaders into saints is common today in Judaism as well as Christianity. In the ancient world, it did not exist.)

In the time of Elkanah and his wives, a slow evolution took place in the mode of worship practiced by the forefathers of Genesis. The personal, spontaneous ceremonies held on roadsides continued, but in parallel, institutionalized worship began to develop in permanent locations. The Israelites built such worship centers at Dan in the north of the land of Israel, and at Shechem and Beth-el in the center of the country. They built a small temple at Shiloh in Samaria, also in the center. Religious ceremonies, which until then took place under the open skies, were now held, at least in some cases, between walls and under roofs.

As opposed to his forefathers, Elkanah did not go out into the field to gather a small pile of rocks into a one-time altar. Rather, he made an annual pilgrimage to a tiny temple in Shiloh. Another difference between the forefathers of Genesis and Elkanah is that while the forefathers held ceremonies throughout the year to commemorate events in the lives of the worshippers, Elkanah and his family visited the temple on a regular annual date (verses 3, 7, and 21). Apparently, they did so in order to hold a ceremony that was related to one significant date. Although Elkanah still performed the ceremony himself, the temple in Shiloh was managed by a priest together with his two sons. The authority of their roles and their new status are revealed through their behavior.

In the year of the story that is related in the book of Samuel, Elkanah followed his lifetime habit. He visited the temple along with Peninah, who bore him sons and daughters, and Hannah, whom the text describes as barren. As usual, he dismembered the sheep or the goat with his own hands. He placed the fatty part on the altar for God. For the ancients, who ate meat only rarely, the fat was considered the choicest portion of the animal. Then he divided the meat among his wives and children. Such was his practice every year, and he repeated it this year as well.

The book of Samuel recounts that Elkanah deeply loved Hannah, his childless wife, who was apparently much younger than Peninah. One of his expressions of love for her was performed on the day of the sacrifice. When Elkanah distributed the meat to his family, he doubled the portion of meat he gave to Hannah:

> It happened on the day that Elkanah brought offerings that he gave portions to Peninah, his wife, and to all her sons and daughters. But to Hannah he gave a double portion, for he loved Hannah and the Lord had closed her womb. (4–5)

Elkanah's habit of doubling Hannah's portion provoked Peninah, and so she made sure that the meat on Hannah's plate was salted amply with tears. As much as Elkanah showered Hannah with his love, so Peninah treated the younger woman with scorn and malice due to her barrenness. This year as well, when Elkanah doubled the portion of meat on his beloved wife's plate, Peninah, as usual, doubled the portion of poison in her mouth. When Hannah could no longer bear the love of one and the hatred of the other, she rose, weeping bitterly, and poured out her sorrow before God. God listened to Hannah's pleas, and one year later, she gave birth to Samuel, her firstborn son.

From the distance of time, Hannah's broken heart and the mark of shame she wore on her forehead is painful for us as well. Just as we identified with Rachel's anguish, so we identify with Hannah's grief and condemn Peninah for acting hostile toward her because of her barrenness. But I must admit that if I were Peninah, I would have behaved the same way!

Peninah was Elkanah's first wife, and her status was much higher than Hannah's. Peninah, not Hannah, bore him sons and daughters, placing him at the head of a sound patriarchal household. Thanks to her, he was respected in his community. Thus if one of his wives had the right to a double portion of meat, it was Peninah. The double portion of meat that Elkanah gave Hannah amounted to discriminatory and unfair treatment of the woman who bore him sons and daughters. The endearments he heaped upon his beloved younger wife reached Peninah's ears and humiliated her. Peninah, who was her husband's property, could do nothing except take out her anger on Hannah.

But Elkanah loved and indulged young Hannah. With this behavior, he became a paradigmatic example of the man who establishes his life beside the bride of his youth, only to grow older and abandon her for a younger, prettier wife.

In the ancient world, a man did not need to divorce his first wife in order to marry a younger woman. He could simply marry an additional wife and ignore the first one. He could behave like Abraham, who, after Hagar was given to him as a wife, behaved indifferently toward Sarah, who followed him devotedly through the desert.

Peninah's eruption of fury due to the double portion of meat seems ridiculous to us today. What was so important about a portion of meat that it succeeded in enraging Peninah each time afresh? The historical truth is that this was no small matter, and Peninah had good reason to harass Hannah on festival days. In biblical times, sheep pens, chicken coops, and industrial farms for fattening cattle did not exist, as they do today. Meat was not an item on the ancients' daily menu. A family kept several sheep or one cow for the daily milk needs of the household. They ate meat only on festive occasions, when the animal was slaughtered, or when it was about to die. Eating meat was a rare event, saved for special occasions. Thus Peninah had good reason to feel snubbed by Elkanah when he doubled Hannah's portion on festival days.

The theological justification for Hannah's childlessness is identical to that which applied to her predecessors Sarah and Rachel: God closed her womb and did not allow her to conceive. But if we ask practical questions, we will get practical answers.

If Hannah married at age ten or eleven, as was accepted in her day, and did not conceive until she was seventeen or eighteen, she already was considered barren. During that time, Peninah had ample opportunity to poison the many double portions of meat with which Elkanah indulged his young wife. But possibly, aside from love, Elkanah had another reason to behave as he did.

The connection between marriage age, a rich diet, and fertility was known to the ancients. The Bible intentionally relates beauty and physical health to fleshiness. Thinness, by contrast, is associated with poverty, hunger, and illness.[26] If Elkanah cared about his young wife's health, and wanted to help her mature and become strong, so that she would be able to bear the expected pregnancies, he was astute to place a double portion of meat on her plate. If we assume that Samuel, Hannah's eldest son, was born when she was an "old" woman of twenty, not the usual fourteen, then he was born to a healthy, strong woman who had reached full physical maturity. Objectively, such a woman was in an ideal position to bear additional children. Indeed, after Samuel was born, Hannah gave birth to five more children and aside from Leah, she was the most fertile woman mentioned in the Bible.

---

[26] Chapter 41 of Genesis describes Pharoah's dreams, which amply illustrate the relationship between fullness and health, and thinness and illness.

Chapter Thirteen

JUDAH AND TAMAR

(GENESIS 38)

Like all the other stories about women in the Bible, the story of our next heroine, Tamar, tells of a woman who fought for her life and for position in her family and society. But unlike other stories we have examined, Tamar was not barren. She did not struggle against her husband's other wife, and no one humiliated her. Tamar's story is of a young woman widowed shortly after marriage, before she was able to conceive, and apparently before she even had relations with her husband.

Tamar's widowhood raises a fundamental problem that reaches far beyond her private situation: what was the legal status of a woman who was widowed before she had children, and before she had established her position in her husband's home? What was her social and familial standing?

Under today's norms, she would be free to marry again, but this was not the case in biblical times. We recall that the bride-price paid by the groom's father (or the groom himself) to the bride's father made her the exclusive property of her husband. Her virginity, her sexuality, her children, and her entire life belonged to him. The commandment in Exodus declares: "You shall not covet your fellow's house. You shall not covet your fellow's wife, his manservant, his maidservant, his ox, his donkey, nor anything that belongs to your fellow" (20:14). This clearly states that a woman, like a home, maidservant (slave woman), ox, or donkey, was the property of her husband. The story of Tamar, and that of Ruth and Orpah, which we will examine in the next chapter, demonstrates that the husband's purchase was a legal acquisition in every aspect. If he died, ownership of his wife passed to his family, and thus the widow did not become a free woman permitted to remarry as she pleased.

The future of a woman who was widowed after she had children was ensured. She had fulfilled her obligation toward the family that had paid her bride-price, and "earned" the food she ate. If she were a young woman who could still bear children, one of her deceased husband's relatives could marry her. Her children by her first husband remained in their father's home, but because their mother remained in the same household, the connection between them was preserved.

The position of a widow without children was much more difficult. If she had left her father's home after she got married and gone to live in a distant settlement, her situation was even bleaker. In her new location, she did not have access to the protection systems offered by her extended family. In such a case, the widow remained like a prisoner in her husband's family, who could do with her as they saw fit. Because she was their property, she was not permitted to remarry at will. Because she did not have children, she was not earning her daily bread, and because she lived far from her father's home, the protection of her extended family did not apply to her. No one protected her or her rights; no one owed her anything.

Tamar fell into this complicated trap.

This is her story:

Judah, Leah and Jacob's fourth son, married a woman from the daughters of Canaan, called "the daughter of Shua" since her father's name was Shua.[27] This daughter of Shua bore Judah three sons: Er, Onan, and Shelah. The text does not relate where Judah and his family lived, but it does say that Judah kept a flock of sheep in a distant village called Timnah, and that he went there every year in order to shear his sheep. When Er, his eldest son, reached marriageable age (thirteen or fourteen), Judah married him to a young woman from Timnah named Tamar. As was the practice in those days, Tamar left her father's home and moved to the village where Judah and his family lived.

If Tamar and Er had led normal lives, their marriage would have tied the first connecting cord between two unrelated families that decided to unite and become one extended family. Over the years, that first cord would have become a thick rope. The two families would have expanded their mutual marriage ties, and several generations later, they would have become one family, forever united. But the scenario imagined by Judah and Tamar's father was never realized. Just after the marriage of the young couple, the thin cord that connected the two homes broke. For reasons we will explore below, God judged Er to be evil, and caused his death. After Er died, Tamar fell into the trap we outlined above: she was left in a distant village, childless, defenseless, and held by a patriarchal household that was not part of her extended family.

---

[27] In biblical language, only sons were given the appellation "son of" following their fathers' name, like the modern English use of "Junior." Apparently, Shua's daughter was thus named because her real name was lost.

THE LAW OF LEVIRATE MARRIAGE
(DEUTERONOMY 25:5–10)

The trap into which Tamar fell returns us to the question we raised earlier: What was the legal status of a young woman who was widowed before she conceived?

The lawmaker, God according to the Bible, addressed this issue and defined a solution for it. In order to enable the widow to remarry and rebuild her life, and to preserve ownership of the woman by the dead husband's family, the lawmaker instituted the law of levirate marriage. This law is one of the most complex and astute laws in the Bible. The law of levirate marriage plays a central role in this story, and therefore we must stop for a while on the side of the road and explain the principle at its foundation. Following is the text of the law:

> *When brothers dwell together and one of them dies, and he has no child, the wife of the deceased shall not marry outside to a strange man; her brother-in-law shall come to her, and take her to himself as a wife, and perform levirate marriage. It shall be that the firstborn – if she can bear – shall succeed to the name of his dead brother, so that his name not be blotted out from Israel. But if the man will not wish to marry his sister-in-law, then his sister-in-law shall ascend to the gate, to the elders, and she shall say, "My brother-in-law refuses to establish a name for his brother in Israel, he did not consent to perform levirate marriage with me." Then the elders of his city shall summon him and speak to him, and he shall stand and say, "I do not wish to marry her." Then his sister-in-law shall approach him before the eyes of the elders; she shall remove his shoe from on his foot and spit before him; she shall speak up and say, "So is done to the man who will not build the house of his brother." Then his name shall be proclaimed in Israel,*

"The house of the one whose shoe was removed!" (Deut. 25:5–10)

The law of levirate marriage operated on behalf of the widow, the family of the dead husband, and the deceased himself. It specified that if a man died before his wife conceived, his brother was required to marry her. The widow profited from such a marriage because it saved her from widowhood, allowing her the opportunity to remarry and bear children, and thus rebuild her life. The family profited through the children the widow bore their other son, for these children remained in the family's possession. Finally, the deceased also profited.

One of the goals of the lawmaker was to commemorate the dead and preserve his economic rights: "It shall be that the firstborn – if she can bear – shall succeed to the name of his dead brother, *so that his name not be blotted out from Israel*." In order for his memory and rights to be preserved, the lawmaker determined that the first son born to the widow and the deceased's brother would be considered as the firstborn of the deceased. The son would inherit his official father's status and property, and continue the chain that had been broken as if he were his natural son.

The levirate law should not be understood only in the social and economic contexts, which are readily observable. We must also consider the family laws related to it, and the religious context of the time in which it was created.

As we mentioned before, ancient society took a positive view of marriage between relatives, as well as of men marrying multiple wives. Thus it was necessary to define the women with whom a man was forbidden to have sexual relations. According to biblical law, a man who had relations with a woman who was forbidden to him committed a sin against God. The forbidden sexual act created impurity, and this was transferred to the holy land and defiled it. The only way to purify the land from this impurity was to execute the sinners (see chapter 5).

The book of Leviticus states clearly and emphatically that a man is forbidden to have relations with his brother's wife:

The nakedness of your brother's wife you shall not uncover; it is your brother's shame. (Lev. 18:16)

A man who shall take his brother's wife, it is loathsome; he will have uncovered his brother's nakedness, they shall be childless. (Lev. 20:21)

In order for a widow to marry her deceased husband's brother, the lawmaker established one exception to the strict list of forbidden relations, and permitted the levirate marriage. This special exception applied only on condition that the widow had no children. To be clear, a woman who had children, or who was pregnant when her husband died, was permitted to marry again, but she could not marry her late husband's brother, because he was in the category of forbidden relations.[28] The lawmaker who permitted one of the forbidden marriages did not do so lightly. He used threatening language in order to clarify that the levirate marriage was an obligation, not a recommendation. This was not a case of, if he wanted to marry her, he would, and if not, he did not have to do so.

The threatening language of the law reveals the lawmaker's awareness that the deceased's family might exploit the situation of the widow as a virtual prisoner in their home, and forbid their other son to marry her. As we noted, if the family did not permit the widow to remarry, she could not rebuild her life. In order to prevent the deceased's family (or the brother-in-law) from treating the levirate marriage lightly,

---

[28] The Bible does not specify the law of a widow whose late husband did not have a brother who could marry her. We may assume that such a widow did not return to her father's home, but married another of her late husband's relatives. We will expand on this question in the next chapter, when we discuss the book of Ruth.

the lawmaker held a stick over their heads. He ruled that in such a case, the widow was permitted to approach the elders – the heads of the respected families – and ask for their assistance. The elders would listen to her, and then invite the recalcitrant brother-in-law to the place of judgment, at the gates of the city, and demand that he fulfill his duty. If the brother-in-law continued to be rebellious, he had to undergo a public ceremony of humiliation held in the presence of the elders and the local population. As part of the ceremony, the widow went to the place of judgment and removed his shoe in front of the townspeople. She then spit in his face and reproached him publicly. After the humiliation ceremony, the elders would stamp the mark of disgrace on the home and family of the insubordinate brother-in-law, calling it "the house of the one whose shoe was removed."

Public humiliation, at the hands of a woman to boot, does not exist anywhere else in the Bible. We must recall that ancient society was traditional, and women were considered inferior to men. A man who was humiliated publicly by a woman could not show his face due to absolute disgrace. The elders intentionally chose the most shameful means of reproach imaginable in those days – spitting in the face and public censure by a woman.[29] A family humiliated in this manner could not simply disappear into a crowded city, as in our day. Such a family had to continue living on its land, within a tiny community that held it in contempt for violating the law of levirate marriage and the command of the elders.

Now, after we have clarified the principles that lie behind the law of levirate marriage, we are able to return to the story of Judah and Tamar.

---

[29] When Miriam criticized Zipporah, Moses' Cushite wife, God refers to spitting in the face as a method of shaming: "The Lord said to Moses, 'Were her father to spit in her face, would she not be humiliated for seven days?'" (Num. 12:14).

The Story of Judah and Tamar

The death of Er, Tamar's first husband, created conditions appropriate for levirate marriage. Judah, described as an authoritarian father who ruled his family with an iron fist, ordered Onan, his second son, to perform the levirate marriage with Tamar:

> Then Judah said to Onan, "Go to your brother's wife and enter into levirate marriage with her, and establish offspring for your brother." (8)

Onan did marry the young widow as the law required, but each time he came to her tent, he refrained from having relations with her, and so God had him killed as well (10–11).

Before we continue, we must place this story in the context of the time when it took place, as we always do. If Tamar married at age eleven, and each of her husbands was around thirteen when he married her, possibly the young husband did not yet know what he was expected to do with the girl given to him as a wife, and died before he ever learned. At any rate, after Er and Onan died, Judah had to decide what to do with the wife-girl-widow who remained in his possession. He had two possibilities: free Tamar from the bonds of the bride-price that connected her to him, and allow her to return to her father's home and remarry; or keep her. If he chose the option of keeping her, then Shelah, his third son, would have to marry her according to the levirate law. Apparently, Judah did not want to lose the price he had paid for Tamar, and so he chose the second option. But because Shelah was still a small boy who had not yet reached marriageable age, Judah decided that Tamar should return to her father's home in Timnah. He ordered her to wear widow's clothing and wait in the village of her birth until her infant groom shed his down and grew a few feathers:

THE WORLD OF THE WOMAN

*Then Judah said to Tamar, his daughter-in-law, "Remain
a widow in your father's house until my son Shelah grows
up." …So Tamar went and lived in her father's house. (11)*

We may assume that at this point, Tamar had reached the
age of twelve, even thirteen. Like every girl who grew up in a
traditional society where the father was the authority figure,
Tamar was obedient. She clothed herself in widow's garb and
returned to her father's home. As Judah had ordered, she
waited until her infant groom grew up and become her second
levirate husband.

A year passed, and another year, then many more, and
still Tamar waited. Shelah matured and reached marriageable
age, and Tamar continued to wear her widow's clothing and
to wait. At a certain point, she began to be gnawed by the fear
that Judah had broken his promise, and did not intend to
allow Shelah to marry her. Next, her fear became a certainty.

At that point, Tamar understood that she was trapped.
Although Judah barred Shelah from marrying her, he continued to keep her in his grip, and prevented her from moving
forward and rebuilding her life. He acted in complete opposition to the lawmaker's purpose in creating the law of levirate
marriage.

Before we recount what this clever, brave woman did in
order to recover her life, we must examine her legal status
during the years when she stood before the entrance of her
father's tent camp each morning and gazed at the horizon,
anticipating a messenger who would arrive and ask her to
return to Judah's home.

During that time, Tamar's status was similar to that of a
betrothed woman who had not yet been given to her husband.
In other words, Tamar had the status of a promised woman
who had a husband, but whose marriage had not yet taken
place. If she had had relations with any other man aside from

her designated groom, she would have been considered an adulteress, and for this sin she would have paid with her life (Deut. 22:13–22).

When Judah decided to break his promise to have Tamar marry his third son, yet keep her under his dominion, her status changed. Tamar became an *agunah*. This term is derived from the Hebrew word *ogen*, meaning "anchor." An anchor keeps a ship in place and prevents it from moving. An *agunah*, or "anchored" woman, is a married woman who is confined to a marriage that is not consummated in the present and is not expected to be consummated in the future. Like an anchored boat, the *agunah* cannot free herself from the chains that bind her, preventing her from continuing her life. She is like a woman who is simultaneously married, yet unmarried.

The purpose of the levirate marriage was to prevent one of the forms of "anchored" women. When the widow had a brother-in-law, she was forbidden to marry any other man. But if the brother-in-law refused to marry her and also refused to free her, she became "anchored" – and this was exactly Tamar's status. Tamar was trapped, "anchored," stuck in one place, promised to a man who did not marry her and had no plan to do so.

Tamar had no place in the world. She had no home, no husband, and no children.

If Judah and her father had lived in the same village, this would have been the time to approach the elders of the community and request their assistance. The elders would have demanded that Shelah fulfill the promise his father made to Tamar years ago. If Shelah, following his father's orders, had continued to refuse, Tamar would have gone to the place of judgment. There she would have removed his shoe, spit in his face in front of the community, and cursed him. The elders would have placed the mark of shame on Judah's home, calling it "the house of the one whose shoe was removed," and Judah and Shelah would have been humiliated before the villagers.

Unfortunately for Tamar, after her second husband died, she returned to her father's home in Timnah. The elders of that village could not help her, because their legal authority was limited to their settlement and family. So they could not call Judah to judgment and order him to fulfill his promise.

Tamar had no way out.

She could not ask for assistance from any authority that had the ability to melt Judah's heart of stone and force him to have Shelah marry her, or else free her from his possession. Like an old dusty box abandoned in a storehouse, she was forgotten, and her widow's clothing became faded and worn with age.

One day, Tamar discovered that Judah was coming to Timnah to shear the sheep he owned in her village – and this was her opportunity. Tamar realized that if she did not act, she would remain desolate until the end of her days. Desperate to save herself, Tamar, who in the meantime had become a woman, took courage, and did something unthinkable in traditional society: she removed her widow's garb and disguised herself as a harlot. Then she hid her face with layers of shawls so that no one would recognize her, and went out to the side of the road to lie in wait for Judah.

When Judah reached the site of the ambush, a mysterious, veiled harlot suddenly appeared and indicated her interest in him. Judah was captivated by her twisting movements, her curvaceous legs and posterior, and the scent of desire she gave off, and he gave in to her seductions. But before the anticipated act could take place, they had to agree on a price for her generous services. Judah considered a goat kid was appropriate payment for the mysterious lady's trouble, but he did not have one with him. Apparently, the payment issue did not worry the prostitute, who suggested that he leave her a deposit until he could send her the agreed-upon amount:

> *When Judah saw her, he thought her to be a harlot since she had covered her face. So he detoured to her by the road, and said, "Come, if you please, and let me come in to you," for he did not know that she was his daughter-in-law. And she said, "What will you give me if you come in to me?" He replied, "I will send you a kid of the goats from the flock." And she said, "Provided you leave a pledge until you send it." And he said, "What pledge shall I give you?" She replied, "**Your signet, your cord, and your staff that is in your hand.**" And he gave them to her, and went in to her, and she conceived by him. (15–18)*

Tamar did not disguise herself as a whore in order to obtain a kid. She wanted to conceive through Judah, and she needed his personal items in order to prove the identity of the man through whom she conceived. The deposit he gave her was comprised of three items: his signet or seal, the cord with which he tied it to his belt, and the staff that bore his marks. These items were equivalent to the modern driver's license and passport. They were her insurance certificate, and Tamar never intended to return them for a kid, nor for any other form of payment.

Three months passed after Judah parted from the veiled harlot, and her movements and scents of desire faded and were forgotten. He completed his business in Timnah and returned home. Then, one sunny afternoon, the sky fell on him. Judah was informed that Tamar had conceived "through harlotry"!

His prisoner had broken the barrier he had placed before her and had relations with another man, and she was going to bear that man's child! Judah, shocked by the scandalous act that humiliated him publicly, felt as if a stone had fallen from the sky onto his head. He was so shaken by the news that he could not imagine there might be any connection between the Tamar who had disappeared from his memory years ago and the harlot who had disappeared from his memory just three months earlier. Judah came to a rude awakening, as if by an evil wind blowing in his face: his prisoner had committed adultery against his son and disgraced him in front of everyone he knew! A man of Judah's pride could not allow such a humiliating act to pass in silence. He rushed to the field and gathered dry twigs for a bonfire on which to burn his impudent daughter-in-law.

Legally, justice was with Judah. The fact that he had anchored Tamar and did not intend to relax his iron grip from her neck did not make her a free woman. She was forbidden to commit adultery against her intended husband, even if Judah kept him from her. She was forbidden to violate one of the most severe prohibitions in the Bible, which forbade relations with the father of her dead husbands. Tamar was an adulteress who had conceived through a man not her husband (Judah did not yet know the man's identity), and thus he decreed that she must be burned at the stake. But at the last minute, just before his plan was realized and Tamar rose to the sky in pillars of fire and smoke, a dramatic turn took place. She revealed the deposit she had kept for this very moment, and declared:

> As she was taken out, she sent word to her father-in-law, saying: "By the man to whom these belong I am with child." And she said, "Identify, if you please, whose are this signet, this cord, and this staff." (25)

When Judah saw his possessions in her hand, he was stunned:

> Judah recognized; and he said, "She is right; it is from me, inasmuch as I did not give her to Shelah my son," and he was not intimate with her anymore. (26)

Tamar was not thrown onto the pyre, nor did her body turn into ashes that scattered across the earth. Instead, she returned to Judah's home and gave birth to the twins she carried in her womb – Perez and Zerah.

THE SINS OF ER, ONAN, AND JUDAH

The story we have analyzed here raises many questions that the author, who relied on his reader's knowledge of the customs of that time, did not feel the need to explain.

According to the text, God was responsible for the deaths of Er and Onan, due to their sins. But what were these sins? And why did Judah admit that Tamar was right, although she deserved to be executed after knowingly violating the most severe relationship prohibition? After all, she had committed adultery against the man to whom she was promised, and conceived through his father, who was also the father of her two dead husbands. In addition, why did Judah bring Tamar back to his home but refrain from having further relations with her?

According to biblical theology, "death by divine decree" takes place only when God acted as judge and punisher of a person who sinned against Him, or when the elders had no authority. In Tamar's case, both conditions were fulfilled: Judah's sons sinned against God, and the elders of Tamar's native village could not offer her legal aid. Regarding Er's death, the text says:

> But Er, Judah's firstborn, was evil in the eyes of the Lord, and the Lord caused him to die. (7)[30]

---

[30] The names of Er and Onan are another example of how the main character's name enriches the story and contributes to its meaning (see chapter 11). Er is the Hebrew word for "evil" spelled backwards.

Onan means "to masturbate," and according to the text, he let his seed "go to waste on the ground" – so his name expresses this act. Undoubtedly, these are not real names, but rather literary names that reveal the negative attitude of the writer toward these figures.

Similarly, the text says of Onan's death:

> *But Onan knew that the seed would not be his; so it was,*
> *that whenever he would go to his brother's wife, he would*
> *let it go to waste on the ground so as not to provide offspring*
> *for his brother. What he did was evil in the eyes of the Lord,*
> *and He caused him to die also. (9–10)*

Still, what sin had the two brothers committed that made them liable to the death penalty? The author of Genesis did not answer this question, and so we again turn for assistance to the book of Jubilees, which we introduced in chapter 9.

The author of Jubilees (c. 250 BCE) repeated the family stories of Genesis in his own words, but changed parts of them as he saw fit, and adapted many sections to his particular ideology. What is important to us here is that the Jubilees author had details that seem to belong to an "original" book of Genesis, which for some reason were not included in the version we have today. The assumption that these are authentic details is based on two important justifications. First, they supply relevant answers to open questions in Genesis. Second, these answers do not support the ideology of the Jubilees author, and thus we cannot suspect that he included these details for ideological reasons.

The Jubilees author had the missing link from the book of Genesis that explains why Er did not have relations with Tamar, and why Onan preferred to spill his seed rather than consummate relations with her. According to Jubilees, Er hated Tamar, so he refused to have relations with her. This was his evil act (Jubilees 41, 1–3).

By contrast, the name Tamar reflects the author's positive opinion toward the heroine of the story. "Tamar" is a palm tree, which together with the olive played a central role in the Israelites' diet. Tamar is named after the sweet, tasty fruit of this tree, the date – and she was certainly worthy of her good name. While Er and Onan are not used as Hebrew names, Tamar remains one of the most popular and beloved names in Israel today.

Er's hatred for Tamar was not considered a sin, just as Jacob's hatred for Leah was not considered a sin. In the ancient world (and in Third World countries today), fathers chose marriage partners for their children, and the question of whether they knew or loved each other was not part of the marriage transaction. Clearly, then, the hatred of a young man for a young woman forced upon him against his will was no proof of his wickedness. But when Er refused to have relations with Tamar, he took over the right to "close" her womb, a right reserved only to God. From all aspects, Er "anchored" Tamar, for although he was her husband, he prevented their marriage from being consummated. Onan's sin was even more severe, because he married Tamar in levirate marriage, and he was obligated to give her a son who would be considered the firstborn of his deceased brother. But Onan scorned the levirate law, and through his behavior, he also "anchored" Tamar. The refusals of each of the brothers to have relations with the woman they married meant she was forced to remain barren. They expropriated her right to bear children and build a life in the home to which she had been brought and in her new community. We must recall that Tamar's "anchored" status did not prevent the brothers from marrying other women who would bear them children and ensure their status in society. This fact made their acts one-sided and even more evil. Since Tamar lived in Judah's village at the time she was married to Er and Onan, the elders of her family could not help her, and therefore God Himself decreed their punishment and caused their deaths.

The third sinner in this story might seem to be Tamar, not Judah, since she seduced him to have relations with her. In this, she not only committed adultery against Shelah, but added insult to injury. Tamar led Judah to commit an act he would never have performed, had he known the identity of the whore who hid her face behind many shawls. The author describes Tamar as acting resolutely and intentionally in order to have relations with the father of her two dead husbands and intended groom, even though this was one of the prohibited relations. The Bible emphasizes that Tamar was aware she was committing a sin (and thus covered her face), and that she would pay for it with her life. Still, Judah admitted that she was right:

> Judah recognized; and he said, "She is right; it is from me, inasmuch as I did not give her to Shelah my son," and he was not intimate with her anymore. (26)

As to why Tamar was right, the text answers simply: because Judah did not have his third son marry her under the levirate law. The fact that Judah prevented Shelah from marrying Tamar meant that he, like his two dead sons, "anchored" and prevented her from having children and continuing the names of Er and Onan, who died childless.

As far as we can judge from this story, the lawmaker considered Tamar's violation of a prohibited relationship to be less severe than Judah's violation of the law of levirate marriage, since "anchoring" a widow without children prevented her from having any form of life. It relegated her to the living dead, and the law of levirate marriage was designed to prevent this situation. Furthermore, since Tamar conceived through Judah, she did not violate his right of ownership of her, because he was the man who had paid the bride-price to her father. Yet despite the biblical author's vindication of her actions, her legal position was complex.

The twins, Perez and Zerah, belonged to a patriarchal household led by Judah, and for this reason, he brought her back to his home. When Tamar became the mother of two sweet little boys, she had a home and a world – but she did not have a husband. She was never freed from her "anchored" condition, and so her legal status remained complicated until the end of her days.

Let us explain.

The fact that Er and Onan were dead did not change the fact that Judah was forbidden to have relations with Tamar. At first, Judah did not realize that the harlot who seduced him was his daughter-in-law. But when her identity was revealed, he honored the prohibition, and thus had no further relations with her and did not give her any more children.

Shelah could not perform the levirate marriage with Tamar, because as soon as she became pregnant, the levirate law no longer applied to her. Levirate marriage could not be performed with a woman who had two children. Furthermore, Shelah could not marry a woman who had conceived through his father, because this was also one of the prohibited relationships:

> The nakedness of your father's wife you shall not uncover;
> it is your father's shame. (Lev. 18:8; 20:11)

In short, Tamar never escaped her "anchored" status. But after she bore Judah's children, she had a home, and she had earned the justification of her existence and her status in her family and community. Furthermore, in a roundabout way, Tamar fulfilled one of the most important principles underlying the levirate marriage law: she commemorated the names of Er and Onan.

As we explained above, the law of levirate marriage determined that the firstborn son of the brother-in-law and the deceased's widow was considered the firstborn son of the deceased (Deut. 25:5–10). Because Judah's two sons had died before having children, both of their names had to be memorialized. In accordance with the principle underlying levirate marriage, Perez, the first son to break out into the world, took the place of Er, and thus he inherited the primogeniture of Judah's household. Perez replaced Shelah, who was many years older. Indeed, Judah's dynasty continued through Perez, Er's "firstborn son," instead of through Shelah.

THE BEAUTY OF THE BIBLICAL WRITING STYLE

The family stories in the Bible, especially those in Genesis, seem easy to understand. Some say they are as simple and naïve as children's fairy tales. As we have seen, and will see below, the opposite is the case.

The biblical authors were not naïve, and they certainly did not write fairy tales. They were brilliant creators, and they wrote for intelligent people who were aware of the legal methods practiced in their time, and who were able to understand the finest nuances of their writing. The story of Judah and Tamar is a wonderful example of this. From all aspects, this is an exceptional textbook on the biblical art of writing.

The story above is told in only thirty verses, into which the author compressed a long list of events: Judah's marriage to Shua's daughter; the births, marriages, and deaths of his sons; the banishment of Tamar from his house; her disguise as a scheming harlot; Judah's plan to burn her; the climax of the story in which Tamar pulls out the proofs of Judah's fatherhood; and finally, the birth of the twins. Thirty verses were enough for the author to recount a dramatic life story, packed with events, lacking no detail vital to our understanding of it.

How could the author write such a long story in so few words?

The answer is that the definition of short and long stories depends on the period and writing style of that time, not only on the number of words it contains.

If the author had lived in our time, he would have needed a thousand pages in order to write what the biblical author wrote in thirty verses. This is because the modern writer does not write only for himself and those in his close circle, but for "the whole world." Because "the whole world" is his potential reader, his words must be understandable to Finnish readers, Chinese readers, and readers from myriad other cultures and languages. The modern author must explain his intentions in detail, otherwise a reader who lives on the other side of the ocean will not understand what he means. In addition, the modern author does not write stories, but books. He is well aware that a short story can never be a best seller, because best sellers are not told in only thirty verses.

Because the modern author must transform a story into a commercial product, he would dedicate dozens of pages to explaining why Judah had dominion over Tamar, the law of levirate marriage, and the definition of an "anchored" wife. Descriptions of the scenery of the dusty tent camp where the characters lived would take up dozens more pages. Still more pages would describe every detail of the physical appearances of Tamar, Judah, and his three sons. Still more pages would describe the complex emotions underlying their deeds. The characters would talk to each other and to themselves for several hundred pages. And finally, of course, the description of the sexual act that led to Tamar's pregnancy would merit particularly intensive treatment. The high resolution of the sections I have outlined here would have added volume to the story, transforming it into a hefty tome. This would have enabled the reader to plunge into the depths of the story that took place thousands of years ago, and to feel as if the characters stood here and now in real life, sweaty and exciting, as if they were acting out their roles at this very moment.

The biblical authors worked in just the opposite manner. They knew nothing of the rest of the world, and did not write for it. They wrote for the people who walked alongside them, on the same clods of earth, for their neighbors who shared the same way of life and cultural milieu. The biblical authors relied on their readers' knowledge, and so they did not have to explain the law of levirate marriage, or why Tamar was not permitted to marry as she pleased – thus saving dozens of pages of descriptions and explanations. Their respect for the characters they wrote about prevented them from revealing their emotional world, and from writing pornographic descriptions, and this fact also significantly shortened the story. Finally, the biblical authors wrote short stories, not novels, because in their time, authors did not write books that took up hundreds of pages. Since they intended from the start to write short stories, they had to consider every word. Furthermore, they wrote on parchment made of animal skin, which was costly, and this was another reason why they kept the number of words to the absolute minimum.

When we explore the thirty verses that contain the story of Judah and Tamar, we find that they are no more than thirty subtitles. The story of the life and death of Er is comprised of only three subtitles. Er was born, got married, and died. Onan did the same: he was born, married Tamar according to the levirate law, and died for his sin. Each subtitle describes another chapter in the life of the character, and the rapid and precise progression from one subtitle to another creates a feeling of swift movement and passing time.

Another writing technique that is almost unnoticeable but very efficient is the rapid change of roles between the main characters. This creates the feeling that "a long time" has passed, but adds not one word to the story. In the first part of the story, Judah is the dominant figure. He stands at the head of his family, while the rest of the characters are frozen in place. Judah does not ask anyone's opinion, and needs no one's acquiescence. He is the only active figure. Tamar, the female heroine, is an obedient girl who follows orders like a marionette attached by a string to her handler.

Suddenly, in one verse, they switch roles. The original obedient Tamar who was tossed around like a rag doll from one groom to another, the girl who was forgotten in her father's house, disappears, and from within her shell bursts a daring, vibrant woman, whose strong will drives the rest of the plot.

In one verse, Tamar is transformed into a level-headed, manipulative woman who took her fate in her own hands and went out to seduce the man through which she wanted to conceive in order to save herself. Her rapid maturation and unexpected behavior creates a feeling of time passing rapidly. The fact that each verse describes a different drama creates a continued tension and the feeling that we are accompanying the characters over many years.

Today, every beginner student in a creative writing course learns that the first thing he must do is to write a title. Then he must write many lines underneath, to flesh out the story. If the biblical authors had sat in on one of these courses, they would have been thrown out in disgrace, because to them, the title was the entire story.

Chapter Fourteen

THE BOOK OF RUTH

The book that bears the name of Ruth the Moabite[31] is considered the most beautiful story in the Bible and one of the most exquisite pieces of world literature. Indeed, it is an incomparable pearl. At first glance, the book of Ruth seems no more than a simple love story between a wealthy man and a poor girl, similar to countless other stories of this genre. But we already know that the Bible does not tell simple stories. The book of Ruth is a complex work, like all the other stories we have studied. It is based on the social laws of the Bible, through which we can learn about daily life in the period to which it refers.

The story has three main characters: Ruth, the young widow from the land of Moab, from whom the book takes its name; Naomi, the elderly mother who lost her two sons, the first of which was Ruth's husband; and Boaz, the wealthy farmer who met Ruth after she was widowed, and gave her and her beloved mother-in-law his protection.

---

[31] Moab was a small kingdom located to the east of Israel more than three thousand years ago. Ruth is called a Moabite because she was born in Moab.

Like all the Bible stories, as in our own lives, the book of
Ruth contains great sorrow. It contains shaking hands that
dig the grave of a man who was alive one day, dead the next.
It contains separation and longing. But it also has something
else that is not so common: optimism, kindness, and love
that unites the three main characters. This story contains
triumph, growth, and a ray of light that illuminates a world
of mourning whose lights were all extinguished. Here we will
not find the white-hot iron that scorched Sarah's heart when
her arrogant slave woman spoke insolently to her. Here we
will not find the visceral hatred that Jacob felt toward Leah,
or Judah's arbitrary behavior. Ruth, Naomi, and Boaz will
take us to a place of softness. With caressing hands, they will
assuage their broken hearts, and perhaps comfort some of us
as well.

The book begins with the tale of a small family that lived
in Bethlehem, in the region of the tribe of Judah, near present-
day Jerusalem. Thus they originated with the tribe of Judah
and the town where David would eventually be born. The
head of the family was Elimelech, his wife was Naomi, and
their two sons were Mahlon ("illness") and Chilion ("annihilation"), whose names expressed their bitter end.[32]

During one of the drought years that plagued the region
of Judah, Elimelech fell into heavy debt and was forced to
mortgage his land. He and his family left their village and
went to a place called the Fields of Moab (in the modern
kingdom of Jordan). The family lived in Moab for ten years,
and during that time, Mahlon and Chilion married two local
women: Ruth and Orpah. Soon afterward, Elimelech died,
leaving Naomi a widow. Then, before the two young brides
conceived, Mahlon and Chilion also died, leaving behind
a family of three poor, isolated widows whose world had

---

[32] As we mentioned in chapter 11, these are literary names, not literal ones, which the
author chose in order to hint at their tragic deaths.

shattered. Shortly after this disaster, Naomi decided to return to her native village in Judah, where Elimelech's family lived. This was also the site of the family land, which had been mortgaged to a creditor whom the Bible does not name. Before Naomi could turn her back on the land where she had buried her husband and two sons, she had to decide the fate of her daughters-in-law. As was the custom in that time and place, the bride-price paid for Ruth and Orpah made them the property of the men who had married them. After Mahlon and Chilion died, ownership of the two young women passed to Naomi. Naomi could keep them in her possession, as Judah did with Tamar, or free them and allow them to go their separate ways. Because the heart that beat between her ribs was different from Judah's, she chose the second option:

> Then Naomi said to her two daughters-in-law, "Go, return, each of you to her mother's house. May the Lord deal kindly with you, as you have dealt kindly with the dead and with me. **May the Lord grant that you may find rest, each in the home of her husband.**" She kissed them, and they raised their voices and wept. (1:8–9)

Naomi's sad words sound like a statement of parting from loved ones. But they also had legal significance. In her speech, Naomi declared that she was dissolving the formal relationship between herself and her daughters-in-law. From that moment on, the familial and legal relationship between them ended, and the two young women were free to go their separate ways and remarry.

When Ruth and Orpah heard Naomi's speech, they did not break out in cries of joy at being freed from the bonds of the bride-price that had confined them. Rather, they broke out in bitter tears, as if they were little girls whose mother wanted to leave them behind – and perhaps they really were little girls. They did not thank Naomi for her generosity, nor did they go their separate ways. Instead, they refused to go out into the world without the kind woman who had been a mother to them. They begged Naomi to allow them to return with her to her native land. But Naomi was a mature, wise woman, and she refused to give in to their pleading. Naomi knew that if these young girls traveled the roads with her, the chances that they could remarry and rebuild their lives were very slight. She knew that if her daughters-in-law did not remarry and have children, their lives would have no hope and no future. Naomi knew that she could not secure the futures of the two young women who grasped the hem of her robe and refused to leave her. She valued their lives, and not the remainder of her own, and so she adamantly refused their begging and demanded that they return to their fathers' homes:

> But Naomi said, "Turn back, my daughters. Why should you come with me? Have I more sons in my womb who could become husbands to you? Turn back, my daughters, go, for I am too old to have a husband. Even if I were to say, 'There is hope for me,' and even if I were to have a husband tonight – and even bear sons – would you wait for them until they were grown up? Would you anchor yourselves for them, not to marry anyone else? No, my daughters! I am very embittered on account of you, for the hand of the Lord has gone forth against me." (1:11–13)

On occasion, we must stop in place to scent the perfume of the biblical writing, or else to express our annoyance at the fact that the authors who polished their story with a thin file shaved off details that might have shed light on the world of the biblical characters. So we will camp for a few moments under an elderly olive tree and listen to the sweet voice of this author, who bequeathed to us one of the most beautiful stories ever written.

In comparison to the stories we discussed earlier, the book of Ruth is characterized by long monologues. Naomi's speech is a superb lesson in rhetoric, for it demonstrates how a speaker can convince the listener to do something against his will.

The author divided the speech into two interrelated parts. In one part, Naomi describes her situation in sharp, realistic words; in the other, she encourages the two young women to leave her, using kind, convincing phrases. Naomi alternates between referring to herself and her daughters-in-law. The intertwining of the two sections creates a blend of bitter statements enveloped in sweet cajoling.

The opening sentence is delicate and gentle, and appeals to the hearts of the two young women: "Naomi said, 'Turn back, my daughters. Why should you come with me?" The use of the phrase "my daughters" emphasizes her love for her daughters-in-law and creates the feeling of a close relationship, like that between a mother and her daughters. After the subtle opening comes a raw, accusatory rhetorical question, highlighting her own brokenness: "Have I more sons in my womb who could become husbands to you?"

The author of these words lived in times when the law of levirate marriage applied. He and his readers knew that if Naomi had a son in her womb, he would become a groom for her daughters-in-law. Naomi made it clear that this was not the case. Again she pushed the young girls gently away: "Turn back, my daughters, go." When these words also fell on deaf ears, Naomi sharpened the message and described her situation even more outspokenly: "For I am too old to have a husband. Even if I were to say, 'There is hope for me,' and even if I were to have a husband tonight – and even bear sons." She then turned the spotlight back to her daughters-in-law and asked them: "Would you wait for them until they were grown up? Would you *anchor yourselves* for them, not to marry anyone else?"

Supposing, said Naomi, that I remarry tonight, and even conceive. Would you wait for this child, like two anchored women, until the baby who does not yet exist grows up and marries you according to the levirate law? An anchored woman, as we saw in the previous chapter, is a woman who has a husband, but whose marriage is not implemented. Because the woman is the property of her husband, or promised to him (if he or she has not yet reached marriage age), she cannot free herself from him, and thus she is an anchored woman.

Naomi's question raises a complex problem that Ruth and Orpah did not notice. As long as she did not free them from her ownership, they were anchored women in any case, just as Tamar was anchored by Judah. If Naomi had acquiesced to their request to stay with her, they would have continued to be anchored – and she did not agree to this. At the next bend in the road, Naomi again addressed herself rhetorically, and concluded her speech with biting words of persuasion: "No, my daughters, for I am very embittered on account of you, for the hand of the Lord has gone forth against me." When she finished speaking, the three women united in their shared mourning. They shed tears for the men who had died and left them to pick up the pieces of their lives. They wept for the friendship and love they felt for each other, which at that point was breaking apart. Finally, Orpah rose and went on her way, to meet her own fate.

At this point, Naomi, the matriarch who until now had played the lead, left center stage to make way for Ruth. Her measured words had fallen on the closed ears of her daughter-in-law, who dug her two heels into the ground, and like an obstinate girl refused with all her might to part from Naomi. The great love of this stubborn girl for her mother, perhaps the only mother she had ever known, touched the heart of the author, and he gave her the finest of gifts. One by one, he strung together on a fine thread the most exquisite words of love in the Bible. He placed this strand, shimmering with delicate pearls that have endured for thousands of years, around the neck of the sweet girl who refused to listen to any voice except the one within her own heart. Ruth said:

> *Do not entreat me to leave you*
> *To turn back from following you.*
> *For wherever you go, I will go;*
> *And wherever you lodge, I will lodge;*
> *Your people will be my people,*
> *And your God, my God.*
> *Where you die, I will die,*
> *And there I will be buried.*
> *Thus may the Lord do to me,*
> *And so may He continue,*
> *If anything but death separates me from you. (1:16–17)*

In Ruth's devotion to the isolated, elderly woman, she reveals her great kindness. With the fine thread Ruth wore around her neck, the fates of the two women became intertwined. They laced their fingers together firmly, and went on their way to the land of Canaan.

In the spring, at the beginning of the barley harvest, the two women came to Bethlehem and settled there.[33] Soon afterward, Ruth said to Naomi,

---

[33] Barley, like wheat, belongs to the cereal family and is a primary source of carbohydrates. Barley and wheat grow well in Israel because they require little water. Barley ripens in early spring, around April. Wheat, its nobler sister, follows about two months later. Bread made from barley is inferior in taste and quality to wheat bread, and thus in biblical times was considered "poor man's bread."

"Let me go out to the field and glean among the stalks of grain behind someone in whose eyes I shall find favor." She said to her, "Go, my daughter." So she went. She came and gleaned in the field behind the harvesters. (2:2)

One who is unfamiliar with the social laws of the Bible will certainly be surprised by this statement. How could a foreign woman think of entering the field of a stranger to gather grain? But Ruth's words are appropriate under ancient Israelite law.

The book of Deuteronomy lists four social classes that were considered society's weakest and poorest: the widow, the orphan, the foreigner, and the Levite. Widows and orphans had no husband or father to support and defend them. A foreigner had no extended family for mutual connections of support, and thus had no one to come to his assistance in times of need. The status of the Levites during the biblical period was particularly problematic, because they did not own their own land. According to the definition in Deuteronomy, Ruth and Naomi belonged to the weak layer of society. They were widows, and Ruth was also a foreigner in the land of Canaan.

The ancient lawmaker, God according to the Bible, was aware of the plight of the poor, and ensured that Israelite society would take responsibility for supporting them. One of the social laws he created concerns the "gleanings," "corner," and "forgotten produce" of the grain harvest (Lev. 23:22; Deut. 24:19–22; 26:12–13). The gleanings were the barley or wheat that accidentally fell from the harvester's hands. The corner was the edge of the field or orchard. Beginning from the time of planting, the produce that grew there was designated for the poor, and the owner was supposed to leave it untouched. The forgotten produce was that which was accidentally left behind. According to the principle that governed

the harvesters or pickers, they walked only in a forward direction. They did not go back in order to gather the ears of grain
that fell, or a bunch of grapes that was forgotten. Whatever
was left behind became the property of the poor.

Thus one spring day, Ruth went out to the area where the
poor gleaned and struggled over a few ears of grain that would
make the difference between hunger and famine.

The first days of spring in the land of Israel are temper-
ate and balmy. The fields, washed by the winter rain, are
still green, and the ground is soft and pleasant to the touch.
The burning summer sun, which in a few weeks will turn
the ground into a desolate field of clods, hard as rock, awaits
its turn patiently, while its mild spring sister warms the air
gently. On one of these sky-blue days, the guiding hand of
fate directed Ruth to the path leading to the field of Boaz, a
wealthy farmer and the third character in the book, who now
takes center stage. Toward noon, Boaz went out to the field,
where Ruth darted after the few stalks that remained behind.
Noticing her, he asked who she was:

> Boaz then said to his servant who was overseeing the
> harvester, "To whom does that young woman belong?"
> The servant who was overseeing the harvesters replied,
> "She is a Moabite girl, the one who returned with Naomi
> from the Fields of Moab; she had said, 'Please let me glean
> and gather among the sheaves behind the harvester.' So
> she came, and has stood since the morning until now; and
> this minute amount is all she was able to collect to take to
> her home." (2:5–7)[34]

---

[34] The accepted English translation of the last verse is quite different: "[Except for] her
resting a little in the hut." According to the original Hebrew, the servant actually informs Boaz that Ruth arrived in the field in the morning, and until that point, managed
to collect only a few sheaves. In Hebrew, as in English, many words have multiple
meanings, and we understand the meaning of a word through its context. In this case,
the translator has chosen a literal translation. But this choice of words does not fit the
rest of the story. Our translation above is based on the exact same words, but is fits the
meaning of the story.

Boaz, we will now reveal, was from Elimelech's family, and news of the disaster that had affected Naomi reached his ears. When he discovered the identity of the young woman gleaning in his field with the other poor, he warned the harvesters not to disturb or harm her. He then invited Ruth to return to glean in his fields in the coming days:

> Then Boaz said to Ruth, "Hear me well, **my daughter**. Do not go to glean in another field, and do not leave here, but stay close to my maidens. Keep your eyes on the field that they are harvesting and follow after them. Have I not ordered the servants not to touch you? Should you become thirsty, go to the jugs and drink from that which the servants have drawn."
>
> Then she fell on her face, bowing down to the ground, and said to him, "Why have I found favor in your eyes that you should take special note of me, though I am a foreigner?"
>
> Boaz replied and said to her, "I have been fully informed of all that you have done for your mother-in-law after the death of your husband – how you left your father and mother and the land of your birth and went to a people you had not known before. May the Lord reward your deed, and may your payment be full from the Lord, God of Israel, under Whose wings you have come to seek refuge."
>
> Then she said, "May I continue to find favor in your eyes, my lord, because you have comforted me, and because you have spoken to the heart of your maidservant, though I am not even [as worthy] as one of your maidservants."
> (2:8–13)

To the delight of those well versed in the hidden meanings of biblical writing, Boaz addressed Ruth using the familiar form "my daughter." The designation "my daughter" (or "my son") does not necessarily indicate family relationship between parents and children, but is understood as an expression of patronage and affection of a person of senior status toward a young person of lower status. In using the appellation "my daughters," Naomi expressed her love for her two daughters-in-law. Even after the formal relationship between them was dissolved, Naomi continued to call Ruth "my daughter" each time she addressed her. At this point, in the barley field, Boaz used this heartwarming designation toward Ruth, hinting that a ray of light might yet shine on the gloomy lives of the two women. During the afternoon break, Boaz again spoke to Ruth and invited her to sit beside him and eat with the harvesters of his field.

> At mealtime, Boaz said to her, "Come over here and partake of the bread, and dip your morsel in the vinegar." So she sat beside the harvesters. He handed her roasted grain, and she ate and was satisfied, and had some left over. Then she rose to glean. (2:14–15)

Roasted barley was a simple, carbohydrate-rich food that ancient harvesters might eat at noontime.[35] In his quiet, protective way, Boaz made sure that Ruth ate her fill of the roasted barley and even left some aside. He knew that she would take the remainder to Naomi to eat late that night (2:18). After the meal was finished, Boaz advanced his connection with the foreign young woman to the next stage:

> Boaz ordered his servants, saying, "Let her glean even among the sheaves; do not embarrass her. And even deliberately pull out some for her from the heaps and leave them for her to glean; do not rebuke her." So she gleaned in the field until evening, and she beat out what she had gleaned; it was about an **ephah** of barley. (2:15–17)

---

[35] Almost certainly, roasted barley was a main staple that nourished Sarah, Abraham, and Lot on their journey many years previously. Barley grew all along the route of their journey – except for the Sinai Desert, where nothing grows.

The section above has far-reaching legal significance. It shows that Boaz ignored the rules specified in the Pentateuch of gleanings, corners, and forgotten produce, which would have limited the foreign woman to the area of produce reserved for the underprivileged classes. From that point on, Ruth would not have to compete with the other poor for the last stalk that remained behind. Rather, she could take as much as she could carry from the field's produce, including the sheaves that had already been gathered and tied into heaps, and none of Boaz's workers would dare to embarrass or rebuke her. Once these limitations were removed from her, Ruth collected "an ephah of barley," or about twenty-four liters of dry grain (equivalent to one bushel), enough to nourish her and Naomi amply for several weeks.

Evening came, and Ruth returned to Naomi's tent. When the old woman saw the great quantity of barley her daughter-in-law had brought home, she asked for the identity of the generous field owner who had extended his patronage to her beloved daughter. When she heard the man's name, she declared:

> "Blessed is he to the Lord, Who has not failed in His kindness to the living or to the dead." Naomi then said to her, "The man is closely related to us; **he is one of our redeeming kinsmen**." (2:20)

Like every detail in the book of Ruth, Naomi's answer sheds light on one of the laws of the Bible. Naomi revealed to Ruth that her knight in shining armor was not a foreigner, but a relative of Elimelech and a "redeemer." This reference directs us to one of the most important family laws of the Bible – the law of the redeemer.

As we have said, in the biblical period, the family was the highest institution in Israelite society, and the patriarchal households in a group of extended families were responsible for each other. This is also the reason that all the social laws in the Bible are family laws, not national laws. The law of the redeemer stated that if one of the patriarchal households of the extended family became impoverished due to economic crisis, then his closest relative was obliged to redeem his household:

> *If the means of a sojourner who resides with you shall become sufficient, and your brother becomes impoverished with him, and he is sold...after he has been sold, he shall have a redemption; one of his brothers shall redeem him; either his uncle, or his cousin shall redeem him, or a relative from the family shall redeem him; or if his own means become sufficient, he shall be redeemed. (Lev. 25:47–49; see also 25:25, and Neh. 5)*

According to the order of redemption determined in Leviticus, the impoverished man's brother was the first to redeem him. If the man had no brother (or if the brother could not help), then his uncle must assist him. If he had no uncle, the obligation of redemption fell to his cousin; and if he had no cousin, the closest relative from the extended family had to assist him.[36] Naomi's reference to Boaz as redeemer reveals that the order of redemption in Elimelech's family passed through him. Furthermore, use of the term "redeemer" confirms what we said earlier: in one of the drought years, Elimelech had fallen into heavy debt, and in order to repay it, he had mortgaged his ancestral heritage to an unrelated creditor.[37] After Elimelech lost his land, he and his family had no place to live, and this is why they left their native village for the Fields

---

[36] The rules of redemption in the Bible also apply to "blood redemption": in case of murder or rape, one of the victim's relatives is responsible for executing the murderer or rapist (see chapter 4).

[37] The fact that Elimelech and his family were not themselves indentured (as the passage in Leviticus describes) reveals that mortgaging the land was enough for them to repay their debt.

of Moab. In order to redeem the land from the creditor and return it to the family's ownership, Elimelech's debt had to be repaid, and this was what Naomi meant when she referred to Boaz as "one of our redeeming kinsmen."

According to the text of the book of Ruth, the two women reached Bethlehem at the beginning of the barley harvest, about the middle of April. Throughout the three months of the harvest, Ruth went out to Boaz's fields, and the love that budded between them sprouted and matured together with the grain. After the harvest season ended, Naomi decided that it was time to reap another, final harvest. She said to Ruth:

> My daughter, shall I not seek rest for you, that it go well with you? Now Boaz, our relative, with whose maidens you have been, will be winnowing barley tonight on the threshing floor. Bathe and anoint yourself, don your finery, and go down to the threshing floor, but do not make yourself known to the man until he has finished eating and drinking. When he lies down, note the place where he lies, and go over, uncover his feet, and lie down. He will tell you what you are to do. (3:1–4)

The rhetorical question "Shall I not seek rest for you, that it go well with you?" echoes Naomi's exhortation to her two daughters-in-law on the day she freed them to return to their fathers' homes and rebuild their lives. Naomi was clear about the identity of the man who would give her daughter respite and security. She was also well aware that on that night, Boaz would be sleeping alone on the threshing floor, and that showers of silver stars shining in the skies would illuminate the dusty path leading to him. So, with careful words, the wise woman sent Ruth out on that bright path, to lie beside Boaz and curl up in his embrace. With this act and with the exact words that Naomi instructed Ruth to say, both women's futures lay in the balance. Well after sunset, Ruth left Naomi's tent:

> *In the middle of the night, the man was startled, and turned about – and behold, there was a woman lying at his feet.*
>
> *He said, "Who are you?"*
> *And she answered, "I am your handmaid, Ruth. Spread your robe over your handmaid, for you are a* **redeemer***."*
> *And he said, "You are blessed of the Lord, my daughter.... And now my daughter, do not fear; whatever you say, I will do for you; for all the men in the gate of my people know that you are a worthy woman.... Now while it is true that I am a redeemer, there is also another redeemer closer than I. Stay the night, then in the morning, if he will redeem you, fine. Let him redeem. But if he does not want to redeem you, then [I swear] that as the Lord lives, I will redeem you. Lie down until morning."*
> *So she lay at his feet until the morning, and she arose before one man could recognize another, for he said, "Let it not be known that the woman came to the threshing floor." (3:8–14)*

We have already noted that the Bible contains no descriptions of the art of love. The author ensured that the darkness of night and a long-forgotten sense of modesty would conceal the details of the couple's meeting. But he did record the conversation that took place between them on the bed of crushed grains that rustled with every movement. As we see, Ruth was careful to call Boaz "redeemer," and so we may conclude that the issue Naomi wished to settle was the redemption of Elimelech's property. On his part, Boaz continued to call Ruth "my daughter," revealing that his deep affection for her remained constant. We can also see that Boaz recognized the fact that the order of redemption passed through him, and that he himself understood the intention of the two women.

A problem arises in Boaz's next statements. His answer creates the impression that Ruth has asked him to redeem her, but he replies that she has a redeemer closer than he: "Now while it is true that I am a redeemer, there is also another redeemer closer than I. Stay the night, then in the morning, *if he will redeem you, fine. Let him redeem. But if he does not want to redeem you, then [I swear] that as the Lord lives, I will redeem you.* Lie down until morning."

Undoubtedly, a mistake has entered the text here, and it is corrupt. It is not possible that Boaz meant that another man would redeem Ruth, because this would have been in opposition to the story's intent. It is inconceivable that Boaz would agree that the young woman who lay in his arms on the rustling grains would fall into the hands of another man. Furthermore, from a legal point of view, Ruth's "redemption" was completely impossible. The law of redemption is a family law based on mutual responsibility among the patriarchal households that belonged to the same extended family. As we saw above, this law specifies a blood relationship between the redeemer and the redeemed. Ruth was not a relative of Boaz, nor of anyone else in the land of Canaan. She did not belong to any family framework that might offer her redemption or protection. Legally, Boaz could marry her, but not redeem her.

Ruth's isolation explains why she was so surprised when the wealthy farmer approached her and offered her his protection. It also explains why Boaz, recognizing her complete lack of defense, gave her his patronage, and warned his workers not to harm or rebuke her. Ruth's vulnerable state also explains why Boaz and Naomi did not want her to go gleaning in the fields of any other farmer. Certainly, Ruth's weakness gave Naomi no rest, and for this reason, she wanted Boaz to marry her beloved daughter. Naomi knew that if Boaz married Ruth she would become part of an extended family that would grant her protection and security. But Naomi hoped for something else as well: for Boaz to be the man who would redeem Elimelech's land – and this was his intention as well. Boaz's answer to Ruth reveals that he recognized that the order of redemption of the property passed through him, but that there was another redeemer for Elimelech's property who preceded him.

REDEMPTION AND LEVIRATE MARRIAGE

Before the sun rose, Boaz held a private ceremony – perhaps a distant echo of payment of the bride-price, or a kind of marriage proposal. Boaz asked Ruth to hold out her shawl, and placed several sheaves of barley into it, a gift to Naomi. The sheaves he placed inside the shawl contained all the answers that Naomi had hoped to hear, from the day Ruth first went out to glean in his field. Ruth said to Naomi:

> "He gave me these six measures of barley, for he said to me, 'Do not go empty-handed to your mother-in-law.'" Then [Naomi] said: "Sit, my daughter, until you know how the matter will turn out, for the man will not rest unless he settles the matter today." (3:17–18)

Naomi guessed correctly: when morning came, Boaz would go to the place of judgment at the city gate, where the elders gathered, and find a way to connect the redemption of the land with his marriage to Ruth – and reality surpassed her expectations. Boaz indeed went to the city gate and waited for the arrival of the man who preceded him in the order of redemption. (We do not know the name of this first redeemer, since the text refers to him only as "Anonymous.") At any rate, after the involved parties had gathered at the place of judgment, Boaz addressed Anonymous and revealed to him that Naomi was trying to "sell" (the text should read, "to redeem") Elimelech's land. Because Anonymous was the first redeemer, Boaz inquired whether he intended to perform the redemption:

> [Boaz] said to the redeemer, "The parcel of land that belonged to our brother, Elimelech, is being offered for sale by Naomi, who has returned from the Fields of Moab. I resolved to inform you of this: Buy it in the presence of those sitting here and in the presence of the elders of my people. If you are willing to redeem, then do so. But if it will not be redeemed, tell me, that I may know; for there is no one else to redeem it but you, and I am after you." And [Anonymous] said, "I am willing to redeem." (4:3–4)

When the first redeemer heard Boaz's speech, he immediately declared his willingness to redeem the land. Then Boaz, who had prepared himself in advance for this possibility, pulled a small rabbit out of his hat. To the surprise of all present, he added a new clause to the issue of the redemption, which he had not included in his first speech, turning on its head the legal matter for which they had gathered:

> Boaz said: "The day you buy the field from the hand of Naomi and from Ruth the Moabite, wife of the deceased, **you have bought it to perpetuate the name of the deceased on his inheritance.**" (4:5)

Until this moment, those present at the judgment thought that the topic under discussion was the redemption of Elimelech's mortgaged property. But at that point, Boaz connected the redemption of the land with the law of levirate marriage. In other words, Boaz tied together two completely unrelated laws, creating one intact issue that could not be divided.

To explain what he did:

The principle underlying the law of redemption says that the member of the family closest to the impoverished man should pay his debts and redeem his mortgaged land. The land that was redeemed returned to the ownership of the extended family to which it had always belonged, but it did not return to the ownership of the individual patriarchal household that had lost it. Rather, it became the property of the relative who redeemed it (if not, he would have no incentive to redeem it).

The law of levirate marriage was designed to uphold the deceased's family's right of ownership over their son's widow, and also to grant her the right to remarry and bear children. Furthermore, it was intended to preserve the deceased's right of inheritance. The deceased's brother married the widow, and their firstborn son was considered the son of the deceased. He thus became the inheritor of his official father's property and status.

Although these are two disparate laws designed to solve two different problems, Boaz wove them into one. He asked that Anonymous pay Elimelech's debt as obligated by the law of redemption, and marry Ruth through levirate marriage.

The combination of these two laws into one was a sneaky tactic. If the first redeemer had been tempted to follow Boaz's suggestion, he would have paid Elimelech's debt and married Ruth, but the land he had redeemed would not have become his. Under the law of levirate marriage, the land would return to Elimelech's family, because the son born to him and Ruth would be considered the son of Mahlon, Ruth's late husband:

> It shall be that the firstborn – if she can bear – shall succeed to the name of his dead brother, so that his name not be blotted out from Israel. (Deut. 25:6)

Boaz's legal scheme was unprecedented, and for this reason, he brought the issue to judgment. If the elders had protested against his intent, he would have had to retract his demand.

Here we must add another issue: from a legal standpoint, the law of redemption indeed applied to Anonymous, because he was Elimelech's closest living relative. But because he was not Mahlon's brother, the levirate law did not apply to him. The levirate law was designed to offer a solution for a child-less woman owned by her deceased's husband's family. But as we recall, Naomi had released her two daughters-in-law from the bonds of the bride-price, and therefore Ruth was free to remarry as she pleased. This means that implementation of the levirate law was unnecessary in the first place, and at any rate, Anonymous was not obligated under it. For this reason, the elders were not authorized to force him to perform levi-rate marriage with Ruth.

Anonymous, who was a clever man, refused to fall into the trap that Boaz set for him. He refused to pay Elimelech's debt and give up ownership of the land he redeemed to a son who would not be considered his. Undoubtedly, if he had insisted only on redeeming the land, without marrying Ruth, the law would have been decided in his favor. But apparently, he did not need the land, or else the atmosphere of the judg-ment favored Boaz, and so he decided to withdraw from the deal:

> The redeemer said, "I cannot redeem for myself, lest I imperil my own inheritance. Take over my redemption responsibility on yourself, for I am unable to redeem." Formerly this was done in Israel in cases of redemption and exchange transactions, to validate any matter: One would remove his shoe, and give it to the other. This was the process of ratification in Israel. So when the redeemer said to Boaz, "Buy for yourself," he drew off his shoe. (4:6–8)

The public ceremony of shoe removal by a woman as described in Deuteronomy was intended to humiliate an intractable brother-in-law and shame his family. In our case, however, only one component of the ceremony applied: Anonymous was the one to remove his shoe, thus symbolizing the ter-mination of any legal relationship between him and Ruth.

But he was not humiliated before the community. Ruth did not come to the place of judgment, and certainly did not spit in his face or rebuke him. The shameful title "house of the one whose shoe was removed" was not applied to Elimelech's relative. The judgment ended with Anonymous publicly declaring that he gave up the obligation of redemption, and then he peacefully went on his way. When the way was cleared for Boaz, he rose and declared before all present that he intended to fulfill what he had asked Anonymous to do:

> *Boaz said to the elders, and to all the people, "You are witness this day that I have bought all that was Elimelech's and all that was Chilion's and Mahlon's from the hand of Naomi. I have also acquired Ruth the Moabite, wife of Mahlon, as my wife,* **to perpetuate the name of the deceased on his inheritance, that the name of the deceased not be cut off from among his brethren, and from the gate of his place.** *You are witnesses today." (4:9–10)*

When the elders and villagers heard this festive declaration, they cheered in his honor and declared in unison:

> *Then all the people who were at the gate, and the elders, said, "[We are] witnesses! May the Lord make the woman who is coming into your house like Rachel and like Leah, both of whom built up the house of Israel. May you prosper in Ephrat and become renowned in Bethlehem; and may your house be like the house of Perez whom Tamar bore to Judah, though the offspring which the* LORD *will give you by this young woman." (4:11–13)*

Ruth and Boaz married, and the love story that sprouted and ripened with the grain ended for the best. The foreign woman who left her people and followed her heart to a strange land married a wealthy man who loved her deeply. Shortly after the wedding, Ruth gave birth to a son, thus ensuring her place

and status in Boaz's home. But the story did not yet reach its
final happy ending.

The connection of the law of redemption with the law of
levirate marriage had legal ramifications for Naomi as well,
and she also profited greatly. Boaz paid off Elimelech's debt
to the creditor and redeemed his mortgaged land – and the
redeemed land returned to Elimelech's household because he
married Ruth in levirate marriage. Obed, their son, was legally
considered Mahlon's firstborn and Naomi's grandson. Eventually, he would inherit the land that had been returned to his
"grandfather's" household – and this had great importance.

Almost certainly, Ruth was not Boaz's first wife, but
his last. If Boaz had other children through another wife (or
wives), each one of them preceded Obed in the order of inheritance in Boaz's household. The fact that formally, Obed was
considered Mahlon's son and Elimelech's grandson ensured
that he would not begin life empty-handed, but would inherit
the property of his legal father, which his biological father had
redeemed.

The final verse of the book of Ruth returns us to the
opening one. As we recall, before Naomi returned to the land
of Canaan, she freed her daughters-in-law from the bonds
of the bride-price and thus ended the formal ties between
them. Orpah returned to her father's home in the land of
Moab, and we can only hope that fate was kind to her and
that she also found a kind man like Boaz and rebuilt her life
at his side, as Noami wished for her. Simultaneously, Ruth's
devotion to Naomi's fate did not change the fact that the
legal-familial relationship between them ended on that very
day. But the formal relationship between the two women was
restored, because Obed was considered the firstborn son of
Mahlon, Naomi's son. Thus Boaz's act before the public that
gathered at the city gate had dual consequences: he redeemed
Elimelech's land, and he also gave Ruth a son who was legally

Naomi's grandson. Thus the connections that were untied at the beginning of the story were retied at the end:

> The women said to Naomi, "Blessed is the Lord Who has not left you without a redeemer today! May his name be famous in Israel. He will become your life restorer, to sustain your old age; for your daughter-in-law, who loves you, has borne him, and she is better to you than seven sons."
>
> Naomi took the child, and held it in her bosom, and she became his nurse. The neighborhood women gave him a name, saying, "**A son is born to Naomi**." They named him Obed; he was the father of Jesse, the father of David. (4:14–17)

Naomi clasped the infant in her embrace, and her deep sorrow was comforted.

THE BEAUTY OF THE BIBLICAL WRITING STYLE

The love story that developed under the bright blue skies of ancient Israel is like many other Cinderella stories. Like all of these, the book of Ruth describes a poor, lonely girl whose hardships end when a wealthy, kindhearted man falls in love with her and marries her. But our Ruth is not one of the dull, cookie-cutter Cinderellas created en masse on a production line. Certainly, the author of this book, who lived three thousand years ago, was not repeating a hackneyed, overused literary style. Instead, he created a new one. He wrote the first Cinderella story, the most beautiful of all. The book of Ruth is apparently the earliest and finest source of the writing form we know as the romance. But several important issues differentiate this story from every other standard Cinderella tale ever written.

The book of Ruth is considered a superlative work of literature, and is justly included among the most beautiful short stories ever written. The book is not just a charming love story, but like all the other family stories in the Bible, it is based on complex family laws, and has depth which cannot be found in any of the other Cinderella tales that crowd the shelves of bookstores.

One of the most exquisite and masterful elements is the integration of many biblical laws within the story, without the author stating any of them overtly. The reader who does not know the laws of the Bible reads a story that is lovely, but flat. But one who does know them reads a story with deep layers, much longer than the number of words it contains.

For example, Naomi made the speech freeing her daughters-in-law because of the law that bound a widow to her husband's family, even after his death. She asks a series of rhetorical questions: "Have I more sons in my womb who could become husbands to you? ...Would you wait for them until they were grown up? Would you anchor yourselves for them, not to marry anyone else?" (1:11–13). These multiple questions teach us that the levirate law was practiced in the period of authorship of this book. The reason why Naomi refused the request of her daughters-in-law to remain with her is clear only to the reader familiar with the levirate law and the lawmaker's opposition to anchored women.

Another example is Ruth gleaning in Boaz's field – this reveals her and Naomi's poverty, and that they had to base their sustenance on the social law of gleaning, corners, and forgotten produce. Boaz instructed his harvesters to allow Ruth to take as much as she could from the sheaves. The reader who is familiar with the laws of the Bible will recognize that in doing so, Boaz removed from Ruth the limitation of the poor to a designated area. Boaz repeatedly warned his harvesters not to harass Ruth, demonstrating the vulnerable situation of the foreign girl, who did not belong to any patriarchal household that would protect her. The quiet way in which Boaz gave his protection to the two women also shows the great importance of the extended family, in a period preceding national institutions that took responsibility for caring for the poor.

Ruth and Naomi refer to Boaz using the title "redeemer." This indicates that Elimelech's land was mortgaged to an unrelated creditor, and teaches us about the method of redeeming property in ancient Israel. Boaz used a clever legal tactic to connect the law of redemption and the levirate law. Only those who know these laws and the principles underlying them will understand this legal ploy. One who is well-versed in biblical law will realize that when Boaz took upon himself to fulfill both laws, he created an inheritor for Elimelech's family, and recreated the formal relationship between the two women who were like mother and daughter to each other.

Another literary element in this beautiful book is the relationship between Boaz and Naomi. Two of the three main characters in the story never meet, and never exchange a word. The relationship between Naomi and Boaz takes place through Ruth's movement from one to the other, which creates the feeling that they are actually conversing and coordinating their positions. The ability to create a conversation between two central characters that never meet is also evidence of the author's genius.

Another important point differentiates the book of Ruth from every other cookie-cutter Cinderella story. The Cinderella stories we know from childhood contain a classic triangle: the girl, the prince, and the witch who tries to harm Cinderella.

The girl symbolizes virginal, helpless good. She is always beautiful, pure, and phlegmatic. The witch, or the wicked stepmother, symbolizes the satanic element in human nature. She is almost always ugly, and always evil. She is jealous of Cinderella and tries to kill her; she makes her work like a slave and banishes her from her home. She tempts her to eat a poisoned apple, disguises herself in the form of a wolf, or pricks Cinderella's finger on an enchanted spindle. Because Cinderella is a weak figure who is powerless to help herself, she falls victim to the witch's plots. She scrubs floors, sews coats of nettles with her bare hands, or wanders from place to place in dirty, tattered clothing. Particularly gifted Cinderellas even manage to die for a while. Helpless Cinderella is the perfect victim, and her weakness is what opens the door for the prince – the strong, brave savior who represents the powers of light. The prince is attracted to spineless Cinderella's weakness, and endangers his life to save her. He battles against the evil and vanquishes it, then marries her, and they live happily ever after.

By contrast, the triangle in the book of Ruth is the antithesis of the Cinderella stories. Each one of the three main characters is kind and infuses the other two with his goodness and compassion. The characteristics of the three balance each other perfectly to form an equilateral triangle.

Our Ruth is not a weak, frail Cinderella. Although the author describes her as a young girl who still needs a mother, Ruth is stubborn. She knows what she wants and cannot be deflected from her goal. Her devotion to Naomi does not come from a position of submission, but rather from a position of love, assertiveness, and decisiveness. Ruth is the only female character in the Bible who is given the option of choosing her fate, and she chooses not to return to her father's home, but to go with Naomi and bear the burden of supporting them both.

Naomi represents the image of the good and loving matriarch. She is the direct opposite of the figure of the stepmother who tries to harm her stepdaughter. Naomi is a warm woman in whose lap Ruth can lay her head, close her eyes, and fall asleep after long day working in the field. A woman like Naomi would not hesitate to send her beloved daughter, on a night lit with sprays of silver shining stars, to the man she had chosen, if she had decided he was the best man for her.

Boaz, the male side of the triangle, is a true fairy-tale prince. Boaz did not save Ruth by banishing the wicked witch from her path, but by becoming the glue that reattached two ribs that had come apart. The expansive heart that beat in his breast was big enough to embrace the two women as if they were one entity.

In summary, the book of Ruth is a charming love story that any reader can enjoy on its surface level. But the reader who is aware of the legal foundation on which it stands reads a deeper narrative, based on the biblical system of social laws that were designed to aid the weak.

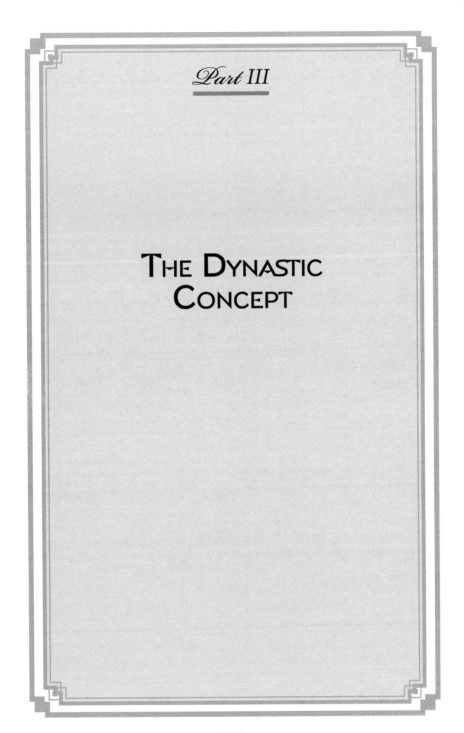

Part III

THE DYNASTIC CONCEPT

Chapter Fifteen

PASSING THE DYNASTIC TORCH

T he Bible recounts the stories of the forefathers and foremothers as separate short narratives. The connection between the different stories is tenuous, almost imperceptible. The Bible does not contain complex family sagas that branch into multiple subchapters. It does not include romances with complex plot twists. Although the family ties between the biblical characters are known to all, they are not described as a series of day-by-day, extended relationships. Rather, these relationships are momentary connections, like cars that stop beside each other at a red light, to continue the next minute on their separate routes.

Bible readers know that Abraham was the father of Isaac, who was born to him late in life, and so we intuitively think that their relationship was close. Perhaps it really was. But in Genesis, Abraham's story is separate from Isaac's, and they meet only once – in the story of the binding of Isaac. Isaac's narrative is separate from that of his sons, Jacob and Esau. The act of stealing the blessing allows us a peek into the complex relationships within his household.

The scanty detail the Bible offers about the characters' family relationships inspires us to ask: What importance do these connections have? Why is it important for us to know that Abraham was Isaac's father and Jacob's grandfather? Why do we need to know that Isaac, not Ishmael, was Abraham's successor? And that Jacob, not Esau, inherited Isaac's position?

We know that Abraham was a special person, because he made the journey from distant Ur to the land of Canaan. But what unique characteristics can we attribute to the credit of Isaac, Jacob, Judah, Boaz, and the others? What is so important about the stories of these simple nomadic shepherds and farmers?

The Bible, as we have noted, is a male work, and women have only a marginal place within it. Why, then, does it include the stories of the foremothers? None of them did anything special or unusual that might justify her inclusion in the holy book and the right to be remembered within it forever. Why did the authors of the Bible decide to record their stories? We have already noted that the family stories in Genesis were written in a very concise style, yet strangely, beside them we find long, involved genealogies that list names of people who play no role in the Bible stories.

In this chapter I address the question: What lay behind the choice of characters that were included in the Bible? Why are the family stories it relates so important? The same question applies to the genealogical list and the female characters of the Bible.

At first glance, the stories seem disparate, the connections between the names incidental. But from a bird's-eye view, the stories flow one into another, combining into a hidden, twisting river that traverses the expanses of time – from the beginning of creation until the end of history. At the first spring stands Adam, whom God created on the sixth day of

Creation. At the other end of the mighty river stands David, the legendary king of Israel. After David, the river continues to flow onward until the end of time, when a redeemer will arise, the Messiah of the house of David (Is. 11:1–10). From the height of a bird's flight, we find that the characters in the book of Genesis were not at all ordinary, everyday people, as their stories might indicate. Rather, they were chosen individuals. They were David's ancestors, and they represent central junctions in the flow of time, from the dawn of creation and throughout Israelite history to David, God's chosen king.

PROCESSION OF THE FOREFATHERS

The Bible mentions two dynastic lists. The first is in Genesis. The second introduces the book of Chronicles, and sprawls across nine long, exhausting chapters that only lovers of complex genealogies, like me, find fascinating. These genealogies have a shared introduction, which says that all humanity originates from the union of Adam and Eve, who were created by God. Both lists give the names of the forefathers who lived in the first generations after Creation. They then split into two directions with two different worldviews.

The list in Chronicles is like a family tree that begins from one trunk and grows multiple limbs that branch out into a broad fan. The intertwined branches – the names in the list – indicate the heads of major families in the Israelite tribes over many generations. Because this list has no particular message of importance for us, we will continue. If the list of forefathers in Chronicles is like an oak tree with many branches fanning outward from one trunk, the list of forefathers in Genesis forms a column. We may compare it to a train of cars attached to an engine that races along a straight track, from the first visible point on the horizon to the last – from the beginning of time until the end. According to this list, God chose the royal dynasty at the time of Creation. Ever since, as in a torch relay, each member of this dynasty passed the torch to one chosen son, until it reached David, Israel's greatest king.

In this chapter, we will trace the torch procession of the royal dynasty. We will find that it reflects a theological and ideological worldview – not necessarily a historical one. It is a secret, hidden march, and only from a bird's-eye view do we notice that it began in the time of Adam and Eve and came to light in the time of David, only to sink again into mystery. Ever since the time of David, and even at present, the dynastic torch procession continues secretly. It forges its path toward the last station, when the Messiah of the house of David will be revealed to all. The Messiah will redeem Israel and the other nations, and bring eternal peace:

> A staff will emerge from the stump of Jesse and a shoot will sprout from his roots. The spirit of the Lord will rest upon him – a spirit of wisdom and understanding, a spirit of counsel and strength, a spirit of knowledge and fear of the Lord. He will be imbued with a spirit of fear for the Lord; and will not need to judge by what his eyes see nor decide by what his ears hear. He will judge the destitute with righteousness, and decide with fairness for the humble of the earth. He will strike [the wicked of] the world with the rod of his mouth, and with the breath of his lips he will slay the wicked. Righteousness will be the girdle round his loins, and faith will be the girdle around his waist.... It shall be on that day that the descendant of Jesse who stands as a banner for the peoples, nations will seek him, and his resting-place will be glorious. (Is. 11:1–10)

Pursuit of the torch procession highlights two fascinating points that we will address in this chapter. First, God chose not only David's forefathers, but his foremothers as well. Second, characters who did not belong to David's dynasty rose momentarily to the stage of history, then disappeared after they fulfilled their roles.

Let's begin to trace the magnificent procession of the dynastic torch.

The book of Genesis recounts that after Adam and Eve were expelled from the Garden of Eden, they had two sons, Cain and Abel. Because Cain killed Abel, the dead brother's line ended and had no continuation. The dynasty of Cain, however, continued to develop. But because he was the first murderer in human history, paving the way for all murderers who followed him and who are still to come, he did not deserve to be one of David's forefathers. Like an evil plague, Cain's numerous descendants spread afar, implanting malignant growths in the heart of every religion and faith. The dynastic torch thus passed from Adam to his third son, Seth, born after Abel's death:

> *Adam knew his wife again, and she bore a son and named him Seth, because "God has provided me another child in place of Abel, for Cain had killed him." As for Seth, to him also a son was born, and he named him Enosh. Then to call in the name of the Lord became profaned. (Gen. 4:25–26)*

Seth's successor was Enosh, the successor of Enosh was Kenan, and then came Mahalalel. Each one of these ancestors had many sons and daughters, but the dynastic torch was passed through only one chosen son, in the column pattern described here:

> *This is the account of the descendants of Adam – on the day that God created Man, He made him in the likeness of God.... When Adam had lived one hundred and thirty years, he begot in his likeness and image, and he named him Seth. And the days of Adam after begetting Seth were eight hundred years, and he begot sons and daughters. All*

the days that Adam lived were nine hundred and thirty years; and he died.

Seth lived one hundred and five years and begot Enosh. And Seth lived eight hundred and seven years after begetting Enosh, and he begot sons and daughters. All the days of Seth were nine hundred and twelve years; and he died.

Enosh lived ninety years, and begot Kenan.... All the days of Enosh were nine hundred and five years; and he died. Kenan lived seventy years, and begot Mahalalel. And Kenan lived eight hundred and forty years after begetting Mahalalel, and he begot sons and daughters. All the days of Kenan were nine hundred and ten years; and he died. (Gen. 5:1–14)

This list reveals that the author was interested only in the son who inherited his father's position, not his brothers or sisters. After mentioning his name, the writer continued to the chosen son of the next generation, without adding any details about his life. Still, from time to time the author found reason to stop and explain important issues. For example, he recounted that in the time of Noah, humans corrupted their ways, and so God opened the windows of the heavens and burst the fountains of the great deep. The water that poured down from above and seeped up from below flooded the earth, purifying it from humanity's sins. The only righteous man in that generation was Noah. Due to his merit, God saved him and his sons from the flood. Noah's importance in the history of the dynasty is that he was one of David's ancestors. He passed the torch from the age of creation to the post-flood period.

Noah had three sons: Shem, Ham, and Japheth. God chose Shem, his eldest son, to follow him, and he passed the torch to his son Aram, an important figure. According to the biblical narrative, Aram was the ancestor of the Arameans, who lived in the region of Aram, in today's Syria and Turkey.

This region is the site of the village of Haran, to which Abraham and his family would eventually travel. Four important women would be born in the region of Aram: Rebecca, Leah, Rachel, and apparently Tamar as well. After Aram went to his last resting-place, many generations passed in which nothing worthy of mention happened. Generations came and went, and the torch passed from hand to hand until it reached Terah, father of Abraham, and here at a long last, we must give Terah the respect he deserves.

According to the order specified in Genesis, after the creation period, the dynastic torch traveled through the region of today's Iraq and Turkey. To get to the land of Canaan, the torch had to leave the region of the Tigris and Euphrates and go on another journey, a journey to a new land in which a red-haired young man, handsome and bright-eyed, would be born one day. A hidden voice that Terah did not hear or recognize somehow entered his head and instructed him to get up and walk toward this distant land – and so he got up and walked:[1]

> Terah took his son Abram; and Lot the son of Haran, his grandson; and his daughter-in-law Sarai, the wife of Abram his son; and they departed with them from Ur of the Chaldees to go to the land of Canaan, and they came as far as Haran and settled there. The days of Terah were two hundred and five years, and Terah died in Haran. (Gen. 11:31)

Terah carried the dynastic torch out of thriving, prosperous Ur. But since he died in Haran, he was not the one to complete the mission. The torch passed to Abraham, one of David's most important forefathers. Abraham grasped the torch in his right hand, and along with Sarah and Lot, carried it through hills and blinding plains for more than 1200 miles

---

[1] In chapter 2, we explored the economic, practical reasons that explain why the family left Ur. In this chapter, I address the theological explanations.

(1930 km), until he reached the land that God showed him
and planted the torch in its destined ground. Perhaps God
revealed Himself to Abraham in Haran because Terah died
before his time, and because He had appointed this chosen
son to complete the most tortuous part of the journey that
the torch had begun at the beginning of time. At any rate,
Abraham, God's faithful messenger, collected his few belongings, and went on his way without question, even though he
did not know why he had been commanded to do so. From
unfathomable heights, God kept His eyes on His faithful,
brave son, who like all the torch carriers was a simple man,
unaware that he was just one link in a divinely determined
historical process. Isaac, Abraham's successor, was the first
forefather born in the land of Canaan, and he passed the
torch to Jacob. Jacob passed the torch to his fourth son, Judah
– although three others preceded him in birth order. Judah
passed it to Perez, the son born to him through Tamar. In all
the generations after Perez, the torch continued its hidden
progress until it reached Boaz. When Obed, the son of Ruth
and Boaz, was born, the torch rose above ground for a moment
and revealed its light:

> Now these are the generations of Perez: Perez begot Hezron;
> and Hezron begot Ram, and Ram begot Amminadab; and
> Amminadab begot Nahshon, and Nahshon begot Salmah;
> and Salmah begot Boaz, and Boaz begot Obed; **and Obed
> begot Jesse, and Jesse begot David.** (Ruth 4:18–22; 4:17)

"And Obed begot Jesse, and Jesse begot David" – the torch
procession that had begun its journey at the dawn of time
finally reached its destination.

Only when we view the list of forefathers from above do
we realize that the Bible tells the story of one family, one
dynasty. All the other dynasties that arose in Israel disappeared as if they had never existed. Every character that was

not one of David's ancestors appeared momentarily on the stage of history, then vanished after playing his role. His descendants were swallowed in the tangled branches of the Chronicles genealogical tree, and became part of the anonymous community of Israel.

Let us examine this assertion.

Moses was a descendant of the tribe of Levi, which was named after Jacob's third son. Undoubtedly, Moses was one of the outstanding leaders of biblical times. Many argue that he was Israel's greatest leader, even greater than David. God chose him to take His people out of Egypt and bring them to the land of Canaan. At the climactic moment when Israel became a nation, Moses went up to the mountain of God and received the Torah.[2] Moses was the only man who stayed with God for forty days and forty nights, and the only one who saw something of God's hidden presence (Num. 12:6–8; Ex. 33:17–23). Yet although we cannot overestimate his special status, Moses was not chosen to be one of David's ancient ancestors, and his line has no continuation. His two sons, Gershom and Eliezer, did not succeed him in the leadership position, and neither of them played any significant role. Almost certainly, Joshua, the judges, and the prophets also had sons and grandsons, but their descendants did not take over their positions, and the Bible does not tell us what happened to them.

The tradition regarding Aaron, Moses' older brother, somewhat complicates things. The book of Exodus relates that God gave Aaron and his sons the priesthood for eternity (Ex. 28 onward, and this is also the main concept in Leviticus). The book of I Chronicles says that Aaron began a dynasty of high priests (5:29–41). But when we look for

---

[2] According to tradition, Moses received the Five Books of Moses, or the Pentateuch.

support for this in the other parts of the Bible, we meet with failure.

According to Exodus, Moses wanted to avoid the mission God gave him. He excused himself, arguing that he was "heavy of speech," and so Aaron was sent to speak for him and serve as his mouthpiece (Ex. 4:10–16). But despite his modesty, Moses was perfectly able to speak for himself, and at no point did Aaron speak in his stead. Exodus and Numbers state that God spoke to Moses hundreds of times, while He spoke to Aaron only a few times. Both books describe Moses as a dominant figure who acted almost alone; at most, Aaron is described as his second. Furthermore, those who read Leviticus closely will discover that God never revealed Himself to the priests, who were the sons of the tribe of Levi and Aaron's descendants. To expand further on this point, we note that while God never appeared to the priests and never talked to them, He did appear to the prophets, who operated outside the Temple and none of them began a dynasty that bore his name.

Aaron's dynasty is not mentioned in the books of Joshua or Samuel, which are named after leaders who were not members of the tribe of Levi, but rather of Ephraim. Aaron's dynasty is not mentioned in Judges or in Kings. The books of Prophets also avoid this family (Ezekiel was from a priestly family, but God appeared to him in his role as a prophet, not as a priest). Thus, although Exodus and Leviticus ascribe great importance to the dynasty of Aaron, we find that it never played a significant role, not in Moses' time, and not afterwards.

I believe that the reason why the Bible follows only one leading dynasty and ignores the others is both historical and theological. Researchers assert that most of the books of the Bible were written by authors from the tribe of Judah, which was David's tribe. Naturally, the Judaic writers recorded the foundation story of their own tribe, their own king. This assumption explains the theology that underlies the dynastic torch procession, whose entire goal is to prove that the royal family was designated by God during the creation process. God chose the family of kings that descended from the tribe of Judah. It was to this family, and no other, that God gave the monarchy for all time (II Sam. chapter 7).

The torch procession reveals another issue of equal importance. The royal dynasty, which began at the beginning of time and to which the forefathers of Genesis belonged, still continues today. It leads to the end of time, when the Davidic Messiah will arise to redeem Israel and the entire world.

The concept of the Messiah as a descendant of David is an underlying principle in Christian messianic thought, which developed its theology as a continuation of the Old Testament. In the Christian view, the torch procession ended when it reached Jesus, the messiah, who was a descendant of the Davidic dynasty (Matt. 1:1–17; Luke 3:23–27; the New Testament mentions dozens of times that Jesus descended from the dynasty of David). However, the messianic concepts of Judaism and Christianity differ on one central issue. According to the New Testament, Jesus was born, lived, and died, then was resurrected and rose to heaven – and there he sits beside God, until the day when he will return to live among human beings. By contrast, Jewish tradition holds that the torch still continues its hidden journey toward the future redeemer, the unknown descendant of the greatest king Israel ever knew.

BIBLICAL LIFESPANS
Our journey in the footsteps of the biblical characters has reached the point where we must stop in our path, as is our habit, to explain an issue that we have encountered, for although it may seem tangential, it is in fact important for

our purposes. This is the moment to set down our packs underneath an ancient fig tree, lie under its shade, enjoy its sweet fruit, and explain the lengthy lives of the forefathers of Genesis.

According to the genealogical list in Genesis, the ancient forefathers lived eight or nine hundred years, even longer. The "young" ones who died before their time only lived to celebrate their six hundredth birthday. Because we know that in the ancient world, men lived an average of thirty-five years (according to the highest estimates), the hundreds of years recorded in Genesis give rise to a healthy measure of ridicule. But alongside the scoffers, others have tried to offer a logical explanation for the tremendous lifespans. The most common explanation is that in the ancient world, the year was calculated using a different method than today. Another explanation is that the authors of the Bible added an additional zero to the real age, so that a person who lived for eighty years was recorded as living eight hundred years. These solutions are creative, but incorrect.

People in the ancient world worked the land, and farmers always knew that a year contained 365.25 days. Even a farmer who did not know how to write his name could count the number of days in the agricultural season. He knew when he had to sow the fields, and how many times the sun would rise and set until harvest day arrived. One year in the life of a human being has always been identical in length to an agricultural year, which is calculated according to the solar calendar. Thus we have no reason to assume that in the time of the ancient forefathers, the year suddenly shortened, then gradually returned to its usual length. Furthermore, we have detailed calendars from ancient peoples who lived in Mesopotamia and Egypt thousands of years before the biblical period, as well as ancient calendars discovered in South America. These calendars reveal that ancient peoples had all the mathematical knowledge necessary in order to make exact calculations of the length of the year.[3] We can reasonably assume that educated writers such as those who authored the Bible were well aware of the number of days in a year. We cannot logically argue that they gave the forefathers such long lifespans because they lacked the knowledge held by simple farmers, who would mark in the ground with a small stick the days passed from sowing until harvest. We also cannot reasonably suppose that they added a zero to the real age, either unintentionally or through lack of knowledge.

In my opinion, the forefathers' protracted lifespans were not intended as exact measures of years, but to account for the time that passed from the time of Adam until Abraham, when biblical history began to stabilize. I think that each one of the forefathers that the Bible mentions by name is a collective name for multiple torchbearers, whose individual names the author did not feel the need to mention. Every forefather who lived eight or nine hundred years represents a period in which nothing much worthy of mention happened, except for the fact that the dynastic torch passed from generation to generation. Evidence of this is found when the torch reaches the time of Terah and Abraham. After them, the forefathers' lifespans are significantly shorter and gradually become more moderate. The Bible says that Terah died when he was "only" two hundred and five years old. Abraham died at the "ripe old age" of one hundred and seventy five (Gen. 25:7–8). Moses died at one hundred and twenty (Deut. 34:7); Joshua at one hundred and ten (Josh. 24:29); and the priest Eli at ninety-eight (I Sam. 4:16). The Bible does not relate David's age at death, but implies that he died of old age and emotional

---

[3] The Hebrew calendar, which Jews continue to follow today, is identical to the Babylonian calendar. The Gregorian calendar, which the Christian world follows, is an almost exact copy of the calendar used in Egypt six thousand years ago.

collapse at age seventy – a realistic, acceptable age (II Sam. 5:4; 19:32–38; Ps. 90:10).

PROCESSION OF THE FOREMOTHERS

Following the dynastic torch reveals that God chose not only David's male ancestors, but the female ones as well. At five important junctions, the threat arose that a successor born to an undeserving woman would divert the torch from its path. At these five junctions, five chosen women arose and ensured that their son would succeed his father and continue the procession toward the goal determined at the dawn of time. Possibly this is why the stories of their lives were included in the Bible. Like the forefathers, the foremothers did not know that God had chosen them to play a role in His historical plan. They did not know that their hands also grasped the torch of hidden light, and that God had placed them at the sides of the track to ensure the procession would continue on its path unhindered. Without knowing why, they stood guard and fulfilled the important role God designated for them.

The first foremother was Eve. From our point of view, a woman created by God's own hands is certainly worthy of being David's ancient ancestress, and thus Eve stands beside Adam at the first post of the dynasty. Later in time, she would be joined by Sarah, Rebecca, Leah, Tamar, and Ruth, whom we praised in the previous chapters and whom we will continue to extol.

SARAH

Sarah was Abraham's half-sister and his blood relative, as we read, "Moreover, she is indeed my sister, my father's daughter, though not my mother's daughter; and she became my wife" (Gen. 20:12). Sarah walked with Abraham on the entire journey from Ur to the land of Canaan, and stood beside him throughout all his trials. In theory, she should have been aware that God had destined her to be the mother of the next torchbearer, since He says so outright:

And God said to Abraham, "As for Sarai your wife…I will bless her; indeed I will give you a son through her; I will bless her and she shall give rise to nations; kings of peoples will rise from her." (Gen. 17:15–16)

God apparently appreciated this as a good jest. The celebratory promise that she would give rise to kings sounds like a cruel joke at the expense of the most well-known barren woman in the history of the Western world. After Sarah's barrenness became a synonym for humiliation and shame, she took desperate measures and gave her Egyptian slave woman to Abraham as a wife. Sarah hoped to be built up through Ishmael, to strengthen her shaky position in Abraham's household. But in reality, she strengthened Hagar's position and created a competitor for Isaac, who was the dynastic torchbearer chosen to succeed Abraham.

The view that David's forefathers and foremothers were chosen by God does not allow for an Egyptian, daughter of slaves, to become a mother of the royal dynasty. Clearly, the mother of the Davidic dynasty had to be withered, long-suffering Sarah, who had walked thousands of miles in order to carry the torch out of Ur to the land of Canaan. But Sarah was exhausted and desperate, the target of mockery. She knew nothing of the torch, and did not know that God, conductor of the historic train, had chosen her to stand beside Abraham at the most important junction of the journey. Eventually, God "visited" her, and she conceived and gave birth to Isaac, and so the promise made to her so many years earlier was fulfilled. But at that point, Isaac had a competitor, and Sarah had to correct the distortion she had caused. She had to remove Ishmael from Isaac's path, and ensure that on the day the torch passed from hand to hand, the young son dozing in her arms would be the one to step onto the racetrack. As soon as Ishmael and his mother were banished from Abraham's household, the threat to Isaac was removed. Sarah fulfilled her historic mission and ensured that the torch would reach the next station safely. When she passed away, Rebecca, the next guardian of the torch, took her place at the side of the track.

Rebecca

The viewpoint that God chose David's foremothers means they cannot be slave women or the daughters of any of the peoples that God forbade Israelites from marrying. This explains why Abraham sent his servant Eliezer to Haran to find a bride for Isaac from his brother's family, and why he so strongly objected to Isaac leaving the land of Canaan and marrying a Canaanite woman:

> Now Abraham was old, well on in years.... Abraham said to his servant...: "Place now your hand under my thigh. And I will have you swear by the Lord, God of heaven and God of earth, that you not take a wife for my son from the daughters of the Canaanites, among whom I dwell. Rather, to my land and to my kindred shall you go and take a wife for my son, for Isaac."
>
> The servant said to him: "Perhaps the woman shall not wish to follow me to this land; shall I take your son back to the land from which you departed?"
>
> Abraham answered him, "Beware not to return my son to there.... [The Lord] will send His angel before you, and you will take a wife for my son from there. But if the woman will not wish to follow you, you shall then be absolved of this oath of mine. However, do not return my son to there." (Gen. 24:1–7)

The faithful servant went on his master's mission to Haran, to the home of Nahor, Abraham's brother, to find an appropriate bride for Isaac. When Eliezer arrived in Haran, he decided on a sign for himself: the young woman who would give water to him and his camels would be the bride God intended for Isaac. No sooner had the servant determined this sign, when Rebecca came out to meet him: "And it was when he had not yet finished speaking that suddenly Rebecca came out – *she who had been born to Bethuel, son of Milcah, wife of Nahor, brother of Abraham*" (Gen. 24:15). Chapter 24 emphasizes twice more that Rebecca was Nahor's granddaughter, and that her grandmother was Milcah, Nahor's niece whom he married. The connection of Rebecca with Abraham and Sarah, leading players in the torch dynasty, confirms that the lineage of the foremothers of the monarchy was highly important.

The Bible recounts that in Rebecca's first years of marriage, she had difficulty conceiving. After Isaac poured out his pleas to God, Rebecca finally conceived twins, who tussled in her womb. Rebecca did not understand the agitation inside her, and asked God to explain it.

God, we must admit, was hardly enthusiastic about speaking with the wingless creatures He had created in His image, even less so with women. In the biblical period, a direct answer from God was considered a special sign of grace, even more so when He took the trouble to speak to a woman. Apparently, then, if God made an exception to His usual silence and bothered to answer Rebecca, this was a sign that He ascribed great importance to her question. God revealed to Rebecca that in her womb she bore twins who would eventually separate from each other and become the ancestors of two nations:

And the Lord said to her: "*Two nations are in your womb; two regimes from your insides shall be separated; the might shall pass from one regime to the other, and the elder shall serve the younger." (Gen. 25:22–23)*

Rebecca did not understand God's answer, but when the twins were born, Isaac developed a preference for Esau, the firstborn, while she favored Jacob but never knew why.

Years passed, the boys grew up, and their parents aged, while Rebecca continued to stand guard.

Isaac became blind, and Rebecca continued to stand guard.

One day, the alarm system God had buried inside her went off, and she went on high alert. Rebecca heard her elderly husband ask Esau to go out hunting and prepare delicious foods for him. After he ate, he would bless Esau and give him the status of firstborn:

> *And it came to pass, when Isaac had become old, and his eyes dimmed from seeing, that he summoned Esau, his older son, and said to him, "My son." And he said to him, "Here I am." And he said, "See, now, I have aged; I know not the day of my death. Now sharpen, if you please, your gear – your sword and your bow – and go out to the field and hunt game for me. Then make me delicacies such as I love and bring them to me and I will eat, so that my soul may bless you before I die."*
>
> *Now Rebecca was listening as Isaac spoke to Esau his son; and Esau went to the field to hunt game to bring."* (Gen. 27:1–8)

When Rebecca heard this, she rose to fulfill a role of which she was unaware, but for which God had chosen her. She and Jacob deceived an old, blind man – her husband, his father. Her elder son, his twin brother. But the dynastic torch passed to the chosen son, avoiding the danger that it would fall into the hands of the incorrect successor.

In chapter 10, we gave many examples to show that the author of Genesis did not give Jacob even one positive quality, nor say one word against Esau – but still, Jacob, not Esau, was the one chosen to carry the torch.

Why? What defect did Esau have that made him undeserving of joining his ancestral torchbearers? Esau was the firstborn son of the senior wife, and logic would dictate that he was his father's natural successor, as was the custom in the ancient world and as Isaac had indeed planned.

The answer is found within the text itself: Esau was disqualified from continuing the dynasty because he married three Hittite women (36:1–3; 26:34). The Hittites were one of the seven ethnic groups given the general name "Canaanites," whom the Israelites were forbidden to marry. Esau's fourth wife was the daughter of Ishmael, who was the son of an Egyptian slave, and who married an Egyptian woman (28:8–9).

Esau was not the only biblical character who married women from the forbidden nations, but he was the son of the chosen family, and this was enough to prohibit him from taking his father's position and becoming one of David's ancestors. Indeed, the Bible takes an exceptionally disparaging attitude toward Esau's Hittite wives (Gen. 26:34–35; 27:46), but remains indifferent toward other characters who also took foreign wives. For example, the Bible makes no objection to the fact that Abraham married and had a son through an Egyptian woman, since her son was not designated to be one of David's forefathers. Moses and Joseph both married and had children with Egyptian women, and the Bible finds no fault with their marriages either, because neither was meant to join the dynasty of forefathers. But where the royal family is concerned, the Bible's attitude changes from one extreme to another. We can assume that Esau's marriages to forbidden women disqualified him from participating in the torch procession. Thus, in order to ensure that no Canaanite woman would push her son into the royal dynasty, Jacob had to take the blessing away from Esau. This theft, carried out with Rebecca's full support, forced Jacob to flee to Haran, to his mother's family, where the third royal foremother waited: Leah.

Leah, not Rachel.

LEAH AND RACHEL

For almost four thousand years, we have been telling the great love story of Jacob and Rachel. For almost four thousand years, we have been mourning the death of the young mother and feeling the pain of her parting from the two young children who were left motherless. For almost four thousand years, we have identified with Jacob's bitter disappointment when he discovered that Leah had reaped the fruits of his tremendous effort to marry her beautiful sister. Because we have studied the family stories as separate units, attaching no particular significance to the connection between them, we have not noticed that each one of the characters described in Genesis is related to the torch procession we are following here.

We have repudiated Laban, who hid Leah in Rachel's bridal bed, yet we have failed to notice that God chose Leah to be David's foremother. Just as Rebecca had the responsibility to ensure that Jacob would receive his father's blessing, Laban had to make sure that Leah would marry Jacob first, in exchange for the bride-price he received for Rachel.

The author does not tell us what was defective about Leah's eyes, or what he meant when he described her eyes as "tender." No matter what her disability was, Leah was not eligible for a bride-price or to marry at the status of a senior wife. Rather, she was supposed to have married as a concubine. But if Leah had been given to Jacob at concubine status, then Rachel would have been his only senior wife. If that had been the case, the status of Joseph and Benjamin, born to her after long years of barrenness, would have been higher than that of Judah, whom God chose to be the forefather of David. Just as the theology of the Bible does not permit David's foremothers to be Egyptian or Canaanite, it does not allow them to be slave women or concubines. In order for the torch dynasty to pass from Jacob to Judah, his mother had to marry at the status of a senior wife, even if this came at the expense of Rachel's bride-price.

From a theological viewpoint, Jacob's love for Rachel was mistaken, and blurred the picture before him. All the evidence that the book of Genesis has given us shows that God chose Leah, and that Jacob's love for the wrong woman led to her downfall. We need only recall that Leah was the mother of Judah, forefather of the royal dynasty, and of Levi, founding father of the priestly dynasty, in order to decide which of the sisters was chosen by God. But there is additional evidence that supports our contention.

In chapter 11, we noted the role of names in the story of Jacob's family members. We asked how it was possible that the name Laban, whose root means "white," symbol of truth and honesty, was given to a cheater. But Laban actually behaved correctly. The night Laban plied Jacob with wine and put Leah in his wedding bed, he loyally fulfilled the momentous role that God had given him. Thanks to Laban, Jacob married the mother of both the royal and the priestly dynasties, at the status of senior wife, and so his name is appropriate for him.

Since God saw that Jacob loved Rachel and hated the woman whom He had destined for him, He opened Leah's womb and prevented Rachel from bearing. The opening of one sister's womb and closing of the other's was necessary because God suspected that Jacob would avoid the woman he hated, forcing her to remain childless. Due to this doubt,

God delayed Rachel's pregnancies until Leah's seven children were born.

Here is additional proof:

For some unknown reason, the author of Genesis chose to sully Rachel's name slightly, adding a pinch of disgrace to her cup of misery. According to the text, when Jacob's family fled Haran and traveled toward Canaan, Laban pursued them. When he caught up with them, he blamed Jacob for stealing his household idols. But Jacob was not the one who stole Laban's idols – it was Rachel (31:19–35).

Another proof:

After Sarah died, Abraham purchased a family burial cave in Hebron – the cave of Machpelah (Gen. 23). Abraham buried Sarah in this burial cave, and he was also buried there. Later, Isaac and Rebecca were buried there, as well as Leah and Jacob.

Leah, not Rachel.

Rachel died toward the end of the journey from Haran to Canaan, near Efrat (near Jerusalem). Jacob buried his beloved wife on the side of the road, and continued his journey along with his entire family. Those unacquainted with the landscape of Israel might imagine that Rachel's burial place is distant from the cave of Machpelah in Hebron. But in truth, the distance between the two burial sites is only 14 miles (23 km). If Rachel's proper resting-place had been in the burial cave of the former torchbearers, Jacob might easily have buried her alongside them, instead of on the side of the road.

At a later point, Jacob and his family joined Joseph, who was alive in Egypt. When Jacob sensed his last day approaching, he called his sons to him, and made them swear that they would bring him to burial in the cave of Machpelah in Hebron. Jacob's deathbed request was highly significant: he asked to be buried not beside Rachel, but beside Leah, David's foremother (Gen. 49:29–33; 50:13).

In order to bury Jacob in the cave along with the previous dynastic torchbearers, his sons had to carry his bones from Egypt and travel hundreds of miles. To bury Rachel in the family burial cave, Jacob would have had to walk for only one day – yet he did not bother to make the effort.

The struggle between the two sisters continued secretly even without them, and reached its final resolution hundreds of years after their deaths, during the time of Saul and David. Saul was from the tribe of Benjamin, named after Rachel's youngest son. Saul, the first king of Israel, was a respected, honest king, and undoubtedly the most admirable descendant of Rachel, his ancient foremother. The man who led to his downfall was none other than the most admired descendant of Leah. This was the man who represented the highlight of the torch dynasty that began in the dawn of time, and to whose hands it will return at the end of days – David.

TAMAR

The fourth guardian of the torch was Tamar. This time as well, the woman God chose to be one of the foremothers of the monarchy was unloved and undesired by any man. In Tamar's time, the torch procession was blocked, but thanks to her wisdom and courage, the path was cleared for the following generations.

Judah, father of the eponymous tribe, inherited the dynastic torch from his father, Jacob. For some inexplicable reason, he did not hear the inner voice that instructed the former torchbearers not to marry women from among the peoples forbidden to Israel. Judah married the daughter of Shua the Canaanite, and he had three sons through her (Gen. 38). The unavoidable result of their marriage was that Judah had three sons, but no successor. Not one of the three sons of the Canaanite woman was worthy of joining the procession of forefathers. Thus Judah had to add a new branch to his family and have another son, this time with an appropriate woman.

The Bible does not recount who Tamar was or on what merit she was chosen to be the mother of the kingly dynasty. It does not specify the unique characteristic possessed by this excellent woman, whose character and strength went unnoticed by everyone other than God.

In order to offer an explanation for the choice of this special woman, we must again return to the book of Jubilees, which we cited when we examined the story from a sociological perspective (chapter 13). When the author of Jubilees repeated the story of Judah and Tamar in his book, he added one important detail. Er hated Tamar because unlike his mother, she was not from Canaan but from Aram (Jubilees 41:1–3) – and this is our missing link.

In the land of Israel in the first centuries BCE, it was an accepted tradition that Tamar was from Aram, the native region of Rebecca, Leah, and Rachel, Sarah's relatives. A text from the late second century BCE, entitled *Testament of Judah*, states this clearly:

> And after these things, my son Er took to wife **Tamar, from Mesopotamia, a daughter of Aram**. Now Er was wicked, and he was in need concerning Tamar, **because she was not of the land of Canaan**. And on the third night an angel of the Lord smote him. And he had not known her according to the evil craftiness of his mother, for he did not wish to have children by her. In the days of the wedding-feast I gave Onan to her in marriage; and he also in wickedness knew her not, though he spent with her a year. And when I threatened him he went in unto her, but he spilled the seed on the ground, according to the command of his mother, and he also died through the wickedness. (10:1–5)[4]

---

[4] R.H. Charles, ed., "Testament of Judah," in *The Apocrypha and Pseudepigrapha of the Old Testament* (Oxford, 1913).

According to the genealogy in Genesis (10:22), and the tradition known to the author of the text above, Aram was the name of one of the torchbearers (as well as a region). The tradition that Tamar was a daughter of Aram is not mentioned in Genesis. But as we have already mentioned several times, researchers argue that different versions of the same story reached the editors of the Bible. These versions were preserved for hundreds of years by various groups that lived in the ancient land of Israel. Possibly, the tradition of Tamar's Aramean origin was common, but for some unknown reason, it did not enter the text of Genesis. Another possibility is that this tradition was included in Genesis, but somehow lost in the long chain of transmission. However, we have no way of determining whether at one time, this tradition was included in the "original" text of Genesis. Still, it answers several major questions that Genesis raises, and so possibly, this tradition did in fact belong to it.

The assumption that God chose Tamar, daughter of Aram, as the mother of the monarchy sealed the fates of her two husbands. It would be unacceptable for a son of a Canaanite woman to have a child with one of the chosen foremothers. This assumption also explains the author's meaning in his statement, "Onan knew that the seed would not be his" (38:9) – Onan was right, the woman he married was truly not meant for him. In addition, if Judah had fulfilled his promise to Tamar and permitted Shelah, his third son, to marry her – God would have caused Shelah to die as well. Judah's fear explains why he went back on his promise, and did not allow Shelah to marry her according to the levirate law:

> Then Judah said to Tamar, his daughter-in-law, "Remain a widow in your father's house until my son Shelah grows up" – for he thought, "**Lest he also die like his brothers**."

> *So Tamar went and lived in her father's house. (Gen.*
> *38:11)*

The argument that Judah did not have a son to succeed him,
and thus he had to have a son through Tamar, explains why
he did not remove the bonds of the bride-price that tied her to
him. According to the theological conception that underlies
the torch procession, Judah was the only man of his generation who could have a child with Tamar, and thus he could
not free her from her "anchored" status and permit her to go
free, remarry, and have a child with another man. Like Judah,
Tamar also could not conceive through a man who was not a
torchbearer, for she was a chosen woman. This data implies
that in order for the torch to proceed to the next generation,
Tamar had to burst through the barrier that Judah created
when he had his three sons through the Canaanite woman.
Tamar thus hid her face with many veils and went out to wait
for him at the side of the road. As a result of this daring act,
she gave birth to twin sons, Perez and Zerah. When Perez
grew up, he took the dynastic torch from his father and carried it securely forward on the path leading to David. As for
Tamar – the Bible rewards her for her suffering and grants her
a place of honor beside her sisters, Sarah, Rebecca, and Leah.

Ruth

Judah and Tamar reached their ends, and their son Perez
passed the torch to his son without disturbance. Generation
followed generation until the time came for Boaz to join his
torch-bearing forefathers. Almost certainly, Boaz had Israelite
wives that the Bible does not mention. But it was Ruth the
Moabite, a daughter of one of the nations from which the
torchbearers were forbidden to take wives, who was chosen
to stand beside him:

An Ammonite or Moabite shall not enter the congregation of the Lord, even their tenth generation shall not enter the congregation of the Lord, to eternity.... You shall not seek their peace or welfare all your days, forever. (Deut. 23:4–7)

Why a Moabite woman?

We can propose various answers to this question, but the one I like best is that God chose Ruth because she chose Him. As we recall, when Naomi began her return to the land of Canaan, she freed her two daughters-in-law from the bonds of the bride-price, and so Ruth was free to return to her father's home and remarry. Ruth was not from the same family as the four foremothers who preceded her, and she had no obligation to stand on the side of the road on which the torch procession passed. She did not have to break any barriers in order to fulfill the role that God gave her – for He did not give Moabite women any role at all. No one blocked her way. No one hated her and no one refused to marry her. No one forced her to wander dusty roads with the impoverished Naomi. But a silent melody, mysterious and lovely, played in the heart of this foreign girl – and Ruth chose to listen to that melody and follow Naomi. She chose Naomi's fate, she chose her people, and she chose her God. From the moment she made the decision, no one could change her mind or divert her from her path. God, so I like to think, appreciated her choice and her determination, and rewarded her generously for her goodness. He allowed her to return with Naomi to Bethlehem, the village where David would be born – and Jesus, one thousand years later. One early spring day, when the ground was still soft and the sun still merciful, God sent her to collect barley in the field of the dynastic torchbearer of her generation:

Now these are the generations of Perez: Perez begot Hezron; and Hezron begot Ram, and Ram begot Amminadab; and Amminadab begot Nahshon, and Nahshon begot Salmah;

*and Salmah begot Boaz, and Boaz begot Obed; and Obed
begot Jesse, and Jesse begot David. (Ruth 4:18–22)*

CONCLUSION

The torch procession we have followed in this chapter represents a determinist theological worldview, in which the first
families the Bible describes are links in a historical process
determined by God at the dawn of creation. According to this
conception, the procession did not stop when David grasped
the torch, but continues to advance, mysteriously progressing
toward the end of time, when the Messiah of David's house
will arrive and bring peace and brotherhood to the world.
The messianic concept accepted by the Christians holds that
the journey has already ended. Jesus, who according to the
New Testament was a descendant of the Davidic dynasty, is
the messiah referred to in the writings of the prophets. The
Christians believe that the messiah was already born, died,
and resurrected, and he waits in heaven beside God for the
day when he will return to walk among human beings.

Researchers of the Bible believe that most parts of the
Bible were written and edited by authors from the tribe of
Judah, who were recording the foundation story of their tribe
and of their great king. The writers wanted to perpetuate the
Davidic dynasty as the only legitimate monarchic dynasty.
In this chapter, we have seen how the torch dynasty justi-
fies the opinion accepted by these researchers. The choice of
David's family explains why the descendants of other characters, although of national stature, disappeared from the
Bible. The biographies of Moses, Samuel, the judges, and the
prophets are more impressive than those of most of the torchbearers, but they had no successors. Their descendants joined
the branching genealogical tree that fills nine long chapters in

Chronicles, and became part of the anonymous community of ancient Israel.

The Bible authors were not the first to assert that God chose the royal family at the beginning of time. Thousands of years before them, the ancient Egyptians held that their kings, the pharaohs, were descendants of the sun god Re, head of their pantheon.

The ancient Near Eastern kings made similar claims: each king, according to his own religion, asserted that the god in whom he believed had chosen him as ruler, and thanks to this choice, he and his sons had the right to rule eternally.

In contrast to this broad concept, none of the biblical characters knew that he was chosen, that he had a mission, or that he was a person of stature. The Bible describes David and his forefathers as simple, ordinary individuals, despite their essential role in the torch dynasty. The fact that the biblical authors preserved the simplicity of the characters enables us to know them through their everyday lives and to overcome the distance of time. Every act they performed could have been done by any other person, and so their deeds reveal the social norms practiced during the period the Bible addresses.

In my opinion, one of the most fascinating elements of the torch procession is the fact that not only David's forefathers were chosen, but his foremothers as well. This phenomenon is found only in the Bible. The choice of the mothers is especially intriguing in the context of a book with such a prominent masculine orientation. Had the biblical authors not granted importance to the origins and status of the foremothers, there would have been no reason to record their stories. If the author had not thought that David's fore-mothers were chosen women, then Hagar the Egyptian or one of Esau's Canaanite wives could have joined the torch procession.

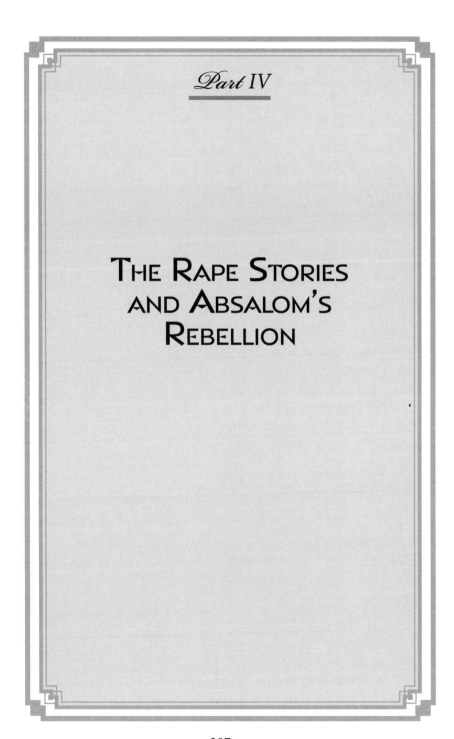

Part IV

THE RAPE STORIES AND ABSALOM'S REBELLION

Chapter Sixteen

INTRODUCTION TO THE RAPE STORIES IN THE BIBLE

T he next four chapters trace four incidents of rape that the Bible describes at some length: the rape of Dinah, Jacob's daughter, by Shechem, son of Hamor (Gen. 34); the rape of Bilhah by Reuben, son of Jacob (Gen. 35:22); the rape of the concubine at Gibeah (Judg. 19–21), and the rape of Tamar, daughter of king David, by Amnon, her older brother (II Sam. 13).

There is something discordant, even disturbing, about the inclusion of stories about serious sex crimes in a holy book. Sanctity and sex crime are not supposed to dwell together under one roof. The place of sanctity is in the sanctuary; the place of sex offenders is in the sewer. In order to remove any question that there might be something polluting about including stories of rape in a sacred book, we must emphasize one of the most important principles that underlay the work of the writers and editors of the Bible.

According to the Bible, sanctity is the sole property of God, and He does not share it with human beings.[1] The forefa-

---

[1] This contradicts the viewpoint of the New Testament, which asserts that Jesus was the son of God. Because God is holy, Jesus was also holy, and lacked any blemish.

thers, foremothers, kings, prophets, and priests were ordinary mortals. Each of them had his own positive character traits and defects. Even the first couple, whom God created with His own hands and placed in the splendid Garden of Eden, violated the sole prohibition He gave them and ate from the forbidden tree.

The assertion that none of the biblical characters was holy is evidenced by the fact that none of the torchbearers, male or female, was free of faults. Even David, the great king toward whom the torch was aimed from the dawn of time, committed adultery with Bathsheba, Uriah's wife, and was severely punished for his sin (II Sam. 12). Moses, one of Israel's most important and faithful leaders, was punished by God for expressing doubt at His ability to produce water for the travelers in the desert (Num. 20:12). For forty years, Moses led the Israelites in the desert and unwearyingly bore their complaints and impatience. But according to the biblical story, he sinned, and thus God prohibited him from entering the land of Canaan. On the day of his death, Moses ascended Mount Nebo, the exact location of which is not known. In the last moments of his life, which he had dedicated to leading the nation in the desert, he gazed at the land spread out before him – the land God did not permit him to enter (Deut. 34:1–4). His elder brother Aaron, who according to the tradition in Exodus served as high priest, was punished along with Moses, and he also died in the desert (Num. 20:23–24).

We could add many other examples to the ones above. All demonstrate one of the major principles of the Bible's theology: only God is sacred. For this reason, the authors of the Bible had no interest in raising human beings above their true characters or hiding the fact that within the families they described, dark deeds took place, identical to those that happen in every human society. Each of the human weaknesses that lies hidden within us is present in them as well.

The major difference between modern and ancient society is not the absence of petty criminals and offenders who carried out horrifying deeds, but in the legal methods that existed then as opposed to the justice systems of modern times.

Today we live in a society that has established national institutions, and that has made the judiciary branch the only body authorized to judge and punish whoever has violated the laws of the state and harmed its citizens. In Western nations, the judge is the only person with the authority to imprison a senior politician who has emptied public coffers into his own pocket, a criminal driver who has slaughtered an entire family with his wild escapades, a thief who has broken into a house and stolen property, or a dealer caught selling drugs to our children outside a schoolyard.

The society in which we live has expropriated from its citizens the authority to take revenge. None of us is permitted to harm a person who has destroyed another person's life or the life of an entire family. The judiciary system we so lavishly praise has erased from the dictionary two terms that are fundamental to the ancient legal system: "an eye for an eye," known as the concept of "natural justice":

> *A man – if he strikes mortally any human life, he shall be put to death. A man who strikes mortally an animal life shall make restitution, a life for a life. And if a man inflicts a wound in his fellow, as he did, so shall be done to him: a break for a break, an eye for an eye, a tooth for a tooth.... There shall be one law for you, it shall be for the foreigner and native alike, for I, the Lord, am your God. (Lev. 24:17– 22; see also Ex. 21:23–25)*

While we wholeheartedly praise our modern legal system, we avoid addressing the contradiction that severe crime in our city streets increases yearly. Although in Western countries, leaders are chosen in democratic elections, many of them are suspected of corruption.

Moses, the respected leader, did not hold democratic elections among his people. Rather, he selected the best and most honest of them to serve alongside him in leading and judging the people:

> You shall discern from among the entire people men of accomplishment, God-fearing people, men of truth, people who despise monetary gain, and you shall appoint them leaders of thousands, leaders of hundreds, leaders of fifties, and leaders of tens. They shall judge the people at all times, and they shall bring every major matter to you, and every minor matter they shall judge. (Ex. 18:21–22)

The judge of our day wears a black ceremonial gown that emphasizes the honor and gravity of his position, but he is subordinate to the book of law that lies in front of him. From the outset, he is not expected to mete out justice, but rather to broker a compromise with the lawyers of the accused parties, who make mockery of him and the justice system. In contrast, the elders who sat at the city gates did not wear ceremonial clothing, nor did they conceal themselves behind a platform that separated them from the accused. The accused did not have the assistance of lawyers or other wonder workers. A trial that began one day did not end seven or eight years later, as today. The elders were not obligated to abide by thousands of complicated laws, but rather by a simple command that the Bible repeats dozens of times, which obligated them to rule justly: "You shall not commit a perversion of justice; you shall not favor the poor and you shall not honor the great; with righteousness shall you judge your fellow" (Lev. 19:15).

The Bible demands that the judge do justice, not reach a compromise.

Implementation of justice is not the only difference between the ancient and modern legal systems. In our time, it is inconceivable that a judge sit trial for an accused who is his relative, who belongs to the same social group, or who is known to him in some other way. By contrast, the elders judged only the members of their own community, who were their relatives. We have already explored the reason for this: in biblical times, government institutions that superseded the family did not exist, and so the respected elders served as the judges of the families they headed. Still, the elders did not take the place of our police or prison systems. In case of a serious crime that required execution of the criminal, the elders permitted his execution, and the blood redeemer bore the responsibility for carrying it out (Num. 35; Deut. 19; Joshua 20). The blood redeemer was one of the victim's relatives, usually his brother. Permission for executing the criminal restored balance to the family and society, and also served as a deterrent. Above all, it created a feeling that "natural justice" had been carried out, so lacking in our times.

Another significant difference between the modern and ancient justice systems is in the case of rape, especially of an unmarried young woman.

In our time, the court considers the raped woman to be the victim of the rapist. Although the judges recognize that her parents and close family are secondary victims of the trauma the girl experienced, the judges do not attempt to quantify her relatives' suffering, and they are not a factor in the legal discussion. Usually, in rape cases, the lawyers perform their juggling acts before the judges, whose role is limited to deciding how many years the rapist spends in jail, if at all. In many cases, the rapist is jailed for only a few years. Such punishment is not only insulting, it also intensifies the damage done to the girl by the rape, and increases the public's lack of confidence in the ability of the legal system to perform justice.

We must not assume that in the ancient world, the rapist got off with a ridiculously light punishment, as in our time. This cannot be the case, because in biblical times, rape was equivalent to murder, and so the punishment for the rapist was death (Deut. 22:26–27). But in the biblical period, a woman who was raped was not considered a victim in today's legal sense. The reason for this is that throughout her life, a woman was considered property, and this reality exactly describes the situation of women in the Third World today. While still a girl, a woman was the property of her father, who gave her in marriage to a man he chose, in exchange for the bride-price. After she married, she became her husband's property, like his home, donkey, or ox (Ex. 20:14; 22:8). Just as a homeowner today is considered the victim of the crime if his house is robbed or his donkey stolen, so was the man of biblical times considered the victim if his daughter, sister, or wife was raped.

While a girl still lived in her father's home, the direct victims of the rape were her brothers. Their honor and the honor of their father's household were desecrated, and they were obligated to heal the fracture created in their lives and to execute the rapist. If the brothers did not do so, this was a tacit admission of their failure and of their family's weakness, and they had to bear the burden of their community's scorn. If a woman was raped after she was married (or if she willingly had relations with another man), then her husband's honor was sullied. The Bible does not reveal the fate of the rapist, but it does tell us that the husband never again had relations with his wife (Deut. 24:1–4).

One of the fascinating differences between the modern justice system and the ancient one relates to a woman's rights over her own body. The modern legal system recognizes a woman's right over her body, but determines the punishment of the rapist based on his ability to pay a lawyer's fees. In contrast, the ancients, who never recognized a woman's rights over her own body, executed the rapist who harmed her. The reason for this was that no man would marry a woman who had had relations with another man (the legal status of a divorced woman and a widow was different).

Unlike every other legal issue that the Bible addresses, in cases of rape where the woman had brothers or other male relatives who could execute the rapist, the elders apparently yielded their judicial authority and did not discuss whether to permit the execution. Their judicial role was rendered irrelevant, since rape cannot take place accidentally or unintentionally. Nevertheless, the book of Deuteronomy introduces a limitation showing that in the case of a young woman who had no brothers or other relatives who could punish the rapist, the elders took upon themselves the right to pass judgment. They instructed him to pay her father the bride-price and marry her, and forbade him from ever divorcing her. Because the bride-price was given only for senior wives, this means that the raped girl was married at senior-wife status.

> If a man will find a virgin maiden who was not betrothed, and takes hold of her and lies with her, and they are discovered, then the man who lay with her shall give the father of the girl fifty silver coins [as the bride-price], and she shall become his wife, because he afflicted her; he cannot divorce her all his life. (Deut. 22:28–29; see also Ex. 22:15)

The elders became involved because rape was (and still is) considered the most serious sexual crime in society. They could not permit an act of rape to pass unpunished, simply because there were no men in the girl's family to demand compensation from the rapist. But because the elders did not act as the executive branch, they did not have the authority to execute the rapist themselves. Still, they did have the authority to force him to marry the girl and to forbid him from banishing her from his home after the marriage.

Possibly, the law that forced the rapist to marry the girl
he harmed arouses our disgust and aversion. Was it possible
to have a woman marry the man who raped her?

The answer is yes.

If the rape victim had any luck, that is indeed what
happened.

As we remarked earlier, no self-respecting man would
have his son marry a stained woman whose virginity had
been taken by someone else. The practical significance of this
is that the young woman was pushed out of the cycle of marriage, simply because there was no one who would marry her
and have children with her – and to the lawmaker, this was
equivalent to murder.

If the social dynamic operated as it should, the brothers
settled the account with the rapist and healed the rift in their
lives: the criminal was executed, and natural justice was carried out. But in so doing, they deepened the crisis in the life of
their sister, for the only man who could marry her was dead.
Their sister was swallowed up between the black sides of
the tent, and there she ended her days. By contrast, a young
woman who came from a weak family that did not have the
power to uphold its honor and act as an executive authority
received the support of the elders. In a manner inconceivable
to the Western mind, the only man who could marry her was
the rapist himself – and the elders ensured this. If the young
woman married him and had children with him, in the final
account she rehabilitated her life, and her position in society
was guaranteed. In the same absurd manner, her status was
infinitely superior to that of a girl from a strong family, whose
brothers preserved the family honor but executed the only
man who could marry their sister.[2]

---

[2] The laws of the Bible reveal that the lawmaker related to the rape of a betrothed girl
(Deut. 22:23–27) differently than that of a girl who was not betrothed. The reason for
this is unclear, given that the result in both cases was identical: the girl never married
and never had children.

Chapter Seventeen

THE RAPE OF DINAH
(GENESIS 34)

A t the heart of the story of the rape of Dinah, daughter
of Jacob and Leah, lies the ancients' belief that the
rape of a young woman was a crime that first and
foremost damaged the honor of her brothers.

This is the story:

About twenty years after Jacob fled to Haran in fear of his
brother Esau's vengeance, he gathered his wives and many
children, and they journeyed over 560 miles (900 km) until
they reached Shechem. The city of Shechem lay at the heart
of the land of Israel, in a region with choice pasture and a rich
water supply, an ideal location for a family of shepherds – and
Jacob was a shepherd. He thus went to the leader of Shechem,
purchased a piece of land on the outskirts of the city, and
settled there (33:18–20).

I must admit that referring to Shechem as a "city" is
somewhat misleading. In biblical times, it was the district
capital of ancient Israel's central region, due to its location
on one of the main commercial routes between Syria and
Lebanon in the north and Egypt in the south. But despite its
important role in the history of the biblical period, Shechem

297

was nothing more than a village whose inhabitants lived in tents or small stone houses. It was never comparable to the royal cities that dotted the length of the Tigris and the Euphrates at that time. It had no magnificent edifices such as the palaces and shrines of Egypt, nor did it influence the culture or economic life of the ancient Middle East in any way. If it had not been mentioned in the Bible, no one would know that Shechem had ever existed.

We may assume that in Jacob's time (around the seventeenth century BCE), Shechem was populated by one large extended family, or perhaps a few extended families. In any case, because the area was inhabited, the newly arrived Jacob could not purchase land in the center of the city where the old, established families lived. Instead, they settled on the outskirts. We may also assume that if not for the act of rape that forced the family to abandon this location and continue walking southward, Jacob and his sons would have built their lives quietly and modestly on that land. If everything had gone as expected, the immigrant family that had just arrived from Haran would have created marriage ties and economic agreements with the local residents, and become integrated with them. One or two generations later, Jacob's family would have become just one thread in the tapestry of inhabitants of the region, like every immigrant family that puts down roots in a new place.

But something went wrong.

Shortly after Jacob and his family members settled on the piece of land they had purchased, Dinah, Leah's daughter, left her family's living quarters and entered the heart of the city, "to look over the daughters of the land." Apparently, Dinah, who had been surrounded all her life by a passel of brothers, was acting out her desire to make some friends among the other girls of her age who lived in Shechem. We may also suppose that she headed toward the well, the meeting place for young people in those days.[3] But we do not know if she ever arrived. The only thing we can assert with any certainty is that the girl's curiosity led her into a strange town in which her father had no relatives or alliances. True, Jacob had been born in Canaan, but he had spent his entire adult life far away in Haran. When he returned to his birthplace, the defense alliances and mutual dependencies that his family had built up in the past no longer existed. Because Jacob did not belong to any extended family, none of the traditional defense networks were available to him in Shechem, and so his daughter was completely vulnerable.

When Dinah entered the town, she met a young man named Shechem, who bore the name of the village where he was born. Shechem was the son of Hamor, leader of the village, and so he was born to the strongest and wealthiest local family, perhaps even the most powerful in the entire region. Shechem exploited the difference in status between himself and the young immigrant girl, and raped her. After fulfilling his needs, he kept Dinah in his possession, and prevented her from returning to her home – thus sending a double message to her family members and the inhabitants of his village.

The first message was intended to clarify the pecking order to Jacob and his sons: who stood at the top of the social ladder, and who was at the bottom. With the rape of Dinah and imprisonment of her in his house, Shechem signaled to the immigrant family that they were weak and defenseless, and that he had the power to crush them into the dust with his heel – let's just see them come to take their revenge and restore their honor! The second message was directed toward the inhabitants of his town. Shechem was his father's eldest son and the future inheritor of his position (34:19). With this

---

[3] Jacob met young Rachel next to the well (Gen. 29:1–10). Many generations later, Moses also met Zipporah and her sisters next to the well (Ex. 2:15–22).

act, he demonstrated his power and authority. He was the dominant male of the herd, and he feared no one.

We should not assume that Shechem raped a young, defenseless girl because he was a sexual deviant who discharged his sick desires in this manner. Through the act of rape, Shechem was demonstrating his strength and authority, and he did what countless other rulers and landowners have done before and after him. He did what conquering armies have always done to the women of the lands they occupied. We need only recall the feats of bravery of warring armies in the last hundred years to realize that nothing about this despicable display of authority has been moderated or improved. Because the rape of women in a weak population is a political declaration and public demonstration of power, Shechem considered it important to make his act known to a large number of people. The news that he had imprisoned Dinah in his home must have spread throughout the region, adding to his reputation as a powerful man who scorned the traditional ways and inspired fear.

The Bible, for reasons we will soon explore, gives a completely different reason to explain why Shechem kept Dinah in his possession. According to the text, after the rape, he "fell in love" with Dinah and thus did not allow her to return to her father's home:

> Shechem, son of Hamor the Hivvite, the ruler of the region, saw her [Dinah]; he took her, lay with her, and violated her. He became deeply attached to Dinah, daughter of Jacob; he loved the maiden and spoke kindly to the maiden. So Shechem spoke to Hamor, his father, saying, "Take me this girl for a wife." (34:2–4)

From a psychological and sociological point of view, this citation is absurd! Love and rape are two conflicting principles that can never go together. A man who loves a woman does not rape her. He does not kidnap her, violently overpower her, or imprison her in his house. He does not frighten her or penetrate her with force. A man who loves a woman does not carry out the vilest of sex crimes against her. We can determine beyond a shadow of a doubt that if Shechem had truly loved Dinah, he would have treated her gently and protected her, just as Boaz protected Ruth. Like Dinah, Ruth was also an unprotected, foreign girl in the village, while Boaz was one of the strongest and wealthiest men, and so he protected her and provided for her and her mother-in-law. If Shechem had loved Dinah, he would have looked out for her best interests, respected the traditional ways, and married her, just as Boaz respected the traditional ways and showed his concern for elderly, impoverished Naomi. If Shechem had loved Dinah, he would have sent sheaves to Jacob, as Boaz did to Naomi, to imply his good intentions. If Shechem had loved Dinah, he would have made her brothers his friends and allies. He would not have humiliated them and turned them into his enemies.

Whatever our view on this matter, the text states that after the rape, Shechem became deeply attached to Dinah and asked his father to arrange their marriage. When Hamor heard his enamored son's request, he rushed to the field where Jacob lived, to convince him and his sons to accede to his request.

Hamor's visit to Jacob's home does not follow accepted tradition. It is not acceptable for a person who stands at the top of the social hierarchy in his habitation to take the trouble to visit the home of a person who stands at the bottom. As if this were not enough, while Hamor made the visit, his son held Dinah prisoner in his home, thus amplifying the humiliation of Jacob and his sons before the entire village. At any rate, Hamor had a mission to fulfill, and he went to the field where Jacob lived in order to obtain his agreement for

Dinah to marry his son. The text reveals that Hamor thought Dinah worthy of marrying his son at senior-wife status, and thus he offered to Jacob and his sons three financial proposals that he intended as her bride-price:

> Hamor spoke with them, saying, "Shechem, my son, longs deeply for your daughter – please give her to him as a wife.
> "Intermarry with us; give your daughter to us, and take our daughters for yourselves.
> "And among us you shall dwell; the land will be before you – settle and trade in it, and acquire property in it."
> Then Shechem said to her father and brothers, "Let me gain favor in your eyes; and whatever you tell me – I will give. Inflate exceedingly upon me the bride-price and gifts, and I will give whatever you tell me; only give me the maiden for a wife." (34:8–12)

Let us examine the financial significance of this bride-price:

The first offer stipulates that Jacob and his sons forge a marriage alliance with Hamor and the people of Shechem: "Intermarry with us; give your daughter to us, and take our daughters for yourselves." Such a marriage alliance usually connected two families of similar economic and financial status (in academic terminology, "alliance of equals"). Each side would marry its daughters to the sons of the other side, and in this way both sides would be equally strengthened. But such was not the case, since Hamor was much wealthier and more powerful than Jacob. The economic and social gap between them might explain why Jacob would want to connect his family to the village chief, and thus benefit from Hamor's connections and defense alliances in Shechem. But what equivalent advantage did Jacob have to offer Hamor? What profit could Hamor obtain from the young women of his village marrying Jacob's sons? And since when did the strongest, wealthiest man in the area want to forge an alliance with the weakest one?

The second provision of the marriage proposal makes Shechem's trade contacts available to Jacob and his sons: "And among us you shall dwell; the land will be before you – settle and trade in it, and acquire property in it." In the ancient world, kings held the monopoly over the trade routes and the caravans that passed through their kingdoms. The kings provided services to the caravans, and collected taxes in exchange for the right to cross their lands. Thus, in addition to property, the trade routes were one of the king's most important sources of wealth. Because one of the ancient commercial routes passed through Shechem (Joseph was sold to one of the caravans that traveled along it), probably the village chief and his people maintained commercial ties with the merchants who traveled through their region. If Hamor stood to earn a profit from opening his trade routes to Jacob and his sons, then we might understand the logic behind his generous offer. But Jacob was only a poor immigrant. Why should Hamor offer economic partnership to a man who had nothing to offer in exchange?

The last item in the marriage proposal indicates that Hamor was willing to pay Jacob any price he asked, if he would only agree to give Dinah to his son in marriage: "Inflate exceedingly upon me the bride-price and gifts, and I will give whatever you tell me; only give me [my son] the maiden for a wife."

The book of Deuteronomy stipulates that a rapist must marry the woman he harmed, and he had to pay her father fifty silver coins (22:28–29). Hamor did not limit himself to this sum, but announced that he was willing to pay any price, if only Jacob would agree to his son's request. But why should Hamor offer any bride-price at all for a girl who came from a family inferior to his? Poor girls who married men of higher socioeconomic status than their fathers were given away for free at the status of concubines, not as senior wives. Indeed, why did Hamor want to pay a bride-price for a girl who had lost her virginity, who was already in his home, and whom no man other than his son would ever agree to marry?

Examining the three provisions of the bride-price reveals that they benefited Jacob, but gave nothing of value to Hamor – and if Hamor earned nothing from the transaction, why should he offer such generous conditions?

As if the questions we have raised are not enough, the rape story becomes even more complex. The more complicated it becomes, the more it appears imaginary and disconnected from the reality of the time in which it took place.

The impression created by the rest of the story is that Jacob was inclined to accept the village chief's offer, but his sons were harder bargainers than he. The sons were not enticed by the excessive offers meant to tempt them. Instead, they agreed to the marriage of their sister on condition that all the men of Shechem undergo circumcision, as was the Israelite custom. Because Hamor was desperate to fulfill the request of his enamored son, he hurried back to the people of his village to convince them that they wanted nothing more than to become circumcised. Three nights later, after all the men of Shechem had been through the operation, two of Jacob's sons, Simeon and Levi, attacked the village and took revenge against the inhabitants while they slept peacefully in their beds. The two heroic brothers killed Shechem and his father, then butchered all the men of the village. Apparently, at some point the rest of the brothers joined them, and together they freed their little sister from her prison. As part of their revenge, the gang captured the beautiful girls of the village, and plundered the property of the inhabitants, who were lying in their own blood. After the brothers took out their anger against the inhabitants of Shechem, they returned victorious to their father's home. Undoubtedly, the honor of Jacob's sons, which had been ground into the dust, was restored. They executed the rapist and all the men of his village, and the crisis in their lives was resolved.

The heroic story we have described here raises one small problem: it is not logical. It adds unacceptable assertions to the inflated bride-price that Hamor seemingly offered Jacob.

When we remove the details of the rape story that do not fit the customs of that time and place, and leave only the portions that could have taken place in reality, we are left with a different story than that told in Genesis.

From a historical point of view, we may accept the testimony that Jacob and his family purchased a parcel of land on the outskirts of the city and settled there. The story that Dinah left her family's living area, entered a strange village where she was defenseless, and was raped there fits the test of human culture, which has been ornamented with such acts ever since the sixth day of Creation. Shechem son of Hamor merely did what many others did before him – and what many more have done after him.

The difficulties raised by this story begin when the chief of Shechem takes the trouble to visit Jacob's habitation, and asks, in accordance with tradition, if he would agree to give Dinah to Shechem in marriage. In a curious manner, the rape of Dinah and her imprisonment in Hamor's home is not mentioned at this meeting. Jacob and Hamor behave as if this severe incident never even happened. Furthermore, the exaggerated bride-price that Hamor offers Jacob conflicts with the fact that under the conditions, the best thing that could have happened to Dinah was for her rapist to agree to marry her. No man but Shechem would ever have married Dinah after she had been raped and imprisoned in his home, where she most certainly was the victim of further rapes. The illogic of this story continues to the daring act of revenge of Jacob's sons against the inhabitants of Shechem.

As we read above, three days after the men of Shechem circumcised themselves, Simeon and Levi went out in the middle of the night to take revenge against the rapist and the inhabitants of his village. The two brothers executed Shechem and his father, then slaughtered the rest of the men in the village. They freed Dinah, plundered the village, took the women and children captive, and looted their homes as well as the sheep and cattle pens.

Historical logic does not accept this arrogant description. Although the men of Shechem were still in pain after circumcising themselves, the story does not say that in addition to their foreskins, they cut off their right hands. Furthermore, it is not logical that two people, as brave as they might be, used wooden swords to kill dozens of men.

The illogic of the vengeance story indicates that the tale must have ended in a very different way.

If Dinah was indeed raped and taken captive by Shechem, son of Hamor, then Jacob and his sons would have had no choice but to evaluate their situation carefully, and decide whether they had the strength to take revenge against him and restore their honor. According to the story, after their daring act of vengeance, Jacob said: "I am few in number, and should they band together and attack me, I will be annihilated – I and my household" (34:30). This declaration is an exact representation of the power relationships between Jacob's family and the local inhabitants. Logic dictates that this should have been said *before* his sons supposedly went out to attack the villagers – not afterward. Furthermore, the Bible relates that immediately after the stunning victory, the family gathered its belongings and traveled south, to a small and distant settlement called Beth-el. The reason for their departure was in order to make sacrifices to God and thank

Him for His kindness to Jacob when he fled from Esau and went to Haran.

> God said to Jacob, "Arise – go up to Beth-el and dwell there, and **make an altar there to God Who appeared to you when you fled from Esau your brother.**" So Jacob said to his household and to all who were with him, "...Then come, let us go up to Beth-el; I will make there an altar to God Who answered me in my time of distress, and was with me on the road that I traveled." ...They set out, and there fell a godly terror on the cities which were around them, so that they did not pursue Jacob's sons. (35:1–5)

Curiously, the reason for the family's departure to Beth-el was to make sacrifices in honor of an event that had taken place over twenty years earlier – not to thank God for the great victory that He had granted to Jacob's sons the day before. Why did Jacob not thank God for delivering the people of Shechem into the hands of his sons? In addition, after the family finished the sacrifices in Beth-el, why did they not return to their plot of land in Shechem, but rather continued journeying southward to an even more distant location? Why did Jacob abandon the enormous amount of property that was in his possession after his sons had plundered the village?

Apparently, the fact that the family left Shechem and the land it had purchased strengthens the assumption that the rape story ended differently than what was recorded.

Jacob's family was poorer and weaker than the village chief, who was one of the most powerful men of the region. Therefore, we cannot logically accept that Hamor visited Jacob's home and offered him excessive financial conditions without receiving anything in exchange. It is unreasonable to suppose that Jacob's sons were in a position to demand that the village chief and his people circumcise themselves, or to dictate any conditions to them at all. We cannot believe that

Simeon and Levi attacked the village in the dead of night, butchered all the men, plundered their possessions, and took their women captive.

Logic determines completely opposite circumstances: the brothers did not attack the city, nor they take revenge or restore their honor. Logic states that the story ended with the family packing its bags and leaving Shechem and the land they had purchased, in humiliation and defeat. Like weak subjects crushed under the feet of powerful masters, they pressed their lips together firmly and did nothing. Dinah remained behind, and no one knows what became of her. Her brothers distanced themselves from her and from the place where their pride was beaten into the ground, never to return.

THE TENDENTIOUS ASPECT OF THE VENGEANCE STORY

The story of the rape of Dinah contains a strong tension between an event that could have happened – that always happens – and a myth designed to extol heroes from the distant past and transform them into superhuman figures.

Many myths of ancient peoples are based on modest seeds of truth that expanded and grew, developing into stately trees – and such is the case with this story. In films and children's fairy tales, justice always vanquishes evil, and the good guys always beat the bad guys. In reality, other forces are at work: the strongest win, while the weak lose and are humiliated even further. Justice, as we know, does not hold a position on the playing field of real life. If so, why did the author find it necessary to recount an act of heroism that is unacceptable, whose tendentious character is so obvious?

The answer to this question is somewhat complex, and returns us to what we have already said about the way in which the Bible stories came together.[4] The story of the rape of Dinah was not recorded on the day it took place. Rather,

---

[4] See chapter 3, "Camels and Historical Writing," and the final chapter.

hundreds of years of oral transmission passed until the story was first recorded. After that, it underwent centuries of repeated copying, until it reached our hands in the present form. Possibly, the first generations that lived after Jacob and his sons recounted this story as it took place in reality. But after their period, and after the many generations that followed them, society changed. The people who lived in a later era in the land of Israel needed heroic figures from the distant past whose brave acts would serve as models for their children. They needed heroes and deeds with which they could identify.

When the text before us was recorded, the tradition that Jacob's sons were the founding fathers of the Israelite tribes was already deeply rooted in the Israelites' consciousness. Thus the biblical author felt an urgent need to enhance the image of the brothers and to conclude the story in a way that would satisfy the author and his readers. The copyist did not delete the story of Dinah's rape. Instead, he used it as leverage to magnify the role of Simon and Levi, to present them as heroes who restored the family's honor. The fabrication of the revenge story is intended to present Jacob's sons as a significant power in the Shechem area, and the village chief as willing to ingratiate himself to them, to circumcise himself and his people, and to pay any price to appease them.

If the rape story had ended without the glorification of Jacob's sons, then they would have been engraved in our memory as a miserable band that was crushed to the ground in the most degrading manner. They would be remembered as having fled Shechem because the imprisonment of their younger sister in the home of her rapist shamed them daily. They would be forever remembered as people who lacked the power to avenge the rape and restore their honor – and this was not the memory that the author wanted to preserve. From such material, one cannot create valiant figures worthy of the title "forefathers of the nation." The story of the daring revenge erased the stain from Jacob's sons, and cloaked them in a cape of superpowers. The updated version presented them as heroes who defended their family's honor and religion, and thus were worthy of serving as symbols and role models to their descendants.

We must make note of a final detail in this story. The author particularly highlights the bravery of Simeon and Levi, and thanks to their daring act of revenge, they have enjoyed eternal commendation. But according to other sections of the Bible, Simeon and Levi were the forefathers of the two weakest tribes in Israel. The tribe of Simeon was integrated into the tribe of Judah, and never existed as an independent tribe. The tribe of Levi disintegrated into its component families, and belonged to the poorest sector of society. Apparently, then, attributing the great revenge to Simeon and Levi was intended to add a bit of blush to the cheeks of the brothers who gave their names to the two palest tribes of Israel.

Although the author of this story exploited the rape of Dinah in order to advance his ideological and social goals, the story preserves some of the social customs which we have described above. It reveals that in ancient times, rape was considered a blow to the honor of the brothers, not the woman raped. Therefore, it is the "heroism" of the brothers, and not the fate of Dinah, that interests the author. The story demonstrates that in a time when a government executive branch did not exist, the brothers had the responsibility to execute the rapist. If they were unable to do so, then they had to leave the area in disgrace. A family that did not restore its honor was considered weak – and this, as we have noted, is what the author wanted to erase from our memories.

The story of the vengeance of Jacob's sons against the inhabitants of Shechem is a hero myth. Thanks to similar myths, every community has its bag of legends containing the hero stories of its founding fathers, in whom it takes pride and in whose image it educates its children – and this is as it should be. These characters from the distant past are the superheroes of their people. Their acts of glory never grow old or lose their validity. They become stories of heritage, and thank God for that.

Chapter Eighteen

THE CONCUBINE AT GIBEAH

(JUDGES 19–21)

The last chapters in the book of Judges tell the story of a bloody fraternal war that broke out like a storm, following a hair-raising rape. The story took place in a settlement called Gibeah, and bears its name – "The Concubine at Gibeah." Gibeah was located north of today's Jerusalem. As in the story of the rape of Dinah, impossible, legendary components seeped into this story and mingled with its historical foundations. A mixture of plausible details and unfeasible ones creates a picture that casts doubt on the credibility of a story that apparently took place in reality.

Following is the story that horrified the Israelites:

Once there was a man from the tribe of Levi, whose family lived in the region of the tribe of Ephraim.[5] Three thousand years ago, Ephraim was one of the largest and strongest tribes living in the center of the land of Israel. Curiously, and in contrast to the accepted writing style, the Bible does not reveal the man's name. So he is known by the general

---

[5] The tribe of Levi was in many ways a "virtual" tribe, because it did not have any property or its own leadership. Thus we cannot relate to it as a tribe, but rather as disparate, scattered families that probably had no connection between them.

appellation of "the Levite man," meaning a man from one of the Levite families. The Levite man married a concubine (a woman given for free, without payment of a bride-price), whose name is also not mentioned. All we know about the concubine is that her family lived in Bethlehem, in the region of the tribe of Judah, and thus she must have been from the tribe of Judah. After marriage, the concubine went to live in her husband's village, where she committed adultery against him.

When she realized that her husband had discovered her sin, she fled to her father's home in Bethlehem. Four months later her husband, the Levite man, went to bring her back. When he arrived at his father-in-law's home, he was received as a welcome guest, and his father-in-law held a feast in his honor that lasted for three continuous days. When dawn broke on the fourth day, the Levite man decided he had had enough of his host's wine, and asked to return home with his wife. Because the kind host, the girl's father, pleaded for him to remain another day, the Levite man agreed. Again the two feasted, again they enjoyed the wine, and between sips and bites, the fifth morning arrived – and the ritual of pleading and feasts was repeated once more. But when evening fell on that day, the wine-loving host's pleas that his son-in-law sleep in his house another night were met with a flat refusal. The Levite man drank a last glass with his host, took his concubine, and began the journey to their home in the region of the tribe of Ephraim.

On the way, the couple neared Jerusalem, which in that period was home to the Jebusites, one of the seven non-Israelite peoples living in the land of Canaan. Since the sun had begun to set, the Levite man decided to continue on to one of the Israelite settlements nearby. So they went on their way, and stopped in Gibeah, in the area of the tribe of Benjamin, where a kindly old man offered to host them in his house for the night.

That night, so the book of Judges recounts, a band of hooligans from Gibeah pounded on the door of the old man, and demanded that he bring his guest out to them, so that they could "know" him.

The language of the Bible often uses the verb "to know" as a polite way of referring to sexual relations (Gen. 4:1, 25; 24:16; I Kings 1:1–4). This allows for the possibility that the mob wanted to sexually abuse the Levite man. The old man with whom the couple was staying fulfilled the commandment of hospitality, and refused to throw his guests out to the depraved crowd. So as not to disappoint them by leaving them empty-handed, the old man offered them a much better deal in exchange. Instead of permitting them to trample the flesh of his honored guest, he would send out his virgin daughter and the man's concubine to cheer them up. The old man's offer was too generous for the rioters, who had only asked to harass the foreign guest a bit, and not, God forbid, to rape any young girls. After a long-winded speech, the old man was convinced that the mob had no interest in his daughter or the concubine, and he went back to bed, to sleep in peace. Unlike the old man, the Levite man was not pacified. He was so touched by the kind-heartedness of the thugs that he felt an uncontrollable urge to compensate them. He thus grabbed his concubine and threw her out to them like a meaty bone thrown to a pack of hungry wolves. After delivering his concubine into the hands of the wild hooligans, the Levite man went back to bed, pleased that he had paid his debt to the gang for leaving him in peace. While he slept serenely, the mob of vandals pounced on his wife and gang-raped her.

When the long night was over and the sun rose, the concubine was still alive. Miraculously, she managed to crawl with her remaining strength to the home of the old man,

where she collapsed on his threshold. Shortly afterward, her
husband also woke up. He opened the door to go on his way
– and lo and behold, his wife had returned to him! He had
no choice but to gather her up, load her onto his donkey, and
leave:

> *The man grabbed his concubine and thrust [her] outside
> to them. They knew [raped] her and they molested her all
> night long until the morning; they sent her away as the
> dawn began to break. The woman arrived toward morning
> and collapsed at the door of the man's house, where her
> master was staying, until it was light. Her master got up
> in the morning, opened the doors of the house, and left
> to go on his way, and behold – his concubine wife was
> fallen at the entrance of the house, with her hands on the
> threshold! He said to her, "Get up, let us go!" but there
> was no answer. He took her upon the donkey, and then the
> man got up and went to his place. (19:25–28)*

When he reached his village, the Levite man began to be
gnawed by doubt that his concubine might still be alive. So
he took a knife, chopped her into twelve pieces, and sent the
parts throughout the lands of the Israelite tribes.

The gang rape and its horrifying consequences terrified
the Israelite tribes, each one of which received a piece of the
carved-up woman. Four hundred thousand warriors were
called from their homes to gather at the meeting place of the
tribes, to try to understand how such an outrageous deed had
taken place among them. At this difficult hour, the Levite
man stood up and, in a voice choked with tears and pain,
recounted the chain of events that had led to the death of his
beloved concubine:

> *The Levite man, the husband of the murdered woman,
> answered and said, "I arrived with my concubine at Gibeah
> of Benjamin, to spend the night. The inhabitants of Gibeah*

rose up against me and surrounded the house against me
at night. They proposed to kill me, and they raped my
concubine so that she died. I took hold of my concubine
and cut her apart, and sent her [body] throughout all the
territory of the heritage of Israel, for they had done an
indecent and disgusting thing in Israel. Here you all are,
O Children of Israel, give your decision and counsel right
here!" (20:4–7)

The reader who compares the Levite man's statement to the
gathering in chapter 20 with the story in chapter 19 will realize that the two versions are vastly different. The first version
(chapter 19) says that the mob was interested in the Levite
man, not his wife, and that he was the one who grabbed her
by force and threw her out to them. Chapter 19 also implies
that while the woman was gang-raped, he was sleeping calmly
in his bed, which he fails to mention in his second version.
According to the first version, despite the terrors of the night,
the woman was still alive in the morning. Possibly, she died
while lying on the old man's threshold, her body shattered.
But by the same token, she may still have been alive when
she reached her home in the region of Ephraim, where her
merciful husband murdered her and cut her into pieces.
According to the husband's version, she died immediately
following the rape. At any rate, when the Levite man stood
before the thousands of warriors who demanded to know how
such an outrage could take place among them, he blamed the
hooligans for the murder of his wife, and begged for justice
to be carried out. When the fighters heard the details in the
improved version, they were furious, and demanded that the
Benjaminites hand over the criminals for execution:

The tribes of Israel then sent men through all the clans
of Benjamin, saying, "What is this outrage that occurred
among you? Now turn over the lawless men who are in

Gibeah, and we will put them to death and eliminate the
evil from Israel." (20:12–13)

When the Benjaminites refused to comply with the demand
of the leaders of the tribes, the gathering of warriors vowed
not to marry their daughters to the sons of the rebellious
tribe. They then united to attack the tribe that had sheltered
the rapists.

Chapter 20 of the book of Judges contains a description of
the internecine war that broke out between the tribe of Benjamin and the other tribes of Israel. No less than four hundred
thousand warriors participated in the battle, and no less than
fifty thousand Benjaminites lost their lives in it. Some seventy thousand fighters from other tribes also died. When the
echoes of battle subsided and the bloody war ended, the Israelites realized that the tribe of Benjamin had been almost
completely wiped off the earth – and then came the weeping
and wailing. The victorious tribes did not rejoice over their
triumph; instead, they mourned the loss of their youngest
brother. They suddenly recalled that the Benjaminites had
never been their enemies.

> *The people came to Beth-el and remained there until*
> *evening before God. They raised their voices and wept in a*
> *loud lament. They said, "Why, O Lord, God of Israel, has this*
> *happened in Israel, that one tribe of Israel should be missing*
> *in Israel today." …For the Children of Israel had relented*
> *toward their brother Benjamin, and they said, "Today one*
> *tribe will be eliminated from Israel! What can we do [to*
> *provide] wives for the survivors? For we have sworn by the*
> *Lord not to give them our daughters for wives!" (21:2–7)*

The leaders of the warriors who had fought with all their
might to kill the Benjaminites now wanted to revive that
tribe. They knew that in order to save their little brother,
who was bleeding to death before their very eyes, they had to

give him new blood. The male Benjaminites, who had just barely survived the war, desperately needed brides to bear children for them and create new lives to replace those that had been cut off. But where would the Israelite tribe leaders obtain women for the Benjaminites? They had vowed in the name of God not to marry their daughters to the Benjaminites, and thus they could not break their promise. The war leaders racked their brains in search of a solution that would enable them to save their dying brother, and at the same time allow them to keep their vow. Finally, after examining every possible and impossible idea, they discovered a new well from which they could draw buckets full of as much new blood as their brother needed!

The war leaders recalled that the inhabitants of a distant community called Jabesh-gilead had not taken the vow that the warriors had, and had not participated in the war. The solution that the battle leaders concocted was creative and clever: the women of Jabesh-gilead would marry the Benjaminites and bear them children, thus assuring a continuation for the stricken tribe. But one small difficulty still bothered them: How would they convince the men of Jabesh-gilead to give their daughters to the Benjaminites?

Marriage in the ancient world was a serious business. Fathers who arranged marriages between their children did so because this served the political and economic interests of the two sides. A family that married its daughters to the men of another family had to receive other brides in exchange, for if not, the family that gave the brides would be weakened. In order to preserve the balance of power between families, marriage agreements usually included exchanges of brides between them.[6] The war leaders had to overcome the problem that the Benjaminites did not have brides to exchange

---

[6] In all likelihood a bride-price was paid only when an exchange of brides was not possible.

with those from whom they wanted to receive. As if that were not enough, the destruction of the Benjaminite cities meant that they did not have enough property left with which to pay the girls' bride-price. The war leaders logically concluded that the men of Jabesh-gilead would refuse to give their daughters to the Benjaminites for free. Their foreheads thus broke into a sweat once again, until they found a way to overcome the expected refusal.

The tribal leaders decided that their warriors would not return to their homes, but rather go straight from the battle that had taken place in Benjamin to attack the inhabitants of Jabesh-gilead in the north (about 124 miles [200 km] from the battlefield). They would smite all the men and the married women, leaving only the virgins alive. After the carnage was successfully concluded, they would take the girls with them and bring them to the young men of Benjamin. This excellent idea was readily accepted by the crowd, and the battle cry was sounded. The blood of the inhabitants of distant Jabesh-gilead saturated the earth, and four hundred young women who were kidnapped from their homes joyfully gave up their virginity to the Benjaminites, saving the tribe from annihilation (21:8–25).

REALITY AND IMAGINATION

We may easily demonstrate that the author who recorded the rape story mingled the credible with the imaginary and the exaggerated. In order for us to relate to the incident here as an event that stands the test of time, we must, as is our habit, separate the probable elements from the improbable ones.

From a historical viewpoint, adultery stories that end with the woman fleeing from her husband to take refuge in her father's home are a dime a dozen. Thus we have no difficulty accepting as a true component the story of the concubine's flight to her father's house, after her husband discovered that she had been unfaithful. It is also possible that the father offered his daughter shelter for four months until the Levite man came to take her back. But from here on, illogical elements penetrate the story and accompany it to its bloody conclusion.

According to the story in chapter 19, when the Levite man arrived at his father-in-law's home, he was given a surprisingly warm welcome. The father of the concubine behaved as if his guest's visit was a joyful event to be celebrated. He held banquets in his honor and served him wine, which in biblical times was done only during a feast. But the Levite man did not go to his father-in-law's home in order to celebrate with him. Rather, he went to kill his adulterous wife – and the wine-loving host was well aware of that. The father knew that his daughter had been unfaithful to her husband and had desecrated his honor before his family, his other wives, his children, and the members of the community in which he lived. The father was well aware that if his son-in-law did not kill his daughter, he could not return to his village or show his face in public due to the disgrace. Yet instead of donning sackcloth and spreading ashes on his head in accordance with mourning custom, he held a feast in honor of the Levite man! How was this possible?

Some might say that the father held the four days of feasting in order to make peace between the couple and begin a new page in their relationship. But such a reading would be anachronistic.

In an anachronistic reading, the reader interprets the text according to the standards accepted in his time and by the society in which he lives, not according to the criteria of the time and place in which the event happened. Someone unfamiliar with the ways of ancient society might certainly think that the Levite man was pining away for his wife, and that he went to appease her and return her to his embrace. After all, who among us does not know couples who committed adultery and in the end reunited? But we are not talking about permissive Western society. Instead, we are discussing an event that took place thousands of years ago in a small, closed, traditional community. The historian, and we along with him, will argue that the Levite man did not go to bring back his concubine in order to begin a new page in their relationship, but to execute her.

The Levite man could not forgive his concubine, because the act was known to the public and the social dynamic permitted him only one reaction. Furthermore, because his concubine had had relations with another man, she was forbidden to him, and so in any case, he could not bring her back to his home to have relations with her.

If the Levite man had wanted to restore his position and the honor of his family, he would have had to do what he in fact did: return his concubine to his village and execute her in public. The public character of the execution would have removed any suspicion that he had forgiven her. This was vital for the restoration of his honor and the honor of his family, while simultaneously serving as a cautionary measure.

Because the participants in the story knew that the girl's fate was sealed as soon as the Levite man arrived in Bethlehem, the festive atmosphere in the host's home contradicted the gravity of the situation, and demands explanation. For this purpose, we must stop at the side of the road for a few moments, and as is our habit, to take note of the mysteries of biblical writing.

The Bible relates positively to the consumption of wine: as the author of Psalms wrote, "Wine gladdens a man's heart" (Ps. 104:15), referring to what every wine-lover knows well. At the same time, the Bible relates the excessive drinking of wine to drunkenness, confusion of the senses, and loss of self-control leading to sexual abandonment. For example, when Noah and his family left the famous ark, Noah planted a vineyard. When the grape clusters ripened, the good man pressed the fruit and made the juice into wine. Noah, who had spent many long days in the small, crowded ark, surely longed for a bit of comfort and oblivion. He tasted a drop of his wine, and then another drop, until his mind was blurred. After he was inebriated, he rolled into his tent, naked as the day he was born, and until the effects of the wine wore off, he remained unaware of the extent to which he was disgraced before his sons (9:18–25).

Another story that connects the drinking of wine to sexual licentiousness is that of Lot and his two daughters. In the time of Abraham, God decided to destroy the inhabitants of Sodom and Gomorrah, after the news of their sins reached His seat on high. Lot and his two daughters were the only survivors of the fire and brimstone that God rained down on the two cities. The three refugees took shelter in a distant, isolated cave, not knowing what or whom they awaited. Many (or a few) days later, the young women began to fear that aside from their father, no man was left in the world to marry them and give them children. Thus the resourceful sisters decided to give their father wine and conceive through him while he was drunk (19:30–38).

Another example leads us to the most well-known adultery story in the Bible. Those who are familiar with the late afternoon shadows that fall over Jerusalem will bear witness to their mysterious and delightful charm. During one of these enchanted hours, King David climbed up to the roof of his house and noticed the profile of a beautiful woman bathing on the roof across the way. Although David knew that this woman was married to Uriah, the captain of his army, he ordered to have her brought to him. Bathsheba was brought to David and conceived through him.

When David discovered her pregnancy, he sent for Uriah to be brought from the battlefield, declaring that he wanted to hear his captain's report about the war situation (II Sam. 11:6–7). David's intention in bringing Uriah to Jerusalem was to place the responsibility for Bathsheba's pregnancy on him. David thought that if Uriah went home, he would have relations with his wife, thus creating the impression that he was the father of the child she way carrying. Undoubtedly, Uriah heard the rumor that his wife and king had committed adultery, and stubbornly refused to go home and be alone with her. Uriah was willing to be killed for his king on the battlefield, but not to create for him the desired impression that he was the baby's father. Uriah knew that an army captain whose wife had committed adultery and conceived through another man was an army captain who had lost his honor, in his own estimation as well as that of his fighters. He thus refused to cooperate with the king who had humiliated him.

When David realized that Uriah was adamant not to be seen with Bathsheba, he plied him with wine, in the hope that his resistance would wane while under the influence:

> Then David summoned him, and he ate and drank before him; and he made him drunk. [Uriah] went out in the evening to lie down in his place among his lord's servants, but did not go down to his house. (II Sam. 11:13)

Uriah did get drunk, but he did not go home and did not see his wife. He had two ways to restore his honor: to kill both parties to the adultery, or to arrange his own death. Faithful Uriah chose the second option.

After we have shown that the Bible relates drunkenness to the relaxation of sexual inhibitions,[7] we can return to the question raised above: Why did the concubine's father give his son-in-law wine for five days straight?

---

[7] We noted the connection between drunkenness and blurring of the senses in our discussion of Jacob's wedding feast.

We have already said that the Levite man's purpose in going to Bethlehem was clear to all. So it is not possible that the five feast days were intended to celebrate a happy occasion. Therefore, we can assume that the host wanted to do to his guest what David tried to do to Uriah – to dull his senses. Possibly, the concubine had conceived through her lover, and her father was trying to create the impression that she had conceived through her husband while he was drunk. A second possibility is that the host wanted to create an atmosphere of debauchery in his home, in order to humiliate his guest even further, so that he would not be able to return home. So every time the Levite man recovered from his inebriation, he found his concubine lying next to him. Under this option, the cuckold's shame would be intensified by public disclosure of the fact that he had behaved licentiously, forcing him to remain in his host's home indefinitely.

The assumption that the Levite man went to his father-in-law's house to retrieve his concubine and kill her stands the test of time, and explains several events that took place afterward. Possibly, the lovers' path was disrupted, and they met up with a band of hooligans. If such was the case, then the fact that the Levite man threw his concubine out to them is understandable, if horrific. Logic dictates that after she had committed adultery against him, and after her father had plied him with wine for five days and confused him, the Levite man wanted to take revenge against both of them in a particularly cruel manner. Therefore, instead of trying to save his concubine from the mob of rioters, he grabbed her by force and threw her at them. We know that when morning arrived, the woman was still alive, but this does not have much significance because her fate was already sealed. One thing lies beyond doubt: after the husband chopped her into pieces and distributed her body parts, his desire for revenge was satisfied. The villagers could be certain that the Levite had restored his honor, and he could walk through the town with his head held high.[8]

From a point of view that takes into account the social and historical background of this story, the analysis of events we have proposed above is feasible and fits the reality of the times. With this, the story should have ended, but instead, it expanded beyond the boundaries of the possible. It tells of a war that broke out between the other Israelite tribes and the tribe of Benjamin, origin of the mob that raped the concubine.

According to the text, hundreds of thousands of warriors marched to the battlefield and spilled each other's blood. The calculation of the number of victims from the two camps reaches 120,000. The problem that these numbers raises is that in the period of the judges (eleventh-twelfth centuries BCE), the land of Canaan was populated by small tribes. Researchers estimate that the population numbered between 150,000 and 400,000, including women and children. The assumption that the number of warriors who participated in the war was higher than the total population of Canaan is somewhat problematic. Furthermore, in order for 120,000 soldiers to lose their lives in war, the fighters would have had to use weapons of mass destruction. But the weapons available to them were wooden spears, bows and arrows, and slingshot stones – and mass killing is not possible with these.

Even if we agree that the number of fighters and victims was much smaller than the numbers in Judges, we still gain the impression that the tribe of Benjamin was large and powerful, and that it had the power to fight alone against all the other Israelite tribes. The truth is just the opposite. Benjamin was the smallest of the Israelite tribes, and the land on which

---

[8] The Bible does not say this, but it is possible that the Levite man went to his concubine's house only four months after she had fled because in the interim he was busy pursuing the man who had had relations with her, and executing him. From a historical and social point of view, only the execution of both of the adulterers would restore the Levite and his family's full honor.

it settled was a thin strip squeezed between two substantial tribes: Ephraim in the north and Judah in the south. Such a small tribe, which in the best case numbered several thousand people, could not feasibly attack and fight its brothers from the larger tribes. In addition, we must recall that the elders of Benjamin shared the same social code followed by the other tribes. If the rioters had come from their tribe, they would have handed them over to the Levite man, so that he and his family would execute them. The Benjaminite elders would never have gotten involved in a tribal war on behalf of a few ruffians.

To these absurd details that the author employs, we must add a few small items, equally strange. According to the book of Judges, some fifty thousand soldiers from Benjamin lost their lives in the war. But somehow, after the war was over, the tribe lacked women, not men!

We also cannot accept that the leaders of the victorious armies decided to heal the tribe of Benjamin by destroying the inhabitants of Jabesh-gilead. Jabesh-gilead was located in the region of the tribe of Menasseh, one of the largest and strongest of the Israelite tribes. It would be absurd to assume that the warrior leaders would consider declaring war against the tribe of Menasseh in order to kidnap brides for the Benjaminites. Finally, we must take into account one more detail: the Levite man was of the tribe of Levi, and thus he belonged to one of the poorest families in the land of Canaan. Possibly, for this reason the Bible does not bother to mention his name, the name of his concubine, or the name of his village (a phenomenon found nowhere else in the Bible). We also must reject the theory that the tribes of Israel went to war because of a private incident that took place in the life of an insignificant man, and which at any rate had to end with the execution of the woman.

The above is enough to cast doubt on the historical credibility of the fraternal war that broke out following the gang rape, which also seems dubious. If so, why did the author bother to expand the story beyond the limits of possibility, and fabricate such a strange, exaggerated war story?

According to researchers, the story of the concubine at Gibeah and the resultant war never took place. In their view, the tale is a falsified plot designed to blacken the name of the tribe of Benjamin, from which Saul would be born. The author intended to create the impression that Saul originated from a tribe with a dubious past, and thus did not deserve to become king of Israel – and the events of the war we have summarized here confirm this hypothesis.

In conclusion, the story of the woman who fled from her husband after she committed adultery repeats itself in one form or another, everywhere that men and women are attracted to each other, fall in love with each other, hate and envy one another. The Levite man's journey to retrieve his concubine and execute her preserves the true foundations of ancient society, since this was the punishment for an adulterous woman. However, the story of the gang rape by the thugs from the tribe of Benjamin, and the story of the fraternal war that broke out after the Benjaminites' refusal to hand them over, does seem like a plot fabricated to slander Saul's tribe. The Benjaminites followed the same laws and customs as the other tribes. If the mob had in fact come from among them, the elders of Benjamin would not have granted them shelter, and would most certainly not have gone to war and sacrificed their lives in order to defend them. The imaginary details added to the tale strengthen the impression that the section about the gang rape and the subsequent bloody war never actually took place.

Chapter Nineteen

THE RAPE OF BILHAH
(GENESIS 35:21–22)

The book of Genesis gives a very short description of another rape, almost forgotten, which took place within Jacob's family. According to the text, shortly after Rachel died, Leah's oldest son Reuben raped Bilhah, Rachel's slave woman:

> Israel [Jacob's other name] journeyed on, and he pitched his tent beyond Migdal-eder. And it came to pass, while Israel dwelt in that land, that Reuben went and lay with Bilhah, his father's concubine, and Israel heard. (35:21–22)

This act of rape, which is compressed into one short sentence, raises significant difficulties. The book of Genesis does not reveal the background of the act, or how Jacob discovered it. It does not relate how Jacob reacted when he heard about the scandal that had taken place in his house. The biggest problem is that Reuben was not punished for both committing a sex crime and violating a forbidden sexual relationship, despite the fact that according to biblical law he deserved execution.

Based on the single verse that remains as testimony to Reuben's despicable act, we cannot solve these conundrums, but we can address several of the issues it raises.

One difficulty is actually easy to solve. The text refers to Bilhah as a "concubine," which is incorrect. Bilhah was not a concubine-wife, but a slave-wife. She was the daughter of slaves, given to Rachel as a gift (29:29). Because Bilhah was Rachel's property, Rachel could use her for her needs and marry her to Jacob, as she did. If Bilhah had been a concubine, this would have meant she was born to a free father, who would have married her to Jacob without a bride-price. In such a case, her position would have been inferior to that of Rachel, but she would not have been Rachel's property. Under that scenario, Rachel would not have been able to marry her to Jacob and be built up through her sons. Bilhah's sons would have belonged to their mother, and to no other woman. But whether concubine or slave, Reuben was still forbidden from having relations with her, because she was his father's wife.

The second problem relates to the absence in the Hebrew text of the verb 'a.n.h., the term that the Bible uses for every other rape it describes. This raises the question of whether this was indeed a rape, or whether Bilhah consented to the encounter.

Despite the absence of the verb "rape," we can determine with certainty that this was indeed an act of rape. If it had been consensual, Bilhah would not have survived to see the light of the next day. Since Jacob discovered the act, she would have shared the fate of the Levite man's concubine, which we discussed in the previous chapter. In addition, this rape story is mentioned in other places in the Bible, and each time, the text places full responsibility on Reuben.

One of the biggest difficulties is to find a motive for Reuben's act. Possibly, the answer lies within the meaning of his name (see chapter 11, pp.187–88).

As we explained earlier, each of the names of Leah's children represents a stage in her life, from lowest to highest. Each name that Leah gave to a new son demonstrates how her fertility enabled the hated wife to establish her position in Jacob's house, leaving beloved Rachel far behind. Because Reuben was her oldest son, his name represents the lowest, most painful stage of her life. When Leah named Reuben, she used the Hebrew term *'onyi*, hinting that Jacob had raped her:

> *Leah conceived and bore a son, and she called his name Reuben, as she had declared,* **"Because the Lord has discerned my humiliation [*'onyi]*,** *for now my husband will love me." (Gen. 29:32)*

Even if we absolve Jacob from such a serious crime as rape, the text reports that he behaved extremely harshly toward Leah. Even the meaning of the name of Simeon, her second son, in which she admitted that her husband hated her, reflected an improvement in her position. While we may be willing to be lenient with Jacob and ignore the cruel explanation that Leah gave for Reuben's name – he did not forgive his father. Possibly, Reuben, whose name commemorates his birth as a result of rape, repaid Jacob measure for measure, and raped Bilhah in revenge for what Jacob did to his mother.

A second possibility asserts that the rape of Bilhah is another link in the chain of power struggles between the two sisters (I think this possibility is closest to the truth). As we have noted, the life and sexuality of a woman were the property of her husband – they represented his "honor." A man who raped another man's wife humiliated her husband. The husband whose honor was sullied in this manner could no longer have relations with his wife. This, I believe, is what Reuben wanted to achieve – and he did so.

At the time of the rape, Rachel was no longer alive, and so Bilhah to a certain extent took her place. She headed Rachel's camp, which numbered only four sons, while Leah's camp was twice as large, with eight sons and one daughter. With Rachel gone, Bilhah did not have a mistress to control the number of children she would bear. Jacob could have relations with her as long as he desired her, and give her additional sons, thus strengthening Rachel's camp. In raping Bilhah, Reuben blocked Rachel's camp from expansion. Although the Bible does not say that Jacob refrained from having relations with Bilhah after the rape, the fact is that she had no more children. I suggest the reason was that after she was raped, biblical law no longer allowed Jacob to have relations with her, of which fact Reuben was well aware.

The major problem that this story presents is the absence of punishment. The rape of Bilhah was not only forbidden as a rape – it was also an act of forbidden sexual relations. For this type of sin, the Bible mandates the death penalty for both the man and the woman involved:

> *Any man shall not approach his close relative to uncover nakedness; I am the Lord.... The nakedness of your father's wife you shall not uncover; it is your father's shame. (Lev. 18:6–23)*

> *A man who shall lie with his father's wife will have uncovered his father's shame; the two of them shall be put to death, their blood is upon themselves. (Lev. 20:11; see also Deut. 23:1)*

Despite the clear wording of the law, the punishment of Reuben, who violated one of the most severe sexual prohibitions, ended with the mere loss of his status as firstborn son and his father's successor (I Chron. 5:1–2). The dynastic torch, which according to birth order was supposed to pass to him, went instead to Judah. But punishment of the kind the law demanded was not carried out. I can suggest two explanations for the absence of punishment – one theological, the other emotional.

According to tradition, the twelve tribes of Israel were named after the twelve sons of Jacob. If Reuben had received his punishment, then one of the tribes of Israel would have been destroyed – and the authors of the Bible feared this eventuality:

> No tribe shall depart from Judah...until Shiloh arrives, and his will be an assemblage of nations. (Gen. 49:10)

According to the exact meaning of the Hebrew, Reuben's act would be resolved eventually, but at the end of days, not at the time when it took place. Moses spoke in the same vein:

> May Reuben live and not die, though his dead be but few. (Deut. 33:6)

The stance expressed in these statements explains why Reuben was not executed, and the eponymous tribe prospered and became one of the largest tribes in ancient Israel.

The emotional reason for why Reuben was not executed is that according to ancient custom, Jacob was the victim of the rape. In the absence of any judicial or executive authority above the family, he was the only person authorized to punish Reuben for his crime. But no sane man would ever execute his son, even if that son were a horrible person who deserved to die for his actions. Apparently, then, Reuben was not punished for the same reason that many rapists who abuse their relatives are not punished: it is easier for a father to absorb a harsh blow from his son than to settle accounts with him. This leads us directly into another rape story that took place within the family: the story of the rape of Tamar by Amnon, her eldest brother.

Chapter Twenty

THE RAPE OF TAMAR
(II SAMUEL 13)

D avid was the legendary king of Israel toward whom the torch procession proceeded from the dawn of time, and to whom it will return at the end of days. David married many women, some from distinguished lineages, others from not so distinguished ones.[9] His first wife was Michal, daughter of Saul, king of Israel, with whom he had no children, apparently so as to prevent new branches in Saul's lineage. In addition to Michal, he married Ahinoam the Jezreelite; Maacah, daughter of the king of Geshur; Hagit, Avital, and Eglah. They were joined by Abigail, former wife of Nabal the Carmelite, and Bathsheba, former wife of Uriah. Aside from these women whom the Bible mentions by name, David had ten anonymous concubines.

These numerous women bore him sons and daughters, but of them, the Bible follows the biographies of four sons and only one daughter. The Bible tells the stories of Amnon, David's eldest son, born to Ahinoam the Jezreelite; Absalom

---

[9] The fact that David married the daughters of kings and many concubines demonstrates that he was considered a man of great political and military power. Regional kings and respected leaders considered it important to make alliances with him, and so they gave him their daughters as his wives.

and Tamar, born to Maacah; Adonijah, son of Hagit; and Solomon, son of Bathsheba. The book of Kings dedicates long chapters to Solomon, David's youngest son, who inherited his throne. For unknown reasons, the Bible does not tell us what became of David's other children. But if we recall the high infant mortality rate in the ancient world, we may assume that many of them did not reach maturity. Another possibility is that they did nothing worthy of mention, and thus the Bible does not follow their lives.

The rape we will discuss here took place in the king's palace, and involved three of his children: his firstborn son Amnon, his daughter Tamar, and Absalom, her brother through the same mother. Amnon raped Tamar, his half-sister, and Absalom executed him. Following this, Absalom rebelled against his father and almost destroyed his kingdom, and in the end, he paid with his life.

In contrast to the story of the rape of Dinah, in which the rapist demonstrated his power to Jacob's family and to the inhabitants of Shechem, the story of Amnon's rape of Tamar contains all the components of what we call today "rape within the family." Tamar was raped within the family's lodgings, in a place where she was supposed to be protected from all harm. She was raped by her eldest brother, who took advantage of her innocence and her trust. In a twisted way, familiar to us from similar incidents screaming from the news broadcasts, David, the rapist's father, protected him until his other son put him to death.

According to the Bible, the reason that Amnon raped Tamar was that he "loved" her. The justification of the rapist's love for the rape victim repeats itself endlessly in cases of rape within families. Fathers who rape their daughters, and brothers who commit the same crime toward their little sisters, do not do so because they hate them or because they want to take revenge against them. These rapists are disturbed, or severely insane. They know that what they are doing is despicable, and that they are ruining the lives of their daughters or younger sisters, although in some way they really do love them. When their "love" takes control over them, they release it on the girl, cruelly and mercilessly. Rapists who use their children's bedrooms as torture chambers do not act out of hatred for the victim, but through a twisted impulse that they cannot control, which their disturbed minds understand as love.

Another characteristic of rape within the family is the age difference between the rapist and the victim. One of the reasons that a man is sexually attracted to his daughter or younger sister is because of her youth, vulnerability, and immaturity. He is obsessed by the idea of picking the fruit before it is ready, and he takes advantage of their difference in age in order to impose silence on her. The fear he inspires in the young girl gives him the feeling of power and control that he so lacks. Amnon's love for Tamar was just such a sick and abnormal love.

This is the story that the Bible tells:

Amnon, David's eldest son and the natural candidate to inherit the crown, "loved" Tamar, his younger half-sister, who was a virgin. His intense, desperate love for the forbidden girl gave him no rest. Tamar was like an irritating column of ants that crawled up his nostrils, marched into his head, and made every cell in his brain itch. She invaded his dreams and deranged his nights. She drove him to distraction in the mornings, when he followed her around the palace, picturing in his mind's eye how he would overpower her, penetrate her, and pierce her hymen. His desire for Tamar drove him insane, and made him sick with a craving that did not wane and could not be satisfied.

One morning, as he lay feverish and hallucinating about the thousand forms of his little sister, his friend and advisor

Jonadab came to visit him. When the faithful advisor saw the look on the face of the tortured prince, he was frightened, and begged him to reveal what was on his mind:

This is what happened afterwards:

> *Absalom, son of David, had a beautiful sister whose name was Tamar, and Amnon son of David loved her.* **Amnon lusted to the point of illness for his sister Tamar, for she was a virgin,** *but it seemed impossible for Amnon to do anything to her. Amnon had a friend named Jonadab, the son of David's brother Shimeah, and Jonadab was a very cunning man. He said to him, "Why are you so downtrodden, O son of the king, morning after morning? Will you not tell me?" So Amnon said to him, "I love Tamar, my brother Absalom's sister." (13:1–4)*

When Jonadab heard the desperate prince's secret, he did what any wise advisor must – he told him what to do. Jonadab advised Amnon to pretend to be ill and wait until his father visited. When the king asked how he was feeling, all Amnon had to do was to say that he needed only one thing for a speedy recovery: to eat dumplings. Not just any dumplings, but dumplings that the little sister he lusted after would prepare in front of him.

Jonadab, of course, did not propose that Amnon rape Tamar the moment she walked into his house. Such a sly advisor was well aware that such a plot could cost him his life. He made do with hinting at a way for Amnon to isolate Tamar from the rest of the family, and did not expand on the question of what would follow.

As expected, the evil advisor's plot succeeded.

Amnon indeed lay in bed burning with fever, real or imagined, driving the worried king to rush to his eldest son's abode. Apparently, Amnon did not have to make much effort in his role as the patient, since the sharp senses of the king, which had saved him from multiple threats, failed to perceive the signals of deceit flashing from his son's bed. The king, as well as all those involved in the incident, paid a terrible price for the betrayal of his senses.

Shortly after the king took his leave of Amnon, he met up with Tamar, and ordered her to go to her brother's house immediately. Little girls are accustomed to obeying their fathers, and accordingly, Tamar rushed to her brother's house, to make the dumplings required for his recovery.

When she reached the threshold of his home, she stood like a tiny butterfly on the edge of the trap he had set. Tamar, of course, did not sense the danger that awaited her at his hands.

Why should she feel any danger?

Amnon was her eldest brother and the natural candidate to inherit the crown when the time came, and she undoubtedly admired him for that. But Amnon was a spider. And the spider, its mouth dribbling sticky, foaming saliva, was focused on the prey that quivered in the thin silver threads of the web he had spun. At that moment, he had to plan how he would lead his sister into the trap he had set for her, to the place where he would attack and devour her.

Tamar trusted him.

She was a young, naïve girl, and Amnon, who could not take his eyes off her, was her eldest brother. Her father, the king, had sent her to make dumplings for him so that he would recover quickly.

What could be more innocent?

At first, Tamar was in the main room, along with Amnon's friends and other relatives. That was also where she made the desired dumplings. But when she served them to him, surprisingly, he refused to accept them, and ordered his guests to leave the house:

Tamar went to her brother Amnon's house, where he was lying down. She took some dough and kneaded it and prepared it in his sight, and she cooked the dumplings. She then took the pan and poured it before him, but he refused to eat. Amnon then said, "Remove everyone from before me"; and everyone went away from before him. (13:8–9)

The visitors walked out, slamming the door behind them, and Amnon was left alone with the girl who had ignited the crazed bonfire in his brain. Their brothers and sisters and other relatives who constantly surrounded her melted into the silence. Suddenly she was completely alone, and completely his. For the first time ever, not one member of their large family stood beside her. No one could disturb him from watching the film in which Tamar, and forever Tamar, played the leading role.

At last.

Perhaps Tamar could still have fled for her life. The trap had not yet closed on her, and the door was open. But she was too young, and the warning sirens that blared from every wall in the house did not reach her ears. Tamar trusted Amnon. She could not imagine the ghosts that raged behind the eyes that remained glued to her. She did not know that her vague form, available but unattainable, tortured her brother during the night, when his fantasies wandered to the room where she slept peacefully. She did not see the silver saliva, dribbling sticky and foamy from his mouth as he watched her playing with her sisters in the family living quarters.

Tamar did not know that at that moment, at the very second when she stood before him in her full physicality, he would seize her and punish her for the terrible suffering she was causing him in her childish wickedness, naïve and self-righteous. Amnon ordered her to bring the dumplings from the main room into the inner room. There, so he said, he would lie in his sickbed and eat the delicacies she had prepared:

Amnon then said to Tamar, "Bring the restorative meal into the room, so that I may recuperate from your hand"; so Tamar took the [dish of] dumplings that she had made and brought it to her brother Amnon, into the room. (13:10)

Once she entered that room, Amnon closed the mouth of the trap he had set for her, grabbed her by force and demanded that she lie with him:

She was serving [them] to him, when he grabbed her and said to her, "Come lie with me, my sister!"(13:11)

All at once, the horror about to take place exploded in her face. In panic, Tamar realized just where she was stuck, and what her brother wanted as he forcibly clutched her, grunting feverishly in her ears. She knew that if she lost her virginity, her life would be over. She would be lost between the walls of the palace, never to return to the bustling crowds under the blue skies of Jerusalem. Tamar begged for her life:

But she said to him, "No my brother; do not violate me, for such things are not done in Israel. Do not commit this despicable act! Where could I go with my shame? And you – you would be considered in Israel as one of the despicable men!" (13:12–13)

When Amnon refused to listen to her voice of reason, she begged him to marry her:

So now, speak to the king, for he would not withhold me from you [in marriage]. (13:13)

The little butterfly proposed marriage to the spider – what a bizarre and horrifying idea!

The Bible forbids marriage between siblings, but their father was the king, and he had the power to solve this problem. Such a marriage, although twisted, was the only opening that could save her from ostracism and isolation. But just as Amnon refused to listen to her first words, he also refused to listen to her last. He grabbed her by force and raped her.

After Amnon fulfilled his terrible need, his mood changed entirely, and he no longer desired his forbidden sister to the point of illness. The fuel that had ignited the flames of insanity in his brain had burned up, and in an instant, love was transformed into hatred:

> And Amnon hated her with very great hatred, for greater was the hatred with which he hated her than the love with which he had loved her. So Amnon said to her, "Get up and go away!" (13:15)

Tamar had been raped. She had lost her virginity, and her fate was sealed. A last spark of hope remained to her, and she clutched at it, until it also died. Tamar knew that no man except Amnon would ever marry her. Shockingly, the only place of refuge remaining to her was the putrid lair of the evil beast that had just dismembered her. Tamar knew that if she were thrown out, it would be her last chance to walk among the crowds of Jerusalem. She would be locked behind the palace walls, there to stay until her days were ended. There was still a chance that Amnon might succumb to her pleas and save her from the worst fate of all, but his feelings had completely changed, and he refused to listen to her. Amnon called to his servant, and ordered him to throw her out of his house and lock the door behind her:

> But she said to him, "Do not do this greater evil than that which you have already done to me – to send me away!" But he refused to listen to her. He called in his attendant who ministered to him, and said, "Send this one out from

me now, and lock the door behind her!" ...His attendant
took her out and locked the door behind her. (13:16–17)

Tamar was thrown out, and her fate was sealed. The last
ember of hope for her life died, and she left, wailing:

> *She was wearing a colorful tunic, for such robes were worn*
> *by the maidens among the king's daughters[10].... Tamar put*
> *dirt upon her head and tore the colorful tunic that was on*
> *her; she put her hand to her head and left, crying out as*
> *she went. (13:18–19)*

Ancient Israelites practiced three mourning customs: tear-
ing their clothes, wearing sackcloth, and placing dirt on their
heads. Tamar tore her clothes and placed dirt on her head –
her life was over, and she mourned for it.

THE SPIDER

We can wager that the author who recorded this story was not
a graduate of the psychology department of any university.
Still, he had a sharp, sensitive eye, and left us with a hair-
raising documentary of a man with a disturbed personality,
blind to the accepted family and social norms.

Rape within the family is a clear expression of serious
mental illness and a release of forbidden drives, and there is no
reason to suppose that the case here is different. Sane brothers have a natural defense mechanism that protects them
from the kind of "love" that Amnon felt toward his sister. A
normal person can distinguish between the permitted and

---

[10] The colorful tunic worn by the king's daughters is an interesting detail offered by the
Bible. Colorful cloth was highly valuable in the ancient Middle East. The blue-purple
color known as *techelet* in the Bible was made from a specific species of snail found
mainly on the coast of today's Lebanon. The fact that David's daughters wore colorful
tunics bears witness to his wealth, as only the wealthy were able to purchase colorful
cloth. Jacob expressed his great love for Joseph by giving him a colorful tunic, which
served as visible proof of his preferred status and aroused his brothers' jealousy (Gen.
37:1–3).

the prohibited, and from the outset does not feel attracted to forbidden targets. The normative behavior of an older brother toward his little sister is protective. Her natural proximity to him does not cause him incessant sexual tension. He does not develop a crazy obsession to pierce her hymen, nor is he tortured by the fact that she is beyond his reach and that he is unable to touch her. A mature, sane brother does not set a trap for his sister, pushing her into it and destroying her life. The author describes Amnon longing to the point of illness for the unattainable image of his virgin sister, and gives a frighteningly exact description of a psychopathic man with something evil exploding in his brain.

Tamar, as expected, refused to accede to her brother's outspoken demand that she have relations with him. Amnon interpreted her logical reaction as threatening, hostile behavior, purposely intended to anger him. From his point of view, Tamar did not respond to his agonized love for her with the proper respect and encouragement, and this gave him the "justification" to punish her cruelly.

As in any disturbed person, as soon as Amnon's lust was sated, the fire of insanity in his brain died out, and he no longer needed the object of his desire:

And Amnon hated her with very great hatred,
for greater was the hatred with which he hated her
than the love with which he had loved her. (13:15)

The author who wrote these words accurately described the instantaneous mood changes of a deranged attacker. The moment Amnon's desire was fulfilled, he had to separate himself from Tamar. All at once, the queen of his dreams was transformed into a stranger who occupied not one line in Amnon's biography. He did not remember that he had desired her, attacked her, or raped her. He did not know what she was doing in his home or how she had come to be there. His little sister ceased to be an object of desire, and in an instant became an object of revulsion, filthy and nauseating. He had to get rid of her and purify his house from the pollution she had brought inside. The spider had to return his home to its previous, satisfactory condition. He thus ordered his servant to open the door and throw her out of the house.

If Amnon had been graced with a shred of sanity, he would have recalled that in the society in which he lived, rapists were liable to only one punishment. He would have realized that Absalom, Tamar's brother, would pursue him, and that he had to flee Jerusalem and run for his life. But Amnon did not flee Jerusalem, because flight from mortal danger would have been normal behavior. Amnon remained in Jerusalem for two more years, until Absalom's sword finally reached him.

And Tamar?

Tamar took her shame to the house of Absalom, her good brother, who took her in and sheltered her as one would protect a small candle whose last light flickered between the palms of his hands. But the storm was too strong, and her flame was too fragile. It wavered and died between his palms. Absalom named his daughter after his beloved sister, and the Bible relates that she was a beautiful woman (14:27).

David found out about the rape that had taken place in his home. He was furious, but he did nothing. David remained silent, and his silence ended the lives of two of his sons, and almost brought an end to his own life and regime.

David found himself in a tragic position. He was a king whose son had raped his daughter. His honor was not sullied by any stranger or enemy who wanted to humiliate him, but by his eldest son, the natural candidate to inherit his throne. If he had been an ordinary citizen, possibly the rape might have been swallowed up inside the walls of his house as a terrible secret. After all, the walls of homes in our times

hide many of the rapes that take place within. But David
was no ordinary man. He was a king, the leader of the Israelite nation and chief commander of the army. News of the
rape that took place in his home spread, and an entire people
looked to him in anticipation of the reaction of the greatest
king that ever lived in Israel. Yet David chose to do nothing.
In order to understand the disastrous consequences he might
have chosen, we must place them in the social and historical
context of his time.

In David's era (c. 1000 BCE), the monarchy in Israel was
just beginning. The government institutions that he established, such as a national administration and a professional
army, had just begun to develop. One of the most important
changes at the beginning of the monarchic period was in the
judicial system. In the ancient world, the king served as the
highest judicial authority in his kingdom – and this was the
case in ancient Israel as well.[11] When David became king,
he became the supreme judge of the land. At the same time,
because the Israelite kingdom was still young, the elders continued to serve as judges, and their judicial role was preserved
throughout the monarchic period. But while the elders judged
only members of their own communities, the king held the
highest judicial authority in his kingdom, and had the authority to judge the citizens of the entire nation.

We might assume that the first legal judgment David was
called upon to make was the fate of his firstborn son – and in
the ancient world, there was only one punishment for rapists.
Furthermore, in the absence of an executive authority that
stood above the family, the harmed family bore the responsibility of executing the criminal. The tragic result of this
reality was that David had to fulfill the role of both judicial

---

[11] Remnants of these customs are still preserved today. For example, the president of
the United States is also commander-in-chief of the army, and he has the right to grant
pardons.

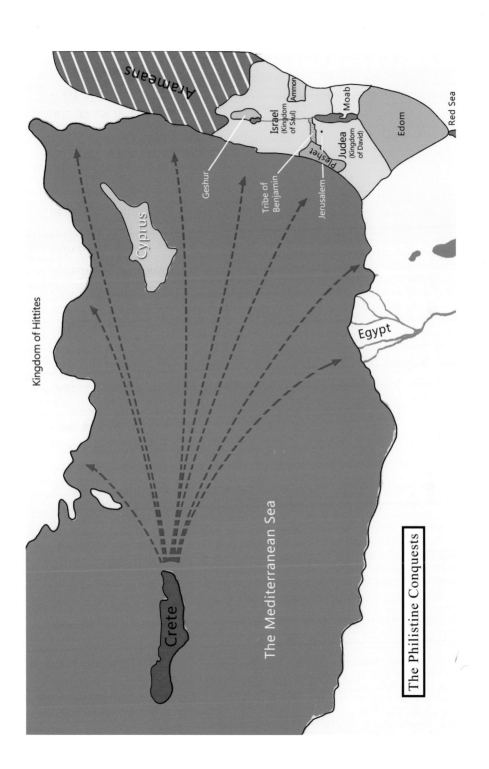

The Philistine Conquests

and executive authorities. He was the only person who had the authority to judge his son, and the only person authorized to order one of his warriors to execute him.

Blind fate and the accepted norms of his time demanded that the great king do something his emotions would not allow him to do. David (like Jacob before him) preferred to bear the weight of shame rather than sign with his own hand the order to execute Amnon. But the choice he made aroused the most dangerous of his enemies from slumber – his son Absalom, Tamar's full brother.

Among the four sons the Bible describes, Absalom was the one who most resembled David. Absalom was an improved version of his father – and David was wrong in not taking that into account. Just as Amnon deserved to be called a spider, Absalom warranted being called a lion cub – and he really was a proud and beautiful lion, the likes of which Israel had never seen before:

> There was no one in all of Israel as praiseworthy for his beauty as Absalom; from the bottom of his foot to the top of his head there was no blemish in him. (14:25)

In biblical language, usually so concise in its visual descriptions of the characters, this should be interpreted as lavish praise of much more than Absalom's physical beauty. Like his father, Absalom was graced with bravery, patience, and discretion. He knew how to plan his steps quietly and wisely. He knew how to lie in the bush motionless, not even a muscle twitching under his skin. He knew how to wait patiently until his prey made its first mistake – and then pounce on it and grab it by the neck. One bite of a molar, one pulverizing shake – and it would all be over. Absalom inherited another characteristic from David that some might call charisma; he charmed people and inspired their trust. Yet another trait he inherited from his father was his long memory: he never forgot anything, and did not know the meaning of forgiveness. Absalom knew that his father lacked the emotional strength to judge Amnon – and he could not forgive him for this.

We may suppose that Amnon's status as firstborn was taken away from him after the rape, and that he was no longer a candidate to replace his father. According to the order of inheritance, next in line for the kingship was Chileab, David's second son (II Sam. 3:3). But Chileab disappeared from the biblical story, and we have no idea what befell him. The third son thus advanced to first place – and the third son was Absalom. However, the fact that Amnon remained alive was a bone in Absalom's throat, and prevented him from being considered an apt successor to his father. The military commanders and warriors would never swear allegiance to a weak, humiliated king who was unable to execute the man who had raped his sister. The elders and the people would never accept the authority of such a king. Absalom was well aware of this, and David knew it as well.

Two years passed from the time Tamar was raped. The Bible does not relate what went on in the royal household during this period, but one thing is clear: in order for Amnon to add days to his miserable life, someone had to have protected him from Absalom – and that someone must have been David, no one else.

The moment of revenge arrived.

One day at the beginning of summer, the shearers finished shearing Absalom's sheep. As was traditional in those days, a celebration was held at the end of the sheepshearing, and Absalom and his men planned a large, festive celebration. After the preparations were complete, Absalom presented himself in his father's house and invited him and his brothers to share in his celebration. Following the accepted manners of the royal court, Absalom addressed the king in third person:

Absalom came to the king and said, "Behold they are shearing for your servant; let the king and his servants accompany your servant." (13:24)

This time, David, who was a wise and experienced man, identified the source of danger. He knew Absalom well, and recognized that he was lying in ambush, tensed in anticipation of the moment of revenge against the king. David did not intend to fall again into a trap set by one of his sons, and politely refused the invitation:

The king said to Absalom, "No, my son, let us not all go, so that we do not overburden you." He [Absalom] importuned, but he would not consent to go, but he blessed him. (13:25)

David's gracious refusal did not conclude the conversation, but rather sharpened it even further. David undoubtedly realized that as long as Amnon was alive, the rape incident could not reach closure, and Absalom would continue to lie in wait at his doorstep. Furthermore, David knew that in giving Amnon shelter, he was humiliating Absalom before the people of Jerusalem, and thus he could not begin to train him as his successor and plan for the day when the kingdom would pass into his hands. David knew that the incident had to reach its conclusion, and that he had no choice but to part from Amnon. But he feared, justly, that Absalom would not be satisfied with that. From Absalom's viewpoint, his father's polite refusal to come to his celebration only postponed his vengeance against the king. But this could afford to wait a while longer, while Amnon's execution had to be performed immediately:

*Absalom said, "If not, then **let my brother Amnon go with us**". But David said, "Why should he go with you?" Absalom importuned him, so he sent Amnon and all the king's sons along with him. (13:26–27)*

The biblical author, as usual, summarized a long, harsh conversation in one short sentence: "Why should he go with you?" But the dissembling question reveals the agreement that they had silently reached. It shows that David understood that Amnon's time was up, that he had no choice but to permit the execution of his firstborn son and send him to his death. If Amnon had been able to think logically and read the map of reality, he would have understood that the moment he left the king's house, he was going to fall into Absalom's hands. But because the warning button in his confused brain was switched off, he happily confirmed his attendance at the shearing party. When he arrived at the place of celebration, Absalom's men killed him.

Amnon died, but for some unknown reason, the rumor that reached David's ears was that Absalom had killed all of his brothers, down to the very last one. When the king heard this terrible news, he tore his clothing and fell to the ground, stricken with grief. At that moment, Jonadab, Amnon's crafty advisor, declared:

> Let my lord not think that they killed all the young men, the king's sons, **for Amnon alone is dead; for Absalom had issued that order since the day [Amnon] violated his sister Tamar**. And now, let my lord the king not take the matter to his heart, saying, "All the king's sons have died"; for only Amnon is dead. (13:32–34)

With artificial naiveté, Jonadab tried to assuage the grief of the king, who for a moment believed that Absalom had killed all his sons. No, Absalom did not kill all the king's sons, Jonadab promised the king, who was collapsing in pain. What the crafty advisor failed to mention was that his evil advice led to the rape of Tamar and in direct continuation, to the death of Amnon as well.

Chapter Twenty-One

ABSALOM'S REBELLION AND DAVID'S RISE TO KINGSHIP

(II SAMUEL 14–19)

T he book of Samuel relates that after Absalom killed Amnon, he fled to the kingdom of Geshur, his mother's birthplace. In Geshur he took shelter in the home of his grandfather, King Talmai son of Ammihud, where he remained for the next three years (13:37–38). The modern reader usually understands his flight as due to fear of the results of his act, but Absalom behaved according to the societal norms of the times. He was Tamar's closest relative, and so he bore the responsibility for executing the man who had raped her, thus desecrating his honor as well as that of his family. Furthermore, David, who was unable to judge Amnon, finally permitted Absalom to kill him – this is witnessed by the fact that he did not pursue Absalom or attempt to punish him in any way. But instead of Absalom returning to Jerusalem victorious and preparing for the kingship that awaited him, he fled north to his grandfather in the kingdom of Geshur.

Why?

The author of this story did not answer this question, nor did he reveal what Absalom was up to throughout the three years of his exile. Like the other biblical authors, this one provided many unrelated details that do not fit together, and we cannot determine why they were included in the story. Yet the author gave us the final, concluding line of the story, which enables us to put these details into place and reconstruct the steps that led to that ending.

According to the book of Samuel, three years passed from Amnon's execution until Absalom returned to Jerusalem from exile. Although the king longed to see his beautiful son, two more years went by until they met. When Absalom finally stood before his father, the king kissed him on the cheeks, thus indicating that the events that had tormented them throughout the last five years were relegated to the past. At that point, so the king believed, life had returned to normal, and he could open a new chapter in his relationship with his son and begin training him for the demanding role that awaited him. Absalom was first in line for the kingship, and the great events that awaited him beyond the horizon highlighted the importance of an improvement in their relations.

Yet Absalom, as we discover, had completely different plans. Although he had settled his debt with Amnon, the account with his father, who had sheltered the rapist and thus humiliated him in front of the entire population of Jerusalem, remained open – and in order to carry out his revenge, Absalom had to go to the kingdom of Geshur. Since the story of Absalom's revenge against his father is intimately related to the events that preceded his lifetime, we must go back in time to explain one of the most ambiguous periods discussed in the Bible, the period of David's rise to the monarchy. The rape of Tamar and Absalom's rebellion are a central link in the chain of events surrounding the rebellion.

SAUL AND DAVID

The tribal population that lived in the land of Canaan was divided into two large groups: northern and southern. The tribe of Judah, to which David belonged, occupied the Judean desert that extends south of Jerusalem. Between the northern tribes and the southern tribe of Judah lay Jerusalem, home of the Jebusites, one of the Canaanite peoples. When David became king, he made Jebusite Jerusalem into his capital, because it formed a natural divide between the tribe of Judah and the other tribes of Israel. A narrow belt north of Jerusalem was home to the tribe of Benjamin – birth tribe of Saul, Israel's first king. The other tribes stretched behind Benjamin to the north, and their northeastern border hugged today's Syria and Lebanon. Their eastern border was today's Jordanian Kingdom.

About two hundred years before the period of Saul and David, a foreign, predatory element penetrated the eastern coast of the Mediterranean Sea: the Philistines (thirteenth–twelfth century BCE).[12] The Philistines, originally from Crete in Greece, took over the enormous kingdom of the Hittites, which spread across the territory of today's Turkey and Syria. They laid waste to it, and the ancient kingdom, which had existed for over five hundred years, collapsed, never to rise again. In addition, the Philistines sailed their boats along the coasts of modern-day Lebanon and Israel, and large numbers reached the coast of Egypt, almost destroying the regime of the Pharaohs. A small part of the Philistine force that invaded the kingdoms along the eastern coast of the Mediterranean also penetrated into Canaan, today's Land of Israel.

---

[12] Despite the similarity in name, the Philistines and the Palestinians are not the same people and should not be confused. The Palestinians of today are Arabs, and they originated in the desert regions of Saudi Arabia and Egypt. The Philistines, as explained above, arrived from Crete or the Greek islands.

Over one hundred years passed after the Philistines reached Canaan. During this time, they attempted to banish the Israelites from their villages and take over their land.

As a result of the heavy pressure they placed on the Israelites' living areas, the respected elders, leaders of the tribes, realized that the era of tribal society had come to an end. The elders understood that tribal society, in which each tribe acted on its own and defended only its own territory, was unable to face a powerful enemy such as the Philistines.

They understood that if they valued their lives, they had to unite and appoint a king who would transform the disparate armies of the individual tribes into a united army, uniform, skilled, and efficient. The elders had to lead a social revolution in order to transform their tribal society into a monarchy. They thus approached Samuel, the religious leader of that time, and asked him to appoint a king. Samuel did not view the political changes of his day as a true threat to the continued existence of the tribes of Israel, and so he supported the traditional form of leadership, tried to dissuade the elders from this step, but to no avail. He finally capitulated, and chose Saul of the tribe of Benjamin to serve as the first king of Israel (I Sam. 8–9). The book of I Samuel describes how after the first hesitant years of kingship, Saul succeeded in establishing control over his kingdom. The text clearly shows that Saul, who was appointed king in order to fight the Philistines, invested most of his strength in battling them – and this was his great and bitter mistake!

At first glance, the battle against the Philistines seems justified, because they were a thorn in the sides of the villagers of central Canaan. But the battle did not take place in a vacuum, though we may get that impression from reading the book of Samuel. As we noted above, the Philistines directed their primary military force toward the powerful Hittite kingdom, scattering its inhabitants in all directions.

Aramean tribes, who until then were under Hittite control, exploited the collapse of the Hittite regime to establish their own independent kingdom in what is today part of Syria.

Those who study historical atlases will discover that the territory occupied by the Aramean tribes was twice as large as that of the Israelite tribes all together. The maps also reveal another dangerous detail: the Aramean tribes shared a border with the northern tribes of Saul's kingdom. The destructive potential of such enormous tribes, which had just been freed from the yoke of the Hittite kingdom and had begun to coalesce as an independent kingdom, was obvious to all – except for Saul.

The author of the book of Samuel omits one vital detail: while Saul was tirelessly battling the Philistines in the center of Canaan, a new kingdom was developing unhindered, alongside the territories of the northeastern tribes of Israel. [13] Saul ignored the process taking place over the border, and behaved as if it were not happening.

At that point in time, Saul had to decide which group was the Israelites' most dangerous enemy: the Philistines, who pressured his people from within, or the Aramean tribes, who were then still peaceful. Saul determined that the Philistines were the greater threat – and this, as we have said, was a bitter mistake that led to his tragic downfall.

---

[13]The historical reality was much more complex. The collapse of the northern Hittite kingdom in the thirteenth century BCE enabled the Aramean tribes to establish an independent kingdom of their own. At the same time, a similar process was taking place in the south. Wall writing and wall paintings discovered in Egypt demonstrate that great numbers of Philistines arrived in Egypt from the Mediterranean Sea. The Egyptians defeated the Philistines, but as a result, the Pharaonic regime was severely undermined. The weakening of Egypt enabled distant tribes that had previously been under its authority to rise up and become independent kingdoms. Edom, Moab, and Ammon were among the kingdoms that arose in that period. Here I focus on Aram and not on other kingdoms that arose in parallel, because Aram represented the true threat to the continued existence of the Israelite tribes.

We must recall that the Philistines penetrated Canaan over a century before Saul's time, and their presence within the Israelite settlement was already a given. Although they were a constant irritation, their powerful momentum, which led to the destruction of the ancient Hittite kingdom and the weakening of Egypt, eventually dissolved. Despite their interference, the Philistines lacked the power to banish the inhabitants of even the small villages, or to take over their territories.[14]

Saul's big mistake is apparent only when we realize that the tribes' process of unification into a kingdom did not take place in one day. This was a slow process that occurred over decades, accompanied by dramatic internal changes. Apparently, this is why the author of the book of Samuel had a mild opinion of the Arameans, and he gives us no idea of the power of their threat. But the author of the book of Kings, which relates to the period beginning about forty years after Saul's death, describes Aram as a vast and mighty kingdom that repeatedly attacked the northern Israelite tribes, cruelly smiting their inhabitants and gnawing at their territories.

The historical reality in which Saul found himself forced him to recognize the danger amassing beyond the borders of his kingdom, and to use the time he had in order to prepare to face it. He had to end the war against the Philistines, make agreements with them regarding the areas where they would settle, and plan together for war against Aram, their joint enemy. Furthermore, logic dictates that the Philistines themselves wanted to reach some sort of agreement with Saul, since the protracted war against him brought them no real

---

[14] The Philistines' dispersal across such a broad region finally led to their downfall: they scattered in all directions, and in the end, their enormous power dissipated. The Philistine arm that penetrated Canaan encountered a tiny village population. Even so, they were not able to expel the village inhabitants, which demonstrates that they had lost the power they had enjoyed one hundred years earlier.

success – and Aram was as great a threat to them as it was to the Israelite tribes.

At this fateful moment, Saul had other reasons to conclude the endless war. Like all the peoples of Greece, the Philistines were experienced sailors. They had extensive commercial relations with distant lands, from which they imported iron ore. The Philistines were also skilled and experienced smiths, and they forged the ore into iron weapons. Thus while Saul's army was still fighting with wooden swords, his enemy was using advanced weapons made of iron:

> Now there was no smith to be found anywhere in the entire land of Israel, for the Philistines said, "Lest the Hebrews produce a sword or spear." ...Thus it was on the day of war that there was not to be found sword or spear in the possession of any of the people who were with Saul or Jonathan; but they could be found with Saul and his son Jonathan. (I Sam. 13:19–22)

In addition to iron weaponry, the Philistines were also well versed in sophisticated war techniques they had acquired in Greece. By contrast, the army Saul founded was a ragtag group of villagers with almost no previous military experience. All the while, Aram was rapidly gaining power beyond the northern border of his kingdom.

The argument that the continued war against the Philistines was a mistake sheds light on the period preceding David's arrival in Saul's house, and explains several issues that the author of the book of Samuel mentioned briefly but did not bother to explain.

The book of I Samuel describes how Saul unleashed his full strength in battle against the Philistines. In parallel, it also describes how much he and his army feared them – and now we understand why. The Philistines had cast-iron weapons, and Saul had no counter to this advantage.

Another central issue that the book of Samuel does not bother to explain is the deep rift in the relationship between Saul and his eldest son Jonathan, who was destined to inherit the kingdom. The book of Samuel describes Jonathan, himself a powerful warrior, as mocking his father, ignoring him, refusing to consult with him, and even blaming him that he was destroying the country (I Sam. 14). In traditional society, in which the father has the status of all-powerful ruler over his family, a son must have a powerful reason in order to reject his father, especially when the father is king. The only reason for a crown prince to act with hostility toward his father is a deep disagreement. Such a disagreement may have been Jonathan's opinion that the continued battle against the Philistines was unnecessary, draining the army's blood and preventing it from preparing for future battles. Almost certainly, Jonathan believed that his father should make a peace agreement with the Philistines and take advantage of their technological and military know-how. When this did not happen, their relationship reached a crisis. The book of Samuel relates that God abandoned Saul, and so a spirit of melancholy and horror began to torment him. In addition to the theological explanation, a practical reason may have led to Saul's downcast mood. Perhaps Saul sensed that in addition to Jonathan, opposition was also beginning to form from within his inner circle, and this intensified his dejected mood and suspicion toward those close to him.

The miserable reality we have described above is intensified by a central new player: David.[15]

---

[15] Many readers of the Bible point the finger at David for rebelling against Saul and leading to his overthrow. But this accusation does an injustice to the great king. Court overthrows, or military coups by army commanders against their kings, follow a regular pattern that repeats itself countless times throughout history. A rebel who wants to become king takes the life of the reigning king (and usually, the members of his family as well). Such was the case in the ancient Near East, as well as in China, Japan, Russia, and Europe. We may easily argue that this model does not describe our case.

The book of Samuel gives two different versions of the first meeting between Saul and David. According to the first version, the king's servants searched for a talented musician who would play before the king and dissipate his melancholy, and David was this man. According to the second version, the two met after David killed Goliath the Philistine, who had copper armor and iron weapons (I Sam. 17:1–7) and inspired terror in the hearts of Saul's soldiers.

The two versions strengthen the feeling that Saul's kingdom had begun to crack even before David reached his household. But analysis of the issues we have presented above leads to another possibility: David went to Saul's house in order to convince him to end the war against the Philistines and make a peace agreement with them (which David did as soon as he became king).

Like Jonathan, David was aware that the northern borders of the Israelite kingdom were porous. Should Aram penetrate deep inside Israelite territory, it would threaten the existence of southern Judah. Readers of the book of Kings will readily note that this is indeed what happened. In my opinion, the courageous friendship that developed between David and Jonathan was based on their agreement that Saul's method of rule was endangering the existence of the Israelite kingdom. The assumption that Jonathan despaired of his father's ruling method explains his rebellious attitude, and the fact that he willingly relinquished his position as crown prince in favor of David (I Sam. 23:16-18). This picture of the situation also explains why Saul's love for David when the young man first came to the palace quickly spoiled, turning

---

When Saul's love for David turned into hatred, he gathered his army and began to pursue him, intending to kill him. During his flight, David had opportunities to surprise Saul from his hiding place and kill him, thus ending the lengthy pursuit of him. Yet although David was surrounded by warriors, he refused to attack the king, and forbade his soldiers to do so (I Sam. 1:24; 26:1–20).

into suspicion and threat. The king justifiably interpreted the friendship between his son and David as a betrayal of him:

> *Saul's anger flared up at Jonathan, and he said to him, "Son of a pervertedly rebellious woman! Do I not know that you choose the son of Jesse, to your own shame and the shame of your mother's nakedness?" For all the days that the son of Jesse is alive on the earth, you and your kingdom will not be established! And now send and bring him to me, for he is deserving of death!"*
>
> *But Jonathan spoke up to his father Saul, and said to him, "Why should he die? What has he done?"*
>
> *Saul hurled his spear at him to strike him. Jonathan then realized that his father had decided to kill David. (I Sam. 20:30–33)*

After this, Saul gathered his army and began to pursue David, with the goal of executing him.

The rift between Saul and Jonathan, and the melancholy spirit that began to affect Saul, create a strong impression that the opposition to Saul began to take shape even before David arrived in his household. At the same time, David's arrival at court no doubt hastened the end of Saul's monarchy. David, who was blessed with a charismatic personality, drew toward himself the circle of individuals who surrounded Saul, and strengthened the opposition that arose within the royal abode.[16] The vise encircling Saul's neck explains why, at the height of his battle against the Philistines, he led his warriors on a chase to catch and kill David. The soldiers, who apparently considered the hunt a waste of their time, did not even bother to hide the fact that they were making no effort

---

[16] The assumption that the opposition to Saul arose from within his own household is also evidenced by the behavior of his daughter Michal, David's first wife. It was Michal who revealed to David that her father had sent people to their home in order to kill him, and she helped him to flee (I Sam. 19:11–17).

to catch him. Understandably, Saul vilified them for betraying him, as his son did (I Sam. 22:6–8).

As we know, Saul's last battle against the Philistines cost him his life and the lives of his three sons, including Jonathan. After the king and his sons died, David took over the Israelite kingdom with power and determination. He mercilessly crushed Saul's inner circle and his followers, and recruited the forces of the Cherethites, the Pelethites, and the Gittites, who were Philistine warriors. After this, he moved rapidly north toward Aram and defeated it. David's army crossed the length of Aram and stopped near the Euphrates, which served as a natural border between Aram and the kingdom of Assyria.[17]

A general overview of the events that took place after his time reveals the logic behind the war David initiated. Analysis of the war reveals that David attempted to achieve two major goals. Both goals bear witness to his brilliant ability to read historical processes precisely and at their inception. They also document his heroic attempt to prepare for them in advance.

David's rush to defeat Aram shows that he decided to weaken that nation before it could gain power and threaten the Israelite settlement. A weak Aram, with David's army hanging over its neck, could not smite the inhabitants whom Saul had abandoned to their fate during the years when he battled the Philistines and pursued David.

The second goal David attempted to achieve is revealed by the fact that he crossed the length of Aram with his army and stopped beside the Euphrates, which, as we said, formed the natural border between Aram and Assyria. David understood that Aram's rise to power was the lesser evil, and that

---

[17] David defeated the rulers of the kingdoms that lay to the east of the Israelite kingdom, but he believed it was not they, but Aram that represented the true danger to Israel.

a greater one was rapidly forming on the other side. The Assyrian kingdom, which lay on the other side of Aram (in today's Iraq), had begun to gather power, the likes of which the ancient world had never known. David understood that when the Assyrian wave reached its full height, it would roll forward, crashing over the lands that stood in its way and washing them off the map. First Assyria would conquer the kingdom of Aram that shared its border. Then, the shock of the blow that Aram absorbed would cause a chain reaction. Like one wave crashing into another, Assyria would defeat the northern Israelite tribes, then overpower the southern tribe of Judah. The only way David could stop the Assyrian wave from crashing over the Israelite kingdom was to turn Aram into a partition area that would separate the Israelite kingdom on one side from the Assyrian kingdom on the other.

When we map the details in the book of Samuel onto the period when they took place, we gain the impression that even if Saul had not been killed by the Philistines, and even if David had not gone to his house, his kingdom stood on the brink of collapse. In the ancient world, all kings were warriors and chiefs of their armies. Their first and foremost role was to protect the borders of their kingdoms. The king had the responsibility to identify the dangers threatening his kingdom in time, and to organize his people to face them – and Saul failed in both of these. The obsession with the Philistine war in the center of the country sucked him in and forced him to abandon the northern borders of his kingdom. As a result, cracks began to appear in the primary circle of support that ordinarily assists a king in stabilizing his regime.

In contrast to Saul, David was a world-class king. Like every great king, David placed his kingdom's security at the top of his list of priorities, and led his army to protect its borders. His military operations reveal that he was graced with long-range vision. Like an arrow shot from a bow, he

sped north in order to brake the rise of Aram, and to transform it into a security partition between Assyria and Israel.
When we compare the operational methods of the two kings,
we find that Saul was a local, village-level king, while David
was a leader of international standing. We also find that if
ever there was a king who tried to save Saul's kingdom from
both the immediate Aramean danger and the future Assyrian
danger, that king was David.

THE RAPE OF TAMAR AND ABSALOM'S REBELLION

In the end, David failed in his desperate and heroic attempt
to block the impending end with his own bare hands. David
rose to kingship late in the game, when the changes taking
place beyond the borders of the Israelite kingdom were already
at their height. Thanks to the harsh measures he took, in his
time Aram was quiet and weak (as were the other kingdoms
that bordered on ancient Israel). But shortly after his death,
Aram freed itself from the burden David had placed on it and
began to smite the northern Israelite tribes and gnaw at their
territories. Soon, the Assyrian empire reached the height of
its power, and David's great fear was realized. First, Assyria
wiped the kingdom of Aram off the face of the earth. Then
it erased the kingdom that Saul had established, and with it
the Philistines, whom Saul had fought throughout his entire
reign (c. 732–724 BCE). The Babylonian empire ultimate-
ly replaced Assyria and completed the work of destruction,
laying waste to Jerusalem and to the Temple that Solomon
had built, and banishing the inhabitants of Judah from their
land (c. 586 BCE).

David's late rise to kingship is not the only reason for
his failure to weaken Aram to such a point that it could not
threaten the Israelite tribes. His plans had two serious flaws
for which he himself was responsible.

The first flaw was that David built up his strength within Saul's family and among the army commanders close to him. According to the book of Samuel, David operated only within the region of the tribe of Benjamin, in the center of the country, and did not go north to forge ties with the elders who led the northern tribes. Possibly, Jonathan was supposed to have convinced them to cooperate with David.[18] But when Jonathan was killed, David was left without his main source of support within the royal family. The northern elders viewed southern David as a foreigner, not one of their own, and did not want him as their king. They continued to maintain their loyalty to their dead king, and preferred that his son Ishbosheth, Saul's fourth son, rule them. But Ishbosheth was a puppet king, murdered shortly after he was crowned.[19] Because Aram was screaming in David's ears, he did not take the time to pacify Saul's supporters, but suppressed them by force – and he paid a heavy price for this in the time of Absalom's rebellion.[20]

---

[18] After the deaths of Saul and his three sons, Ishbosheth, Saul's fourth son, became king. Ishbosheth was a weak king (possibly, he was still a child when he took the throne) and an inappropriate replacement for his father. In practice, Abner, Saul's uncle and army commander, led the Israelite kingdom. When Abner understood that Ishbosheth was unable to stand in his father's shoes, he decided to unite with David, and convinced the northern elders to end their opposition to David, and join him (II Sam. 3; also 13:17–21). The cooperation between David and Abner never took place, because Abner was murdered. But the book of Samuel clearly states that Abner's role was to convince the northern elders to join David, supporting the assumption that this was Jonathan's role from the outset.

[19] The name Ishbosheth is derogatory, and it based on the word *bushah*, "shame" – meaning that such a king was shameful to Israel. In chapter 11, we pointed out that many times, the Bible authors changed the original names of some characters, giving them new names that described their personalities. The name Ishbosheth is such a name.

[20] Undoubtedly, the protracted war against the Philistines exhausted the northern tribes. Possibly, one of the reasons for the elders' opposition to David was that they wanted to enjoy a bit of peace, instead of beginning a new war against the Aramean tribes, who had never harmed them. Like Saul, they did not predict that their quiet neighbors would suddenly change their tune and attack them.

The second impediment to David's plan was Absalom himself – and this is the time to complete the circle we have made and return to Jerusalem and the story of the rape of Tamar, which occurred at the height of the period we have described here. David, the military genius with the political vision who feared no man, was unable to order one of his warriors to execute Amnon. In this, he created his own bitterest enemy: the son who most resembled him, Absalom.

From a historical point of view, long after the events have reached their conclusion, we can determine that from the day David offered shelter to the rapist, the clever political plan described above began to fall apart. In the end, the immediate danger that threatened his life's work did not lie in wait for him from afar, but rather inside his own home, because Absalom overturned the kingdom. David must have known that a man like Absalom would never forgive him for protecting Amnon and thus humiliating him before the entire population of Jerusalem. Indeed, the desire for revenge that boiled in Absalom's veins explains his actions during his exile in the kingdom of Geshur and in the years following his return to Jerusalem.

As we recall, after Absalom executed Amnon, he "fled" to his mother's family in Geshur, where he remained for three years. Yet the flight was unnecessary, both because he was acting according to the legal procedures practiced in his day, and also because his father did not pursue him.

The kingdom of Geshur was a tiny enclave located about 124 miles (200 km) north of Jerusalem, on the border of the northern Israelite tribes. From Geshur, Absalom contacted the Israelite elders, who remained faithful to their late king and did not want David to rule them. He created a group of supporters among them who aided him in his plan to overthrow his father. Without their support and the military forces they placed at his disposal, he would have no warriors (the army that David had founded, including the Philistine mercenaries, remained loyal to him). Clearly, then, in order to prepare for the rebellion, Absalom had to be in the northern area of the country.

We must admit that the Bible, with its usual reticence, does not relate that Absalom contacted the northern elders from within the kingdom of Geshur, but it does confirm this assumption in a roundabout manner. It says that when Absalom raised the banner of rebellion, the kingdom of Saul answered his cry and stood beside him in all its might. But with this, we are getting ahead of ourselves.

Two years passed after Absalom returned to Jerusalem until his father summoned him and they made their peace. But this peace was for appearances only, because the covert cooperation between Absalom and the leaders of the northern families continued. Absalom did behave as if he were willing to begin a new chapter in his relationship with his father, and even began to plan for the time when the crown would pass to him. In order to strengthen the desired impression, Absalom began to take over some of the king's roles, the first of which was to stand at the city gate every morning and judge the people who came to be judged by his father. In addition, Absalom drove around the streets of Jerusalem in a horse-drawn chariot, with fifty men announcing his arrival, as befitting a crown prince making a public declaration that he was first in line to the crown:

> It happened after this, that Absalom prepared for himself chariot and horses, and fifty men to run before him. Absalom would arise early and stand by the way toward the gate [the city gate was the place of judgment]; and it happened when any man who would have a dispute to bring to the king for judgment, Absalom called to him and said, "**Which city are you from?**" **And he said, "Your servant is from such and such tribe of Israel**." Then Absalom said to him,

"Look, your words are good and proper, but there is no one before the king to understand you." Then Absalom said, "If only someone would appoint me judge in the land, and any man who had a dispute or a judgment could come to me – I would judge him fairly!" And it was that whenever anyone came near him to prostrate himself before him, he would stretch out his hand and take hold of him and kiss him. Absalom did this sort of thing to all of Israel who would come for judgment to the king; and Absalom stole the hearts of all the men of Israel. (15:1–6)

This quotation is nothing but a ruse revealing that Absalom had poured a sleeping potion into his father's goblet and put him to sleep. David assumed from the enthusiastic coquetry of his handsome son that he was interested in succeeding him as king of Israel – but David made a bitter mistake. He did not evaluate his son's character correctly, and did not suspect that the royal manners Absalom had adopted were part of a brilliant scheme of fraud designed to buy him the additional time he needed to complete his preparations for rebellion.

In David's time, and throughout the years of the monarchy, the elders continued to hold their traditional positions as judges of their communities. Since the monarchy was new, judgment before the king was a new procedure, and it took place in parallel to the traditional legal process. Thus Absalom's habit of standing at the city gate in order to judge the people did not fill any legal vacuum.

According to the citation above, Absalom would first verify the origin of each and every man who came to be judged before his father. If the answer was "One of the Israelite tribes," he persuaded the man to be judged by him. The answer "Your servant is from *one of the Israelite tribes*" sounds neutral, but the opposite is the case. It reveals that the man who came to be judged was not from the tribe of Judah, but rather from one of the northern tribes that remained loyal to Saul.

Until the time of Saul and David, the Bible relates to Israel and Judah as one entity, referring to them with the general name "Israel." But after that period, the name Israel relates only to the tribes that lived north of Jerusalem, who appointed Saul as their king. The name Judah applies exclusively to the tribe of Judah, which lived in Jerusalem and southward of Israel, in the region of the Judean and Negev Deserts. This means that at the time we are studying here, the Bible related to Israel and Judah as two separate territorial and social entities, which David wanted to unite under his reign. If a man coming for judgment before the king replied to Absalom that he was from one of the tribes of Israel, he revealed that he lived in northern Israel, and that he was not from the tribe of Judah.

But why would a northern man go south to Jerusalem for judgment? Why should he submit to judgment by David, and not go to the elders of his community, as was the time-honored practice? Furthermore, why did Absalom convince the man to be judged by him, and not by his father?

The fact that the northern tribes supported Absalom during the rebellion seems to offer the answer to these questions. It strengthens the supposition that Absalom's position at the place of judgment was in fact camouflage for his preparations for rebellion. It hints that the northern men who came to Jerusalem for "judgment" were in fact messengers who relayed communications between the rebel leaders in the north and Absalom in the south. We can determine with a high level of certainty that the expression "Absalom stole the hearts of the men of Israel" means that the court he operated was actually the headquarters of the rebellion. When the preparations were complete, Absalom blew the horn, and the rebellion broke out in the kingdom of Israel:

Absalom then sent spies throughout all the tribes of Israel, saying, "When you hear the sound of the trumpet, announce, 'Absalom has become king in Hebron.'" ...The conspiracy was powerful, and the people with Absalom continually increased. The bearer of news came to David, saying, "The heart of [every] man of Israel has turned to Absalom." (15:10–13)

When we look at the goal of the rebellion from the perspective of time, we find that Absalom did not want to kill his father in order to speed his path to kingship, or because he suspected that one of his brothers might compete with him for the crown. If Absalom had wanted the monarchy, he would have received it on a golden platter. If this were the case, he would have done well to preserve the stability of the regime in Jerusalem, strengthen his positive relations with the elders of the north, and fortify the security strip that his father had established within the kingdom of Aram (which reared its head just after David's death – I Kings 11:23–25). If Absalom had wanted the monarchy, the best thing for him to do would have been to extend his training period until the day when the scepter passed into his hand in an organized fashion. The fact that he chose to destroy everything David built means only one thing: revenge. It also reveals that he could not forgive the king for giving shelter to the son who had raped his sister, and evading the responsibility of executing him. Absalom did not want to allow David to end his reign in peace; he wanted war, and war he made.

The significant support Absalom enjoyed from the northern elders shows that they could not forgive David either. In their case, they could not forgive him for crushing the remaining members of the king's family and his supporters. The elders' support of Absalom confirms what we noted above: David made a severe mistake in neglecting his relationship with them and leaving them out of his plans, which were designed to save them first (though I argued that he did not have time to do this). The northern elders were so furious with David that they were willing to betray the alliance they had made with him, and make a new alliance with his son to bring about his downfall. As evidence, throughout the years that passed from the day Absalom returned to Jerusalem and until he sounded the horn, they kept his secret, and did not send informants to Jerusalem. On the fateful day, they stood by his side with all their might.[21]

In the end, Absalom's rebellion failed. In the midst of the war, while riding his mule, Absalom's head became entangled in the branches of an elm tree, suspending him between heavens and earth. When Joab, commander of David's army, saw Absalom hanging by his neck, he took three sharp branches and thrust them into his heart (18:14).

Absalom died.

But before that, he succeeded in humiliating his father in the same way he and his sister had been humiliated. When David fled Jerusalem, he left ten of his concubines to guard his house. At the height of the rebellion, Absalom entered his father's house, took the concubines up to the roof, and there, in full view of the inhabitants of Jerusalem, he raped them, one after another:

> Ahitophel advised Absalom, "Consort with your father's concubines, whom he left to keep the house. All of Israel will hear that you have totally repudiated your father, and all who are with you will strengthen their resolve." So they pitched a tent on the roof for Absalom, and Absalom consorted with his father's concubines before all of Israel. (16:21–22)

---

[21] After the rebellion failed, the Israelite elders wanted David to rule them. Apparently, they finally realized the seriousness of the threat from Aram, and they wanted to prepare for it (II Sam. 19).

THE BEAUTY OF THE BIBLICAL WRITING STYLE

We will now leave the story of Absalom's rebellion, allow the heroes to rest peacefully in their graves, and rest from the ordeals and struggles of their mighty but terrible days. They need complete rest, and they deserve it. We will approach them slowly, bow before them in final appreciation, and press our lips to the edges of the faded cloaks that envelop their war-weary bodies. We will then turn our backs on them with silent steps, and return with deep love to the beauty of biblical writing.

The biblical authors hid their identity from us, but their dim reflection is revealed by the way they described the characters and their deeds – and this is to our great fortune. Each portrayal pushes back a few inches of the heavy screen that conceals them, revealing a small portion of their selves. Suddenly, from a distance, we hear an echo of their voice, well hidden behind the monumental events they recorded. The voice of the biblical authors is like the soft melody of the cello, deep and resonant. The reader who desires to listen to the dark sound of the cello, and through it, to hear the authors' whispers, must listen with great caution – and this is what we will do.

After David's loved ones and enemies died, he mourned their deaths, composing poems of grief in their honor. Tradition forever ascribes the most beautiful of these elegies to him. As long as the history of the Western world continues to progress, the concise, haunting lamentations that he wrote will weep for us in times of grief. When we are unable to find our own words to express our broken hearts, David's laments will speak for us.

Saul knew that as long as the cooperation between his son Jonathan and David continued, his dynasty would not be firmly established, and so he pursued David with the goal of killing him. But when the king was killed along with his son, David voiced these words of mourning, engraved forever in our minds:

> *O mountains of Gilboa – let neither dew nor rain be upon you,*
>
> *nor fields of bounty,*
>
> *For rejected there was the shield of mighty ones, the shield of Saul,*
>
> *as if unanointed with oil.*
>
> *From the blood of the slain, from the fat of the mighty,*
>
> *the bow of Jonathan would not recoil,*
>
> *the sword of Saul would not return empty.*
>
> *Saul and Jonathan, beloved and pleasant in their lives,*
>
> *and in their death not parted.*
>
> *They were swifter than eagles, stronger than lions....*
>
> *How have the mighty fallen in the midst of the battle.*
>
> *(II Sam. 1:17–27)*[22]

David wept over the deaths of his friend and the strong-willed king who had pursued him and tried to kill him. Saul erred in his battle against the Philistines, as well as in his pursuit of David. Still, Saul was an honest, daring king and a respected enemy. After Saul was killed, David eulogized him in the manner of noble warriors who mourn for other noble warriors, even if they are enemies. Abner son of Ner was Saul's military commander, and like his leader, he was also a bitter but respected enemy. When Abner was murdered, David lamented the dead warrior:

---

[22] Ancient eulogies followed fixed rules, and David's eulogy for Saul and Jonathan adheres to them strictly. A eulogy praises the dead in exaggerated language, and never disparages him. These rules explain why the eulogy praises Saul's bravery and loving relationship with his son, while the historical chapters of the Bible paint the opposite picture.

Should Abner have died the death of a knave?
Your hands were not bound and your feet were not placed
in chains;
As one who falls before villains have you fallen! (II Sam.
3:33–34)

Not long afterward, David delivered his most terrible of eulogies. He lamented the death of his son Absalom, who was killed at the height of the battle he led, after raping the royal concubines in the sight of all Jerusalem. David knew that Absalom hated him, and he also knew why. David knew that his son was not attacking him because he was power hungry, but because he was a proud lion cub who could not forgive his father for humiliating him in public. David knew that Absalom could not be bribed – not with chariots, not with the crown, and not with kingdoms. Absalom was the son of a lion, and the only thing David could give to pacify him was his own head. After Absalom died, David mourned. Ever since, his heartbreaking lament has been repeated by an endless procession of fathers who have accompanied their sons to the grave:

"My son, Absalom! My son, my son, Absalom!
If only I could have died in your place!
Absalom, my son, my son!"
…The king covered his face, and the king cried out in a
loud voice, "My son, Absalom! Absalom, my son, my son!"
(19:1–5)

When David heard of Amnon's death, he fell to the ground and wept bitterly, but he did not eulogize his death. Amnon was a sex offender, a psychopath worthy of oblivion, not poetry.

From a historical point of view, we cannot be certain that David himself wrote the exquisite eulogies attributed to him.

Possibly, they were written by anonymous poets who offered him the lamentations they wrote, enabling the magnificent king, who embodied every type of weakness and every type of greatness, to mourn the noble dead, and above everyone else, his son Absalom.

We will never know the absolute truth regarding the identity of the authors of the eulogies. But this is not important, because we possess these wonderful creations, which were attributed to the only king deserving of them. To us, it is important to conclude our words with a final statement. The author who recorded the story of Absalom's rebellion against his father described the lion cub in words of incomparable beauty:

> There was no one in all of Israel as praiseworthy for his beauty as Absalom. From the bottom of his foot to the top of his head, there was no blemish in him. (14:25)

The author was right – Absalom had no defects.

Not in his looks, nor in his sense of honor, nor in his gentle and protective love for his sister. Nor in his wild revenge that almost destroyed the monarchy his father had built, and which cost him his life.

Part V

INHERITANCE STORIES

Chapter Twenty-Two

INHERITANCE AND VITAL RESOURCES

THE LAW OF THE FIRSTBORN

The property that passes by inheritance from parents to their children is made of dangerous, flammable material. It is like an explosive packed into a cartridge: one careless movement can ignite its destructive power and lead to fraternal war. This is the case today, and this is the way it has always been. Each of us knows that at some point in life, always earlier than we would like, the time will come when we will have to address the question of what to do with our property after we move on to the netherworld. In our day, many parents prepare a will, documenting their desire for their property to be divided equally among their children. After all, the last thing we want is for our dear children, knives in hand, to invade our homes an hour after we are brought to burial and empty them of our possessions.

Because the feelings of parents toward their children, like other emotions, are not time dependent, we have the intuitive sense that our ancient forefathers also divided their property equally among their children. But in the biblical period, equal division of family property among multiple heirs was impossible, and thus did not exist. This is because ancient society was agricultural, and land was the only property that was inherited. Land was not divided among multiple heirs, but passed down in its entirety to one son, usually the firstborn. This means that the heir's brothers went out into the wide world empty-handed. The difficulty with this law is that it conflicts with another biblical law called "the law of the firstborn," which determines that each one of the sons born to the same father had the right to inherit a fixed portion of his property:

> *If a man will have two wives, one beloved and one hated, and they bear him sons, the beloved one and the hated one, and the firstborn son is the hated one's: then it shall be that on the day that he causes his sons to inherit whatever will be his, he cannot give the right of the firstborn to the son of the loved one ahead of the son of the hated one, the firstborn.* **Rather he must recognize the firstborn, the son of the hated one, to give him the double portion in all that is found with him; for he is his initial vigor, to him is the right of the firstborn.** *(Deut. 21:15–17)*

According to this law, all the sons (meaning only the sons of the senior wives) have the right to inherit a portion of their father's property. In order to preserve the special status of the firstborn, the law states that he will inherit a portion double in size than that of his brothers: "For he is his initial vigor, to him is the right of the firstborn." We have the intuitive sense that this law deals justly with the firstborn as well as with his younger brothers, who also receive a defined portion of their father's land. But in truth, this is a terrible law. It would impoverish the family and harm each of the sons, and thus it was never implemented.

To prove this assertion:

Let us assume that a certain father had four sons, and one hundred acres of land that supported him and his family generously. When the father grew old, he decided to divide his land according to the law of the firstborn. In order to give his oldest son double the amount that his brothers received, the father divided his property into five equal parts. The firstborn received two of these parts, or forty acres of land, and each of the three other brothers inherited one part, or twenty acres. We will assume that the four brothers decided to follow the path their father forged, and in their old age, they also adhered to the law. If each of them had four sons, then they divided the same one hundred acres among the sixteen inheritors. At most, the fourth generation of inheritors might have room to place a small footstool on their portions, where they could sit and gaze at each other in dismay.

This illustration is enough to point out the great failure inherent in the law of the firstborn. The law in Deuteronomy ignores the fact that in agricultural society, the inherited property was land. While the number of inheritors increased in subsequent generations, the size of the land remained fixed. Repeated partition of the inheritance reduced it to nothing. The father who served as our example ended by impoverishing his sons, and even in the first generation of division they were much poorer than he. Clearly, if he wanted to deal justly with his sons, he had to give his entire property to only one of them. In this way, the land preserved its value, and it was enough to support the inheriting son and his family, as well as a number of other families who served as the regular labor force of the farm.

We also find that the law of the firstborn could not be implemented in a society of shepherds, in which the main property given in inheritance was the flocks and not land. Although the size of a flock of goats is not static, and it can be divided and then multiplied, such an act would weaken the family just as quickly as our imaginary father weakened his sons.

Traditional shepherds, such as those who lived in ancient times, lived in areas of poor pasture and little water. This fact forced them to wander from one sparse pasture to another.[1] If Abraham, Isaac, and Jacob, who lived in the dry Negev area (in today's southern Israel), had divided their flocks according to the law of the firstborn, the obstacle we explained above would repeat itself. They would multiply their flock beyond the capacity of the pasture, and the unavoidable result of this would lead their sons to fraternal war.

One of the stories that best illustrates our meaning here is that of the disagreement between Abraham and Lot (Gen. 13).[2] As we recall, Abraham, Sarah, and Lot made the long journey from Ur to Canaan together. For twenty years, the three marched side by side. For twenty years, they slept under the same sky and divided the same loaf of bread. From every aspect that can be analyzed and measured, they were masters of survival. They survived the exhausting, danger-ridden journey because they carefully calculated the scarce vital resources available to them, and utilized them wisely and carefully. Their strength was in their unity, in the uncompromising recognition that each served as guarantor for the lives of the others. None of them had any living relative except for the two others. No one could allow himself to tire of the others and take shelter with another loving relative. No one could eat the other's bread ration in secret. Abraham, Sarah, and Lot were all the family in the world to each other, and

---

[1] Shepherds who lived in areas rich in water and pasture, such as those who settled beside the great rivers, exchanged their nomadic life for regular settlement in one place, and became part of agricultural society. For them, land was the main property that was given in inheritance.

[2] The fact that both had neither father nor son is not relevant to the discussion.

logic dictates that they had to preserve this unity, even after they reached Canaan and set down their wanderers' sacks. But in the last chapter of the journey, something went wrong, and Abraham and Lot had a serious disagreement.

When the three exited the Sinai Desert and entered the Negev area, they were overcome by a strange feeling of well-being, and they divided their flock of goats between them. After the division, each one increased the number of goats he owned – and the result of this hasty act was not long in coming. Abraham and Lot continued to pasture their flocks in the same area and quickly overused the resources at their disposal. As a result, they began to compete with each other for the water sources and for every green leaf in the pasture area. Finally, the two had an argument, which left them no choice but to separate and dismantle the long-term partnership between them:

> So Abram went up from Egypt, he with his wife and all that was his – and Lot with him – to the south. Now Abram was very laden with livestock, silver, and gold.... Also Lot who went with Abram had flocks, cattle, and tents. **And the land could not support them dwelling together, for their possessions were abundant and they were unable to dwell together.** And there was quarreling between the herdsmen of Abram's livestock and the herdsmen of Lot's livestock.... So Abram said to Lot: "Please let there be no strife between me and you, and between my herdsmen and your herdsmen, for we are kinsmen. Is not all the land before you? Please separate from me: If you go left, then I will go right, and if you go right, then I will go left." ...So Lot chose for himself the whole plain of Jordan...; thus they parted, each from his brother. (Gen. 13:1–11)[3]

---

[3] The description of Abraham and Lot leaving the Sinai Desert driving full herds of sheep and cattle is impossible. The physiologies of cows and sheep are not suitable for long periods of walking, certainly not for crossing 250 miles (400 km) of dry desert like the Sinai. The shepherd who attempts to lead cows and sheep through the desert

In order to demonstrate the connection between Abraham and Lot's quarrel and the law of the firstborn in Deuteronomy, we will adapt the story for a moment to fit our needs. For the purpose of illustration, let us suppose that Abraham's flock numbered one hundred goats. Let us also suppose that Sarah, our blessed foremother, had no difficulty conceiving, and during the years in which she traveled the long roads, she gave birth to four healthy sons. Let us also imagine that the members of this happy family left the Sinai Desert and went straight to the place where Abraham and Lot had their argument. We will make a last supposition, and say that just at that spot, Abraham decided to organize his affairs and divide his property among his sons exactly according to the law of the firstborn in Deuteronomy.

In such a case, Abraham's firstborn would have inherited forty goats, and each of the three younger sons would have inherited twenty goats. Even if the sons were satisfied with the number of goats they inherited, each of them would be much poorer than Abraham, who owned a flock of one hundred goats. If each one of the brothers decided that in order to support his wives and children, he needed one hundred goats, then the argument between Abraham and Lot would have broken out among them as well. This is because the pasture area that barely supported one family of shepherds and one hundred goats would then have to support four families and four hundred goats, all crowded into the same area. From this, we clearly understand that if Abraham wanted to ensure that his sons would not begin a fraternal war for the available resources, he would have to give the flock and tenancy of the pasture to one son alone. Each of the other three sons would receive a few goats as a gift, and leave almost empty-handed

will kill them within a day or two. In chapter 3, we discuss the biblical author's intention of presenting Abraham as a wealthy man.

to find himself other, available pastures – and according to the biblical narrative, this is indeed what happened.

The book of Genesis relates a story that few recall: after Sarah died, elderly Abraham marries a woman named Keturah, who bears him six sons. As if this capable wife was not enough, Abraham went on and married concubines, who also had many sons (25:1–6). The historical credibility of this strange chapter is doubtful, but unimportant at this point. What is important is that this ancient source reflects the practice of only one son inheriting his father's property, even in a society of shepherds:

> *Abraham proceeded and took a wife whose name was Keturah. She bore him Zimran, Jokshan, Medan, Midian, Ishbak, and Shuah.... All these were the descendants of Keturah. Abraham gave everything he had to Isaac. And to the sons of Abraham's concubines, **Abraham gave gifts; then he sent them away from Isaac his son while he was still alive**, eastward, to the land of the east. (Gen. 25:1–6; see also II Chron. 21:1–4)*

Undoubtedly, the best plan for Abraham and each of his supposedly numerous sons was to preserve their family unity. If this had happened, then the dynastic thread that was almost broken during the journey would have been strengthened, and his children really would have been as numerous as the sand on the seashore. But in the ecological reality practiced in the area of the Negev where he settled, this was impossible. Thus Abraham had no choice but to leave his property to one son: the firstborn of the senior wife – Isaac. His other sons had to wander afar to find their own land, where they would not compete with the inheriting son nor with each other.[4]

---

[4] Genesis contains two accounts that seem to be different versions of the same story. These stories reflect the connection between the vital resources of the Negev's poor pastures and the number of people and size of the flocks inhabiting those areas. The first version relates that even after Abraham and Sarah reached Canaan, they

Another story, almost forgotten, illustrates the assertion that two shepherd families cannot graze their flocks
together in a desert region. Chapter 36 of Genesis offers its
own version of the reason why Jacob and Esau parted paths.
According to this version, Jacob never stole Esau's blessing,
nor did Esau attempt to murder his twin brother. The reason
why the brothers parted ways, in love and friendship, was
because both established large families and had large flocks,
so that one pasture was not sufficient to support both families. In order to prevent fraternal war, Esau left Canaan and
settled in Edom:

> *And these are the descendants of Esau.... Esau took his*
> *wives, his sons, his daughters, and all the members of his*
> *household – his livestock and all his animals, and all the*
> *wealth he had acquired in the land of Canaan – and went*
> *to a land because of his brother Jacob. For their wealth was*
> *too abundant for them to dwell together, and **the land of***
> ***their sojourns could not support them because of their***
> ***livestock**. So Esau settled on Mount Seir; Esau, he is Edom.*
> *(Gen. 26:1–8; Edom is in today's kingdom of Jordan)*

The examples above reveal that inheritance laws must fit the
economic and ecological reality of the place where they are
practiced. In our time, when most of the population in the

---

continued to wander in the Negev region. During their wanderings, they reached a
settlement named Gerar, located southwest of Beersheba (20:1). Abraham dug a well
in Gerar, but the local king's servants blocked it and did not permit his flocks to drink
from it (21:22–34). The second version recounts a similar story: Isaac and Rebecca
also go to Gerar and settle there. This version says that Isaac had several wells that he
inherited from his father, and in addition, he controlled fields where he grew wheat
(Gen. 26). Isaac's fields and flocks prospered, disrupting the delicate balance among
the limited vital resources in his living area. In response, the king's shepherds battled
him and filled the wells with dirt. The two versions say that Abraham and Isaac vanquished the shepherds who harassed them, but they both conclude by stating that the
two left Gerar. These two versions illustrate the relationship between the number of
people and herd animals living in one area, and the land's ability to support them.
The moment one shepherd disturbed the delicate balance, conflict broke out between
him and the local residents.

Western world lives in cities and makes a living outside the family, an inheritance divided among numerous heirs comes in addition to what each person earns alone. The situation is completely different in an agricultural society, in which land is the inherited property. Repeated division of that heritage breaks it into pieces, and after a few generations, it is no longer sufficient to support any family. This rule is also followed by families of shepherds, in which the property given in inheritance is the flock. Because pasture and water sources remained static, the father was obligated to pass down his property to only one son.

SONS WHO DID NOT INHERIT

The situation we have described above required each brother who was not included in the inheritance to make a decision about his future. The best possibility was for the brothers to acquire available property in the area near their father's home, and establish a kind of family village. Indeed, the first villages that developed in Canaan, like almost everywhere in the world, were family villages originating with one forefather. Brothers who established satellite patriarchal households alongside their inheriting brother preserved their family unity and the traditional framework. Over time, the family expanded and its elders became the leaders who directed the extended family's internal and external affairs.

Available territories near the father's habitation were naturally limited, and depended on the existence of reserve land and water resources. As the family expanded and resources dwindled, the situation we described above returned: the population grew, but the size of the land remained constant. Eventually, the option of acquiring territory nearby was no longer a possibility, and this obligated the father to bequeath his property to only one son. The brothers who did not inherit had to choose among three other possibilities, and the Bible shows that all three were practiced.

We discussed the first possibility above: in arid areas, family unity was almost impossible to maintain, and so the sons who did not inherit had to travel far away and find a new habitation.

The second possibility available to them was apparently much more common, and is more appropriate for a farming society than for families of shepherds. According to this possibility, the brothers remained on the land of their eldest brother, the heir, and became part of the regular labor force on the farm. Although the brothers were not the property owners, they enjoyed the advantages of family unity and they did not have to travel far away and search for a new place to build their lives. Furthermore, the short lifespan of people in the ancient world and marriage among relatives undoubtedly created new opportunities for inheritance that did not exist at the time when the land was inherited.

The third, final possibility was to rebel against the inheriting son and try to depose him from his position and the property. It appears that rebellion within families of herders or farmers was a very rare phenomenon. But within royal families, in which the kingdom was the heritage, rebellion against the crown prince was common (a kingdom is never divided among several inheritors). The rebellion usually ended with the heir identifying the particular brother who was endangering his rule – and destroying him. If the heir did not identify the source of danger to his kingdom, he paid with his life.

Chapter Twenty-Three
THE THEFT OF THE BLESSING

The image of Jacob in Genesis is like a six-sided cube – and we are attempting to trace each side. We have discussed Jacob's love for Rachel and his hatred for Leah and for Laban, father of his two wives. In this chapter, we will discuss how Jacob stole Esau's blessing, and how the author presents his image in this story. In the next chapter, we will discuss his exaggerated love for Joseph, Rachel's elder son.

Genesis gives two different versions of how Jacob received the status of firstborn, usually reserved for the eldest son of the senior wife. Both versions relate that Jacob acted in roundabout ways in order to obtain the desired inheritance, to which he was not entitled since he was the younger twin. The property that Isaac would eventually bequeath was no more than a small field and a burial cave that Abraham had purchased, a flock of goats, and possible tenancy of several wells near Beersheba. Despite the meagerness of this property, the flock and the arid territory where Isaac herded his flocks were enough to support him and his family, and were also supposed to support the son who would inherit from him. This scanty property was the thin line that separated

between very little and nothing – and Jacob desired this little
for himself.

SALE OF THE BIRTHRIGHT FOR A MESS
OF POTTAGE (GENESIS 25:19-34)

The first version that relates how Jacob expropriated his
brother's inheritance is known as "the sale of the birthright
for a mess of pottage." Long ago, the expression "sold for
a mess of pottage" crossed the boundaries of the Bible and
entered our language. Such a deal requires two participants:
one intelligent and cunning – played by Jacob; the other, foolish – played by Esau. The cunning conspirator will always
try to convince the foolish person to do the very thing that
will cause him the greatest damage, and in most cases, he
will succeed. Because the foolish one believes everything, he
legally sells the conspirator the most valuable property he
owns, at the price of a "mess of pottage." In other words, he
gives it away for free. In this manner, according to the first
version of the story, Jacob purchased from Esau his right to
inherit from his father.

One day, Esau returned from the hunt, hungry and tired,
and discovered that Jacob had prepared a mess of pottage.
This was lentil stew, a simple, cheap food. Three thousand
years ago, as today, it was hardly considered a meal that a
hungry man would crave after returning home from chasing
deer all day long. But Esau was ravenous and exhausted, and
every muscle in his body cried out in agony. The blazing sun,
which had scorched the top of his head since morning, now
began to burn from the inside. Esau wanted nothing more
than to eat and rest. But his beloved mother, who loved his
twin brother better, did not bother to prepare a decent meal
for her elder son, who was supplying game for her household.
Finding no appropriate food other than the lentil stew, Esau
was willing to eat what was available.

Jacob, an intelligent young man, did not intend to feed his brother for free, even if preparing the stew did not involve any intense effort. The payment he demanded for the miserable meal was no less than the firstborn status. Esau, who was very hungry and not very intelligent, agreed to the deal, although it would impoverish him of all the property Isaac meant to bequeath to him:

> Jacob simmered a stew, and Esau came in from the field, and he was exhausted. Esau said to Jacob, "Pour into me, now, some of that very red stuff, for I am exhausted." ... Jacob said, "Sell, as this day, your birthright to me." And Esau said, "Look, I am going to die, so of what use to me is a birthright?" Jacob said, "Swear to me as this day"; he swore to him and sold his birthright to Jacob. Jacob gave Esau bread and lentil stew, and he ate and drank, got up and left; thus, Esau spurned the birthright. (25:29–34)

The manner in which the author presents Jacob's cunning and Esau's recklessness in scorning his position as firstborn and inheritor destroys the realistic foundations of the story. Almost certainly, this is a popular tale designed to amuse the listeners, and not much more. At any rate, the sale that the two agreed upon was invalid, because they were dealing in something that did not belong to them, but to their father. Indeed, on the day of the inheritance, Isaac called Esau to him, not Jacob.

Despite the simplicity of the story, we can learn from it one or two things about the importance of the inheritance in the ancient world. Even between twins who left their mother's womb at almost the same moment, the son who entered the world first was considered the firstborn for the purpose of inheritance. In addition, the story confirms our above assertion: the family property was not divided among brothers, but rather passed in its entirety to one heir. For if not, part of

Isaac's property would have been reserved for Jacob. One last note: the inheritance, even if meager, was always important. Regardless of the economic logic that explained why one son received it and regardless of its value – the son who did not inherit felt deprived.

THE SECOND VERSION:
THEFT OF THE BLESSING (GENESIS 27)

The version in Genesis chapter 27 is known as "the theft of the blessing." In this version of the story, Isaac is described as an elderly man who has lost his sight, and who knows that he is nearing death. Isaac understood that the time had come for him to transfer his property in an organized fashion to his inheritor. He called Esau to him, and requested that he take his bow and go out to hunt game, from which he should prepare the delicacies that Isaac particularly loved. After he had eaten his fill, Isaac promised to bless his elder son. In other words, he would appoint him head of the family and recognize him as his heir and successor. According to the text, Rebecca secretly listened in on her husband's conversation, and because she had a clear opinion of which one of her two sons deserved the inheritance, she decided to push her preference.

Rebecca ran to Jacob, who was sitting in her tent, and convinced him to precede Esau and present himself before Isaac in order to receive the blessing instead of his brother. Rebecca did not need to use much force to convince her son to join her. As soon as she had his agreement, she worked quickly. First, she sent Jacob to the goat pen to bring her two kids, which she used to prepare the dishes that Isaac loved. She then tackled the main problem that threatened to spoil her plan: the physical difference between her two sons. Esau was hairy, while Jacob's skin was smooth. If blind Isaac happened to stroke the arms and face of his younger son and kiss him, he would easily discover the true identity of the man who stood before him. In order to overcome this problem, Rebecca skinned the kids and swiftly sewed the skins into sleeves and a covering for the neck. When she had finished, she dressed Jacob in Esau's clothing, so that the scent of the field and the odor of his sweat would reach Isaac's nose. She then covered Jacob's hands and neck with the kidskin sleeves and collar she had sewn, and attached a false beard to his face.

Disguised as his twin brother, Jacob presented himself before his blind father. Isaac sniffed Esau's clothes, and scents of the field that his beloved son carried with him wafted into his nostrils. He patted Jacob's hands, which were wrapped in the kidskins, and was convinced that they were indeed hairy like Esau's hands. For a moment, Isaac doubted that it was really Esau standing before him, but after Jacob promised him faithfully that he was indeed his brother, the old man fell into the net that his wife and younger son had woven for him. He sat down to eat the roasted meat, and even sipped the wine that accompanied the repast. After he finished eating, Isaac was content. He addressed Jacob, whom he thought was Esau, and granted him the desired blessing.

Almost certainly, the description of Jacob's disguise belongs to the tendentious element of the story we will discuss below, and never actually took place. Isaac, who had been a shepherd all his life, knew how to distinguish between goat meat and game. Undoubtedly, he was able to differentiate between human skin and kidskin to the same extent. It is difficult to believe that the old man's mind was clear enough to arrange his affairs in an organized fashion, but not clear enough to uncover such a childish and ridiculous trick. Thus we will renounce a discussion of whether the kidskin Jacob wore truly led Isaac astray, and return to the realistic foundations of the story.

When Isaac intended to announce Esau as his inheritor, he placed Jacob at a crossroads. Jacob was forced to choose one of the possibilities we listed in the previous chapter.

We must reject out of hand the possibility that Isaac would divide his property between his two sons. As we have seen, inheritance in the ancient world was not distributed among the sons, but rather passed entirely to one of them. The fact that Isaac planned to bequeath all his property to Esau confirms this practice.

Jacob was confronted with three possibilities, and he had to choose the best one for him. The first possibility was to leave the family living area and the region where his father wandered, and search afar for his own place to live. He would kiss his mother and father goodbye and journey forth to meet his fate, as Abraham's many sons had done (Gen. 25:1–6). The second option was for Jacob to continue living in his father's home, and accept Esau's firstborn status and leadership. In such a case, the brothers would preserve their unity, and continue to herd their father's flocks together. But because they would establish large families, and because they had to consider the scarce resources of the arid Negev, they would become much poorer than their father.

The third possibility that Jacob faced was to attempt to divert the inheritance to himself – and this, as we know, is what he chose. In the scene the Bible describes, Jacob stood before his father and received the blessing designated for Esau:

> Then his father Isaac said to him, "Come close, if you please, and kiss me, my son."
>
> So he drew close and kissed him; he smelled the fragrance of his garments and blessed him.
>
> He said, "See, the fragrance of my son is like the fragrance of a field which the Lord has blessed. And may God give you of the dew of the heavens and of the fatness of the earth, and abundant grain and wine. Peoples will serve you, and

*regimes will prostrate themselves to you. Be a lord to your
kinsmen, and your mother's sons will prostrate themselves
to you. Cursed be they who curse you, and blessed be they
who bless you." (27:26–29)*

The blessing that Isaac gave Jacob is very short, but it follows
strict ceremonial rules: it begins with a festive opening, then
follows the blessing as the central concept, and it ends with a
festive conclusion. The main importance of the beginning is
the statement that God serves as witness to the event:

*He said, "See, the fragrance of my son is the like the
fragrance of a field which the Lord has blessed. And may
God give you of the dew of the heavens and of the fatness
of the earth, and abundant grain and wine."*

At the heart of the blessing, Isaac declares in one short, pithy
sentence that his heir will rise above all his brothers:

*Be a lord to your kinsmen, and your mother's sons will
prostrate themselves to you.[5]*

Prostration has always been an expression of self-abasement,
subservience, and acceptance of authority by the weak party
toward the strong one. Prostration is a form of expression of
the worshipper toward his god, the slave toward his master,
and a one-sided show of respect of a weak person toward a
stronger one. The significance of prostration in this case is
a one-sided declaration of allegiance of the brother who did
not receive the inheritance to the brother who has risen to
the status of family leader. The sentence "Be a lord to your
kinsmen, and your mother's sons will prostrate themselves
to you" declares that the brother who chooses to remain in
his father's home must recognize his elder brother as leader

---

[5] Isaac, as we know, had only two sons. In my opinion, the plural form "your mother's sons" is a literary expression. Still, possibly this hints that Isaac had other sons
through wives of lower status, who at any rate were not eligible to inherit from him.

of the family. The third section ends the blessing in a celebratory fashion:

> *Cursed be they who curse you, and blessed be they who bless you.*

When the short ceremony ended, Jacob left, confident that he had succeeded in tricking his old father and exploiting his twin brother. Just as in every well-written drama, the minute Jacob left his father's tent, Esau went in to Isaac, holding the game he had prepared. When Isaac and Esau realized that Jacob had led them astray just a few minutes earlier, they reacted with shock:

> *Then Isaac trembled in very great perplexity, and said, "Who – where – is the one who hunted game, brought it to me, and I partook of all when you had not yet come, and I blessed him? Indeed, he shall remain blessed!"*
>
> *When Esau heard his father's words, he cried out an exceedingly great and bitter cry, and said to his father, "Bless me too, Father!"*
>
> *...Isaac answered, and said to Esau, "Behold, a lord have I made him over you, and all his kin have I given him as servants; with grain and wine have I supported him, and for you, where – what can I do, my son?"*
>
> *And Esau said to his father, "Have you but one blessing, Father? Bless me too, Father!" And Esau raised his voice and wept. (27:33–38)*

We have often utilized tools to understand the biblical writing style, which is so different from modern writing. We discussed how the writers who recorded the Bible stories behaved with extreme circumspection with regards to revealing emotions and the private lives of the characters. The terse, restrained sentences cross an ocean of thousands of generations and penetrate our hearts with the full power of their understatement. But this time, the author, who usually wove webs of

restraint around the suffering and joy of our ancient ancestors, deviated from his custom and described at length Isaac
and Esau's broken cry at the act of theft that took place in
their own house. Such a clear deviation from the usual writing style cannot be unintentional. When we find a section
that describes the characters' emotional upheaval at length,
we must note that the deviation reveals that something
exceptional has taken place.

From a theological perspective that follows the progress
of the torch dynasty, Jacob had to present himself for the
blessing ceremony. But from a practical viewpoint that focuses on the inheritance practices of ancient times, the opposite
is true. Esau was the firstborn son of the senior wife, and
Isaac correctly considered him his successor. The moment
a brother decided to take over the position of firstborn and
divert the inheritance to himself, he was rebelling against
the legitimate inheritor. In this rebellion, as in any rebellion,
the loser pays with his life. It makes no difference whether
the rebel is the son of a king who decides to murder his elder
brother in order to seize the kingship, or the son of a poor
shepherd who wants to take over his father's meager property. A bequest of a small flock of goats, two wells, and a bald
patch of pasture was the entire world of this inheritor – and
of his brother who wanted to disinherit him. This was the
property that would support the heir his entire life, and that
he would hand down to his son.

A brother who rebelled against the traditional methods of
inheritance intended to leave the legitimate inheritor without
any means of survival. A legitimate inheritor who was dis-
inherited could not remain to live with his brother. He had
to flee from his land empty-handed, or else kill the brother.
The opposite is also true: a younger brother who recognized
the authority of the eldest brother could remain to live on
the family land. But if he attempted to divert the inheritance

toward himself, then he would have to kill his elder brother –
otherwise he had no way to ensure his control over the family
property. This reality leads to the conclusion that when Jacob
stood before his father with the goal of receiving his blessing,
he introduced the death penalty into the small family. If Jacob
and Rebecca had calculated their deeds up to the end, they
would have realized that Esau would never willingly give up
his inheritance and flee without a fight. They would have
understood that in order to ensure his inheritance, Jacob
would have to kill his brother, for if not, he would fall into
Esau's hands – and this is the reason for the bitter cry that
burst from Isaac's tent.

Isaac could not retract his blessing from Jacob, because
he gave it under oath, invoking the name of God as his witness. In our day, an oath made in God's name sounds like
the rude joke of politicians or criminals who do not hesitate
to place their right hands on the Holy Bible and swear that
any lie is the truth. But the Bible is the book of belief in God,
not a mockery by which any swindler today may swear. After
granting the blessing in the presence of God, Isaac could not
take it back. Exploited Esau, who had just lost his status and
all his future property, begged his father to grant him a blessing as well. Isaac responded to Esau's request, but gave him
a terrible blessing:

> So Isaac his father answered, and said to him: "Behold,
> from the fat of the earth will be your dwelling and from the
> dew of the heavens above. **By your sword shall you live,
> and your brother shall you serve; and when you rebel,
> you shall break off his yoke from your neck**." Now Esau
> seethed with resentment against Jacob over the blessing
> his father had blessed him; and Esau thought, "**As soon as
> the time for mourning my father draws near, I will kill
> my brother Jacob**." (27:39–41)

Like the first blessing, the second one begins in a ceremonial style, and relates to the earth's bounty. Then comes the blessing itself:

> *By your sword shall you live, and your brother shall you serve; and when you rebel, you shall break off his yoke from your neck.*

Isaac did not retract the first blessing, but in a roundabout manner, the blessing he gave Esau cancelled the validity of the one fraudulently taken from him. First, we note that in Esau's blessing, Isaac did not mention the name of God, thus rendering invalid the pronouncement that Esau would serve his brother. Second, although Isaac repeated the declaration that the inheriting brother was master over his brother, he did not command Esau to bow down to Jacob. In other words, the act that symbolizes submission and acceptance of authority, which is the heart of the first blessing, is missing in the second – and not by accident. Isaac completely absolves Esau of the need to perform the act that symbolizes recognition of Jacob's authority. Finally, Isaac goes so far as to permit Esau to kill Jacob: "When you rebel, you shall break off his yoke from your neck." History reveals that rebellion against an inheriting brother ends in only way: the winner kills the loser. And this is precisely what Isaac intended.

> *Esau interpreted his father's blessing in this way as well:*
> *Esau thought, "As soon as the time for mourning my father draws near, I will kill my brother Jacob."*

Rebecca, who as usual was listening to the conversation from behind the tent sides, realized that her plans had gone awry. She suddenly understood that in order to preserve the inheritance, Jacob would first have to kill his brother, who was much stronger than he. She thus urged her beloved son to flee for his life to the home of her brother in Haran, to the family

of the royal dynasty's foremothers. There he was awaited by
Leah, the woman whom God destined for him.

From a theological point of view that follows the progress of the torch dynasty, Jacob won the inheritance and the
divine plan proceeded according to the path determined for
it at the beginning of time. Still, Jacob and his mother paid a
heavy price for the devious way they played their roles in the
great plan. They made a bitter mistake in thinking they could
succeed in their deception of Isaac, and that Esau would willingly give up his inheritance. Rebecca, who feared to lose both
her sons in one day, did in fact do just that. Jacob went far
north, while Esau went south, to Edom (in today's kingdom
of Jordan). As we understand from Genesis, Rebecca never
saw them again before she died.

Jacob, who so desired the inheritance, was unaware that
he did in truth receive it, just not in the material sense that
he had intended. From the day he stood before his blind father
and declared that he was Esau, he did not enjoy a moment
of peace. For the next twenty years, he worked at hard labor
in the home of his uncle Laban in Haran, who treated him
like the lowest of slaves. Rachel, the woman for whom he
broke his back, died while giving birth to his youngest son,
Benjamin. After he returned to Canaan, his little girl Dinah
was raped by Shechem, son of Hamor. His wife Bilhah was
raped by Reuben, his oldest son. Later, Joseph, the son Jacob
loved more than all the others, was sold by his brothers to
merchants who took him to Egypt. Jacob believed that a wild
beast had devoured his son, and mourned him for many long
years – while his sons who knew the truth allowed him to
remain in his misery.

In his old age, Jacob traveled to Egypt, where he reunited
with his lost son, and where he met Pharaoh and summarized his life with these words:

And Jacob said to Pharaoh, "The days of the years of my
sojournings are a hundred and thirty years. Few and evil
have been the days of the years of my life, and they have
not attained the lifespans of my fathers in their days of
sojourning." (47:9)

Indeed, Jacob's days were harsh and bitter. He paid a heavy
price for the folly of his youth, and for his desire to obtain
the family inheritance. Still, the torch procession continued,
following a hidden course that always reaches the destination
determined by God.

THE BEAUTY OF THE BIBLICAL WRITING STYLE:
THE IMAGE OF JACOB IN GENESIS

Before we move on to the next story, we will stop at the side
of the road as is our wont, and take a look at how the author
formed the image of Jacob.

Outside Genesis, the Bible mentions Jacob in a positive
manner, as befits one of the forefathers of the torch dynasty.
The authors of legends who lived after the biblical period (in
the first centuries BCE and CE), our parents, teachers, and
religious leaders have elevated Jacob to the level of a righteous man, and praised his noble character traits. In legends,
Jacob symbolizes the man of peace, pleasant in character and
manner. He is generous, kind to his fellow human beings,
and his whole life is dedicated to studying Torah. Esau, by
contrast, descends to the lowest of the low. He is the leader
of the forces of evil, of robbery, hatred, and murder. Some
legends describe him as a wild beast that hunts its prey with
its teeth. If the author of Genesis ever witnessed what was
done to Esau by the legend writers who lived one and two
millennia after him, he would be shocked. He would never
have agreed with the world of images built on the backs of
these twins.

The reader who follows the bare bones of the text, free of interpretations, will realize that the author took every opportunity to roast Jacob over sizzling coals. On the other hand, he did not give Esau any particular negative trait, except for the fact that he was foolish.

But perhaps the foolish one was Jacob?

The author uses direct and indirect statements to express his opinion of Jacob. He weaves his images using wordplays and stinging, razor-sharp double entendres. He places Jacob in ridiculous situations, whose entire purpose is to blacken his image – but he leaves Esau alone.

In chapter 11, we discussed the image of Jacob as revealed through the names Leah and Rachel gave their sons. Below, we will add further depth and color, in order to complete the preliminary picture.

The story of Jacob disguising himself as his twin brother was obviously meant to ridicule him. Those who imagine a young man sticking goat skins on his hands and face and declaring aloud that he was not himself will agree that this is a grotesque, mocking image – and there is no reason to assume that the author intended anything better. Another obvious criticism is the insertion of the meaning "swindler" ('*a.k.v.*) into Jacob's name, and the inclusion of this word in many places in the story. His father called him a swindler:

> He said, "Your brother came in deceit and took your blessing." (27:35)

His twin brother also described him in the same way:

> [Esau] said, "Is it because his name was called Jacob that he outwitted me these two times? He took away my birthright and see, now he took away my blessing!" (27:36)

The father of his wives also called him a swindler:

Laban said to Jacob, "What have you done that you have deceived me and led my daughters away like captives of the sword? Why have you fled so stealthily, and cheated me?" (31:26–27)

We may assume that had the author not considered Jacob a swindler, these repetitions would not appear. A slightly oblique critique is the fact that despite his wit, Jacob fell in love with the wrong girl (and so God closed her womb), raising the question of who exactly had "tender eyes."

Another example of the negative portrayal of Jacob is his image as a hothead, not as the calm, gentle man that our teachers have presented to us. Jacob is the only character the Bible describes as hating the wife who bore him children, and whose "anger was kindled" at the woman who did not bear him children. This phrase, as we discussed, is one of the harshest expressions of anger in biblical language. We find support for Jacob's brutal relationship with his wives in the story of his flight from Haran along with his wives and children. When Laban discovered their departure, he and his male relatives pursued and overtook the escapees. A bitter argument broke out between Jacob and Laban, who had never exactly loved each other. The dispute concluded with Laban conceding his demand that Jacob and his daughters return to his home. But before they parted, he had his son-in-law vow not to abuse Leah and Rachel, and invoked God as his witness:

*Then Jacob took a stone and raised it up as a monument…. And Laban declared, "This mound is a witness between me and you today…. He said, "May the Lord keep watch between me and you when we are out of each other's sight. **If you will ill-treat my daughters** or if you will marry wives in addition to my daughters – though no man be*

among us – but see! God is a witness between me and
you." (31:45–50)

Had Laban not feared for his daughters, he would never have
made Jacob vow to treat them fairly.

   The author's subtle criticism is more interesting than the
outright denigration, because it reveals his genius as an artist
of the written word. The story of the theft of the blessing adds
its own secret fuel to the bonfire exposed to all. Jacob, as the
story goes, hesitated to go to his father while disguised as his
twin brother:

> *Jacob said to Rebecca, his mother, "But my brother Esau is*
> *a hairy man, and I am a smooth man. Perhaps my father*
> *will feel me and I shall be as a cheater in his eyes; I will*
> *thus bring upon myself a curse rather than a blessing."*
> *(27:11–12)*

Jacob's fear of appearing before his father disguised as his
brother is understandable to one unfamiliar with biblical language: young Jacob feared that his father would punish him if
he discovered the swindle. But the reader who follows the play
on words the author uses will read the verse in a very different
way. The sentence *"I am a smooth man"* can be understood
in two ways. According to one interpretation, "smooth man"
means a person who speaks in smooth language – flattery and
deceit.[6] A man whose language is smooth is a cheater, a man
who swindles with his words. Indeed, Jacob says of himself
that he embodies his name: "I am a smooth man" means "I
shall be as a cheater in his eyes."

   Jacob's description of himself as a "smooth" man is certainly one of the wisest and sharpest statements in the Bible.
Until very recently, when men began to remove the hair
from their chests and eyebrows and make themselves up like

---

[6] See also Is. 30:10; Ps. 12:3–5; 73:18; Prov. 2:16; 6:24; Dan. 11:32.

women, a "manly" man had a hairy chest and rough hands. A man did man's work and wore manly symbols – he had a beard, he carried weapons. He was a warrior and hunter like Esau, like all warriors, and like the kings in the ancient world. The legendary king Nimrod was called "mighty," a masculine description: "He was a mighty hunter before the Lord; therefore it is said, 'Like Nimrod, a mighty hunter before the Lord'" (Gen. 10:9). When the author described Esau as a hairy man who carried weapons, he was using masculine symbols. But when he described Jacob as a man who had to stick hair in the places where men were supposed to be hairy, he used imagery characteristic of children. A man with smooth cheeks is a young boy. But in our case, this was actually a boy still unable to dress himself, and so his mother dressed him in his elder brother's clothing:

> *Rebecca then took her older son Esau's clean garments which were with her in the house,* **and clothed Jacob her young son***. With the skins of the goat kids, she covered his arms and his smooth-skinned neck. (27:16–17)*

Yet Rebecca's "older" and "younger" sons were twins.

We have discussed the fact that the image of Jacob in our collective memory is as an intelligent man, while Esau is foolish. But it is highly doubtful whether the author of Genesis would have agreed with this distinction. He described Jacob as "a simple man, abiding in tents" (25:27). A wholesome man who stayed in the tents together with the women and other children[7] was the opposite of a man who went out to

---

[7] The authors of the legends noted that Jacob was a "dweller in tents," like one of the women. In order to present their preferred image of him, they said that he sat in "tents of Torah" – that he was a scholar who studied Torah (Pentateuch). The biblical text, of course, offers no support for this idea. There were no study halls in the desert, nor does the Bible mention their existence. According to the Bible, the Torah was given at Mount Sinai, centuries after Jacob's time.

hunt game. He was the reverse image of the warrior, or of the wise and powerful man whom the book of Proverbs admires:

The wise man remains steadfast, and the man of knowledge grows stronger. For through [wise] strategies, you can wage war for your benefit; and salvation is in abundant counsel. (Prov. 24:5–6; see also 20:18)

The following verse also raises the question of which brother the author might consider wise, and which one the less intelligent:

To provide simpletons with cleverness, a youth with knowledge and design; that a wise one may hear and increase his learning, and a discerning one may acquire strategies. (Prov. 1:4–5)

The image of Jacob's "smooth-skinned neck" to which Rebecca attached a false beard is not only a childish image, but also a womanly one. The author had another way to describe Jacob as a womanly man, using images from the kitchen. Bible stories reveal that men were responsible for hunting, slaughter, and sacrifice. In honor of his guests, Abraham slaughtered a "calf" (which was certainly no more than a little kid). During holidays, Elkanah would slaughter a goat and distribute its meat to the members of his family. With his own hands, Esau prepared delicacies for his father from the game he hunted. The ceremonial worship that involved sacrifices was done only by men (Leviticus offers dozens of examples). By contrast, women are identified with vegetarian cuisine. Women baked bread and cooked vegetables. Sarah honored Abraham's guests by baking meal cakes (Gen. 18:6). The baking of bread by women is mentioned in Leviticus (26:26, and in I Sam. 8:13). In our story, the kitchen roles are switched. Rebecca slaughtered goats, while Jacob cooked lentil stew. Cooking lentil stew was women's work. Roasting game over the fire was man's work. After the spoiled days of the young tent dweller ended, Jacob became a talented and diligent shepherd who performed manly labors. Almost certainly, his wives were the ones who cooked the lentil stew in his house.

We could continue in this vein and offer additional examples to demonstrate that the author of Genesis did not lose any opportunity to bite Jacob's heel with his sharp tongue, but the above will suffice. For our purposes, it is important to conclude this topic with two short comments. First, the author, a master talent in the art of writing, intentionally inserted the mockery of Jacob into the text, both overt and subtle. The second comment relates to the manner in which the historical memory of Bible readers has been shaped, both Jews and Christians. Most of us imagine Jacob in the way our parents, teachers, and many generations of commentators and religious leaders have taught us. But when we study the bare text and judge it for ourselves, we see a more complex picture than that which has been etched in our memories. To my mind, the new picture is far richer and more fascinating.

Chapter Twenty-Four

JOSEPH AND HIS BROTHERS
(GENESIS 37, 39–50)

More than all his other sons, Jacob loved Joseph, Rachel's oldest son, and this ignited the brothers' jealousy and hatred toward him. The brothers hated Joseph because their father gave him special privileges in his home, and had stitched for him the famous coat of many colors that symbolized his preferred status.[8] They also hated him because on the long days when they accompanied the flocks to pasture and suffered the cold of winter and the heat of the sun, as well as attacks by plunderers, wild animals, snakes, and scorpions, their spoiled brother remained at home. What is more, they hated him because he exploited their absences in order to slander them to their father. But apparently, more than all these reasons together, the brothers hated Joseph because of his dreams. When they

---

[8] In chapter 20, I explained that colored fabrics were very valuable in the ancient world, since the production of dye from rare natural substances was expensive and required special knowledge. The striped coat that Jacob made for Joseph was apparently colored – and for this reason, it aroused the jealousy of his brothers, who wore simple tunics. In today's terms, Joseph was wearing a garment for special occasions, while his brothers wore the work clothing of simple laborers who perform the hardest physical work.

rose before first light to milk the flock or lead it to pasture, Joseph continued to lie in his bed and dream. When he finally awoke, the spoiled boy rushed to relate that in his dreams, he saw himself ruling over his brothers and obtaining the status of firstborn in their father's house. In his first dream, so he recounted, he saw himself and his brothers gathering sheaves in the wheat field. Suddenly, his sheaf rose up, while his brothers' sheaves "bowed down" before it:

> Joseph dreamt a dream which he told to his brothers, and they hated him even more. He said to them, "Hear, if you please, this dream that I dreamt: Behold! We were binding sheaves in the middle of the field, when behold! – my sheaf arose and also remained standing; then behold! – your sheaves gathered around and bowed down to my sheaf." His brothers said to him, "Would you then reign over us? Would you then dominate us?" And they hated him even more – because of his dreams and because of his talk. (37:5–8)

Like us, the brothers had no difficulty understanding the meaning of the dream. They understood that the sheaves bowing before Joseph's upright sheaf symbolized the brothers who did not inherit submitting to the authority of their inheriting brother. The brothers saw clearly that the lazy boy was trying to exploit their absence and their father's love for him, to make them into slaves in his small shadow. As if the first dream was not enough to incite their anger, Joseph dreamed a second dream, even more infuriating, which he hurried to recount to his family. In the new dream, Joseph's desire to witness his brothers bowing down before him expanded, and he also rose above his father and mother (apparently referring to Leah, since Rachel had died):

> He dreamt another dream, and related it to his brothers. And he said, "Look, I dreamt another dream: Behold! The

sun, the moon, and eleven stars were bowing down to me." (37:9)

If the sun and the moon symbolized his father and mother, and the eleven stars were his brothers, who did Joseph think he symbolized?

God?

The Creator of the universe, Who rules over the heavenly bodies?

When Jacob heard this dream, he gently rebuked his beloved son:

> *His father scolded him, and said to him, "What is this dream that you have dreamt? Are we to come – I and your mother and your brothers – to bow down to you to the ground?" So his brothers were jealous of him, but his father kept the matter in mind. (37:10–11)[9]*

The brothers' fury toward Joseph was justified. Joseph may have been Rachel's elder son, but he was not his father's eldest son. Leah's six sons were born before Joseph, to a senior wife equal in status to his mother, and so each of them preceded him in the order of inheritance. But his tale-bearing lips were close to their father's ear, and the tales he secretly whispered were poisonous. Considering the long hours he spent in their father's company, the special privileges he enjoyed, and the nature of his dreams, the brothers had good reason to suspect that Joseph would divert the firstborn status, and the economic benefits accompanying it, to himself. After the second

---

[9] Many have interpreted Joseph's dreams as an indication that he wanted kingship, and not the firstborn status. I believe that this interpretation is incorrect. Joseph lived about five hundred years before the beginning of the monarchy period in Israel (c. 1600 BCE; Saul lived c. 1050 BCE). Joseph could not have wanted something that did not exist in the area where he lived, and of which he was unaware. His dreams reveal that he wanted to dominate his family, not to declare a certain territory as "the kingdom of Joseph." The first time he was exposed to a monarchic society was when he went to Egypt.

dream, they conspired to kill him and remove him from their path.

At the time when the following events took place, Jacob and his family lived in Hebron, apparently on the plot of land that Abraham had purchased (Gen. 23; 35:27). When the short spring days ended, and the long, dry months of summer lay ahead, the brothers led their fathers' flock from Hebron to the summer pasture in Shechem (modern-day Nablus).

In our time, Shechem is one of the most congested and dangerous places in modern Israel, which is rich in sites that are sacred but volatile. Yet in biblical times, Shechem was a charming, peaceful place, verdant and rich in water. Thus we can understand why the brothers led their father's flocks north to Shechem in the dry summer months. Almost certainly, they intended to stay there throughout the summer, and return to Hebron some six months later, when the rainy season arrived. So while the brothers led the flock to summer pasture, their lazy brother remained behind, luxuriating in his pompous dreams and whispering venomous secrets in his father's ears.

Weeks passed, and Jacob decided that he could put Joseph to good use. One day, he ordered him to go check on his sons and the flock. Joseph accordingly went on his way. Because he was not driving a flock before him, we can assume that the journey to Shechem and back should have taken only a few days. If he had ridden a donkey, the trip would have been much faster and not too exhausting. When Joseph reached Shechem, he discovered that his brothers had continued a short distance north, and he went to find them at the fateful rendezvous.

The meeting between the dreamer and his brothers took place in an area where Jacob was unable to defend his best-loved son from the jealousy and hatred of his other sons. The brothers decided to exploit the fact that the chick had left its safe haven under their father's sheltering wings. They were determined to remove the threat that he might succeed in diverting the desired inheritance in his direction. The plot they concocted was to kill him, throw his body into a nearby watering hole, and then tell their father that a wild animal had devoured him (37:17–20).

Yet for some unknown reason, the brothers gave up the most daring part of their big plan and decided to make do with a more modest solution. As Joseph approached, they grabbed him, stripped him of the coat of many colors, and threw him naked into an empty pit (the fact that the pit was empty strengthens the assumption that the event took place at the height of summer). Afterwards, they sat down to satisfy their stomachs and consult on what to do with the prisoner crying out to them from the bottom of the pit. A short time later, they saw a caravan of merchants passing nearby, on its way to Egypt. After brief negotiation, the brothers pulled Joseph out of his cell and sold him to the merchants, as if he were a simple slave passing from hand to hand. His purchasers took Joseph down to Egypt, where they sold him to a man named Potiphar, who was Pharaoh's chamberlain of the butchers. Meanwhile, the brothers completed the second part of their plot: they slaughtered a kid, dipped the coat of many colors in its blood, and sent it to their father so that he would recognize its owner:

> They took Joseph's tunic, slaughtered a kid, and dipped the tunic in the blood. They dispatched the fine woolen tunic and they brought it to their father, and said, "We found this. Identify, if you please: Is it your son's tunic or not?" He recognized it and he said, "My son's tunic! A savage beast devoured him! Joseph has surely been torn to bits!" Then Jacob rent his garments and placed sackcloth on his loins; he mourned for his son many days. All his sons and all his daughters arose to comfort him, but he refused to

comfort himself, and said, "For I will go down to the grave mourning for my son." And his father bewailed him. Now the Midianites had sold [Joseph] to Egypt, to Potiphar, a courtier of Pharaoh, the chamberlain of the butchers. (37:31–36)

The loss of Joseph broke Jacob's heart, and he mourned his death for many long years. Throughout that time, his sons kept their secret, and never revealed to him that the very hands that tried to comfort him were responsible for his grief. Their father's pain did not soften their hearts, and none of them admitted their sin. None of them planted any hope in the mind of Jacob that perhaps his beloved son was still alive, and in the meantime, he added many miserable years to his life. The brothers remained trapped in their silence and hatred. Their silence reveals that they never forgave their father for preferring Joseph, and for lending a willing ear to Joseph's slander. As we are well aware, sons never forgive their parents for the injustices they commit toward them – and on this point, nothing has changed since biblical times.

THE BIRTHRIGHT
Joseph's buyers sold him into slavery, and his life in Egypt was rough and bitter. Yet after many years, he rose to power, becoming second only to Pharaoh. He donned clothes of office, wore the king's ring on his finger, and was chauffeured around town in the king's chariot with pomp and majesty (41:40–44). Undoubtedly, from an economic point of view, he was wealthier than his father and brothers combined. Eventually, after the many adventures he experienced in Egypt, he even witnessed his brothers bowing down before him, as he had dreamed in his youth. The sense that Joseph received the status of firstborn is strengthened by the tradition that each of the Israelite tribes was named after one of Jacob's sons, while Joseph was honored with two large and powerful tribes:

Ephraim and Manasseh, named after his two sons. Thus it seems that the law of the firstborn, which stipulates that the eldest son inherit a portion twice that of his brothers (Deut. 21:15–17), was fulfilled in Joseph, the forefather of two tribes. The addition of Ephraim and Manasseh to the count of the tribes raises their number from twelve to fourteen, and this demands explanation.

The tradition engraved in our collective memory says that each of the tribes that left Egypt settled in a region named after the tribe's founding father – but this is not exact. Although the tribe of Levi was given the honorary title of "tribe" during the period of wandering in the desert, we cannot define it as a tribe like the others. A tribe was comprised of a group of extended families that lived together, with leaders of their own. When the tribes settled on their designated territories, those areas were named after them. Yet after the Israelites reached Canaan, the tribe of Levi ceased to exist, and its families scattered throughout the other tribes' regions. Levi never owned its own territory, nor did it establish an independent leadership, and so it does not fit the definition of "tribe" (Deut. 10:8–9; Josh. 13:14, 33). Similarly, there never was a tribe, leadership, or territory called "Joseph." The absence of Levi and Joseph from the map of settlement made way for Ephraim and Manasseh and kept the number at twelve tribes, each with its own territory and leadership. Still, this explanation leaves Joseph with a double portion, since Ephraim and Manasseh were his children, and so technically he really did receive the birthright.

Still, the status of firstborn passed to Judah, not Joseph. About a century after David's death, the Assyrian empire strode onto the stage of history (ninth century BCE, in the area of modern-day Iraq). The armies of Assyria that David had feared crashed over the borders of the Israelite kingdom in powerful waves, pushing its inhabitants out.[10] Among the tribes that scattered to the four winds and never returned to Israel were the tribes of Ephraim and Manasseh. Most of the exiled Israelites who returned from exile and built the Second Temple (c. 515 BCE) were members of the tribe of Judah. Thus despite the fact that Joseph was the forefather of two tribes named after his sons, he did not receive the status of firstborn, because his descendants were scattered and we do not know their fate.

To complete our discussion of the birthright, we will return again to the theological worldview of the Bible. First and foremost, the birthright or inheritance in the Bible is theological. Its economic significance is only secondary. Under the theological worldview, the inheritance passes down the line that began at the beginning of time and proceeded unswervingly toward David – and which will return at the end of days to one of his descendants.[11]

To prove that the Bible does relate the birthright to the Judean dynasty, we must again recall that Jacob's last request before he died in Egypt was to be buried in the Cave of Machpelah. This was the burial site of Leah, Judah's mother, and of two other torch-bearing couples: Abraham and Sarah, and Isaac and Rebecca. Rachel, Joseph's mother, was buried on the road, about 14 miles (23 km) from the torchbearers' burial cave. Joseph, like his father, died in Egypt. But while Jacob was brought to burial in the Cave of Machpelah, next to Leah, Joseph was buried in Shechem (Ex. 13:19; Josh. 24:32). Furthermore, in order to remove all doubt that David, son of

---

[10] See our discussion of Absalom's rebellion and David's rise to the monarchy in chapter 21.

[11] The Christians identify with the tradition in the New Testament that Jesus was of the Davidic dynasty. They also view the tribe of Judah as the heir that continued Jacob's dynasty.

Leah's dynasty, was the inheritor of the dynastic torch, and not Joseph, son of Rachel, the author of Psalms wrote:

> *He [God] rejected the tent of Joseph, and did not choose the tribe of Ephraim;*
>
> *He chose the tribe of Judah, Mount Zion, which He loves.*
>
> *And He built His Temple like the high heavens; like the earth He established it forever.*
>
> *And He chose David, His servant, and took him from the sheep corrals.*
>
> *From behind the nursing ewes He brought him;*
>
> *To tend to Jacob, His nation, and to Israel, His inheritance. (Ps. 78:67–72; see also 18:51; 132:10).*

THE BEAUTY OF THE BIBLICAL WRITING STYLE

From a literary point of view, Joseph's sojourn in Egypt is a mirror image of his life in Canaan. Elements found in the first part of the story are repeated in the second part, or presented again, but in an inverted format. Let us again take a deep breath and fill our lungs with the intoxicating scent of biblical writing, and admire its beauty and sophistication.

The story of Joseph in his father's home begins with a description of his preferred status above his brothers, and ends with the story of his downfall at their hands. In Egypt, the schema of the story is turned upside down. Joseph began his experiences there at the lowest point when he was sold into slavery, and ended at the highest point, at which only the king stood above him.

As we recall, Joseph's brothers stripped him of his many-colored coat and cast him into the pit. They then pulled him out and sold him to purchasers who took him down to Egypt, where he was sold to Potiphar, Pharaoh's chamberlain of the butchers. The honored minister gave the young slave the responsibility for managing his household. Soon afterward, the minister's wife revealed her own plans for him. The respected lady asked that between his duties in her household, Joseph find time to pleasure her and restore some of her youthful passion, which she had apparently forgotten long ago. But the handsome Hebrew slave refused to perform this last role. Just as the wife's attempts at seduction intensified, Joseph's refusals increased at the same frequency. Finally, the woman grabbed his clothes and ripped them off – conjuring the image of Joseph, stripped of his clothes a second time. Shocked, he was forced to flee for his life from the furious woman whose honor was sullied by an insubordinate, arrogant slave. But unfortunately for him, he did not run fast enough or far enough.

When the honorable minister returned home that evening, his wife, her voice choked with insult, related that the slave had forced her to sleep with him. As evidence, she showed him the clothes she had ripped from his back. Joseph, who in his youth had slandered his brothers to his father, then learned the extent of the evil of slander for himself. The minister believed his tale-bearing wife, and threw the audacious slave into the prison dungeon (chapter 39) – and Joseph found himself once again in the pit.

In prison, Joseph found two prisoners who had been lowered from high positions to the deepest pit: the chamberlain of the bakers and the chamberlain of the cupbearers. One night, both prisoners had dreams. In their dreams, they saw various symbols whose meanings they could not comprehend, but they were certain of one thing: these symbols encoded their fate. The dreams of the two chamberlains are parallel to the two dreams Joseph had in his youth. Joseph was revealed as a talented interpreter of dreams, and he interpreted the meaning of the symbols that the ministers saw. He informed the chamberlain of the bakers that he would be executed, and revealed to the chamberlain of the cupbearers that Pharaoh would release him from prison and reinstate him in his previous position. His interpretation came to fruition: the chamberlain of the bakers was executed, while the chamberlain of the cupbearers once more filled the king's cup with red wine. After these events, many months passed in which poor Joseph languished in prison, forgotten, and he seemed destined to end his days as a prisoner. But the wheel of his fate made one more turn.

One night, the omnipotent Pharaoh had a dream, and then another – and here we have a third pair of dreams with symbolic elements. Like his two ministers, Pharaoh was certain that the symbols he saw in his dreams had valuable significance. He also did not understand their meaning, and the solutions his wise men offered did not satisfy him. When the king tired of his wise men, the chamberlain of the cupbearers recalled that two years earlier, a young man had given an apt interpretation of his dream. When Pharaoh heard this, he commanded to have Joseph brought to him as quickly as possible – and thus it happened that the dreams that led him into the pit in childhood served to lift him out as an adult.

Joseph interpreted the meaning of the king's dreams. He said that Egypt should expect seven years of plenty, after which would come seven years of severe famine, such as the land had never seen. In order to prepare for the bad years, the king had to appoint a wise man to collect large quantities of food from the entire kingdom of the Nile during the good years. The wheat stored in Egypt's storehouses would nourish the kingdom's inhabitants during the years of famine that awaited them. When the king heard the dream's solution, he recognized at once that Joseph was speaking the truth, and appointed him as the man to implement the great project:

> Then Pharaoh said to Joseph, "Since God has informed
> you of all this, there can be no one so discerning and wise

as you. You shall be in charge of my palace and by your command shall all my people be sustained; only by the throne shall I outrank you." Then Pharaoh said to Joseph, "See! I have placed you in charge of all the land of Egypt." And Pharaoh removed his ring from his hand and put it on Joseph's hand. He then had him dressed in garments of fine linen and he placed a gold chain upon his neck. He also had him ride in his second royal chariot, and they proclaimed before him, "Avrech!" Thus, he appointed him over all the land of Egypt.

Pharaoh said to Joseph, "I am Pharaoh. And without you no man may lift up his hand or foot in all the land of Egypt." (41:39–44)

In his father's home, Joseph wore a coat of many colors that symbolized his preferred status. In Egypt, he again donned clothes that symbolized his high position. He also received trappings even finer than clothes: the king's own jewels, and a chariot in which to perform the important mission that Pharaoh delegated to him.

These opposing images show that Joseph's life in Egypt was the mirror image of the first part of his life. They also lead to another, final image, which I find the most beautiful of all. The first part of the story emphasizes Joseph's negative traits. He is described as an evil little tyrant who lives in a fantasy world. The dreams in which his family bows down to him as if he were God highlight the negative qualities of the boy, who lives a life of idleness and slander. The adult Joseph who attained wealth and wisdom stands in direct contrast to the image of the child he used to be: he is gentle, loving, beneficent, pitying, and merciful toward his family. The wise adult Joseph, who achieved the honor of kings, symbolizes more than all else the good, faithful brother whom each of us would wish for his own.

The years of plenty and the years of famine that Pharaoh saw in his dreams eventually reached Egypt and the surrounding region. The famine stretched as far as Canaan, striking its inhabitants harshly. The starving people fled for their lives to Egypt to purchase food for their households – and among the refugees were Joseph's brothers.

The text relates that Joseph, who at this stage had reached the height of his power, received his hungry brothers and recognized them. The brothers never dreamed that the respected minister standing before them, clothed in official raiment, was the youth whose coat they had stripped off years earlier, and whom they had thrown into a deep pit. They bowed down before the man whom they thought symbolized the royalty of Egypt, doing just what the younger Joseph had dreamed they would do. But at that point, a completely different heart was beating in his breast.

Joseph did mock his brothers mildly for not recognizing him, accusing them of coming to Egypt to spy out the land instead of to purchase food for their starving families. But while the brothers were in shock at the bizarre, baseless accusations the ruler made against them, Joseph walked away from them. Secluded in one of the back rooms in his magnificent house, his heart shattered and he wept for the years he had spent separated from them and his elderly father. All the wealth and power he had attained in Egypt were not enough to salve his longing for the terrified, starving group of men who came to buy food from him. They were his brothers, and the blood that ran in their veins was the very blood that ran in his. The respect they showed him did not dissolve the pain of knowing that his greatness was in fact his punishment.

In secret, without attracting his brothers' notice, Joseph took the burden of supporting them on his own shoulders, and returned the money they had paid for the wheat (42:27–28). The brothers returned to Canaan, and when the grain in their sacks was gone, they went back to Egypt and stood before him a second time, along with Benjamin, Joseph's younger brother. Once again Joseph accused and frightened them, and again he was overcome by his longing and love for them and for his brother Benjamin. Again he sobbed in pain and regret. But this time, seeing the surprised face of young Benjamin, he did not have the strength to control his feelings, and revealed himself to his brothers:

> Now Joseph could not restrain himself in the presence of all who stood before him, so he called out, "Remove everyone from before me!" Thus no one remained with him when Joseph made himself known to his brothers. He cried in a loud voice. Egypt heard, and Pharaoh's household heard. And Joseph said to his brothers, "I am Joseph. Is my father still alive?" But his brothers could not answer him because they were left disconcerted before him. Then Joseph said to his brothers, "Come close to me, if you please," and they came close. And he said, "I am Joseph your brother – it is me, whom you sold into Egypt. And now, do not be distressed, and do not be incensed with yourselves for having sold me here, for it was to be a provider that God sent me ahead of you." (45:1–5)

Joseph, the spoiled boy who rose to the right hand of royalty, learned from his own travails the meaning of pity, the meaning of love, and the meaning of forgiveness. "Do not be distressed," he said to his brothers, "God sent me ahead of you." Joseph rushed to send wagons to Canaan to bring his father to him, along with the rest of the family, before he starved to death or died of old age. When the family arrived in Egypt, Joseph provided for his father and brothers to the end of his life.

Chapter Twenty-Five

INHERITANCE BY WOMEN

I
n the days when the generations marched in formation
and inheritance followed tradition, women did not inherit from their husbands, nor did girls inherit from their
fathers. When inheritance followed the usual rules, girls could
receive land as a gift from their fathers, but they could not
inherit it (Judg. 1:12–15; Job 42:13–15). But the traditional
way of life was fragile and destined for disruption. Every once
in a while, the customs were interrupted, and a girl inherited
from her father. The story of the daughters of Zelophehad in
the book of Numbers addresses just such a case. This story
is particularly important, since it reveals how ancient society
dealt with cases that lay outside the boundaries of traditional
inheritance methods.

This is the story:

There once was a man named Zelophehad, one of the
Israelites who had left Egypt. Apparently, Zelophehad was
from the tribe of Manasseh, and a descendant of a respected family. Thus he was deemed worthy of receiving land in
Canaan. But Zelophehad had no sons. Instead, he had five
daughters. When the time came to divide the land among the

families who entered Canaan, he was no longer alive. Because daughters did not inherit from their fathers, there was no one to inherit the land Zelophehad would have received, had he remained alive. The custom that a daughter could not inherit from her father meant that their father was considered childless, although he had five daughters. Zelophehad's daughters understood this, and so they went before Moses, Eleazar the priest, and the elders of all the Israelite families, asking them to recognize their right to inherit the land to which their father would have been entitled.

> *The daughters of Zelophehad...stood before Moses, before Eleazar the priest, and before the leaders and the entire assembly at the entrance to the Tent of Meeting, saying: "Our father died in the wilderness, but he was not among the assembly that was gathering against the Lord in the assembly of Korah, but he died of his own sin; and he had no sons.*[12] *Why should the name of our father be omitted from among his family because he had no son? Give us a possession among our father's brothers." (Num. 27:1–5)*

The problem that the five daughters raised extends far beyond the limits of their own private incident. The case of a certain patriarchal household having only girls was no rare incident requiring an individual, one-time solution. On the contrary, this was a common occurrence that took place in every era and in every community, and so it deserved a comprehensive, organized solution. After all, if all households with only girls were considered childless, the family would eventually lose its land, and this was untenable.

Moses, as the text relates, understood that the problem the daughters of Zelophehad brought before him demanded

---

[12] The Bible does not explain the nature of Zelophehad's sin. It does say that his punishment was that he had no sons, only five daughters. This statement supports the argument that people in the ancient world related to the birth of girls alone as divine punishment, for such a family was considered barren.

a solution for all of Israelite society. Because he did not know how to respond, he referred their question to God – and this is the answer he received:

> The Lord said to Moses, saying, "The daughters of Zelophehad speak properly. You shall surely give them a possession of inheritance among the brothers of their father, and you shall cause the inheritance of their father to pass over to them. And to the Children of Israel you shall speak, saying: If a man will die and he has no son, you shall cause his inheritance to pass over to his daughter. If he has no daughter, you shall give his inheritance to his brothers. If he has no brothers, you shall give his inheritance to the brothers of his father. If there are no brothers of his father, you shall give his inheritance to his relative who is closest to him of his family, and he shall inherit it. This shall be for the Children of Israel as a decree of justice, as the Lord commanded Moses. (Num. 27:6–11)

The correction identified with the daughters of Zelophehad clearly determines that in a household that had no sons, or in which the son died before his father, the father would pass down his land to his daughters. The inheritance did not pass to his widow, for if she remarried, then the land would leave the ownership of the family to which it had always belonged, and pass into the hands of her second husband. A much worse situation would be created if the widow married a man from another tribe. The land she inherited would be transferred to her second husband's tribe. The most extreme example of this undesirable situation appears in the book of Ruth. If Ruth had inherited from her first husband and then returned to her homeland and remarried one of her fellow Moabites, then the land of a family from the tribe of Judah would have gone to a Moabite family.

The law we have cited above prevents the possibility of the family land passing through the widow to another family, another tribe, or even another nation. Still, the correction of the law does not prevent the eventuality that this might happen through the father's daughter, and this is what the elders of the tribe of Manasseh, Zelophehad's tribe, feared. When Zelophehad's relatives heard Moses' answer, they protested:

> The heads of the...family of Gilead...son of Manasseh... approached and spoke before Moses and before the leaders, the heads of the fathers of the Children of Israel. They said, "The Lord has commanded my master to give the land as an inheritance by lot to the Children of Israel, and my master has been commanded by the Lord to give the inheritance of Zelophehad our brother to his daughters. If they become wives of one of the sons of the tribes of the Children of Israel, then their inheritance will be subtracted from the inheritance of our fathers and be added to the inheritance of the tribe into which they will marry, and it will be subtracted from the lot of our inheritance." (Num. 36:1–4)

Moses understood that the elders spoke the truth, and that the correction of the inheritance law did not close the loophole through which the land could be transferred from tribe to tribe. He thus appealed to God a second time, and returned with a satisfactory answer – if the daughter married one of her paternal relatives, she could inherit her father's land.

> Moses commanded the Children of Israel according to the word of the Lord, saying, "Correctly does the tribe of the children of Joseph speak. This is the word that the Lord has commanded regarding the daughters of Zelophehad, saying: Let them be wives to whomever is good in their eyes, but only to the family of their father's tribe shall they become wives. An inheritance of the Children of Israel shall not make rounds from tribe to tribe; rather the Children of Israel shall cleave every man to the inheritance

of the tribe of his fathers. Every daughter who inherits an inheritance of the tribes of the Children of Israel shall become the wife of someone from a family of her father's tribe, so that everyone of the Children of Israel will inherit the inheritance of his fathers. An inheritance will not make rounds from a tribe to another tribe, for the tribes of the Children of Israel shall cleave every man to his own inheritance." (Num. 36:5–9)

The second correction of the law plugged the remaining gap. It allowed a daughter to inherit from her father, on condition that she married a man from his family. In this way, the land she inherited remained in the hands of one of the patriarchal households in the extended family to which it had always belonged.

The correction of the law did not solve the problem about which the daughters of Zelophehad had approached Moses in the first place. The daughters justified their right to inherit their father's land with an argument that relied on the law of levirate marriage specified in Deuteronomy (25:5–10) and the book of Ruth, which recognizes the deceased's right to inheritance: "To perpetuate the name of the deceased on his inheritance, that the name of the deceased not be cut off from among his brethren, and from the gate of his place" (Ruth 4:10).

As we have said, if Zelophehad had fathered a son, the land would have passed entirely to this boy, and his five sisters would not have inherited anything. But Zelophehad did not have a son – he had five daughters. The law stating that they could inherit the land reveals that it was divided into five parts, and did not pass whole to one daughter. The division of the land cannot "perpetuate the name of the deceased on his inheritance," for only land that was preserved in its entirety could still bear the name of its original owners even after many generations passed. Because Zelophehad's land was divided, each daughter's portion was annexed to her husband's land, and Zelophehad's name was not "perpetuated on his inheritance." We must note an additional detail: the correction of the law above reveals that in a case in which daughters inherited their father's land, the oldest one did not have seniority over her sisters. Thus the land that would usually have passed whole to one inheritor was divided equally among all the father's daughters.

The assertion that a woman did not inherit her husband's land returns us for the last time to the book of Ruth. The question of whether Elimelech's land was mortgaged is not relevant here. Even if the land were not mortgaged, Naomi could not have inherited it, because a woman did not inherit from her husband. Thus after Elimelech and his two sons died, the next closest member of Elimelech's family should have inherited his land, as specified by the law of inheritance in Numbers, which we discussed above. From the story of Ruth, we see clearly that Naomi wanted to create a family tie between Elimelech's land and her beloved, faithful daughter-in-law. She wanted to ensure that Ruth would own land in Canaan, and to guarantee her economic future. The only way to accomplish this was for Ruth to marry through levirate marriage. The law of levirate marriage created a legal relationship between the widow and her dead husband's land. Ruth did not become owner of the land. But because Boaz married her through levirate marriage, their son Obed was considered Mahlon's oldest son, and thus he had the right to inherit the land of his grandfather Elimelech.

Part VI

THE WORLD
OF THE BIBLE

Chapter Twenty-Six

THE BIBLE REALLY HAPPENED

In 1922, Old Testament scholar Hermann Gunkel, a German Protestant, published *The Legends of Genesis*. Despite the years that have passed since his book appeared, to this day it is considered one of the most important and influential works in the academic field of biblical studies. Today, researchers who continue Gunkel's way of thinking head Bible studies departments in major universities in the United States, Europe, Scandinavia, and Israel – and this is proof enough of the book's influence and status.

In his methodological and well-documented book, Gunkel attempted to show that everything written in Genesis, where most of the Bible's family stories are concentrated, is merely a collection of popular legends, transmitted orally over a long period of time until they were assembled and edited. The "legends of Genesis," so the German scholar declared, although beautiful, are myths, not history. They never took place in reality, and thus we can learn nothing from them about the historical period of the Bible or the formation of the Israelite nation. The stories of Genesis are false, from beginning to end.

In many ways, Gunkel's view was evolutionist. As such, he asserted that the highest rung in the ladder of intellectual development is occupied by rational and scientific man, represented by the historian (largely resembling himself) of the modern age. As he argued, the historian is gifted with an organized thinking process. He has a broad education and is well versed in the details of his subject. The historian studies only events that took place in reality, and which have broad national and public importance. The lowest rung of the ladder of intellectual development is occupied by the ancients, whose thinking was primitive. "Primitive humanity" (a term Gunkel used dozens of times) was uneducated, and related to its environment in a naïve, unsophisticated way. As opposed to historians, primitive humans wrote popular legends and stories that could never take place in reality.[1]

Gunkel used Genesis in order to prove his theory of the intellectual evolution of humanity. He presented hundreds of examples to show that the stories of Genesis were impossible, and could not take place in reality. He used many proofs to justify the argument that the authors of Genesis represented the lowest and the most primitive intellectual stage of writing. According to him, they were not able to relate to reality and the environment in which they lived in a realistic manner.[2] Since the authors of Genesis were unable to

---

[1] Hermann Gunkel lived at the same time when Charles Darwin's book *The Origin of Species* stood at the eye of the storm in the academic and religious world in Europe. In his book, Darwin (1809–1882) showed that all forms of life existing today developed from ancient, lower forms of life. The evolutionary process gradually selected out the strongest forms of life, which adapted themselves to their environment, and these developed at the expense of the inferior forms of life, which slowly died out. Gunkel was influenced by Darwin in composing his theory of the intellectual evolution of man.

[2] As an example, he noted the story that God created the world in six days, then stopped to rest because He was tired. Another example tells of the first woman, who had an evil conversation with a snake, just as Little Red Riding Hood spoke with the wolf. According to Gunkel, the authors of Genesis naïvely believed in the existence of a tree whose fruit made humans wise, and another tree whose fruit made them live forever. He also used the example that God gave Noah the exact measurements for

think scientifically, they did not write historical works that required methodical thinking. They did not address topics of broad national importance. Rather, they wrote of "village gossip, what went on beside the water trough, the well, or the bedroom."

As Gunkel said, the family stories of Genesis and other Bible stories do speak of daily life and events that took place in the small tent camp where the characters lived. None of them discuss events of national magnitude or public importance, and so the designation that they are no more than village gossip does not belie the truth.

According to Gunkel, the inferior level of the Genesis authors was further proved by the brevity of the stories they wrote, which sometimes contain no more than a few lines. They used simple language comprehensible to children, or to adults whose developmental level was comparable to that of children. Again, Gunkel gave many examples for this argument.

Besides asserting that Genesis described trifling matters and events that never could have taken place in reality, Gunkel pointed out that each story has only two or three characters, described superficially. The stories do not offer detailed descriptions of the characters, and their dialogues are very short. Their emotional world and the landscape in which they lived are completely hidden from the reader. According to Gunkel, these are characteristics of children's literature, and they emphasize the extent of the gap between the authors of Genesis and the modern author, who describes every detail of his topic.

---

building the ark, into which he placed one pair of all the animals in the world. God then closed the doors of the ark with His own hands. To him, Abraham and Jacob represent the archetypal man of good character. Sarah and Jacob's wives represent the archetype of the jealous, bitter woman. Hagar represents the young, wild desert girl. Gunkel gave dozens of additional examples to prove that compared to modern humanity, the ancients were intellectually inferior.

The extensive evidence Gunkel analyzes in his book, of which I have mentioned only a selection, led him to conclude that the authors of Genesis came from groups that did not have a long tradition of writing, as we do. According to him, in the period in which they lived, they did not possess the words needed to detail the emotional world of the characters. The limited vocabulary available in that period explains why they wrote "village gossip," not historical works. This same reason explains why the authors of Genesis did not write complex stories that branch into subplots with many characters, as is customary in "advanced" works written in our time.

Gunkel did not stop with these erudite analyses. He also declared that the short, simple stories proved that the listeners' ability to absorb material, and the storyteller's ability to invent stories, was limited to just fifteen minutes in length. After this period of time, both the ability of the listener to concentrate and the storyteller's imagination reached their maximum limits.

Among the many examples Gunkel used, one is particularly important for our purposes. Like many researchers both before and after him, Gunkel argued, justifiably, that the legends of Genesis developed in a society that was still illiterate. The stories were transmitted orally over many generations and centuries before they were finally recorded. In his analysis, a story that is passed down orally for such a long period of time cannot be preserved in its original, pure form. A memory recorded as a story is liable to change over time. Every storyteller adds or subtracts something from the story he has heard from his predecessor, and so in each generation, the gap widened between the story told at that point, and the first story that had begun its journey centuries previously. Furthermore, all the family stories in the Bible, not only those of Genesis, took place in the private realm. Except for those directly involved, no one witnessed them or wrote them down as they took place. Thus even if they did have some historical value at the beginning, this was lost over the years in which the stories were carried within the memories of the Israelites.

The first seedling that Gunkel planted put down deep roots, and over the years, it grew into a willow tree. His convincing arguments earned the enthusiastic applause of the academic community, which received them warmly. Many researchers went one step further and insisted that nothing written in the Bible ever took place in reality. In the academic world, the most extreme of these are called "Bible deniers." To date, even if some academics here and there believe that Gunkel and his successors went too far with their conclusions, this is a lone opinion that is not heard, and that dissolves like a pinch of salt thrown into a pot of bowling water.

We may conclude the summary above with a comparison of which I am particularly fond. According to most of the researchers at today's major universities around the world, the historical authenticity of the family stories in Genesis (and the rest of the Bible) is comparable to the stories of Little Red Riding Hood, Cinderella, Pinocchio, and beloved Winnie the Pooh. One who believes that Sarah, Rachel, and Leah were women who really lived must have the pure, naïve soul of a child. Such a person would easily believe that once upon a time, a long time ago, in a land far, far away, there lived a little princess who kissed a frog and then married him.

For Gunkel, it is exactly the same.

Because the arguments I have presented here have become internalized by researchers to the point that they consider them to be absolute truth, I would like to discuss them briefly. We will then set them aside and delve deep into the world of the biblical writers.

The first problem raised by the conclusions of Gunkel and his successors is the absolute negation of the existence of the One God, God of the Jews, the Christians, and the Muslims.

The first verse of the Bible, "In the beginning, God created the heavens and the earth," announces the existence of God to the world. According to Genesis, God revealed Himself to the forefathers, then to Moses, the prophets, and the kings. If God had not revealed Himself to the biblical characters and spoken to them, we would have no way of knowing of His existence. Naturally, the New Testament could not relate that Jesus was the son of God.

No researcher, as bright as he may be, can separate God from Genesis, and argue that everything it says is untrue but that the existence of the God Who this book reveals is true. Similarly, no researcher can separate the New Testament from Genesis, and say that Jesus existed but that his forefathers, including David, were never born. Some things cannot be disconnected, and first among these is the close relationship between God and the book that informs us of His existence.

Gunkel, a religious person and man of the church, attempted to prove "scientifically" that all the Genesis stories, including the story of creation, never happened, but he proved something he never intended to: that the God in which he believed did not exist. The many researchers who follow in his path choose, like him, to negate everything written in Genesis, but at the same time, they are careful not to deny the existence of God, of Whose existence Genesis reveals to the world. But like all other academics, Bible researchers must uphold the conclusions that derive from their research, even if this leads them into open conflict with the members of the community in which they live. As a fact, the researchers who deny the Genesis stories are not brave enough to take another step and to admit that in doing so, they are denying the existence of God and the existence of Jesus, His son.

We will now return to Gunkel's arguments.

The statement that "historical writing" addresses issues of broad national importance, while legend addresses topics of home and family life, is untrue. This definition describes the working method of an academic living in our time, but nothing beyond that. Because the Bible was not written as an academic work, the rules of writing that Gunkel discussed are not applicable to it! The argument that topics of life in the family and the village are legend, not history, erases the past of each one of us with the brush of a hand. It eliminates my grandmother Hinda, a poor peddler who pushed her cart from one village to another, selling sheets and undergarments so that she could feed her numerous children. It also obliterates my grandfather Isaac, a merchant of scrap iron. Such an argument denies the past and heritage of all of us. It transforms our family stories into legends that never took place in reality, and turns us into individuals without any past.

The assertion that "the legends of Genesis" developed from within a public still unable to distinguish between imagination and reality is, in one word – ludicrous. There never was a stage in the history of humanity in which human beings did not distinguish between reality and imagination. There was no era in which human beings did not work to provide food for their families, raise their children, or heal their sick. There was no period in which the human brain lacked the necessary level of development in order to distinguish between what was possible and what was impossible. Human beings always distinguished between reality and imagination, and at the same time wrote legends, and there is no conflict between the two.

The argument that legend is characterized by concise description, short dialogue, a small number of characters, and superficial character development, whereas history is lengthy and complex, transforms some of my most beloved authors into historians. To my delight, according to the criteria that Gunkel determined for historical writing, wonderful writers such as J. R. R. Tolkien and J. K. Rowling, who wrote books extending over hundreds of pages, are really historians! In the worlds of hobbits and magicians, monumental events of immense national importance took place, and the fact that we are not part of that world is no proof that it does not exist. My point here is that a historical work is not characterized by strict rules or the number of words it contains. It can be short, or it can be long. It can address issues of national importance, or issues from the realm of family life. Just as wonderful legends are written in our time, so can ancient society produce historical writing.

Another assertion from Gunkel's school that we have mentioned above is that the authors of Genesis originated from groups that were not well versed in the art of writing. Because the vocabulary they had access to was poor, they used simple language and wrote simple children's stories that were easy to understand.

Only a person expressing an opinion about a work written in a language in which he is not completely fluent, and of whose deep layers he is unaware, could express such an appalling and erroneous argument. A researcher who depends on a word-for-word translation of the Bible into his own language loses the vitality, the wide range of meanings, and the wordplays that the original language enables. Gunkel's scorning the level of writing of the Genesis authors is based on his scanty knowledge of Hebrew. It is comparable to disparaging Shakespeare's use of the English language based on rudimentary knowledge of English. In direct contrast to this, researchers with a strong command of biblical Hebrew assert that Genesis is written in such advanced language that even native speakers of Hebrew have difficulty understanding it.

Wordplays and double entendres are almost impossible to translate from one language into another. Thus the reader who lacks an extensive knowledge of biblical Hebrew misses the levels hidden under the top layer of the story, which many times does seem simple. For this reason, I dedicated a large portion of this book to translating the wordplays and the unique writing style of the biblical authors.

Gunkel asserted correctly that the Bible stories do not contain detailed descriptions of nature, as accepted in today's literature. But Gunkel lived his whole life in Europe. He was not familiar with the landscape of the Land of Israel, and thus was not able to identify the adaption of each Bible story to the landscape and climate in which it took place. If we asked him why Hagar and her son almost died of thirst, and why Jacob's sons who lived in Hebron led their father's flock to Shechem, he would not know how to reply. Gunkel and many of his followers were unfamiliar with the landscape, the climate, and the geography of the Land of Israel. Thus they could not distinguish the transformation of the landscape and movement of the characters from one place to another. It advances from Hebron, in which pasture and water sources are depleted when the summer arrives, to Shechem, rich in water and pasture, even in the dry summer months.

The ancients whose listening ability was "limited to just fifteen minutes" were the same ones who laid the foundations of modern mathematics and astronomy. The pyramids, shrines, and palaces built thousands of years ago bear spectacular witness to the ability of ancient architects to calculate, plan, and execute their ideas. The tens of thousands of clay tablets found in the Near East address issues of justice, state, and economy, as well as poetry and literature. Yet according to Gunkel's evolutionary theory, this vast cultural heritage

– including the Bible – is the product of a primitive people who lived in a period when the human brain had not yet reached the level of development necessary to handle tasks requiring more than fifteen minutes of concentration....

THE ARCHEOLOGICAL PICTURE
Researchers who argue that some of the characters of Genesis (according to the more extreme view, all the characters in the Bible) are legendary figures have received support from several archeologists who have published their findings during the last decades.

Unfortunately, archeological excavations have revealed no fragments that may be dated to the earliest periods described in the Bible. Archeologists have not found the Garden of Eden or the miraculous tree whose fruits were eaten by the first man and woman. They have not found Noah's ark on Mount Ararat (in today's Armenia), or Sarah's tattered sandals in the Sinai Desert. Neither have they found any remains of the first Tablets of the Covenant that Moses shattered, the kidskin sleeves that Rebecca sewed for Jacob, or Joseph's well-known coat of many colors.

Archeologists have invested huge sums and endless hours of work in their never-ending search for remains from the period of the forefathers. But their search has been in vain.

They have found nothing.

Because archeologists have uncovered no finding that might reinforce even one of the Bible's family stories, some of them have vociferously negated the historical validity of the period of the forefathers. To them, "we have not found" means "it did not exist." Yet the principle guiding the archeologist's methodology states that they must base their conclusions on what they find, not on what they do not find. "I have not found" proves nothing. It does not prove that a certain event took place, or did not take place. What was not found today may be found tomorrow. It could be hiding underneath the one stone that the archeologist neglected to turn over.

In actuality, we should not be surprised by the fact that the archeological excavations have found no remnant to support the stories of the forefathers. The tents, clothes, shoes, and other personal items that the Bible mentions were made of soft, biodegradable material. If these items were not placed inside stone caskets or clay pots that were sealed and buried in caves, then they deteriorated and were lost. A goat hair tent or sheepskin cloak had no chance of surviving for over three thousand years under the searing Middle Eastern sun. Because the forefathers used items that deteriorated even during the period in which they were used, I cannot understand what ever inspired the archeologists to search for them in the first place.

The united opinion of scholars who argue that the Bible stories are fabrications has a basic weakness that causes it to collapse. Just as there is no finding that proves scientifically that the characters we have discussed here once lived, so there is no proof that they are imaginary characters. The fact that no side has hard evidence to prove its case moves the argument to the realm of historical probability. In other words, the question is: Could the Bible stories have taken place in reality, or are they illogical and thus impossible?

THE PROBABILITY TEST

As we said before, one of the most important assertions of Gunkel and many Bible researchers is that a tradition preserved in memory and transmitted orally cannot be maintained in its original form over time. The many changes the tradition undergoes over generations render it void of any historical value.

This argument is both true and untrue.

No one argues that memory can preserve the original story for centuries in its initial form. Human memory is not able to preserve long, complex sagas with many characters. It is unable to preserve long conversations. But at the same time, a memory preserved within one group can certainly contain true flashes of its past. It can include short stories and isolated points. Thus, even if the full account of the event is long lost, the essence can be preserved – and as Gunkel rightly pointed out, the stories in Genesis are indeed very short. One of the reasons for this can be because large portions of the entire story were forgotten, and only isolated fragments heroically survived the ravages of time and reached the authors who recorded them in writing.

Academic researchers have reached the general agreement that the Bible stories are a collection of dozens of short compositions that were preserved by various groups. (The "Bible deniers" share this view.) Over the years, the stories were compiled and edited together in chronological order. Under the rule of probability, the moment we agree that dozens of stories found a home under one roof, we must take into account the possibility that some are legends, while others are true stories that survived centuries of oral transmission. We must also consider a third possibility, that on top of a story that actually took place, the editors added legendary components.

For example, any person who does not uphold a strictly religious worldview will doubt the truth of the story that Sarah was ninety years old when she conceived through Abraham, who was then one hundred years old. But the chapters in this book that address the stories of the couple show that the Bible gives many details that could have taken place in reality. The moment we admit that the realistic foundation of the story has been preserved, we cannot state that Abraham and Sarah were legendary figures. It would thus be appropriate for even the greatest skeptic to relate to their story as a true narrative to which legendary aspects were added.

True, we cannot prove that the figures we have discussed here actually lived. No one recorded or photographed what happened between the sides of the tents. No one witnessed what was said between Rebecca and Isaac, or between Tamar and Amnon. Not one of the characters wrote a diary or documented the conversations that the Bible relates in his or her name – and this is what Gunkel said and what his successors say, although in different words and with a different attitude than ours.

Still, although almost every one of us has a camera and advanced recording equipment at home, we also do not photograph or record everything that is said and that takes place between the walls of our homes. Just as we cannot prove the truth of what Ruth said to Boaz on a dark blue spring night, we cannot prove that a conversation that took place this morning between two participants actually happened. Most of us tend to believe the information that enters our knowledge because it is logical. We believe it because it stands the test of logic that serves as a filter for information we capture, and not because we have hard proof that it is in fact true – and this will serve as the basis for the first rule that underlies the continuation of our argument below.

The first rule says that we will place into the drawer of legends only impossible stories, those that reasonable logic refuses to accept. But stories about ordinary topics that might have taken place in reality will remain outside the drawer of legends. We will consider them as true, although we admit that we cannot present hard evidence of their reality.

FAMILY AND SOCIETY

Researchers agree that the land of Canaan was inhabited during the biblical period. Centuries before the time of

Abraham and Sarah, groups of poor nomads came to Canaan, where they pitched their tents and built their lives. Some of the nomads left this searing land and continued to wander to other, shadier regions. Some were banished from their homes by other nomads who took control of their living areas by force. Some dug their fingernails into the hard, stubborn ground, and vanquished the onerous heat and the covetous hands that stretched toward them. Thus in the time of the first forefathers and those who succeeded them, Canaan was not empty of inhabitants.

In direct contrast to Gunkel's assertions, human beings are historical creatures. They always tell their stories, because it is their nature. Whether through etchings on cave walls, pictographs, or other meaningful signs, human beings have always documented the fact of their existence. In any place where humans lived, they wove stories of people, their families, the relationships between them, and their beliefs.

Stories are always connected to the landscape and climate in which they take place, and so they describe that place, and no other. They fit the time of their composition and the way of life practiced in that time, and no other. This is the way it was in the ancient world, and so it remains today. From this we derive the second rule which will guide our discussion below: if a story reveals an accurate connection with the place and time of its occurrence, we will consider it as true.

Let us examine these assertions.

The book of Genesis condensed the story of the journey of Abraham and his two escorts from Ur to Canaan to a list of names of settlements through which the travelers passed. When we placed these points on the map, we learned that the family walked about 2175 miles (3500 km). We also saw that they walked along a route that was in widespread use in the ancient world, not along an imaginary, illogical path that led nowhere.

The question that occupied us was this: Can a person travel such a distance in one lifetime? In order to answer our question, we took into account every component that we thought might influence the length of the journey. The conclusion we reached was that Abraham and his entourage needed about twenty years in order to complete such a journey, and thus they could have accomplished it in one lifetime. Furthermore, the story that Abraham and his family originated from Ur does not serve the ideology of the Bible writers. If the story of the journey were deleted from the book, the reader would not feel its absence. But the historical memory of the biblical writers was pulled to the area along the Euphrates, and thus they mentioned it in other places as well (Josh. 24:2, and elsewhere). From this we may conclude that a short, fragmented memory reached the biblical authors about a real journey that took place long before they lived. The authors recorded the faded remains of this memory in writing, and thanks to their labors, a tiny echo of the most important journey in the history of the monotheistic world was preserved and reached our hands. Although the story of the journey passes the test of probability, this is no proof that it actually happened. At the same time, those who disagree with this conclusion will have to justify why they think the journey never took place. If they cannot prove that the data we have presented is unfounded, then the rules of the scientific method to which every academic is bound will force them to admit that the story passes the probability test and could have taken place in reality.

True, I cannot use the isolated verses the Bible dedicates to Sarah, Rachel, and Hannah to prove that these three women actually lived once upon a time. Possibly, as Gunkel and his successors assert, they really belong in the legends drawer. Still, the story of childlessness that unites the three crosses the ocean of time and penetrates the heart of the modern age

– and because it takes place constantly, it is eternally true. Rachel's desperate plea – "Give me children, else I am dead" – burst from one of the forgotten tent sides that long ago deteriorated and turned into dust. But her heartbreaking cry was not forgotten, and the dry wind that came from the east did not turn it into dust. Even today, at this very moment, it echoes between the walls of the most advanced clinics for fertility treatments. The pain of these three women continues to bleed from the flesh of every woman who ever fought to conceive a child. Thus as long as Rachel's bitter cry continues to echo in our ears, the stories of the barren women in the Bible will be considered true.

From our point of view, there is no difference whether the cry is uttered by a woman wearing a worn and tattered cloak such as Sarah, or by a woman wearing a modern-day designer suit purchased in a classy boutique. The main difference between the biblical women who had difficulty conceiving and their daughters who live among us is in society's attitude toward them. The biblical characters could not establish their status in their husbands' households, while modern women receive looks of pity that embitter them even more. The former were considered a failure and a disgrace to themselves and to the society in which they lived – while their sad daughters feel exactly the same thing. And so, although we do not possess the identity cards of Sarah, Rachel, and Hannah, it is enough that their story takes place in every time, in every village, and in every city, for us to establish that they could be true. The fact that legendary elements penetrated their stories does not make them impossible, and so we will not place the stories of these three important women inside the drawer of legends.

The book of Numbers tells the story of the daughters of Zelophehad, who asked Moses to recognize their right to inherit the property their father would have received had he remained alive. The tradition that daughters did not inherit from their father existed throughout the ancient world (and still exists in various locations). It meant that in households that had only daughters, there was no heir. Because this was a common occurrence, society had to find an organized solution that the coming generations would follow. The solution offered in Numbers enabled a daughter to inherit from her father, and at the same time guaranteed that the land she inherited remained the property of the family. The social and historical logic underlying this law ensures that the story of the daughters of Zelophehad also remains outside the legends drawer.

Let us examine the family stories from a broader perspective:

Human beings established their first permanent settlements near sources of water. Ur and the city-states nearby were built alongside the Tigris and the Euphrates. The ancient Egyptians established their cities alongside the two banks of the Nile, where the population of Egypt remains concentrated to this day. Because settlement beside water sources repeats itself in every time and place, this must also have been the case in Canaan. This means that in the period of the earliest forefathers and their successors, most of the population lived in the water-rich areas in the northern and central regions of Israel. The dry, southern Negev region was populated by poor, isolated families of shepherds who wandered from one poor pasture to another. This picture of human settlement fits the story of the entrance of Abraham, Sarah, and Lot into Canaan.

We have discussed the fact that the three travelers came into Canaan through the northern entrance, which is much richer in water than the southern region. We also noted that because the area suffered a harsh famine when they arrived, the existing population pushed them south to the driest area, so that the newcomers would not use up the last remaining drops of water. At this point, we can expand on this and say that in truth, it makes no difference whether Abraham and his two escorts arrived in Canaan during a famine, or whether it was a bountiful year. Either way, they would have been pushed south. The reason for this assertion is that wherever a group of small, weak immigrants arrives, the existing inhabitants push it to the poor areas of the new land – as is the case in our day as well. From the viewpoint of the established residents, immigrants are foreigners who consume the residents' means of subsistence. The immigrants allow their sheep to graze in the locals' pastures and drink their water. The veterans have no choice but to push the newcomers to the poorer areas so that they will not compete for vital resources.[3]

The Negev, where Abraham and his two escorts stopped at the end of their journey, was (and remains today) the poorest area of the land of Israel in terms of both water and pasture. Therefore, it is logical that the three were pushed to that region. We have no difficulty accepting the Bible's testimony that even settlement in the Negev was not easy, for even this arid region was not completely empty of inhabitants. Abraham and Sarah, who had just arrived, had to compete with the local shepherds for use of the limited water sources found there, and for every blade of grass, however dry. Yet again, although we cannot prove the story that Abraham, and later Isaac, fought with the local shepherds for the right to use the wells, we can determine that a shepherds' battle over use of water is an exact reflection of the present reality in the driest areas of the world.

---

[3] In Europe and Scandinavia, we find an example demonstrating that this process continues in our time. The tens of millions of Muslims who have immigrated there since World War II and until today are pushed out to the poorest suburbs on the edges of the cities.

The story of Jacob and his family moving from Haran to Canaan also fits with our analysis. As we recall, Jacob purchased a plot of land on the outskirts of Shechem in the center of the country, which he left after the rape of his daughter, Dina. Genesis does not reveal why Jacob wanted to settle in exactly that place, but the reason is clear to those familiar with Israel's landscape. In comparison to other areas of the country, Shechem is located in a region of abundant water and pasture, and so it was an ideal place for families of shepherds and farmers. Although the Bible does not relate that Jacob's flocks used the water and pastures of the established residents of Shechem, we can assume that this was what happened. We may reasonably conclude that the residents did not want the foreign family that had just arrived at their borders to draw their water or graze flocks in their pastures. Their desire to banish Jacob and his family could be the reason why Shechem raped Dinah and imprisoned her in his house. The rape can be interpreted as an unequivocal message that Jacob and his family would do well to leave Shechem. In truth, the rape story in Genesis ends differently from the scenario we have proposed. Still, Jacob left the town and continued traveling south to a region whose population was sparser and poorer than that of the central region, and there he succeeded in putting down roots.

The books of Judges and Samuel open a new chapter, and describe the period about six hundred years after the time of the Genesis characters. The social picture painted in these books depicts farming families that lived in permanent settlements in the center of the country. In these books, large families moved to northern areas that were rich in water in comparison to the southern part of Canaan. Again, this principle repeats itself in every country that absorbs foreign populations: the immigrants first settle in the poorest areas, and later the strongest of them move to better living areas.

Thus we find that about six hundred years after the time of the early forefathers, the mass of Israelite settlement moved from southern Canaan to the center and north, conquering areas where the established Canaanite population lived.

We may illustrate this principle in a colorful manner.

The lucky among us were raised on the exciting stories and films of the Wild West, which describe the history of the pioneers who came from Europe to the United States and appropriated land. The pioneers arrived in their famed covered wagons to empty areas, and to areas that were settled by Native American tribes, the established population of the region. The novels and films describe the war of survival of the poor pioneers who drove their stakes into a new land. They tell of their battles against the Native Americans, who had always controlled the land that the pioneers penetrated. These media creations describe a village society that existed without national institutions above it, whose leaders sprung from within. They praise the local heroes that saved their families from the robbers who came to plunder them.

The battles for existence waged by the pioneers in America against the Native Americans are exactly equivalent to the battles for existence of the early forefathers and their successors against the Canaanites who preceded them in Canaan. Like the heroes of the Wild West, the judges were local heroes who defended their families and territory. The role played by the family leaders, whom we have praised in this book, is identical to that played by the leaders who sprung from the families who reached early America.

I, of course, do not claim that the stories about the white settlers who came to the new America are documentary works of exact, faithful historical value. Still, they preserve the settlement experience that took place in reality. They describe the difficulties that the new, poor groups experienced in conquering areas that were sparsely populated and turning them into their own. The thousands of years that separate one pioneer story from another do not erase their parallel principles.

We might expand the survey we have given above and show that the image of society and settlement revealed in the Bible stories repeats itself everywhere a new population penetrates. But if we do so, we will be digressing into areas that this book does not address. The issue I would like to emphasize is that despite the theological purpose for which the Bible was recorded, the image of society and settlement that filters through is appropriate for its time. This picture returns us to the principle that wherever people live, they create stories of people – and these stories always describe the reality of their time, the landscape, and the society in which they took place. Thus, although we have no proof that the stories we have examined here occurred as written, they describe a realistic picture of settlement that is constantly taking place. Although legendary elements were added to them, this does not erase their realistic foundations, and so they can be considered true.

We thus return for the last time to the argument that all the family stories in the Bible, especially those in Genesis, are legendary and lack any factual basis. The distance of time and the absence of any archeological evidence supporting them make the Bible the only source that describes an entire period and lifestyle that took place in an area of the world about 60 miles (100 km) long and 37 miles (60 km) wide.[4]

This is a problematic situation, which leaves us with the self-evidence of a book in which most of the stories were transmitted orally over many centuries until they were first

---

[4] Many readers of the Bible think that the twelve tribes of Israel were spread over a broad territory – but the opposite is the truth. The area they occupied, Jerusalem and the surrounding region, measured about 150 miles (240 km) from north to south and 37 miles (60 km) from east to west. According to the maximum calculation, the stories in the Bible are focused on an area of 62 by 37 miles (100 by 60 km).

recorded in writing. After they were written down, they continued to undergo repeated copying throughout the centuries that followed, until they reached our hands. As regards historical authenticity, no court of law attempting to reach the truth on the basis of hard proof could rely on the evidence of stories that took place at a tiny, distant point on the globe. Possibly, Gunkel and the researchers who follow in his footsteps are correct in their assertion that the family stories and other parts of the Bible are no more than a collection of ancient popular legends. We will never be able to prove otherwise.

But we have an answer to their accusations: the stories we have discussed here stand the test of historical probability. Tendentious and legendary elements were added to the stories, thus blurring the original picture, but they do not undermine their realistic foundations. The legendary outer layer of the stories does not obscure the universal aspects of the family and the social picture they describe. Gunkel and his successors focused on the legendary outer layer, completely ignoring the universal social aspects that repeat themselves in every time and place.

When we connect the details that could have taken place in reality, they form a well-defined picture of a living, breathing, functioning society. A society that lives on its land is a society that writes historical as well as legendary stories. It writes poetry, such as the lyric book of Psalms. It writes profound, daring philosophical works, such as the books of Job and Ecclesiastes. Just as in our time, it writes about every subject on its daily agenda. Thus, even if none of the variety of issues that the Bible addresses has concrete evidence, the general picture formed by the collection of details fits the time and place of its occurrence. The legendary elements that these stories contain do not undermine the historical and social process they outline. Because the details we have explored create a feasible picture, it is possible that they did take place – that the Bible really happened.

THE AUTHORS OF THE BIBLE

The question of the identity of the authors of the Bible celebrated its fifteen hundredth birthday long ago. Possibly, it has celebrated hundreds more such birthdays, of which we possess only shadowy clues. The first to offer an organized answer to this question were the Jewish sages who lived in today's Iraq around the fifth century CE (the authors of the Babylonian Talmud). The sages asserted that most of the books of the Bible were written by its main characters. In their view, God dictated the Pentateuch (the first five books of the Bible) to Moses, except for the last eight verses of Deuteronomy, which describe the elderly leader's last moments. According to the tradition the sages possessed, Moses also wrote the book of Job. Joshua wrote the book that carries his name, as well as the last eight verses of Deuteronomy. Samuel wrote Judges, Ruth, and the eponymous book. David and ten wise men who assisted him wrote the book of Psalms, and so forth.

Orthodox Judaism and Christianity have accepted the tradition that relates the composition of the books of the Bible to its main characters, and they still uphold this tradition today. But the answer of the sages, who lived fifteen hundred years ago, has not satisfied the academic community. Most biblical researchers assert that the Bible, like any other written text, was written by human beings, and that God had no part in its writing. They say that the Bible, which covers a period of 1350 years, was written by hundreds of writers who belonged to a variety of groups. At a certain point, which also lasted for centuries, the stories were collected, underwent an editing process, and were finally arranged by topic and in chronological order.

This book does not address the debate between the religious and the academic approaches to original authorship. I focus here on a later stage, about which both schools agree: the stage when the biblical stories were transmitted orally over a very long period of time, before they were recorded.

Almost certainly, alongside the literature that was recorded, or that was in the process of being recorded, the oral literature continued to pass through the years as it was originally transmitted. The explanation here is that almost everyone in the ancient world was unable to read or write, and the only way for an illiterate society to preserve the memories of its past was through oral transmission. The fate of the written literature was both similar, and different. Like the oral literature, the written literature was also transmitted for centuries from the hand of one author-copyist to his successors, who recopied the text he received. But unlike its elder brother, which continued to climb the ladder of time through oral transmission, the written story underwent polishing and refinement before it was recorded. Apparently, some of the written stories have preserved the borders of their first framework, like the story of Abraham's journey to the land of Canaan. But alongside these are some stories that seem to have undergone extensive expansion by the author-copyist. This expansion was intended to inject into the story the author's personal opinion about the main character, to add some charm and color to the main character's cheeks, or to include legendary or moralistic material.

A good example that illustrates this process is the interpretation of the names of Leah and Rachel's sons. Possibly, the original text simply listed the names of Jacob's sons, and it revolved through many generations unchanged. In the generation when the change was made, this list reached an author of rich imagination and rare poetic talent, who added his interpretations of the names of the sons and placed this interpretation in the mouths of the two sisters. This supposition is justified because the encoding of the name interpretations is so sophisticated and clever that it creates a hidden story within the revealed one (chapter 11). A composition written in such a refined style does not seem to be a tradition transmitted orally over generations and copied word for word. It seems more likely that this is an authentic story that at some point underwent significant expansion at the hands of the copyist, who did not hesitate to weave into it his personal opinion of Jacob.

Another example of such a composition is the story of Joseph's life. The description of Joseph's sojourn in Egypt is a mirror image of his life in his father's home. By weaving many details into the story and then inverting them, the author transforms Joseph from a spoiled, lazy child whispering poisonous lies about his brothers in his father's ear, to a mature, wise, compassionate man. Writing such a complex story demands planning and precision, and this goal is very difficult to achieve in a work preserved in oral tradition.

The elegant, sophisticated language of the Bible stories inspires the question: Who were their authors? And no less importantly, who were their readers?

I must admit that unfortunately, I cannot give a satisfactory answer to this most important question. The Bible authors were not movie stars or football giants. They did not leap out in front of the television cameras, nor did they give autographs to fans. None of them signed his name on the work he copied, or recorded the name of the author from whom he received the texts. Of course, he did not identify the next copyist in line.

The identity of the biblical authors remains an eternal secret. Still, I can propose a partial answer to the question of who they were and for whom they wrote. In addition, I can offer an explanation of why the Bible stories are so short (even those that underwent expansion are still very short), and why they exemplify the well-known and wonderful synergy paradox that "a story is longer than its words."

The general consensus that the stories were preserved over a long period of time by an illiterate public is accepted in both religious and academic circles. But the authors who eventually wrote them down belonged to the educated class, part of the narrow band of the social elite, who served in the palaces and shrines.[5] Such was the situation throughout the ancient world, and such must have been the case in ancient Israel as well.

This leads to the conclusion that the biblical authors wrote for the group of individuals to which they belonged. This highly educated group was literate, and it had access to written literature. Undoubtedly, the authors wrote for people who could read and understand a work written in sophisticated language, which was much different from the everyday language spoken by the simple people. They wrote for people who were capable of enjoying a story whose outer layer was simple and easy to understand, but which concealed complex layers formed of wordplay, double entendres, and contrasts.

To illustrate this point, we will recall Jacob's words to Rebecca:

> But my brother Esau is a hairy man, and I am a smooth man. Perhaps my father will feel me and I shall be as a cheater in his eyes; I will thus bring upon myself a curse rather than a blessing. (Gen. 27:11–12)

In its simple, superficial meaning, Jacob's statement is understandable as the natural doubts of a young man who fears that his father will discover his trick. (This meaning is easy

---

[5] Researchers agree that in ancient times, only about three percent of men living in the large cities were literate. Literacy was professional knowledge preserved within families of scribes that served in palaces and shrines, which were located only in big cities. The remainder of the population was illiterate.

to translate literally into any language.) The hidden meaning of the verse is based on wordplays and double entendres. This inner layer describes Esau as a hairy, masculine man. By contrast, the verses depict his twin brother as a boy, still smooth in the places where a mature man grows hair, and still sitting in his mother's tent with the other children. Only the educated could understand the hidden meaning of the verse. Only they would be aware of the wordplay of Jacob's self-description, admitting he was a man of smooth language who deceived with his words, and that for that reason, his name in biblical Hebrew meant "swindler."

In other words, readers who discerned the entire range of possibilities in such verses read a story twice as long as its words. Undoubtedly, only a virtuoso could write a verse that could be understood in the native language in three different ways, and only a reader as sophisticated as he could enjoy its range of meanings.

The educated elite, who were well acquainted with the Bible's laws, could identify these laws as they were interwoven into each of the family stories. Naturally, these readers were also the ones who asked the big questions – about the creation of the world, the purpose of humanity, and the meaning of reward and punishment. Only the educated elite would recognize the elevation of David's dynasty through the torch procession, embroidered with an almost indistinguishable fine thread that stretched through the stories from the beginning of time to its distant end.

The biblical authors wrote for themselves and for their fellow readers, whose numbers were few, but who shared one language, one culture, and one landscape. They wrote for readers who walked inside the story like a person walking inside his own house. But their stories were restless nomads. They set sail in rickety boats on stormy waves, and climbed high, rocky mountains. They exchanged the blazing, everlasting blue skies that hung above the land of their birth for murky skies burdened with heavy gray clouds. They exchanged the burning sun for snow and frost. On their way to distant regions, they crossed borders, passed through villages and cities, and finally settled in one place. Wherever they settled, they received a certificate of citizenship and were translated into the local language – and a range of wonderful meanings integral to the source language was lost forever.

The authors of the Bible could not imagine that such would be the chain of events. They could not know that one distant day, the memories of their past would reach readers who did not speak their language, who did not understand the wordplays and double entendres they had so carefully added to selected words. They could not know that in the distant future, cultures would arise that would be so different than the one in which they lived, that their new readers would need explanations of what was obvious to their contemporaries.

The assumption that such was the case explains, at least partially, why they wrote such short stories, and why they did not bother to explain themselves. The members of their social groups knew from their own experience that a concubine-wife was a legal wife, not the secret lover of a man who did not marry her. They understood the hierarchy that determined the status of a woman whose husband took additional wives. The biblical authors did not have to explain why elderly, wise Naomi could not inherit Elimelech's property. The educated readers were well acquainted with the social laws of their time, and so they understood why Naomi severed the formal connection between herself and Ruth, and how Boaz retied that connection.

Educated readers of the Bible, contemporaries of its authors, read much longer stories than modern readers. A good example of this is wells. The modern reader lives in a house with running water, and merely has to open a tap at the end of a pipe in order to fill a glass or take a shower. The biblical characters, by contrast, were dependent on wells for their water. Indeed, the Bible mentions many events that took place beside wells, and relates that Abraham and Isaac dug wells. But what is the logic of digging wells in a dry area that receives almost no rainfall, whose rivers are dry almost throughout the year? How are wells filled in a place with no rains, no rivers, and no water?

Most Bible readers today live in countries where heavy rains often cause the rivers to overflow their banks and flood the populated areas. Naturally, inhabitants of these countries think of floods as natural disasters. By contrast, people who live in the Negev, where the forefathers of Genesis lived, consider floods a great blessing. Floods are a gift from God – they are the artery through which the life source flows. Long ago, in the dry areas of ancient Israel, the floods that pounded the Negev once a year were the only thing that enabled human beings to survive.

But the biblical authors did not write about floods – or perhaps they did?

The sparse rain in the Negev falls in short, heavy bursts. Because of the type of earth found in this region, rain that hits it all at once is not absorbed into the ground. Instead, it flows across the earth's surface. Drops of water join together and flow into tiny streams, then continue onward to fill the dry riverbeds. The riverbeds, which stand dry almost the entire year, enjoy a few days of indulgence when they flood with abundant, gushing water. The Negev inhabitants, who were well acquainted with the flood paths, dug pits along them in order to trap the water inside. The water collected in these pits maintained them and their flocks throughout the long summer months. This was the case until the advent of gigantic pumps, which push water in pipes from one end of the country to the other. True, the Bible does not mention the floods that hit the desert like a blessing. However, it does say that Abraham and Isaac dug water pits – and such pits were filled only in one way: by the wonderfully welcome floods that inhabitants of other places in the world consider natural disasters.

Just as authors in our time, even those who write copiously, do not explain to their readers the meaning of "turning on a light," or "stopping at a red light," the biblical authors did not explain phenomena that were self-evident to everyone. After all, a "short" or "long" story is measured not only by the number of its words, but also by the comprehension of its readers, and whether they share the language, time, and culture in which the story was written. Possibly, if Gunkel and many of his followers who lived in water-rich countries had recognized the details we have presented here, their conclusions about the believability of the biblical story would have been slightly more modest – and a bit of modesty, as we know, has never harmed any researcher. The precision of details belonging to such a specific landscape and climate can only be identified by a person from the region, and a foreigner will never notice them, even if we were to tie red feathers to their heads and place them in front of their eyes.

෴෴෴

The family stories in the Bible are indeed very short. Undoubtedly, the talented artists who recorded them could have written much longer stories, if they had wanted to do so. Alternatively, they could have added words to the stories that reached them, as they apparently did with the stories whose writing demanded a high degree of sophistication. Still, the very fact that they are so short seems to support their true foundations. We agree with the argument that memory alone cannot preserve lengthy works for an extended period. Poetic compositions such as the prophetic books and the Psalms, or a complex and daring work such as the book of Job, were apparently recorded at the same time as they were composed, and preserved as is. However, we strongly assert that collective memory can preserve true details from its past, and transmit them faithfully over generations. These details are fragments of history that were preserved, overcoming oblivion. When collected together, the discrete memories expand the borders of individual memory, as well as the border of each separate story. Each one of the memory fragments teaches something about itself, but at the same time, it is part of the mutual conceptual framework of the neighboring memories, and reveals something about them as well. The aggregate value of the compilation of memories and the integration of the legal system within their fabric give us a faithful image of the Israelite nation's first days in its land, its way of life, and its faith.

The biblical authors who immortalized the memory fragments they inherited from their forefathers did not know that their stories would one day be transformed into universal memories, that an entire culture would arise and march forward, carrying them on their backs. They certainly did not know that they were writing the greatest best seller of all time, which would be translated into languages that were not yet invented in their day.

But even if this was not their intention – this is what happened.

Only a few of us know the identity of a distant grandfather who lived three or five hundred years ago. All we can say about the anonymous grandmother who walked beside him is that part of her still lives on, inside the genetic code of her granddaughter. Here and there, she returns from the depth of oblivion and smiles anew from within the green or brown eyes of her granddaughter, who has no idea that her visage bears the stamp of the beloved grandmother whom she has forgotten. But thanks to the memories of the biblical authors, we know who our forefathers and foremothers were. Details of their lives have become individual memories for each one of us, and part of the collective memory of inhabitants of the Western world. Thanks to the magnum opus of the biblical authors, and to their work of compilation, which is unique in human history, we remember something deep and primal about ourselves and our past, which the chasm of time has not erased.

What is the secret charm of these ancient stories? Why, despite the fact that we live in the age of technology with vastly different social and legal norms, do we still cling to these ancient stories, unable to part from them? Why does everyone recognize the family stories, while only a few have read the books of the prophets, Ezra and Nehemiah, and Chronicles?

I believe the answer to this is that the biblical authors wanted to emphasize and praise the wonders of the One God, not of human beings. Because they stood before the infinite greatness of God, they had no interest in elevating the figures about which they wrote, beyond the ordinary characteristics found in every human being. Thus despite the distance of time, we identify something deep about ourselves in these ancient stories – and this is the secret of their great attraction.

Each one of us will easily understand why Abraham preferred the young, fertile Hagar over exhausted, barren Sarah. Every reader will easily understand why Sarah envied Hagar, and why the moment she was able, she banished her from her house.

Sarah did what I and every other woman would do if we had to stand in her place and fight for the lives of our sons. We have no difficulty accepting that Isaac and Rebecca were divided in their love for their sons, because each of us is part of a community of families in which too many parents are

conflicted in their love for their children. In the hidden corners of our hearts, we recognize Jacob's great love for Rachel,
because once, before we became cynical and scarred, we knew
what love was. We knew its gentle appeasements, its bitterness and grief.

In the mutual jealousy between Leah and Rachel, we see
our own jealousy. We recognize the wild revenge of Absalom
against his father in our own lack of courage to carry out our
own revenges. We recognize the possessiveness of Judah, and
the triangle of kindness that bound together the three main
characters of the book of Ruth. In them, we find our own
weaknesses and positive traits, and all the good and the bad
we contain. Even David, the magnificent king who was graced
with supreme wisdom and exceptional merits, is described as
having a full measure of human weaknesses, just like any of
us. In his old age, the cold penetrated his bones, and he suffered from physical and spiritual decay, like many of today's
elderly who are living out their final days. We admire his
intelligence and courage, and at the same time, we recognize
the terrible mistakes he made with his children, because they
are the same mistakes we make every day with our own children. In his greed and lust, we recognize the greed and lust
we harbor within ourselves.

Of course, the technology that serves us is infinitely faster
and more advanced than that of travelers who walked at the
pace of the flock of black goats they drove before them. Yet
when we look into the eyes of our forefathers and foremothers, we see our own faces gazing back at us. Every weakness
and strength they possess, we possess as well – so that they
are also us, in all our simplicity and nakedness. The biblical characters are the profound, original memory of what we
were and who we are, and no one can take this memory away
from us.

The editors of the Bible chose to begin the holy book with a message revealing the existence of the One God. At the end of a long process, this new message that took root within a small nation, which lived in an unbelievably tiny territory, vanquished the religions of the ancient Near East, and eventually spread far and wide. Christianity and Islam, which developed much later, were not to overcome this religion. Rather, they built their own level on top of it. The New Testament cites hundreds of verses from the Pentateuch and the books of the Prophets, and Writings, while the Koran copies dozens of stories from these books. This phenomenon is also unique in the history of humanity. The Bible is the shared foundation for Jews, Christians, and Muslims – no matter whether they are religious people, or people who define themselves as completely secular.

The chapter on creation reveals that just like the top physicists of our day, the ancients grappled with defining the moment of origin of the universe. They asked, where was the turning point at which the primal chaos began to transform into the complex, yet ordered, system in which we live?

The answer that the authors of Genesis gave to this question has been the stimulus for the best scientific minds that ever lived, one of which is chosen every year to mount the stage and receive the Nobel Prize. Their answer has been a strong point of support for philosophers who grasped at the story of the might of the One God, in their everlasting, indefatigable search for one absolute truth that cannot be undermined.

The biblical authors, first among them those who recorded the family stories, transformed the stories of our foremothers and forefathers into a source of inspiration for our greatest artists: for Kafka and Rembrandt, for Bach and for Beethoven. The biographies of our ancestors have been sources of insight for preachers of religion and ethics and street-corner producers of world-class dramas, as well as for schoolteachers authoring the second-grade play.

With their words, the biblical authors sketched a picture of the landscape revealed to them from the openings of their tents and from the reality of their time. Thanks to their magnum opus, we preserve rare evidence of the exhausting life our ancient forefathers and foremothers lived in the hours that stretched from dawn until darkness. They left us with stories that could have taken place, stories of miracles, and other stories that served their religious and social worldview. They left us with veiled criticisms of characters they loved, and of characters they did not love so well. They left us with a spiritual heritage that miraculously continues to grow, becoming deeper and richer with every passing year.

The authors of the Bible bequeathed one last thing to us. To record the stories they inherited from their predecessors, they used language that has no equal in beauty, language that is refined and pure. They weighed each word in gold, and only then did they place it in its own unique position, thus shaping an eternal standard for the definition of a literary masterpiece. In their modest way, exacting, minimalist, full of respect for the written word and for the heritage of their – our – forefathers, the biblical authors laid the foundation stone for the Western culture that was built on their backs.

SELECTED BIBLIOGRAPHY

Averbeck R. E., Chavalas M. W., Weisberg D. B. (eds.). *Life and Culture in the Ancient Near East,* Bethesda, MD: CDL Press, 2003.

Bar-Ilan M. 'Literacy among the Jews in antiquity', *Hebrew Studies* 44 (2003) 217–222.

Berlyn P. 'The journey of Terah to Ur Ksdim or Urkesh?' *Jewish Bible Quarterly* 33,2 (2005) 73–80.

Charles R. H. (ed.). *The Apocrypha and Pseudepigrapha of the Old Testament*, Oxford 1913.

Cohen J. M. 'Displacement in the matriarchal home: A psychological study of the Abraham-Sarah marriage', *Jewish Bible Quarterly* 30,2 (2002) 90–96.

Cohen N. 'The maternal effect on the Twelve Tribes of Israel', *Hakirah* 13 (2012) 97–126.

Cohen R. 'The nomadic or semi-nomadic Middle Bronze Age I settlements in the central Negev', *Pastoralism in the Levant: Archaeological Materials in Anthropological Perspectives,* Madison, WI: Prehistory Press (1992) 105–131.

Dever G. D. *Who Were the Early Israelites and Where Did They Come From?* Grand Rapids, 2003.

Dimant D. 'Judah and Tamar in "Jubilees" 41', *A Teacher for All Generations II* (2012) 783–797.

Dresner S. H. 'Rachel and Leah', *Judaism* 38,2 (1989) 151–159.

————. 'Rachel and Leah: Sibling tragedy or the triumph of piety and compassion?', *Bible Review* 6,2 (1990) 22–27, 40–42.

Faust A. 'The Canaanite village: Social structure of Middle Bronze Age rural communities', *Levant* 37 (2005) 105–125.

Finkelstein I. *The archaeology of the Israelite settlement*, Jerusalem: Israel Exploration Society, 1988.

————. 'The archaeology of the united monarchy: An Alternative View', *Levant* 28 (1996).

————. 'The Rise of Jerusalem and Judah: The Missing Link', *Levant* 33 (2001).

Fortes M. (ed.). *Marriage in tribal societies*, Cambridge University Press, 1972.

Freedman D. N. 'Dinah and Shechem, Tamar and Amnon', *Divine Commitment and Human Obligation* (1997) 485–495.

Galaty J. G. and P. Carl Salzman (eds.), *Change and development in nomadic and pastoral societies*, Leiden: Brill, 1981.

Goldfarb S. D. 'Jacob's love for Rachel', *Dor le Dor* 4,4 (1976) 153–157.

Gordon C. H. *The world of the Old Testament*, Phoenix House, 1960.

Grohmann M. 'Abraham and Sarah: Genesis 11–23', *Great Couples of the Bible*, Fortress Press, 2006.

Gunkel H. *The legends of Genesis*, Chicago: The Open Court, 1901.

Hallo W. W. *The Ancient Near East: A History*, Fort Worth: Harcourt Brace College Publishers, 1998.

————. *The World's Oldest Literature: Studies in Sumerian Belles-lettres*, Brill, 2009.

Hendel R. J. 'A Biblical Approach to Dream Interpretation', *Jewish Bible Quarterly* 39,4 (2011) 231–238.

Hepner G. 'Abraham's incestuous marriage with Sarah: A violation of the holiness code', *Vetus Testamentum* 53,2 (2003) 143–155.

Hess R. S. 'Questions of reading and writing in ancient Israel', *Bulletin for Biblical Research* 19,1 (2009) 1–9.

Holt J. M. *The patriarchs of Israel,* Nashville: Vanderbilt University Press, 1964.

Irons W. and Hudson W. D. *Perspectives on nomadism,* Brill: Leiden, 1972.

Kass L. R. 'Love of woman and love of God: The case of Jacob', *Commentary* 107,3 (1999) 46–54.

Kramer S. N. *History begins at Sumer,* Thames & Hudson, 1958.

———. 'In search of Sumer: A personal account of the early years', *Journal of the American Oriental Society* 103,1 (1983) 337–351.

———. *The Sumerians: Their history, culture, and character,* Chicago University Press, 1963.

Lester L. G. (ed.). *Can a 'History of Israel' be Written?,* Sheffield, 1997.

Mark E. W. 'The four wives of Jacob: Matriarchs seen and unseen', *The Reconstructionist* 63,1 (1998) 22–35.

Mbuwayesango D. R. 'Can daughters be sons? The daughters of Zelophehad in patriarchal and imperial society', *Relating to the Text : Interdisciplinary and Form-Critical Insights on the Bible* (2003) 251–262.

Miroschedji, P. 'At the dawn of history: Sociopolitical developments in southwestern Canaan in Early Bronze Age III', *I Will Speak the Riddles of Ancient Times* (2006) 55–78.

Mundy M. and B. Musallam (eds.). *The Transformation of nomadic society in the Arab East,* Cambridge University Press, 2000.

Na'aman N. 'In Search of Reality Behind the Account of Israel', *Israel Exploration Journal* 52 (2002) 200–224.

Osgood S. J. 'Women and the inheritance of land in early Israel', *Women in the Biblical Tradition* (1992) 29–52.

Perdue L. G. 'The Israelites and Early Jewish Family: Summary and Conclusions', *Families in Ancient Israel,* Louisville, 1997.

Ramsey G. 'Israel's ancestors: The patriarchs and matriarchs', *The Biblical World II* (2002) 175–193.

Rosen S. A. 'The case for seasonal movement of pastoral nomads in the late Byzantine – early Arabic period in the south central Negev', *Pastoralism in the Levant* (1992) 153–164.

Rothstein D. 'Why was Shelah not given to Tamar?: Jubilees 41:20', *Henoch* 27,1–2 (2005) 115–126.

Rudman D. 'Reliving the rape of Tamar: Absalom's revenge in 2 Samuel 13', *Old Testament Essays* 11,2 (1998) 326–339.

Schulz R. and Seidel M (eds.). *Egypt: The world of the Pharaohs,* Ullmann, 2010.

Shectman S. 'Rachel, Leah, and the composition of Genesis', *The Pentateuch* (2011), 207–222.

Snaith N. H. 'The Daughters of Zelophehad', *Vetus Testamentum* 16 (1966) 124–127.

Spanier K. 'Rachel's theft of the Teraphim: Her struggle for family primacy', *Vetus Testamentum* 42,3 (1992) 404–412.

Speiser E. A. 'At the dawn of civilization', *The World History of the Jewish People I,* Rutgers University Press, 1964.

———. *Genesis,* The Anchor Bible, Doubleday, 1964.

———. *Mesopotamian Origins: The Basic Population of the Near East,* University of Pennsylvania Press, 1930.

Spero S. 'Was Abraham Born in Ur of the Chaldees?', *Jewish Bible Quarterly* 24,3 (1996) 156–159.

Spooner B. *The Cultural Ecology of Pastoral Nomads*, Addison-Wesley Modular Publication, 1973.

Swidler L. J. *Women in Judaism: The status of women in formative Judaism*, Metuchen, NJ: Scarecrow Press, 1976.

Tollington J. E. 'Abraham and his wives: Culture and status', *The Old Testament in Its World*, Leiden: Brill (2005) 183–199.

Tucker W. D. 'Women in the Old Testament: Issues of Authority, Power and Justice', *Expository Times* 119,10 (2008) 481–486.

VanderKam, J. C., *The Book of Jubilees* (academic translation), Lovanii, 1989.

Volkmar, F. and Davies R. (eds.). *The Origins of the Ancient Israelite State*, Sheffield, 1996.

Weeks S. D. E. 'Literacy, orality, and literature in Israel', *On Stone and Scroll* (2011) 465–478.

Young I. M. 'Israelite Literacy: Interpreting the Evidence', *Vetus Testamentunm*, 48 (1998).

Zucker, D. J., 'Abraham, Sarah, and Hagar as a blended family: Problems, partings, and possibilities', *Women in Judaism* 6,2 (2009).